The Living Ancestors

THE LIVING ANCESTORS

Shamanism, Cosmos and Cultural Change among the Yanomami of the Upper Orinoco

Zeljko Jokic

berghahn

NEW YORK · OXFORD

www.berghahnbooks.com

First published in 2015 by
Berghahn Books
www.berghahnbooks.com

Library of Congress Cataloging-in-Publication Data
A C.I.P. cataloging record is available from the Library of Congress.

British Library Cataloguing in Publication Data
A catalogue record for this book is available from the British Library

Printed on acid-free paper

ISBN 978-1-78238-817-3 (hardback)
ISBN 978-1-78920-758-3 (paperback)
ISBN 978-1-78238-818-0 (ebook)

*This book is dedicated to the Yanomami people
and especially their shamans Ruweweriwë, Makowë, Enano and others,
who allowed me to step into their world
and take part in their age-old tradition.*

The master shapori Ruweweriwë and his disciple Arawë singing in front of the ceremonial mast – Mountain of the ancestral hekura spirits.

CONTENTS

ILLUSTRATIONS

All photographs taken by the author.

Figures

Title page image: The master shapori Ruweweriwë and his disciple Arawë singing in front of the ceremonial mast – Mountain of the ancestral hekura spirits.

PREFACE AND ACKNOWLEDGEMENTS

This book engages in phenomenologically oriented ethnography, focusing essentially on experiential aspects of Yanomami shamanism, including shamanistic activities in the context of cultural change. Many facets of the topic are covered, ranging from cosmology and shamans' roles and activities to their relationship with spirit helpers and their responses to cultural change, especially their attitudes and reactions towards introduced diseases and the corresponding new forms of treatment that have resulted in a terminal imbalance in the Yanomami lifeworld. At the heart of the book is a detailed ethnographic description and systematic phenomenological analysis of the entire process of body transformation during shamanistic initiation. The book aims to demonstrate how cosmology, on the basis of myths and other oral communications, comes to be replicated in initiatory visionary experiences, while the shaman's body, as an integrated and dynamic whole, comes to provide a model for the integrated and dynamic totality of the cosmos. The study uses an innovative approach that interweaves ethnographic material with a theoretical component of a holographic principle ('part is equal to the whole'), which, I argue, is implicitly embedded in the nature of the Yanomami macrocosm, human dwelling, multiple soul components and shamans' relationship with their embodied spirit helpers.

Among the Yanomami shamans, the established method for accomplishing shamanistic initiations, mastery of trances and the subsequent competence in handling spirits involves the use of certain psychoactive snuff substances. The snuff not only aids shamans in establishing contact with the spirits, but is also conceived as food for their embodied spirit helpers. This procedure is generally known and described in a number of essays and books dealing with aspects of Yanomami and Sanema shamanism and cosmology: Barandiarán (1965); Barandiarán and Brandli (1983, especially Chapter XV); Colchester (1981, 1982) on the Sanema myths and cosmovision respectively, including sections on shamans and the cosmos; Taylor (1976) on Sanema shamanism and ancestral spirits; Chiappino (1995) on Yanomami shamanism, cosmology and conservation of a vital cosmic energy based on his fieldwork in Sierra Parima; Lizot's (1974, 1989) compilation of Yanomami myths, and his more recent article (Lizot 2007) on Yanomami cosmology; and parts of Cocco (1972), Valero (1984) and Biocca (1971) and Eguíllor García (1984) that deal with shamans, ancestral spirits and accompanying cosmological aspects. Barandiarán (1965) outlines shamanistic initiation among the Sanema. Father Luis Cocco (1972) in his book reproduced an account of shamanistic initiation as recounted by Helena Valero. Lizot (1976a, 1985: 87–105) provided a detailed account of shamanistic initiation, while De Pedro (1980) produced an outstanding documentary film on this topic. More recently, a Brazilian shaman, Davi Kopenawa, in collaboration with Bruce Albert published a monumental autobiographical account *The Falling Sky: Words of a Yanomami Shaman* (Kopenawa and Albert 2013), providing an insight into his thoughts and the challenges that the Yanomami today face. I shall refer to these works and other studies throughout. They mainly provide detailed representations of the Yanomami (and Sanema) cosmos, shamanistic practices and spirits. Despite the apparent volume of sources, there has been a paucity of information regarding further systematic exploration of the nature and dynamics of consciousness associated with shamanism (with the exception, to some extent, of Lizot 1976a, 1985). The reason for this deficiency lies in either the lack of interest in shamanism as a subject of investigation in its own right, or in the customary anthropological approach to fieldwork, which emphasises neutrality and detachment rather than personal experiential involvement, which is crucial when studying phenomena associated with changes of consciousness, such as shamanism. By making shamanism a central theme for my analysis, I aimed at producing a more comprehensive, principal book-length study of Yanomami shamanistic practices, cosmology and sociocultural changes than what had hitherto been the case.

In the burgeoning field of multidisciplinary consciousness study there is a growing emphasis on subjective and experiential content (e.g., Baars, Banks and Newman 2003; Hunt 1995; Laughlin, McManus and d'Aquili 1992; Shanon 2002; Wautischer 2008). For this reason, different modalities of consciousness, as experienced in shamanic initiations and ensuing practices, became the main object of my ethnographic investigation and the subsequent subject of this book. My broad intellectual framework, as well as the main research interest, is the general nature of human consciousness. Shamanism as a phenomenon under investigation is a technique of consciousness that in itself includes an array of different modalities of consciousness in transformation. As such, shamanism pushes the boundaries beyond the limits of the Western rational mind and challenges the limitations of the Western philosophical tradition. This study is specifically intended to fill an important gap in the regional ethnography of the Yanomami people, and, more widely, make a significant contribution to Amazonian ethnography. By making consciousness involved in shamanism an object of investigation, I trust this study will contribute to a better understanding of shamanism as a phenomenon, with likely benefits to the general science of consciousness. This book could, therefore, benefit and attract the attention of scholars and university students from various disciplines, such as social and medical anthropology, psychology and consciousness studies. Considering the ongoing extensive interest in shamanism as a way of personal empowerment, this book may also appeal to many readers outside of academic circles who are interested in various esoteric phenomena. The account of shamanistic initiation in Chapter Four is mostly written in the present tense (i.e., it is unfolding in 'ethnographic present'). Certain parts of the book dealing with the dynamics between the Yanomami and the health system are complementary to some recently published works on this subject (Kelly 2011). In the last chapter I refer extensively to Albert's (1985, 1988) analysis of the history of representations of contact among the Brazilian Yanomami, as well as the aforementioned Davi Kopenawa's personal account (Albert and Kopenawa 2013).

The book is based on fourteen months of field research carried out during 1999 and 2000 in two Yanomami villages in the Upper Orinoco region of Venezuela, under the auspices of the Anthropology Department, University of Sydney and funding provided by the Carlyle Greenwell Bequest Fund for which I express my gratitude. I am grateful to Dr Jadran Mimica for his support and guidance; he was and always will be my source of inspiration. In Venezuela, the realisation of my project was made possible through affiliation with several institutions, including the School of Anthropology at the Central University of Venezuela (UCV). I owe a debt of gratitude to Dr Daisy Barreto for her guidance and ongoing friendship. In Amazonas, my research was further facilitated by the Amazonian Centre for Investigation and Control of Tropical Diseases 'Simon Bolivar' (SACAICET) in Puerto Ayacucho, who provided me with the logistical support and enabled the realisation of my project. I am grateful to then director of the SACAICET and coordinator of the ecoepidemiology unit Dr Carlos Botto for his help. I am also indebted to Arelis Sumabila-Tachon for helping me with contacts in Venezuela.

I am grateful for being awarded, in 2006, a writing fellowship from the 'Cross Cultural Centre Ascona' (Centro Incontri Umani Ascona) located in Switzerland to assist me in writing this book. Eight months on from receiving the award, with my book not yet finished, I went back to my native Belgrade to continue writing. A few months later, I received a job offer in Venezuela to partake in the National Programme for Elimination of Onchocerciasis – Southern Focus Amazonas (PNEO-FS), which I gladly accepted. I packed all the necessary equipment and personal belongings, including my laptop and a pen drive with a copy of the unfinished manuscript. After landing at Caracas airport, I took the wrong (fake) taxi and was robbed at gunpoint. All my equipment was stolen. I realised I had made a huge mistake of not leaving a copy of my work in Belgrade; my manuscript had ended up in the hands of the robbers. Disheartened and deeply shaken by this unfortunate incident, but happy to be alive, I went to Puerto Ayacucho where for the next five years I was incorporated into the multidisciplinary team of the ecoepidemiology unit of the SACAICET, dealing with the research and control of onchocerciasis among the Yanomami population of the Upper Orinoco. Due to my heavy work commitments and frequent field trips, I did not get back to working on my manuscript, but I managed to publish a couple of essays on Yanomami shamanistic initiation (Jokic 2006, 2008a) and another, more recent essay (Jokic 2014) on hostile and harmful aspects of Yanomami shamanism.

While in Amazonas, I was acquainted with the developments in the Upper Orinoco since I had left Venezuela in 2001, and this additional information is included as a postscript at the end of the book. As an anthropologist-investigator working for the PNEO-FS, I participated in numerous field trips to various parts of Yanomami territory and on a few occasions briefly revisited my field sites after years of absence. Towards the end of 2012, my work contract with PNEO-FS terminated and I returned to Belgrade where I finally decided to complete this book. I owe a special debt to Olivera Pilipovic for revising and subediting the manuscript.

My deepest indebtedness goes to the Yanomami people of Platanal and Sheroana-theri, who befriended me and allowed me to stay with them. In particular, I owe special thanks to Jacinto Serowë, my main informant and host from Platanal, for looking after me and accepting me as part of his family. I am also grateful to an ex-Mahekoto-theri headman Alfredo Aherowë for allowing me to stay in Platanal and assisting me with my research. I remain forever grateful to a number of shamans for allowing me to participate in their activities: Enano and Makowë from Platanal for teaching me many things about their world and allowing me to participate in their shamanistic sessions, and my heartfelt thanks goes to Ruweweriwë, the principal shaman of Sheroana-theri and my classificatory father, who initiated me and privileged me with access to the world of shamans.

Map • xv

Map of the geographical area of Platanal – Goaharibos Unturán in the Upper Orinoco River region of Amazonas State showing the location of the Yanomami communities that appear in the book; namely, the Mahekoto-theri (upper left corner), the Sheroana-theri and the Toritha-theri, among others (source: PNEO-FS, Onchocerciasis Unit SACAICET).

INTRODUCTION

~~~❦•❦~~~

The known is finite, the unknown infinite; spiritu-
ally we find ourselves on a tiny island in the middle
of a boundless ocean of the inexplicable. It is our
task, from generation to generation, to drain a small
amount of additional land.
— Thomas Henry Huxley, 1887

A shaman is someone who is already dead and thus
has no fear of death or life.
—Don Eduardo Calderon (Peruvian shaman)

Shamanism: Origins and Key Features

Shamans and the phenomena associated with shamanism have
intrigued Westerners ever since the Europeans began returning from
their exploratory voyages of the 'New World' (America) five centuries
ago. They were telling shocking but fascinating tales about individuals
performing peculiar rites and communicating with spirits. Considering
the dominant role of the Catholic Church in shaping people's views at
that time, those individuals were labelled as servants of Satan (Narby
and Huxley 2001). When Russians began colonising the 'wild east' of
Siberia during the seventeenth century, they too encountered people who
were allegedly summoning ancestral spirits by entering a trance, through

singing, dancing and drumming. Those individuals, who were among the Evenki people of the Tungus language family, were called *saman*.[1]

Although the word 'shaman' and its anthropological derivative 'shamanism' was originally a culture-specific term confined to northern and central Asia, it nonetheless became a transcultural category designating a similar set of practices and understandings concerning the cosmos, spirits and human needs that occur in various parts of the world, more frequently in small-scale hunter-gatherer societies (DuBois 2009: 6). However, the original, ethnographically specific meaning of the term 'shaman' has been to a large extent lost. Known through Russian and deriving from the Tungusic term *saman*, it signifies someone who is 'excited, moved, raised'. This is descriptive of shaking – one of shamans' fundamental characteristics (Lewis 1971: 51; Casanowicz, cited in Peters and Price-Williams 1980: 408). The term shaman has been applied so generally and indiscriminately that it eventually became a label for any kind of similar magico-religious practitioners and mystics from other parts of the world (Sullivan 1994: 29; Furst 1994: 5). Shamanism became a broad category, taking many forms and definitions. Consequently, the problem of defining what is a shaman and shamanism and what is not has been a point of a long-standing debate and controversy.

Shamanism has existed throughout time in almost all societies and continents from Australia to South America. It has been eclipsed by dominant religions and political systems while in some places it virtually became extinct and pertinent knowledge was lost due to encroaching modernity. In many parts of the world shamans have been persecuted and brutally killed. Nevertheless, as Vitebsky (2003: 278) commented, shamanism 'is characterised by a chameleon-like elusiveness' and has survived in one form or another until the present day. In many traditional societies shamanic practices are being revitalised and reinvented. Shamanism has not only survived, it continues to arouse academic interest and general curiosity, taking new forms and meanings, especially in the last sixty years. The upsurge of interest in shamanism and shamanic healing in the West took place during a period of major social and political change worldwide and within the context of an increased interest in nature religions and neopaganism of the New Age movement. Shamanism became a spiritual attitude and a prominent approach to self-discovery in a trendy New Age fashion among the Western urban middle classes. In this newly emerging, entirely positive interpretation, shamanism is 'rediscovered' as a way of finding 'our lost' connections with nature, and provides a path of self-realisation, healing and empowerment. Within this framework, certain elements of shamanism, namely its positive aspects, are emphasised and selectively stripped of their cultural contexts, while other, more negative and destructive components were intentionally left out. There is a widespread opinion that great shamans no longer exist. Truly, nowadays it is difficult to encounter shamanism in the way it was practised by the ancestors of various peoples of the Siberian tundra and taiga, North American savannas and deserts or African and Amazonian rainforests.

In Siberia, the sort of grand shamans that existed a few centuries ago are now almost extinct due to severe persecution by the Soviet state. The neo-shamanistic revival during the 1990s influenced by the New Age paradigm and globalisation is an entirely different phenomenon (Vitebsky 2005; see also Jokic 2008b). In South America, Indigenous peoples suffered great population losses from epidemics triggered by European colonisers. Some ethnic groups lost their traditional shamanic knowledge and contacts with their ancestral shamans, while in some parts of Amazonia shamanism took new syncretic forms (Chaumeil 1992; Homan 2011; Luzar and Fragoso 2013).

The Yanomami are one of the last and largest remaining Amazonian groups where traditional shamanism is still widely practised relatively free from outside influences, as it has been practised from time immemorial. Yanomami shamanism is by no means exempt from the peril of disappearing. On the contrary, as this book will show, the living and dead shamans (ancestral spirits) are in danger of vanishing due to an encroaching danger of cosmic proportions. Despite many problems and culture changes that the Yanomami people have been facing ever since their sustained contact with national society in the last sixty years, the vast majority of their population relies on shamans for protection and healing. This book is about them and their practices.

Yanomami Shamanism: A Cross-cultural Perspective

Archaeological evidence suggests that shamans have existed since the earliest Palaeolithic times. Some scholars have speculated that certain Upper Palaeolithic cave paintings related to hunting magic are depicting shamanic visions in trance (Lewis-Williams 2002; Whitley 2009). Shamanism is certainly an ancient and near-universal phenomenon with various culture-specific forms and manifestations. Furst (1994: 2) considers an archaic 'shamanistic worldview as originally the common property of humankind' whose main components include: feminine earth and masculine sky; reciprocal relationships between human beings and spirits; and animals and plants each having their spirit masters or 'owners'. The shamanistic outlook assumes all components of a phenomenal world – including human beings, plants, animals, rivers, mountains, wind and celestial bodies – have their animate soul essences and a certain kind of intentionality of consciousness akin to humans. From those intangible essences of phenomenal appearances the material components of the world originated. Shamans are specific individuals capable of not only perceiving but also manipulating those intangible essences of things. They are the mediators '... between the visible and invisible, the generally known and largely unknown' (DuBois 2009: 82). A shaman's vocation is not only deemed the oldest human profession (Basilov 1997) but shamans are also considered to be 'the world's most versatile specialists' (Dow 1986: 6). Some authors (Furst 1994; Riches 1994) claim that shamanism is the origin and the key to all of the world's religions and all cosmologies; while others (e.g., Gilberg 1984) proposed that shamanism is as old as the human society itself. Verily, in diverse mythopoeic traditions the true origins of shamans derive from a distant, pre-cosmic realm of the original ancestors (Sullivan 1988). Primordial shamans were beings with mixed human and animal qualities, able to change their outer form at will. They are the bringers of knowledge and the founders of culture, providing the model for later human shamans (Kalweit 2000: 9). These original ancestors lost their primordial condition of immortality and transformed into material components of the universe, including human beings, plants and animals. The end of primordium and the emergence of a permanently open cut of human existence resulted in everlasting bifurcation of the masculine sky from the feminine earth. However, the legacy of the primordial epoch became an exclusive property of human shamans. Through various methods of accomplishing trances, shamans have been able to partake in the ever-present primordial condition, undergoing multiple transformations and accessing different cosmic regions (Eliade 1989 [1951]).

There have been many different definitions and interpretations of what a shaman is, but it has been widely agreed that the ability to control spirits and accomplish trances through socially recognised rituals is one of shamans' pivotal characteristics. They are communally acknowledged professionals who have a personal relationship with their spirit helpers, which they employ when dealing with various problems of their clients and communities at large (DuBois 2009). Thus, for shamans, entering a trance is not the goal in itself but a means to an end. Only entranced shamans are able to communicate with spirits or metamorphose into one of them, negotiate or effect cures and undertake trans-corporeal journeys to different cosmic locales in search for missing souls, etc. They are custodians of mythical lore, which they pass on to generations. They are diviners, weather manipulators, psychopomps, healers and harm-doers. But also, they are often skilled hunters and political negotiators. The shaman is a multifunctional being.

Shamans can enter a trance by various means, including meditation, drumming, dancing, chanting, sensory deprivation, fasting and the ingestion of hallucinogenic substances, etc. While the vast majority of scholars agree that an ability to master trance and control the spirits is one of the most prominent aspects of shamanism, they ascribe different interpretations to what constitutes a genuine shamanistic trance. The terms 'trance' and 'ecstasy' have been employed inconsistently and interchangeably to describe shamanistic trance, but they are, as Rouget (1985: 6) argues, two distinctive states in opposition and by no means synonyms. A state of ecstasy, for Rouget, involves a profound, mystical religious experience characterised by sensory deprivation, immobility, silence and solitude. A trance state is the opposite: it is noisy, public, active, frenzied and hyper sensory. Rouget associates trance primarily with possession, dissociation and post-trance amnesia, while ecstasy, for him, is an entirely conscious experience. In the end, he admits that the difference between the two states is not always clear-cut. Therefore, they are regarded as 'constituting the opposite poles of a continuum, which are linked by an uninterrupted series of possible intermediate states, so that it is sometimes difficult to determine which of the two is involved' (Rouget 1985: 11).

For Shirokogoroff (1935: 271), spirit possession is a principal constitutive element of (Tungusian) shamanistic trance, while for others (De Heusch 2007 [1971]; Eliade 1989 [1951]) the main aspect of shamanistic trance (which they call ecstasy) is an extra-corporeal journey into different cosmic regions. Yet Lewis (1971: 49) argues that shamanistic ecstasy may involve both spirit possession and an out-of-body journey; the two phenomena can coexist or exist separately. While Lewis does not differentiate between shamanism and possession, Rouget (1985: 20) argues that there is a fundamental difference between spirit incorporation in shamanism and possession. The main difference between shamanic and possession trance, according to Rouget, is that in shamanic trance shamans gain total control over the spirits they incorporate and consciously journey with the help of those spirits, while in possession trance it is the possessing deity or spirit who completely controls the body of the shaman, dominating the subject, and in the majority of cases the shaman has no memory of what has taken place during the possession period. However, the boundary between the two states is often blurry and both types of experience may occur in one and the same person (Rouget 1985: 23).

The Yanomami equivalent of a shaman is a *shapori* or *hekura*. The latter term also denotes the shaman's auxiliary spirits. All hekura are shamans and all shamans have hekura powers. Both shamans and hekura are of the same nature. The Yanomami shamanistic complex or the sum of shapori activities involving hekura spirits is known as *shaporimou* or *hekuramou*. The common archaic motifs that the Yanomami shamans and others across Amazonia share with their counterparts from other parts of the world include (to mention but a few): fasting, sexual abstinence, initiatory sickness, symbolic death through dismemberment, ecstatic trance, involvement of helping spirits, metamorphosis into animals, soul loss and retrieval, lodgement of pathogenic objects and their extraction through sucking and blowing, a stratified cosmos and cosmic axis, secret languages, great ancestral proto-shamans and culture heroes, divination, telepathy, weather shamanism and assurance of game in hunting (Crocker 1985; Eliade 1989 [1951]; Furst 1987; Wilbert 1972).

Yanomami shapori are predominantly, if not exclusively, men. Save for several reported cases of female shapori in the past, women are largely excluded from shamanistic activities. The ancestral spirits are customarily passed down from father to son or sometimes from uncles to their nephews. In some instances, the spirits are inherited after a shapori's death, when his soul essence fuses with the multiplicity of his personal spirits. Disembodied anew, these spirits wait to become reincarnated into new candidates. Reincarnation of hekura spirits is thus one of the most important aspects of Yanomami shamanism. Caroline Humphrey (1996) similarly observes that the Daur *yadgan* (shaman) after their death fuse with their tutelary spirits, waiting to become re-embodied into some future candidate.

To become a shapori and receive his[2] father's spirits, the Yanomami candidate must endure intense experiences of successive aggressive acts by the ancestral hekura spirits, culminating in death and subsequent renewal. They scorch him with fire, devour him, pierce him with an arrow, cut his body with a machete then reassemble it to form a new person with extraordinary properties. Concurrently, the candidate undergoes self-metamorphosis, implying a radical rupture of consciousness and self-dissolution through ritual death and subsequent holistic renewal. In the words of Kalweit (2000: 1), 'Their [shaman's] nature is bent, broken, reduced to worthlessness, and then immaculately fashioned afresh'. As the future shaman sacrifices himself to hekura, they subsequently become his personal allies imbuing him with a broad variety of powers and capabilities, such as the ability to observe from great distances or look inside others' bodies; to enter jaguars and snakes and direct their movements or transform into an eagle and fly.

Akin to other, similar types of professionals from around the world, the ability to enter a trance and control spirits is one of the key abilities of a Yanomami shapori, and this book, especially Chapter Four, deals at length with this phenomenon. Shamanistic performances, especially the trances of the Yanomami shamans, are very lively, hyper sensory communal events, involving intersubjectively shared experiences. In this regard, they would fit well into Rouget's above mentioned definition of what constitutes a trance, albeit the entranced Yanomami shamans are entirely conscious of their experiences, which for Rouget is the main characteristic of mystical and religious ecstatic states. Mindful of Rouget's differentiation between trance and ecstasy, I do not use these two terms in my study as synonyms. However, I do use the term ecstasy in the more general sense of an emotion of a thrill, excitement, elevation and movement of the shaman's soul that is strongly present in Yanomami shamanistic practices, as will become evident in the book. The shaman's ecstasy, understood in this sense, is also their spirit helpers' ecstasy, for when he is intoxicated his spirits are also intoxicated. They dance and sing together with their host in ecstasy, a movement that stirs up the shaman's soul until he reaches the threshold of death, a gateway to a trance state. We will see how being in a trance is not only a specific state of consciousness equivalent to death but also a 'gateway' for shapori, to the primordial sphere of free transformations. Regarding the subject of spirit possession, Butt Colson's depiction of the Akawaio shaman and his spirit helpers resembles the Yanomami shapori and his hekura helpers. She writes that the spirits dwell in the Akawaio shaman's body permanently, thus he is in a state of 'constant latent possession but only occasionally, at séances, in full trance' (Butt Colson, cited in Lewis 1971: 47).

The Yanomami employ two terms when referring to the effects of *epena* snuff and shamanism: *shi wãri* and *nomai*. The first is a general phrase meaning 'being under the influence of epena snuff' (frequently involving shaking), while the second, more specific term means 'to die', referring to the peak moment when the shaman enters a trance. Therefore, the Yanomami equivalent for trance is consistent with the original meaning of the word. Etymologically, the word 'trance' comes from the old French *transir* ('to go over' or 'to die'), which is similar to the English 'to pass away' (Sansonese 1994: 24). Each time a shapori enters a trance he relives his death, as we will see later. The initiatory death experience or a shapori's first trance opens up his intentionality of consciousness towards new horizons of perception. During this time, they experience themselves journeying to the sky, encountering various hekura beings and receiving knowledge from them. However, during their subsequent activities, the entranced shapori may only metamorphose into various hekura without necessarily departing their bodies. They undertake journeys to different cosmic strata (ascending to the sky or descending to the underworld) to recover missing souls or accompany souls of the deceased to their resting place. But they also frequently travel in spirit to other terrestrial locale (i.e., to enemy villages) to inflict harm or death, as we will see in various examples throughout the book. Therefore, as DuBois (2009: 51) rightfully claims, shamans' journeys are not only vertical movements upward and downward (as they have been frequently described), but also horizontal in a seen, terrestrial world.

Shamanism as a technique of consciousness par excellence has been frequently associated with the term 'altered states of consciousness' (ASC). Ludwig defines ASC as:

> any mental state(s) induced by various physiological, psychological or pharmacological manoeuvres or agents, which can be recognised subjectively by the individual himself (or by an objective observer of the individual) as representing a sufficient deviation in subjective experience or psychological functioning from certain general norms for that individual during alert, waking consciousness. (1966: 225–26)

He identifies the following general characteristics of ASC: alterations in thinking; disturbed sense of time; loss of control; emotional change; change in body image; perceptual distortions (visual and auditory hallucinations); change in what is perceived as meaningful or significant; inability to communicate experience; feelings of rejuvenation; and hyper suggestibility (1966: 229–34). Evidently, for him, 'altered' equals pathological deviance from 'normal', ordinary waking consciousness.[3] Atkinson (1992: 310) writes that in their interpretations of shamanism behavioural scientists '... sceptical about the ontological basis of spirit worlds, have found epistemological bedrock in the concept of altered psychological states'. Crapanzano (1977: 11) warns against such a tendency to reduce and consequently distort the spirit idiom into a secondary, more officially acceptable 'psychological' idiom. Consequently, the entire phenomenon of shamanism, in all its complexity, together with the accompanying cosmological systems and their denizens, has often been reduced to a mere psychophysical functioning. For example, an American psychiatrist Roger Walsh in his book *The Spirit of Shamanism* (1990) provided a thorough analysis of shamanistic states of consciousness, contrasting them with those experienced in some Eastern traditions, namely yoga and meditation. However, he reduced shamanism to a mere psychological state, denying ontological status to anything existing outside of the mind, and regarding, for example, the cosmic layers as mere mental constructions while 'spirits are mind-creations' (ibid.: 43). For Walsh (and indeed many others) to assume that there may exist something outside of the mind it would be 'an enormous philosophical leap' (1990: 11). Thus he prefers to stay on safer ground and avoid such a consideration when defining shamanism. Almost twenty years later, he wrote another book, *The World of Shamanism* (2007), admitting that he never conducted fieldwork or had any direct experiences with shamanism, except in Michael Harner's 'core shamanism' workshops. He is still not sure how to treat the ontological status of spirits (among other things) and introduces the term 'incommensurability' when referring to the problem of interpreting differing worldviews. Thus he writes:

> Ontological indeterminacy implies that we may be unable to determine the precise nature or the ontological status of something: because the available data may be interpreted in many ways (undetermination of theory by data), and we have no absolute method by which to decide which interpretations are best (incommensurability). (Walsh 2007: 148)

Rather than deciding which interpretations are best suited for us, a good starting point is to employ Husserl's method of transcendental phenomenological reduction or epoché, which he laid out in his monumental work *Cartesian Meditations: An Introduction to Phenomenology* (1960 [1906]). In a nutshell, epoché is a mental manoeuvre of bracketing or temporarily suspending the whole self-given objectified world together with an accompanying naturalistic and positivistic attitude to explore the reality of human consciousness and recover the world as a phenomenon. In other words, reduction in a phenomenological sense is a systematic process leading back to the epistemological origin, which, for Husserl, is a concrete transcendental subjectivity that constitutes the world. Bracketing involves 'putting aside', temporarily, questions concerning the rational, objective and ontological status of ideas and beliefs to grasp better the way in which they appear in consciousness. Husserl envisioned transcendental phenomenology as ontology of lifeworlds. The guiding principle employed in regional lifeworld ontologies is the world of a priori structure (Steinbock 1994). This a priori world is the lifeworld – that is, the original, intuitable world of immediate and shared experience existing independently and a priori to any theoretical reflection or objectification. As opposed to the scientific objective world, the lifeworld is given in direct evidence. With such an approach, spirits, dreams, cosmic layers and all other phenomena related to shamanism are treated as empirical realities of human consciousness rather than shamans' interpretations, phantasies or mind inventions.

The Book's Subject Matter and its Guiding Principles

The main focus of my field study has been the systematic inquiry of the nature of consciousness involved in Yanomami shamanism and indigenous responses to cultural changes brought about through prolonged contact with criollos.[4] The subsequent subject matter of this book is centred upon experiential and phenomenological aspects of Yanomami shamanism, shamans' roles, activities, their socio-cosmic position and their shifting roles in the context of culture change. Particular emphasis has been placed on the shamanistic initiation, the gradual mastery of trance, shamans' metamorphic abilities and methods they use for augmenting personal powers through the acquisition of additional spirits. The book also examines the nature of shamanistic engagement with spirits in both ritual and non-ritual contexts and at both the intracommunal level (defensive and protective activities) and intercommunal level (offensive acts). The dialectic between offensive and defensive shamanism forms a significant part of my broader interpretive objectives.

The analysis of shamans' social position on the intra- and intercommunal levels is broadened through examination of their activities and manifest powers within the overall cosmological matrix. The book focuses here on knowledge, in its broadest sense, generated through shamans' personal experiences and their hekura spirit helpers. One of my research objectives was to explore the full extent of sources of shamanistic manifest powers and forms of knowledge, which become accessible to shamans by means of a psychotropic snuff known as *yopo* or *epena*. The book focuses on a symbiotic, interface relationship between shamans and their embodied hekura assistants as sources of a shaman's knowledge, and how this knowledge is further articulated between shamans and members of their community and across various other communities. The knowledge transmission beyond a shapori and his hekura spirits takes place within the context of collective rituals involving interactions between shamans and other co-participants on the level of intersubjectively shared experiences.

Another vital aspect that the book investigates is Yanomami understanding of multiple soul components that together constitute a person, and how they relate to each other as well as to different aspects of the Yanomami stratified cosmos. This is then linked with shamanism and broadened with the analysis of various modalities of the shaman's consciousness and its intentional structure, as well as the nature of the worlds in which shamans operate. Too often shamans are depicted as mediators between the natural and supernatural worlds, as a consequence of the Christian Aristotelian legacy. Therefore, one of the objectives of my field project has been to investigate one tacit ontological premise of the Yanomami cosmos and its spirit denizens. The book subsequently explores the nature of the 'other-worldliness'; other-worldly dimensions are treated as empirical realities of human consciousness and not as 'mental constructions and mind creations'.

In this regard, one of the guiding principles for this study has been the concept of intentionality as the essence of consciousness – one of Husserl's central insights. Intentionality signifies the directedness of consciousness towards the world through intentional acts (perception, imagination, signification) directed at intentional objects (Husserl 1960 [1906]). Consciousness is always conscious of something, and this something is an intentional object. The term 'object' is understood in the widest possible, all-inclusive sense (Gurwitsch 1974 [1967]). There are four main characteristics of Husserl's intentionality. Firstly, consciousness is a continuous flow or a stream containing a raw data in the form of appearances. When intended as objects, such appearances form a straightforward meaning, as they follow one another in sequential order, thus building up the experience of an object and presenting it to our consciousness in its fullness. The pre-given object in this sense is a point of reference from which raw data from the stream of consciousness interprets its meaning (Spiegelberg 1969: 110). Secondly, intentionality works on establishing the identity of, and integration between, different modes of intentional acts intended at various aspects of an object as it appears to consciousness. The third attribute of intentionality is intuitive fulfilment whereby each aspect of an object refers to related aspects of modes of consciousness. This in turn generates a horizon of meaning. Lastly, constitutive intention aims at self-constitution and object constitution. The constituted object from a phenomenological perspective loses its pre-given originality and instead becomes something originating in the act of constituting itself as *eidos* or essence (Husserl 1985: XXV). Intentionality of consciousness discloses its horizonal structure. Consciousness is not a thing in itself but a process constituted through engagement of human beings in the world. In other words, there is no meaning in ego itself isolated from its surrounding environment. The world in its totality is experienced as unity and wholeness. Therefore, the intentional structure of the world is signified by infinity, in a sense of endlessness and openness of our experience towards the world (ibid.: XXXVIII).

One of the key objectives in my field research was to capture the raw data of the continuous flow of the candidate's perceptive consciousness unfolding during shamanistic initiation. In this regard, large segments of Chapter Four are based on the transcription of the initiate's direct experiences as revealed in his chants. This information is presented in the 'ethnographic present'. We will see how the candidate's stream of consciousness unfolding during initiation is directed towards the intended objects of perception; in this case the incoming hekura spirits. Merleau-Ponty (1962: 303), in his study of perception, gives primacy to the experience of perceiving objects; there can be no object without perceiving it first. Things exist only because we can perceive them in the first place. Perception starts with or in the body rather than in objects (or from an objective point of view). Merleau-Ponty calls this pre-objective. Perception is open-ended and indeterminate; there is no limit to what we can perceive.

> If our perception "ends in objects", the goal of phenomenological anthropology of perception is to capture that moment of transcendence in which perception begins, and, in the midst of its arbitrariness and indeterminacy, constitutes and is constituted by culture. (Csordas 1990: 9)

To the extent that my approach to dealing with the essential aspects of Yanomami shamanism is phenomenological, this perspective also applies to the shamanistic activities in an historical and a political context of culture contact and change. The book accordingly explores issues such as the shamans' perception of and responses to introduced diseases, the dynamics of relationships between doctors, shamans and Yanomami patients, and Yanomami attitudes towards biomedicine in a pluralistic setting, such as the rural health post in Platanal. Finally, the last section of the book deals with general crises brought about through epidemics of introduced diseases and shamans' responses thereof, including their changing role in a context of culture change.

The book's central idea is based on a holographic principle,[5] which is implicitly embedded in the nature of the Yanomami macrocosm, the *shapono* (collective house), the human body and shamanism, namely within the shapori-hekura relationship. The term 'hologram' derives from the Greek *holos* meaning 'whole'. The basic premise of a holographic paradigm is that the whole is contained within each of its constitutive parts or that each part is equal to the whole. This is the opposite from the conventional view that the whole is the sum of its parts and therefore greater than each part. Thus, the key focus of the book is the tension between the one and the many; the totality and its fractions or the micro and macro dimensions of existence. The Yanomami perceive cosmos as a stratified totality enclosed within the abdomen of a giant cosmic snake (boa), which is a widespread notion in Amazonian cosmologies throughout the continent. I will argue that the entire Yanomami cosmos is implicitly holographic in its nature, which is explicitly reflected in the name of each cosmic stratum. Specifically, each cosmic layer superimposed on top of the other is a distinct world, albeit interrelated with all other strata. All together, they form different structural parts or changing conditions of the cosmic whole as a set of different stages from new to old and from male to female. In other words, each cosmic stratum represents a state of the cosmos or condition of the totality of a fragmented cosmic boa's abdomen. The topmost layer is cosmos in the making, perceived as the young abdomen akin to a small child's, while the lowest layer is described as an old woman's abdomen. Together, all strata constitute the primal cosmic totality of the 'world body', which is a term for the classical idea of the macrocosm. It is an image of a primordial snake as a holographic whole bounded by the snake's skin, and encapsulating the totality of existence in the past, present and future. It is through the earth level that the male and female cosmic principles converge at the moment of the regeneration, transformation, and death and rebirth of the universe. The earth disc, where the Yanomami live, is a central place of manifestation of cosmic order. The book will show how this mythic image of a cosmic boa becomes fully manifested through the medium of a shaman's body during shamanistic initiation. The shaman's body thus becomes a microcosmic totality bounded by the skin, which is accordingly dotted in the manner that resembles the pattern on the snake. Therefore, the book aims to show how explicit knowledge of the cosmos is generated implicitly through the lived experience of the shamanistic initiation or what I term the cosmogenesis and the construction of the cosmic body, or the shaman's corporeal microcosm, which itself is a replica of the Yanomami cosmos and a template of its full manifestation. The shaman's cosmic body here is not treated as an object upon which culture is inscribed. Nor is the body a source of symbols whose cultural meaning and social significance can be explained in terms of various discourses. Shamans' bodily experiences described and analysed throughout the book are not 'symbolic acts' of something outside themselves. Body is the subjective source and an intersubjective ground of shared cultural experiences. In the words of Csordas (1990: 5), 'The body is not an object to be studied in relation to culture, but is to be considered as the subject of culture or as the existential ground of culture'.

During initiation, the candidate embodies a number of hekura or spirits of the ancestral shamans who enact ritual death and subsequently become his allies and future assistants. In the process, the candidate himself becomes hekura, which is a synonym for shapori (shaman). I argue that the relationship between a shapori and his embodied hekura is implicitly holographic as the book aims to demonstrate. Through initiation, a shapori becomes a unified multiplicity of all his embodied hekura but also one of the hekura. He is simultaneously one and many; a part of the whole but also the whole in itself containing other wholes – all other incarnated hekura. My argument is based on the prevailing evidence of the nature of a shapori's implicitly holographic post-mortem consciousness. A shapori's initiatory death experience involves self-dissolution and the subsequent emergence of a new being reconstituted as a multiplicity of various hekura selves. After his biological death, disembodied hekura disperse into various directions and his soul accordingly multiplies as each hekura retains an imprint of the shapori's persona, thus becoming a carrier of his soul image.

The holographic principle is moreover embedded in the nature of shapono or the Yanomami communal dwelling. More specifically, each shapono is a micro replica of the Yanomami macrocosm and a site of its full manifestation, which becomes fully evident during shamanistic rituals. The multiplicity of shaponos across the Yanomami territory (and hence on top of earth's cosmic stratum) represents a multiplicity of macrocosmic manifestations of a cosmic order. The whole (of the cosmos) replicated in the structure of each shapono is simultaneously manifested as many. The part is equal to the whole. I will also argue that the holographic principle is implicitly evident in Yanomami knowledge of the human self-constitution, namely in some of its immaterial soul essences, as revealed through shamanism. More specifically, each physical body part and internal organ contains a certain amount of its own immaterial vital essence called *pei puhi* and *pei mɨ ãmo*. Each amount of these soul essences is part of the whole body, but at the same time it is in itself whole – both the parts and the whole share the same substance akin to a drop of ocean and the whole ocean. When shapori treat a sick person with their hekura assistants, they repeatedly take 'samples' of vital essence of the whole body to determine which of its parts is affected. The whole is contained in each of its parts. The same principle of part determining or affecting the whole is also evident in so-called 'footprint sorcery'. Here, the sorcerer takes earth with someone's footprint in order to inflict harm and death. The footprint contains an essence or part of that person open to manipulation. The part stands for the whole. Finally, the damaging effect of increased contacts with Westerners has resulted in crises of cosmic proportions, which threaten to bring the Yanomami world to an end. This is articulated as a looming threat of the collapse of the sky and the resulting disintegration of the cosmic order equalling the end of the world. Yanomami shapori claim it is only they who are capable of holding the sky up and maintaining its distance from the earth. If we take into consideration that each shapori is a self-sustained cosmic unit and a micro replica of the Yanomami macrocosm, I argue that the death of each shaman is simultaneously the death of the world. Multiple deaths of shapori and the failure to continue with the process of incarnation of ancestral hekura would eventually result in an overall sky collapse, which only shapori are able to maintain.

Fieldwork Setting and Methodology

Yanomami (or Yanomamö) is the name commonly used to refer to members of an entire ethnic group of 25,000 people living in approximately 350 villages in the border region of Brazil and Venezuela. But, in fact, they are one of four culturally and linguistically related subgroups (the others are Yanomam, Ninam and Sanema), together forming a unique linguistic family. The Yanomami (including to a lesser extent Sanema), numbering somewhere around 13,500, is the most numerous subgroup in Venezuela, living in the Upper Orinoco and Rio Negro municipalities of Amazonas State. Their territory stretches from the Parima Mountains in the east down to the Brazilian border, including the adjacent areas of the Brazilian state of Amazonas. On the northern side, the Yanomami border with their Sanema neighbours around headwaters of the Padamo, Metacuni and Ocamo rivers. The southernmost part of the Yanomami territory in Venezuela (where this research was conducted) incorporates the upper reaches of the Orinoco, Mavaca and Siapa rivers. The majority of their territory is situated within Parima Tapirapecó National Park, in the far south-east corner of Amazonas State, Venezuela, a large section of which was declared the Upper Orinoco-Casiquiare Biosphere Reserve in 1991. In this ecologically rich region, the predominant types of vegetation are dense evergreen lowland, submontane and montane forests and forested mountain ranges, including some secondary savannas in the southern parts of the Parima highlands.

All in all, I spent just over a year living in the two Yanomami communities of the Mahekoto-theri and Sheroana-theri (see Figure 0.1). The first is situated in Platanal, a Salesian Mission established on the riverbank, approximately six to eight hours by boat upriver from the municipal capital La Esmeralda. The mission site was founded in 1950 after the Mahekoto-theri people settled on the left bank of the Orinoco River, where they have remained ever since. Nowadays, Platanal is a meeting place for many Yanomami coming to exchange trade items and visit their relatives. There is a bilingual school for children, a rural health clinic with a doctor in charge and an adjacent hospital building. During the second part of my fieldwork, I lived in a small inland community of Sheroana-theri linked through kinship ties with some Yanomami from the Mahekoto-theri. To get to their shapono from Platanal, one has to travel upriver by boat (for approximately three hours) to the confluence of the Shanishani River and Orinoco where the forest trail begins, then walk for about six to eight hours. Sheroana-theri and other neighbouring communities belong to the area of influence of the Platanal health post. From the point of view of the health system, these communities are considered intermediary by being situated midway between riverine villages with frequent contact with national society and those from the Siapa River Valley to the south with little or no contact.[6] However, during the time of my fieldwork, medical visits to those intermediary communities south of the Orinoco were virtually non-existent. The main reason for this was the strenuous commitment to Platanal and a lack of personnel and logistics to undertake demanding hikes through the forest. The main reason for choosing these two communities for my research was to compare attitudes and responses to health problems among those Yanomami exposed to a permanent medical presence and those with sporadic or non-existent medical intervention. While I was living with the Sheroana-theri, I had a few opportunities to briefly visit the more remote communities of the Toritha-theri and Kayurewë-theri (now called Hyomitha), a one and two day walk respectively to the south of the Sheroana-theri. I gathered some information from their shapori and other Yanomami regarding their attitudes and responses to health problems and participated in a few shamanistic sessions.

I arrived in Platanal for the first time in June 1999, armed with all the necessary government permits, personal equipment, food supplies and obligatory trade items and gifts. To get to Platanal, I first had to catch a two-hour flight in a small commercial aircraft from the capital of Amazonas State, Puerto Ayacucho, to the capital of the municipality of the Upper Orinoco, La Esmeralda. Beyond La Esmeralda, further up the Orinoco River where the Yanomami territory begins, is a restricted area with no organised public transport. I did not have any prearranged transport for the trip from La Esmeralda to Platanal. Before I left Puerto Ayacucho, I went to the Salesian headquarters to meet up with a missionary, Father Jose Bortolli, who spent twenty years living in Platanal. During our brief meeting, he gave me some useful advice and told me that upon arriving in Platanal I should look for Jacinto Serowë – an influential newly emerging Yanomami leader. After a two-hour flight above 'the green ocean', the plane finally touched La Esmeralda airstrip. As soon as I got out, I spotted a Yanomami man standing nearby and introduced myself. It was Jacinto. He did not know I was coming, and commented how he was waiting to pick up some supplies for the Platanal mission site and was returning to Platanal that same afternoon. He agreed to take me with him and offered me a place to stay. Eight hours later we finally reached the Platanal dock and it was already pitch dark. When Jacinto pulled out his flashlight, we saw a group of Yanomami standing on the shore watching us. They helped us unload the boat and then we went to Jacinto's house. Jacinto then took me to the missionary residence where I met Howard and Olga – the couple running the mission. I also met Jacinto's older brother, Alfredo Aherowë – the Mahekoto-theri headman – and a few other Yanomami men. I explained briefly the reason for my visit and showed them my permits. Howard and Alfredo did not object and welcomed me to Platanal; however Alfredo said that he would have to call a village meeting the next day and let the community decide if I should stay or not. 'It is ultimately they who decide, regardless of your government's permits', Howard told me quietly. 'If they reject you, nothing can be done!' The following morning, all Yanomami gathered in the shapono's open area. Jacinto told them how he had found me in La Esmeralda and that I could stay at his house. Alfredo then talked about my interests in shamanism and my intended research objectives; he did not have any objections to my stay in Platanal and asked if anyone was against it. A few men spoke and Alfredo translated to my relief that they all agreed with him. But, before I could get the final green light for my project, Alfredo had to address the shapori, who were sitting together in one corner, watching the meeting. One of them got up and spoke. It was Alfredo's father-in-law, Enano, the most prominent shapori in Platanal. He wanted to know if I only intended to observe their activities or participate as well. I replied that I was interested in both and the meeting ended in my favour.

Jacinto became my host, my translator and a very good friend throughout my stay in Platanal. Over the ensuing days and weeks, I gradually became acquainted with the place, its inhabitants and the dynamics of their quotidian life. From the beginning I noticed certain animosity and competitiveness between Jacinto and Alfredo, which sometimes turned into an open quarrel. The Platanal Yanomami were accordingly divided. At one point, Jacinto and his kinsfolk left the mainstream community after a heated dispute and constructed separate houses nearby. They have been living there ever since. From the outset, this schizoid situation had put me in a delicate situation because both brothers were competing for my attention, food and material goods; I was always trying to keep a balanced relationship between the two. After some time, I got to know all Yanomami personally by their (Spanish) names. Since most of them could speak Spanish we had no trouble communicating with each other. Nevertheless, one of my first priorities was to learn some basics of the Yanomami language before attempting the second stage of my field research in one of the more remote communities.[7] Dr Helen Rodriguez was in charge of the health post, accompanied by two medical students coming from Caracas every two months as part of the government's rotating programme. On a few occasions, I accompanied health teams to upriver communities where I met many other Yanomami. In Platanal, I was able to observe the dynamics of the relationship between the shapori, Yanomami patients and medical personnel, and their attitudes towards each other. Not long after my arrival, I had my first unforgettable experience with epena snuff. Initially I was cautious, taking small quantities and only in a non-ritual context. In time, as I became more confident, I began increasing my epena intake and participating in shamanistic rituals. A few months later, I co-participated in an unsuccessful shamanistic initiation of Enano's nephew, who was from the community of Karohi-theri. Five days into the initiation he suddenly got afraid and disoriented and refused to continue. Enano was very angry and sent him back to his community.

One day, a group of Jacinto's relatives from the inland community of Sheroana-theri arrived for a visit and subsequently stayed for a few days. One of them spoke a bit of Spanish and we befriended each other. Jacinto suggested that I could live in Sheroana-theri the following year and I wholeheartedly agreed. They proposed that I go back with them at once and stay for a few days to get to know the place and its inhabitants. If they could agree to have me there the following year, I could then come back again. It seemed like a good idea so I went and stayed in Sheroana for two weeks. For me it was a big change from Platanal, as Sheroana had only twenty-nine inhabitants. I met their headman Maruwë and the principal shapori Ruweweriwë. After this brief visit, I returned to Platanal but only for a month. One day, a messenger arrived from Sheroana-theri to inform Jacinto that one of my new friends, Arawë, was to be initiated as a shaman. Ruweweriwë knew about my interests in shamanism and thus he invited me to participate. Jacinto recommended that I not miss such an opportunity and he took me upriver to the beginning of the forest trail leading to Sheroana. I waved him goodbye and disappeared into the forest with the messenger. Arawë's initiation (described in Chapter Four) commenced a week later. He temporarily moved out of his house and suspended his hammock next to Ruweweriwë's and mine. To my surprise and delight, the master shapori allowed me to assist Arawë throughout the whole three-week long ordeal. I felt privileged because, apart from Ruweweriwë and his shapori assistant Taramawë from Toritha-theri, I was the only person allowed to be in Arawë's proximity. Not long after Arawë became a shapori and started practising, his progress was interrupted one day after an enemy shapori from a distant community attacked him via his hekura. This near-fatal blow nearly cost Arawë his life, scattering the whole structure of his fragile cosmic body and causing his recently embodied hekura to flee to the nearby mountaintop where they had come from in the first place. This unfortunate event provided me with a unique opportunity to monitor on a daily basis the loss of his abilities, the ensuing bodily sickness and his slow and painful recovery, which extended well into the following year. As my permit to stay in the Upper Orinoco was slowly coming to an end, I was obliged to go to Caracas and renew it.

Upon returning to Sheroana-theri, the Yanomami suggested building me a house adjacent to their shapono. I politely refused their offer, telling them that I would rather stay inside the shapono; they were surprised by my response, but Ruweweriwë immediately 'adopted me', inviting me to join his family and put up my hammock in a corner of his house. Within the overall kin network he became my classificatory father. Arawë fully recovered from the hekura attack and recommenced practising hekuramou. I continued to observe his progress, and participated in shamanistic rituals, becoming more experienced and confident each day. One afternoon, it was my turn to experience a hekura attack and I almost lost my life. The intruding hekura, however, stayed inside my body and Ruweweriwë decided to initiate me, which he did a month later. This spirit intrusion, which the Yanomami initially perceived as an illness, for me was a point of serious entry into the hekura world. I followed Ruweweriwë's instructions, assisted by a Spanish-speaking informant. Due to my limited knowledge of the Yanomami language, I recorded the words of initiatory chants on a piece of paper and memorised them. To be sure, I had the text in front of me for back up during the entire process. Thus I fulfilled one of my most important research objectives of gaining personal experience of transformation of consciousness in shamanistic initiation and subsequent practices. Correspondingly, an experiential, full-participatory approach with emphasis on dialogue with multiple informants became my main methodological fieldwork strategy. However, like other anthropologists, I had a few key informants.

The conventional method of data gathering in anthropological fieldwork has hitherto been 'participant observation'. The legacy of this technique, at least at the level of textual presentation, is grounded in a scientific and positivist attitude emphasising the neutrality of detached observation with minimal interference in the studied culture. Thus ethnographic analysis involves certain positivist expectations, such as being able to generate data that can be interpreted empirically. Without compromising a critical perspective, my ethnographic engagement with the Yanomami was inspired by Reichel-Dolmatoff's (1975) *The Shaman and the Jaguar*, containing a balanced presentation of both Desana experiences and the author's own attempts to get an inside perspective.

A similar fieldwork orientation was undertaken by a group of scholars favouring an experiential, full-participatory approach rather than detached observation (Young and Goulet 1994, and more recently Goulet and Miller 2007). Other authors discuss the relevance of the ethnographer's personal experience and emotions (Davies and Spencer 2010; McLean and Leibing 2007). The advocates of an experiential approach to fieldwork emphasise the importance of first-hand experience of rituals and associated changes in consciousness. The resulting methodological shift involves a change in attitude from traditional 'participant observation' to what Laughlin (1994: 102) identifies as 'transpersonal participant-comprehension'. The focus of data gathering thus shifts from passive observation and interviews to active participation in dialogue and ritual activities. In my view, this kind of methodology is not radically different from the classical notion of 'participant observation'. However, I agree with Jackson's argument that personal experience can be (and should be) used as 'a mode of experimentation, of testing and exploring the ways in which our experiences conjoin or connect us with others, rather than the ways they set us apart' (Jackson 1989: 4). In other words, the new scientific scrutiny, which echoes the Husserlian plea for rigorous scientific philosophy (Husserl 1960 [1906]), would not take informants' information for granted. Rather, it would test its validity (if possible) through intersubjective involvement and experience. Therefore, I do not treat my own experiences as subjective, isolated events of my own intentionality of consciousness but as an intersubjective dialogic product arising within the interpersonal field of social relations. Shamanism for me was a point of intersubjective entry into the Yanomami lifeworld, and the resulting personal experiences are windows providing my own subjective insights into that world. I was careful to separate my own experiences from the rest of the text, based primarily on observation and dialogue, and use them as valid supplementary data that can only be obtained through personal involvement. Some may object that the incorporation of ethnographers' subjective experiences into analysis could tell us more about how foreigners react to rituals and little about the nature of Yanomami experiences. Although this may be true to a certain extent, I follow Goulet and Miller (2007), arguing that these subjective experiences should not be dismissed a priori as irrelevant or biased but treated as viable research tools. In other words, ethnographers' subjective field experiences can reveal certain information about the general nature of human consciousness beyond a particular ethnographic instance. Laughlin, McManus and d'Aquili (1992) in their multidisciplinary analysis of the nature of the human brain and consciousness also used their own as well as other people's subjective experiences mediated by behaviour and cultural meanings as the primary data of consciousness.

The incorporation of anthropologists' subjective experiences into ethnographic analysis is what Goulet and Young (1994: 305) (advocating Husserl, and especially William James) refer to as a 'radically empirical method'. The personal data can then be compared to others' experiences in order to explore our similarities and differences within the intersubjective field of inter-experience (Jackson 1998: 5–16; Merleau-Ponty 1973: 56). Full participation in the lives of others without any preconceived prejudices requires the bracketing of all personal beliefs and suspension of disbelief to open up a part of ourselves to the experience, blocked off from our own cultural assumptions (Young and Goulet 1994). However, opening up to the experience of other lifeworlds involves more than simply the intellect. It is a holistic endeavour involving immersion and engagement through all the bodily senses. An important part of this process is the ethnographer's self-examination and his or her engagement in self-reflexivity, which is best summarised in the following words:

> When I reflect upon myself and my cultural universe ... I cannot delude myself by thinking that everything that my culture is, in some direct way, is also myself ... [l]ikewise, as an ethnographer I encounter and begin to understand that radical other through his or her and my concreteness in which the transcendent cultural meanings are entirely incarnated in each of us. And only in that synthesis the understanding is engendered and objectified. In this process I am appropriating the other just as he is appropriating me. Each ethnographer senses the limits of this process, for it requires the opening of him or herself, and as a consequence there ensues an inevitable sense of alienation. The initial step – the opening up ... – is the crucial momentum ...[i]n the momentum of opening one recognizes that every other is the possibility of oneself, which in effect shapes further assessment of both. (Mimica 1988: 159–60)

Once the fieldworker allows others to teach him or her their culture through experience and involvement, they can claim 'a new organ of understanding ... [and] regained possession of that untamed region of themselves, unincorporated in their own culture, through which they communicate with other cultures' (Merleau-Ponty 1964a: 120).

Throughout my fieldwork, I taped all major parts of shamanistic initiation as well as numerous shamanistic seances carried out by different shamans and for different purposes. The last few weeks in Platanal I spent transcribing this copious material with Makowë's help then translating with Jacinto transcripts of songs and chants from the Yanomami language into Spanish and finally into English. I also took a series of photographs of Arawë's initiation, some of which are included in this book. All data was recorded in a field diary, using different coloured pens for different kinds of information. For example, observations of daily activities and events, including the shamanistic sessions, were recorded with blue pen. Black pen was used for personal experiences, red for dreams, and lead pencil for 'thinking and reflecting' sections of my diary.

The Outline of the Book

The book is divided into eight chapters. Chapter One provides some background information on the Yanomami people; their habitat, the main features of their culture and a brief summary of historical migratory movements. The emphasis is placed on the Yanomami dwelling and their social organisation as well as sociocultural changes brought about by the Salesian Mission and Western medical personnel and their consequences. The chapter also introduces the ethnographic locale of two Yanomami communities (Mahekoto-theri and Sheroana-theri) and the main characters that appear in the book, as well as the local history of contact and regional micro movements of each community respectively, as told by field informants.

To understand the Yanomami lived reality of their cosmos, especially as articulated in shamanistic initiation and later practices, which is the book's central theme, it is necessary to begin with the depiction of the Yanomami cosmos and its origins. Chapter Two accordingly consists of the two main sections. Drawing mainly on different literary sources as well as on my field data, the first part depicts the composite image of the Yanomami cosmos as a holographic, multilayered totality and the relationship between its various components. Particular focus is on the motif of the fallen sky, a significant primordial event marking the end of an epoch. The second part of Chapter Two explores various transformative cosmogonic processes embedded in mythical accounts of multiple creations, contributing to the establishment of ontological order. The prevailing theme of these myths of origin is the multiplicity of transformations of ancestral beings through death and the emergence of different world components, including human beings. Here, I introduce the concept of primordial time or a pre-cosmic dimension in constant flux, which is particularly important for it also manifests itself as a specific state of primordial consciousness associated with death and shamanism.

The process of separation of material from non-material components of the Yanomami cosmos resulted in the bifurcation of the original ancestors into finite, disease-prone human beings on the one hand, and immortal hekura spirits on the other. Chapter Three accordingly analyses the nature and phenomenological manifestation of the ancestral hekura spirits and their relation to shapori, particularly focusing on shamanism in myths and in the contemporary context and the relationship between the shaman and the jaguar. The first part of the chapter explores the holographic relation between the shaman and his personal hekura assistants. This is followed by an analysis of the various entheogenic transformative substances commonly known as epena or yopo; the method of their preparation, ritual use, mythical origins and their experiential aspects. The remaining section of Chapter Three deals with the Yanomami conception of a person, including visible or physical aspects of the body and its invisible components of the multiple soul, as well as their relation to causes of various illnesses.

Chapter Four is a central part of the book. It is a detailed ethnographic description and systematic exploration and analysis of the entire process of body transformation during shamanistic initiation, which I term the corporeal cosmogenesis or metamorphosis of the human body into a cosmic body. The chapter follows the initiation of a young candidate, Arawë, which took place in Sheroana-theri. His ordeal involved an intense experience of multiple deaths through dismemberment by the hekura spirits, and subsequent rebirth as a 'living hekura'. But he also became a multiplicity of embodied hekura, which are his future personal assistants and sources of power, who imbue his post-mortem ego with certain holographic properties. Arawë received into his body the hekura path, their shapono and a corporeal (cosmic) mountain. His body thus became a micro replica of the Yanomami macrocosm. The last section of the chapter explores the concept of the shaman's cosmic body as the 'centre of the universe' and a site of its full manifestation.

Chapter Five follows Arawë's first steps in hekuramou practice, and explores the process of the continual expansion of a shapori's powers and capabilities through incorporation (but also loss) of additional hekura spirits. The main source of acquisition of additional hekura by far comes from dreams and dream-related activities. The chapter thus examines the role of dreams in Yanomami shamanism and analyses consciousness associated with dreaming. The specific focus is on the technique of dream control as a method of further incorporation of hekura spirits, followed by an analysis of dreaming in the context of shamanistic initiation. These issues are examined through a number of dream accounts relayed by the field informants, as well as my own dreams. The final section explores the links between dreams, illness and healing and the shaman's intrusion into other people's bodies through dreams. This is analysed through an account of the death of a boy from Sheroana-theri, who was apparently attacked in his dream by a distant enemy shaman.

The case of the boy's death is the point of departure for Chapter Six, which focuses primarily on the issue of ambiguity of shamans' social position and the application of their personal powers and skills for healing and harming purposes. The chapter examines the dialectics between the defensive and offensive types of shamanistic activities – a dual role that any shaman can assume depending on circumstances. The first section explores – through various ethnographic cases – protective and curative activities that shamans apply on the intracommunal level, including detoxifying poisonous substances, providing assistance during childbirth, retrieving a lost soul and protecting community members from harmful hekura spirits during storms. But, the same shaman can simultaneously engage his personal spirits in lethal assaults on potential victims from other, distant communities. Therefore, the next segment provides various ethnographic examples of hekura attacks and shamans' responses to those attacks, followed by the analysis of shamans' activities to include phenomenology of healing and harming, implicit in the shapori's access to other people's bodies. The remaining part deals with issues of subjectivity and intersubjectivity in relation to shamanism as a practical method of cultural knowledge diffusion first of all from the spirits directly to the shaman and, via him, to the rest of the community.

To the extent that the book thus far explores the essential aspects of Yanomami shamanism, the remaining two chapters deal with shamanistic activities in the bicultural context of medical pluralism; more specifically shamans' changing role in the context of cultural change, especially their attitudes and responses towards introduced diseases (and the corresponding new forms of treatment), which have resulted in a terminal imbalance in the Yanomami lifeworld. Chapter Seven deals with *shawara* epidemics, which Yanomami primarily identify with fever and the arrival of white people. The generic concept of shawara is examined through three major health disturbances (malaria, diarrhoea and respiratory diseases) that continue to be the principal causes of high mortality among the Yanomami of the Upper Orinoco. The chapter also explores the relationship between shamans and medical workers, as well as Yanomami attitudes towards Western medicine, including the ongoing problems associated with prolonged treatment.

The beginning of Chapter Eight refers back to the myth of the great deluge and the disappearance of the primordial twins. Particular emphasis is on shamans' interpretation of the advent of white people and deadly epidemics of previously unknown diseases within the context of Yanomami cosmology. The Yanomami initially interpreted the arrival of white people to the Upper Orinoco region in the mid nineteenth century as the return of their own ancestors or the offspring of their great cultural transformer Omawë to teach them the secrets of white people and bring them manufactured goods. Hence, the first part deals with the ways in which the Yanomami positioned themselves in relation to foreigners. The second part examines the overall process of the decline of shamanism and the shift in the nature of Yanomami leadership, which has paralleled the emergence of new, educated generations of Yanomami men who are now becoming less interested in continuing shamanistic tradition as a form of cultural identity. The last section explores the changing role of the Yanomami shamans and the link between the phenomenon of prophetic revelation and shamanism, which signals a radical shift in the Yanomami consciousness of the colonial context. To this end, the remaining part of the book examines the cosmo-shamanic discourse of the threat of a new collapse of the sky and subsequent 'end of the world' articulated through the shamanistic vision of the Brazilian shaman-prophet and political activist Davi Kopenawa. The situation in Brazil where the Yanomami contact with national society was much more traumatic is then compared to the Venezuelan situation where the threat of the crushing sky or collapse of a symbolic order is directly related to a general decline of interest in shamanism and a gradual decay of the Yanomami cosmos, but which arguably leads to the beginning of a new era.

The final section of the book (postscript) deals with several recent developments in the Upper Orinoco region and provides some updates based on my subsequent visits to field sites.

Notes

1. According to other sources, the word 'shaman' derives – via the Chinese *sha men* – from the 'Vedic *sram-* ('to heat oneself' or 'practise austerities'), and *sramana-* ('practitioner of austerities' or 'ascetic person') (Halifax 1979: 3; Hultkrantz 1973: 26; Lewis 1984: 5). Shirokogoroff and Mironov (cited in Peters and Price-Williams 1980: 398) argue that the word 'saman' is not native to North Asia but arrived there from the south from shamanism that, according to them, evolved from Tantric and Lamaistic Buddhism.
2. I will refer to the Yanomami shamans throughout the book using the male pronoun, mindful of the fact that they are predominantly male.
3. Zinberg (1977: 1) proposed the term 'alternate' as more appropriate than 'altered', because 'different states of consciousness prevail at different times for different reasons'. 'Alternate states of consciousness' is an all-inclusive term, unlike 'usual state of consciousness', which is merely one specific state of ASC.
4. In the State of Amazonas, the term criollo signifies a non-indigenous person.

5. Holography is a special type of three-dimensional lenseless photography invented by Nobel Prize winner Dennis Gabor in 1971. Gabor used holographic film that contained an interference pattern of chaotic light signatures or a hologram. Each illuminated piece of this image-pattern produces the whole three-dimensional, original image.

6. These interrelated communities from the remote Siapa River Valley south of the studied area are known by the collective name Shamathari and they are the traditional enemies of the Orinoco Yanomami.

7. Prior to coming to Platanal, I obtained a copy of Jacques Lizot's (1996) *Introducción a la Lengua Yanomami* and memorised some words and basic grammar rules. In Platanal, my vocabulary expanded considerably, and with Jacinto's help I was soon able to communicate on a basic level.

Chapter 1

LIFE ON TOP OF THE OLD SKY

Yanomami Habitat, Ethnographic Setting and Local
Histories

According to some mythical narratives, contemporary Yanomami and *napë*
(non-Yanomami) descended from the survivors of the great flood who sought
refuge on top of the Mãiyõ Mountain. Other narratives relate to another
significant primordial event – 'the collapse of an old sky' – which became
the earth where the Yanomami live. These are the themes that will be
discussed in Chapter Two. In this chapter, I will outline some basic features
of the Yanomami culture and habitat and provide a reconstruction of the
contemporary Yanomami origin through historical migratory movements
and encounters and the subsequent effects of culture change. The chapter
also introduces the ethnographic locale of two Yanomami communities
(Mahekoto-theri and Sheroana-theri), as well as the main characters that
appear throughout the book and the local history of contact and regional
micro movements of each community as told by field informants.

Yanomami Habitat

The Yanomami reside in shaponos (community dwellings). The terms
shapo-no and shapo-ri (shaman) both share the common root shapo-,
which is associated with domesticity (Lizot 2007: 281). The shapono is

a domesticated cultured space where human beings live, surrounded by wild, untamed forest, while a shapori is an aggregate of domesticated hekura spirit helpers, as opposed to their unruly counterparts. At first glance, a shapono appears as one unbroken circular construction covered with a slanted, leaf-thatched roof, curving around an open central area, but in fact it consists of a number of separate family houses adjacent to each other and all facing a large central patio. The shapono is divided into well-defined public, semiprivate and individual family areas. Each family builds their own section of the shapono. Family life is centred on the fire in the middle of the hearth around which people suspend hammocks, prepare and eat food or sleep, rest and converse. The strip of ground beneath the highest part of the roof and bordering the central patio is reserved for artisanal activities, mortuary rites and shamanistic sessions. The central area of a shapono (hehã) is a public, multifunctional space intended for communal activities and festivities where children play games, people dance, resolve quarrels or receive visitors and exchange gifts (Lizot 2004: 60). Hehã is the focal point of a shapono; everything is open towards it, everyone looks towards it and the life of the shapono revolves around it.

On a broader, macrocosmic scale, each shapono is a self-contained whole whose form mirrors the image of the Yanomami conception of their universe. The shapono is also the site of the direct manifestation of the cosmic order where social and cosmic hierarchies converge. A shapono's central area gapes towards the sky but is simultaneously a celestial arch (ãmo mɨsi) (Lizot 2004: 13), situated directly above the centre of a shapono, towards the roof's edge or the lower part of the sky where it meets the terrestrial cosmic stratum. The circumference of the roof's edge, from a shamanistic perspective, is equivalent to the horizon of a shapori's macrocosmic modality of expanded consciousness. Under the highest part of the roof where the two cosmic strata intersect, shapori carry out hekuramou activities and escort the souls of the deceased to their resting place in the sky after their bodies are cremated. A shapono's ground level includes sheltered family spaces and adjacent outer gardens. It also forms the basis of the flat terrestrial stratum while the subterranean level directly underneath a shapono is inhabited by the ancestral Amahiri (see Chapter Two).

Shaponos vary in size and shape. Depending on the population they can shelter between 20 and 200 inhabitants. The suffix theri contained within the name of each shapono means 'community' or 'a member of a local community', while the name itself indicates a certain animal, plant or nearby geographical feature (Smole 1976). The open type of shapono is the predominant model that continues to be erected without major alterations. However, it is by no means the only model. Communal houses of the eastern Yanomam subgroup are closed, cone-shaped structures with a small opening called *maloca*. In the cooler Parima Mountains, shaponos consist of smaller, rectangular houses with double sloping roofs and walls made of mud.

Shaponos are customarily erected near a water source, such as a river or creek. Near to each shapono is a cultivated, communal area *hikari thëka* with clearly delineated family sections managed exclusively by Yanomami men. The bulk of food supplies come from cultivated plants, therefore gardens are vital for survival. Establishing a new garden is hard work. Men must first fell large trees and then burn down the remaining undergrowth before they can plant crops. The main crops consist of various types of banana tree, plantains, sweet manioc, yautia, papaya fruit and sugar cane. Plantains (*kuratha*) are the staple food, occupying most of the garden – up to 75 per cent (Lizot 2004: 183). According to mythology, in primordial times when the Yanomami ancestors did not know about plantain, one of them by the name of Poreawë cultivated a prototype garden of various species of plantain. Another, ancestor Hõrõnami, stole them from Poreawë and taught others how to cultivate them (Lizot 1989). A special section of each family lot is allocated for tobacco growing. Tobacco (*pee nahe*) is an important element of the Yanomami way of life and a highly valued trade item. All Yanomami develop a lifelong habit and addiction through tobacco consumption. Hãshõriwë or the Ancestor of Kinkajou (also known as the 'honey bear') appears in various myths as the original custodian of tobacco, but Nosiriwë introduced it to the Yanomami. Once he was roaming through the forest, he felt particularly restless. To help him, his fellow ancestors or *no patapi* gave him various fruits, but nothing could satisfy his cravings. Finally, he met Hãshõriwë, who offered him some ready-made tobacco. Nosiriwë put it in his mouth, and then started spitting the juice. Wherever he spat, new plants grew and rapidly spread throughout the area (ibid.).

Another important source of alimentation is a much-esteemed fruit called *rasha* from the peach palm, which is used for making bows and quivers. Every year from December until February, during the harvest of this fruit, the Yanomami hold intercommunal feasts. The period from one harvest to the next is equivalent roughly to one year and this is how the Yanomami count time. For example, to say 'next year' or 'in a year's time' is *ei rasha tëhë*, which literally means 'next time when the peach palm bears its fruits' or 'next rasha harvest'. The original mythical custodian of the peach palm is Violaceous Jay from the crow family. Yanomami derive additional sources of food from fishing, hunting, and the gathering of wild forest fruits and berries, bee larvae, honey, ants, and crabs. The bulk of their meat supply comes from a wide range of game animals, such as tapirs, monkeys, armadillos, various rodents, snakes, bush pigs, anteaters, and a variety of birds. Hunting and gardening are predominantly male activities, while women engage in child-rearing and food-gathering practices.

The Yanomami remain in their shapono throughout most of the year, but during the dry season (from November to April) the entire community undertakes seasonal food-gathering expeditions (wãyumɨ) for a few months, during which time they gather berries, hunt or visit relatives in other communities. While in the forest, the Yanomami construct small provisional camps called tapiri, consisting of various family shelters. Every few years when the shapono's roof has become infested with insects or the garden soil has been exhausted, the Yanomami migrate to a new area where they establish a new garden and shapono.

Social Organisation and the Naming System

Each shapono community is a sovereign whole, interlinked with other shaponos through vast network of kinship ties extending beyond each community. All the inhabitants of a shapono are members of two or more patrilineages or mashi, which is a group of interrelated kinsmen with a common origin whose line of descent is traced through the paternal side of the family (Lizot 2004: 206). Patrilineages extend across various shaponos and within the same community, they are in effect 'the local segments of a dispersed lineage' (Ramos 1972: 193). A lineage comes into being when a group of agnates reside together for some time, and as they grow in numbers they become one generation. Two or more different lineages may merge and form one community. At some point in time, when the population of a shapono reaches a significant number, tension and internal disputes inevitably occur, which leads to some groups leaving the community to establish their own residence elsewhere. After some time, splinter groups will often make peace and become allies against a common enemy. All men within the same lineage are brothers and all women call each other sisters. Men from different lineages are potential marriage partners and they refer to each other as 'brother-in-law'. In addition, father and father's brother(s) are merged into the single classificatory category haye (father) while mother and her sister(s) are all called naye (mother) (Chagnon 1968a, 1968b, 1974; Saffirio 1985). Yanomami men and women are obliged to marry their cross cousins from different lineages or cousins from their parent's opposite sex sibling. Thus a man must marry a daughter of his maternal uncle or father's sister, which obliges him to reciprocate by giving his sister as a wife to the kinship group to which his wife belongs. His son(s) will continue this practice by exchanging their sisters.

Cross-cousin marriages reinforce ties and alliances between different kin groups. The newly married couple continues living matrilocally, with husbands obliged to carry out *siohamou* or son-in-law 'goods and service' duties for many years to come as a form of bride service to his wife. His son-in-law duties may include anything from giving a portion of the hunt to his father-in-law to repairing the worn-out roof of his father-in-law's house. The involuntary nature of arranged marriage partnerships does not prevent some Yanomami men from acquiring an additional, younger wife when their first one passes her reproductive age. The first wife sometimes leaves her husband in protest or out of jealousy and returns to her family. However, if she decides to stay she usually takes an authoritarian stance towards the newcomer. In the beginning there may be some friction and jealousy, even physical confrontations between co-wives, especially if they are not related, but eventually they accept each other. The advantage of polygamy for women is that they are able to share their daily workload. From the male perspective, more than one wife increases a man's social status and prestige. More wives would mean more children, which in turn would increase the possibilities of forming intercommunal conjugal alliances with other groups through female cross cousins as potential marriage partners (Chagnon 1992).

Parents customarily bestow names on their infants in consultation with shapori, based on baby's personal characteristics or some significant event that occurred around the time of their birth. However, children do not receive their proper names until approximately two years of age, because up until then they are not considered as persons, as their souls are not yet fully formed. Once a child receives a proper name and thus becomes a person, it is never pronounced in public. Instead, everyone calls each other by the appropriate kinship term. Yanomami living closest to rural health clinics such as the one in Platanal are more relaxed about personal name taboo while in more remote communities this is not the case. Various shapori told me about the danger of pronouncing someone's name loudly, because an enemy shapori in the distance could hear it and pinpoint the name-bearer causing him or her harm or even death with his hekura (see also Ramos 1972). Thus to confuse hekura, the Yanomami adopt foreign names. The shapori's aggression is facilitated through his victim's personal name and not the introduced foreign name. More powerful and self-confident shapori like Ruweweriwë from Sheroana-theri and Makowë from Platanal have public names because they are not afraid of other hekura. Personal name taboo is particularly strong in relation to deceased relatives. There is a strong prohibition of mentioning the name of a person after his or her death. This seems not to be the case among the Sanema where there is no distinction between living and dead in relation to name pronunciation (Ramos 1972, 1995). Yanomami call the deceased *kamakari*.[1] In Sheroana-theri, I often heard Yanomami publicly naming deceased persons from other communities as a joke, which was sometimes met with disapproval by fellow villagers.

Historical Migratory Movements and Encounters

No one really knows with absolute certainty where the Yanomami predecessors lived before the late eighteenth century. Some scientists have hypothesised that the contemporary Yanomami are solitary remnants of the earliest migrants who gravitated towards the South American continent from the north-west direction until reaching their present location where they remained isolated from other sequential groups and their cultural influences (Layrisse and Wilbert 1966; Wilbert 1963). Others postulate that the Yanomami are descendants of tropical forest and agricultural societies who were forced by other stronger groups to migrate from the central Amazon lowland flood plains northwards via the Rio Negro-Casiquiare Canal (Lathrap 1970). Once they reached the Orinoco River, most of the migratory groups continued spreading downriver while the Yanomami migrated eastwards until they reached the Parima Mountains. These two seemingly opposing theories are not necessarily mutually exclusive, as it has been widely agreed that small hunting bands of Palaeo-Asiatic hunters from north-east Asia crossed the Bering Strait via a land bridge that was connecting the Asian and American continents during the last Ice Age. The new inhabitants then gradually spread out southwards through what is now North America, all the way to Tierra del Fuego at the southernmost tip of South America. On the basis of some oral accounts recorded between 1957 and 1972, Italian linguist Ernest Cesar Migliazza (1972) suggested that the Yanomami ancestors were once part of a large proto-Panoan linguistic group inhabiting the area around the Upper Ucayali River of present-day Peru. They eventually descended towards the Lower Ucayali and then migrated eastward into what is now Brazil. The proto-Yanomami speakers, according to Migliazza (cited in Early and Peters 2000: 19), separated from this larger group and moved northwards along the Rio Negro to its confluence with the Rio Branco where they eventually settled around the area that is drained by various lower Rio Branco tributaries. Migliazza refers to the possible Yanomami origin of the name of one (and possibly more) of the lower Rio Branco tributaries, which Lizot (1984) takes as an indication of the Yanomami presence in this area prior to migrating to Sierra Parima where the actual frontier between Brazil and Venezuela runs through.

In the early colonial days, the region around the Rio Negro and Branco rivers was spared of colonisation processes. This is because the Europeans were too involved in managing coastal settlements and plantations – Portuguese along the east coast of Brazil and Spanish and Dutch on the Caribbean seaside of Guiana. In time, the amount of skilled labourers in coastal plantations became insufficient to meet the demand. From the mid seventeenth century onwards the Portuguese colonial administrators and slave traders navigated the main waterways in search of indigenous slaves and to concretise their territorial claims. Part of their strategy was to persuade mainly Arawakan indigenous groups to help them in their pursuit for new slaves. In the 1720s they eventually reached the Rio Negro – Branco area – and for the next one hundred years the Yanomami experienced a great loss of their population due to violent clashes and new infectious diseases introduced by slave traders and their Arawak helpers. Around the mid nineteenth century, the remaining Yanomami survivors were forced to abandon the area and seek refuge to the north, in the Parima Mountains, which were presumably unpopulated at that time (Ferguson 1995).

Secluded in the Parima highlands away from the major migratory routes of pre-Columbian indigenous groups and new microbial diseases, the Yanomami in the following decades managed to recover their population losses. Despite the inaccessibility of the rugged terrain they never lived in total isolation. They discovered the value of metal goods (axes, machetes, cooking pots) obtained through raids or from trade with neighbouring indigenous groups such as the Yekwana and Mácu, who had more contact with the Europeans. Protected from diseases and with new metal tools that helped to support intensive agriculture, in the following decades the Yanomami experienced a rapid demographic growth. During the first half of the twentieth century, pushed by population pressures and the desire to obtain more Western tools and manufactured goods, the Yanomami began to migrate from the Parima Mountains towards the lowlands. They later expanded their territory (Chagnon 1974; Heinen 1991; Lizot 1984, 1988) to the interfluvial areas around the Ocamo, Padamo, Mavaca and Orinoco rivers in Venezuela, which had apparently been previously occupied by Mandawaca Indians, who migrated southwards towards Rio Negro (Vidal Ontiveros 1993).

From the mid eighteenth century onwards, numerous exploratory expeditions and frontier commissions penetrated the region. The main objective of these undertakings was to reach the source of the Orinoco River, which was believed to be the Lake Parime with legendary El Dorado on its shores. Other aims were to make scientific discoveries or to mark the boundaries of nation states. On their journeys they frequently heard stories mainly from other indigenous groups about the dangerous 'Guahiba' people living around the Orinoco headwaters. In the Upper Orinoco River region of Venezuela, the Goaharibo rapids, situated upriver from today's Platanal Mission post, formed a natural barrier that kept various European explorers from reaching the source of the Orinoco River. The first known European incursion into the Upper Orinoco region was undertaken in 1758 by Francisco Fernandez de Bobadilla, an officer in charge of the Spanish exploratory expedition; however, he did not reach the Goaharibo rapids or encounter any Yanomami (Caballero-Arias 2003). In 1760, Apolinar Díez de la Fuente was in charge of the Limits Expedition, which set out to reach the source of Orinoco. He founded the settlement La Esmeralda but never went further beyond it due to warnings from local Yekwana people about the ferocious 'Guariba' Indians. When German naturalist and explorer Alexander von Humbolt reached La Esmeralda in 1799, he also encountered other local Yekwana. In their stories the ferocious tribe were believed to be 'White Indians' ('Guaicas') but he, too, did not have a direct encounter with them (Smole 1976). In 1886 Jean Chaffanjon, a French explorer, not only reached the Goaharibo rapids but continued his journey upriver to the next big rapids; he named them Peñascal, believing he had reached the source of Orinoco. On his journey he did not encounter any Yanomami.

The first reported contacts with the Yanomami occurred in 1787 around the area of the Upper Parima River in Brazil, by members of the Portuguese Border Commission, led by a military geographer Manuel da Gama Lobo D'Almada. The second reported contacts were made in 1939 by a German-born explorer for Great Britain, R. H. Schomburgk. In 1911, another German explorer and scientist Theodor Koch-Grünberg apparently met two Yanomami groups on the Uraricoera River, a tributary of the Rio Branco. He allegedly went to their villages and provided the first ethnographic information about their way of life (Early and Peters 2000). In 1920, an American geographer Alexander Hamilton Rice reached the Goaharibo rapids where he encountered a group of hostile 'Guaharibos' (Yanomami) warriors. Thinking that they were cannibals, he opened fire killing a few of them, when in fact they were after some manufactured goods.[2] Another American explorer and ethnologist, Herbert Dickey, hoping to reach the Orinoco headwaters, arrived at Goaharibo rapids in 1931 where he met a group of friendly Yanomami with whom he exchanged some manufactured goods.

In the first two decades of the twentieth century, rubber was discovered in the Upper Orinoco and Rio Negro regions. During a short-lived rubber boom the contact between the Yanomami and the rubber tappers and farmers intensified. The incursion of rubber tappers coincided with Yanomami demographic expansion from Parima towards the Mavaca, Ocamo and Orinoco rivers, and their sporadic encounters sometimes led to violent clashes. In 1932 a clash at the Rio Dimití – a tributary of the Rio Negro – between a group of Yanomami from the village of Kohoroshiwethari and a Brazilian farming family resulted in the kidnapping of a 12-year-old girl, Helena Valero. She spent the next twenty years living with the Yanomami, and her story was recorded between 1962 and 1963 by Italian parasitologist and anthropologist Ettore Biocca (1971).

The more Yanomami heard the stories about strange white human-like beings coming by the big river (Orinoco) and bringing with them metal tools and other goods, the more they were willing to migrate to lowlands in search of metal tools. On the other side, the decades before the missionaries arrived in the Upper Orinoco were characterised by an increase in conflicts and sorcery accusations between various Yanomami groups, concomitant with an increase in the presence of new metal tools and previously unknown diseases (Ferguson 1992). From the 1940s onwards, the rubber tappers left the area but were soon replaced by timber workers. In 1946, Juan Eduardo Noguera and his party of loggers went up the Orinoco from La Esmeralda. They discovered a garden with lots of plantains, some distance below the Goaharibo rapids, and met a group of Yanomami from the Mahekoto-theri to whom they gave some metal tools. Noguera named the place Platanal. This Yanomami group was the first to settle permanently on the banks of the Orinoco River where they remain to this day. In 1950, a missionary, James Baker, from the evangelist New Tribes Mission (NTM) arrived in Platanal and founded the first mission post there. The following year, a joint French-Venezuelan scientific expedition passed through Platanal on their way to the source of the Orinoco for the purpose of demarcating the disputed border between Brazil and Venezuela. Following the success of that expedition, the two countries agreed that the entire Orinoco would be part of Venezuela (Anduze 1960). A few years later, Baker encountered a group of Yanomami from the Pishaasi-theri downstream from Platanal near the mouth of the Mavaca River and gave them quantities of manufactured goods and machetes in order to encourage them to settle. He established a second mission outpost at Mavaca where the Venezuelan Ministry of Health erected a malaria control station (Ferguson 1992). In 1957, the Salesian Catholic missionaries Luis Cocco and Alfredo Bonvecchio founded a third mission outpost downriver from Mavaca at the confluence of the Ocamo and Orinoco Rivers and named it 'Santa Maria de los Guaicas', nowadays known as Ocamo. Here the third group of Yanomami from the Iyëwei-theri,[3] who were migrating down the Ocamo River at the time, settled permanently. Father Cocco remained in charge of the mission for the next fifteen years (Cardozo and Caballero 1994; Cocco 1972; Heinen 1991; Steinvorth-Goetz 1969). James Baker stayed in Platanal until 1959 when he handed over the administration of the Mission to the Salesians while he and other North American evangelists moved their headquarters to Sierra Parima and Koyowë. This zone consequently became their main area of influence until 2005 when they were expelled from the country. The fourth mission, Mavakita, on the Mavaca River was founded in 1976.

The Sweeping Winds of Change and its Consequences

Ever since the missionaries established themselves permanently in the Upper Orinoco region the Yanomami have experienced accelerated cultural change along with the general deterioration of their health and subsequent population decline. One of the major consequences of the missionaries' activities and influences has been the alteration of the structure of the conventional Yanomami communal dwelling. The missionaries encouraged the Yanomami to build individual rectangular houses with double-sloped roofs for each extended family. Closed houses protect dwellers from insects that thrive in abundance along the river, but have resulted in the compartmentalisation of social space and the erosion of social cohesion (Lizot 1976b). This change in living arrangements has also affected the outdoor practice of shaporimou, which is now practised inside the house. But this does not appear to be a major problem.

In the early days, the Salesians adopted a paternalistic and protective attitude towards the Yanomami, focusing their attention on 'civilising' them and teaching them religious doctrine. In 1972, Salesian missionaries opened a boarding school for the Yanomami and Yekwana children in La Esmeralda (ibid.). The missionaries brought children from neighbouring communities, separating them from their parents. At boarding school, children were taught Spanish and to read and write in their own language, but the main purpose of the school was to indoctrinate the children in non-indigenous values and to assimilate them into national society and a national way of life. On a broader level, the intention was to train indigenous children to become teachers, who would eventually become the new leaders in their communities. Due to widespread avoidance of school in La Esmeralda, in 1975 the Salesian Mission underwent some internal reforms and adopted a new approach to dealing with local communities by preserving and reinforcing Yanomami cultural practices and traditional values while focusing on a more gradual introduction of cultural and social changes, primarily through education and self-management and continuing to prepare them for integration into national society. However, their work inevitably generated and continues to generate profound social changes regarding basic principles of traditional leadership and social organisation. The following year the Salesians, backed up by the Ministerial Office for the Subject of Frontiers and Indigenous Peoples (OMAFI) – a division of the Ministry of Education – implemented the first intercultural and bilingual educational programme called 'Plan Pastoral'. This ambitious project in fact integrated several programmes concerning education, indigenous teacher training and economic cooperatives (Salamone 1997). New branches of bilingual boarding schools were established for the Yanomami children in all mission centres, including Platanal, together with so-called 'extension schools' in adjacent communities run by the first generation of Yanomami teachers.

During the 1980s, the mission started introducing the Yanomami to the world of commerce and the value of money and paid work. In 1986, the missionaries and some missionary-trained Yanomami leaders founded the Yanomami trade cooperative 'United Shaponos of the Yanomami from the Upper Orinoco' (SUYAO). This initiative was aimed at fostering Yanomami self-management through commerce by engaging most of the riverine communities in commercial activities and promoting the production of handicrafts. On another level, the projected intention of the missionaries was to create a grass-roots Yanomami organisation that would represent their voice and interests in the external world. A branch of SUYAO was created at each mission post where the Yanomami could exchange their artefacts, such as baskets, bows and arrows for machetes, axes, knives, pots, soap, fishing hooks and nylon. As an alternative, Western goods provided by the missionaries could be bought with money; a growing number of Yanomami had salaries from employment by the local government, while others could earn cash by doing various types of work around the mission sites, such as mowing the lawn or washing clothes and cleaning the mission house. The trade activities of SUYAO went far beyond the river settlements, as a two-way trade flow of manufactured goods and handicrafts engaged the Yanomami from more remote inland communities to the south of Orinoco, which was a covert intention of the missionaries. The organisation worked well for some time, until the Yanomami started expressing their dissatisfaction with their subordinate position and the desire and aspiration to gain more economic independence from the missionaries. The SUYAO cooperative certainly contributed to the influx of much-desired Western goods. However, by introducing new values through money it also generated some tensions and social inequalities, as only a few privileged individuals emerged with new social status and economic power.

Another consequence of prolonged contact with outsiders has been the changes in Yanomami diet. The Yanomami from Platanal and adjacent communities became increasingly dependent on food provided by the missionaries, such as pasta, canned sardines, cooking oil, sugar, salt and rice, which they would often receive as a form of payment for their work in the mission. The mission also regularly provides this type of food to children attending boarding schools in Mission centres and 'extension schools' in adjacent communities. Consequently, whole generations of Yanomami children are growing up on an introduced diet. More and more Yanomami now prefer to earn money by working in the Mission and eating the introduced food rather than attending to their gardens or go hunting and fishing. In some instances Yanomami prefer to sell their game and buy food from the shop in La Esmeralda. In addition, more than half a century of a sedentary lifestyle coupled with the introduction of hunting guns has contributed to game depletion around mission posts. As a consequence of this change in diet and a sedentary lifestyle, the Yanomami have introduced more fat into their diet, which has marked detrimental consequences for their general health (Lizot 1976b). Further major change took place from the mid 1990s onwards. The Upper Orinoco region became a municipality with its seat in La Esmeralda. National multiparty politics and the voting system known as 'politica criolla' have crept into the Yanomami and Yekwana communities causing major divisions among the population. In the first place, the first elected major was the Yekwana candidate Jamie Turon, who appointed his own representative for all the Yanomami from the nearby community of Cejal; however their interests were not represented equally. Secondly, the local municipality started to employ some Yanomami with regular salaries as supervisors in their communities or promoters of sports, social services or culture, which further increased the social inequalities and tensions between individuals. In sum, these developments created divisions among the Yanomami population, both on the intra-communal as well as the general macro level. The major disagreement that resulted in the fission of the Yanomami into two opposing blocks took place in 1997 after a conference organised by ORPIA (Organisation of Indigenous Peoples of the Amazon), when Yanomami representatives from Ocamo, Mavaca and Platanal, backed by the Salesian missionaries, proposed the creation of a monoethnic, Yanomami-only municipality by the name of the Yanomami demiurge Omawë with a seat in Mavaca. They argued that they had been marginalized and not adequately represented. Another argument raised at the conference was that the community lacked material goods and money. Others, from Cejal, Warapana and Mavakita wanted to preserve the existing political division. It is beyond the theme of this book to discuss the divisions of these two opposing population blocks at length (see Caballero-Arias 2003), but it is important to mention that they are partly articulated in the animosities and witchcraft accusations that stem from the past. We will see throughout many examples later on how these historic animosities are ongoing in the form of shamanic attacks and reprisals. For the Mahekoto-theri and Sheroana-theri the traditional enemies are the southern Shamathari and for the latter this also includes some communities around Mavaca and Cejal further downriver.[4] The Yanomami-only municipality was never put into place, and political division has remained to the present day.

Health Problems and the State's Responses

One of the main factors that has contributed to the development and transmission of parasitic infections and a general increase of intestinal and respiratory diseases is the radical shift in the character of the Yanomami settlement pattern. From being semi-nomadic people preferring to build their settlements near small inland streams at a medium altitude, they started to build their shaponos along rivers.

> It is generally recognised that large permanent nucleated settlements foster unhealthy conditions by encouraging the concentration of wastes and parasites. They also facilitate the spread of directly transmitted infectious diseases by enabling frequent contacts between individuals. (Polunin, cited in Newson 1993: 258)

Medical personnel working in the area at the time of my fieldwork were of the prevailing opinion that the closed-type of house affected the health of the Yanomami in negative ways. Many Yanomami, especially children, now suffer from asthma and coughs, exacerbated by the smoke, which accumulates inside the house. Closed-type houses also tend to be dirtier, as there is rubbish lying everywhere: banana skins, sardine tins, etc. Doctors as well as many Yanomami are nostalgic for the original, healthier and cleaner open-type of shapono where everyone lived together, though some Yanomami prefer closed-type houses because there is more privacy for lovemaking, fewer mosquitoes and it is warmer at night. Frequent intercommunal gatherings and traditional trade activities at mission centres have further helped the geographical spread of parasites and infectious diseases from sedentary riverine communities to more remote, inland communities.

One of the most detrimental consequences of prolonged contact with the 'outside world' has been an increased exposure to various new diseases, which has greatly affected the health of the Yanomami and resulted in a population decline. The health situation worsened from the late 1960s when more outsiders than ever were coming to the Upper Orinoco, bringing with them various pathogens. One example of the epidemiological consequences of intensifying contact was the 1968 measles epidemic that was introduced by some Brazilians. As a result, the Mahekoto-theri lost around 25 per cent of their population, according to Chagnon (1992: 286). In the early 1970s, the Venezuelan government launched the programme 'The Conquest of the South' (CODESUR) coordinated by the Commission for the Development of the South, whose main objective was socio-economic development and geographical integration of southern parts of the country and its indigenous peoples, including the Yanomami. During this short-lived project, medical dispensaries were built in Ocamo, Mavaca and Platanal. Moreover, an existing airstrip was improved in Ocamo while a new one was cleared in Platanal where from 1971 until 1975 the missionary in charge was promoting tourism, bringing rich tourists from Europe to have 'the Yanomami experience' with around forty Brazilians working on the project. The presence of a large number of outsiders in the 1970s resulted in a general increase in respiratory infections and frequent, severe malaria outbreaks, with a new deadly *falciparum* strain having been introduced into the region, which resulted in severe health crisis and many deaths. Prior to the mid 1980s, there were no resident doctors in the area of the Upper Orinoco and they came sporadically from other parts of the state. Missionaries and malaria service workers were able to provide some basic medical assistance through primary care. The Catholic sisters of Maria Auxiliadora specialised in sanitary assistance and nursing and established the first register of vaccinations, births and deaths, and possible causes of death. As the cases of sick Yanomami around the mission posts multiplied, and with the possibility of outbreaks of epidemics in remote communities, the missionaries decided to hand over the problem to the state. In 1985, the Venezuelan Ministry of Health and Social Welfare created a programme of medical attention called 'Parima-Culebra' aimed at providing health assistance to the Yanomami population of the Upper Orinoco. Under this scheme, young graduate doctors with no prior experience of working with native populations were sent from Caracas to do compulsory one-year rural service to health clinics in La Esmeralda, Ocamo, Mavaca and Platanal. The programme soon ran into various economic and logistic difficulties, but the situation started to improve in 1993 when the Upper Orinoco Sanitary District No. 4 was created under the direct administrative control and responsibility of the Regional

Health Office of Amazonas. Ever since then, a doctor for a one- or two-year period has been assigned as a Chief of the District, responsible for logistics. Furthermore, following an agreement between the SACAICET (Amazonian Centre for Investigation and Control of Tropical Diseases 'Simon Bolivar') and the School of Medicine at the Central University of Venezuela (UCV), a new boost in medical personnel in the Upper Orinoco has been accomplished under the new rotating government programme known as 'Project Amazonas'. Every two months two medical students (and less frequently dentistry students) in their final year of study are sent to each health clinic to practise as part of their degree completion.

In addition to non-Yanomami medical personnel working in health clinics, over the years there has been an emphasis on training Yanomami as part of the health staff. One of the main objectives of this idea is to bridge the gap between medical workers and the Indigenous population, and on a broader scale, the long-term, ongoing aim of the increased incorporation of the Yanomami into the health system is to foster Yanomami self-management of their health. In 1976, the first Yanomami were capacitated as auxiliaries of simplified medicine and since then each health clinic has had one working alongside doctors. In 1995, the first group of Yanomami received training as microscopists for malaria. Nowadays, each health clinic is supposed to be staffed with one resident doctor, two students of medicine, one Yanomami microscopist, a motorist and one or two auxiliaries of simplified medicine.

Platanal and Sheroana-theri at the Turn of the Twenty-first Century

The Salesian Mission post in Platanal consists of a hut with a palm-thatched roof used as a chapel, the missionary residence, an intercultural and a bilingual school with a dining room for Yanomami children and the local branch of the SUYAO cooperative where the Yanomami exchange their crafts for manufactured goods. In 1999, there was no resident priest in Platanal and a young lay missionary couple, Howard and Olga, were running the site. Howard was a caretaker and supervisor of the SUYAO activities, while Olga was a teacher at the bilingual school together with one Yanomami assistant. Father Nelson resided at the Mavaca headquarters and he was in charge of all mission posts. Every Sunday, he would come to Platanal to hold a local mass for a group of around twenty baptised Yanomami. For them, the Sunday Mass was a time to socialise, sing religious songs in their own language and wear their best clothes and body adornments. School would start each day at 8.00 A.M.

with children lined up under the rising Venezuelan flag and singing the national anthem 'Gloria al Bravo Pueblo'. In classes they were taught maths, health-related subjects and Spanish. Classes would run until approximately midday when children would go for a swim in the river and then have lunch. In Platanal children could go up to sixth grade and those who wished to continue their education had to go to the capital of the Upper Orinoco municipality, La Esmeralda. In 'extension schools' located in adjacent communities and run by locally trained Yanomami teachers, children could only go up to third grade and after that they had to continue their education in Platanal.

The Platanal health post has an extensive geographical area of coverage that nowadays stretches all the way upriver as far as the Peñascal rapids and inland south of the Orinoco up to the Sierra de Unturán Mountain range. Altogether it covers twenty communities with populations ranging from 11 to 145 inhabitants (see Figure 0.1). These communities are classified into four main groups according to their distance and accessibility from Platanal: base communities (in Platanal); close (up to 1 hour by boat); intermediate (up to 5 hours by boat) and distant (more than 5 hours by boat and/or walking). During 1999 and 2000, medical workers were only visiting close and intermediate communities every so often due to a lack of fuel and strenuous work commitments in Platanal. Medical infrastructure in Platanal includes a residence for doctors and medical students, a rural health clinic and an adjacent hospital building for patients from intermediary and distant communities that require medical observation. The health clinic consists of an area for consultation, a room with medicaments that serves as a pharmacy, and one separate room with two microscopes for identifying malaria that serves as a laboratory (Figure 1.1).

In 1999, the health clinic and the nearby hospital were in poor condition but the following year both buildings were renovated. The residence for medical staff, situated in front of the clinic, is rudimentary with one kitchen-dining room with a gas stove, a bathroom and two bedrooms where medical workers sleep in their hammocks. Electricity for light and cooking as well as to run the health clinic is obtained through solar panels or a small gasoline-powered generator, which is only used for a few hours in the evening due to chronic fuel shortages. Fuel is primarily reserved for trips to upriver communities within the Platanal area of influence.

Up until the end of 1999, Dr Helen Rodríguez was the resident doctor in charge, with two students rotating every two months as part of the aforementioned 'Project Amazonas' programme. In addition, two Yanomami employees were working in the clinic: malaria microscopist Elias Yakirahiwë and male nurse Julio Vichato. Each morning around 8.00 A.M., one of them would open the clinic and get things ready before

Figure 1.1 Health clinic in Platanal.

the doctor and medical assistants arrived. From the early hours of the morning there would be a row of patients gathered in front of the clinic – mostly mothers with their children – waiting to be examined. Morning work at the clinic terminated at midday when doctors would go to lunch and rest until 2.00 or 3.00 P.M. then the clinic would open again until 6.00 or 7.00 P.M. Sometimes, in the afternoons, Dr Helen would go to a nearby shapono to visit patients who were too sick to come to the clinic or go by motorboat upriver to adjacent communities to do a round of visits and administer treatment. The medical personnel often complained about the numerous problems they encountered working in Platanal, ranging from challenging working conditions in the clinic itself to various difficulties in dealing with the Yanomami. For example, Helen would call by radio the medical headquarters in La Esmeralda and order a medicament, which was about to run out, but the medicine would never arrive before the existing supplies were completely exhausted. She told me about a delicate situation in which antipyretic drugs did not arrive on time and she only had injections, which the Yanomami refused to receive because they were afraid of needles. Another ongoing problem was the aforementioned chronic shortage of fuel, which prevented medical personnel from making more trips to nearby communities.

The main Yanomami authority figures in Platanal at that time were Jacinto Serowë and Alfredo Aherowë – the two siblings with a long history of mutual rivalry and animosity. The whole population was accordingly divided along their kinship lines. The older brother Alfredo inherited leadership of the Mahekoto-theri from their father Okoshiwë, a man of great prestige and an ex-shapori, who was very young when the white people, presumably the rubber tappers, arrived at the upper Orinoco around late 1930s and early 1940s. The mainstream community at the time of my fieldwork numbered 178 individuals living in one large shapono. Alfredo had a reputation of solving disputes with a shotgun and many Yanomami from other communities beyond Platanal feared him. Jacinto and other opponents described him as an aggressive, selfish and greedy leader who liked to impose his power and authority on others. Jacinto, on the other hand, is a missionary-educated man of influence, who has been involved in the SUYAO cooperation and in politics. He obtained approval from the National Council of Indians of Venezuela (CONIVE) in Puerto Ayacucho to organise people. He was also responsible for organising political meetings of Yanomami from the area. After a serious dispute with his brother, Jacinto had decided to leave the community with his immediate kinfolk, including his father-in-law shapori Makowë, Elias the microscopist and their families, and establish a separate community in the vicinity of the Mahekoto-theri shapono. Makowë is a prominent shapori originally from the community of Arimawei-theri, situated in the area of the Manaviche River. He is primarily engaged in protecting and healing members of his own community but he also frequently visits his Mahekoto-theri colleagues and participates in group shamanic sessions or healing rituals. The most powerful and prestigious of all shapori in Mahekoto-theri is Nakiishima, the father-in-law of Alfredo and Jacinto. He is commonly known as Enano ('dwarf'), a nickname that he acquired due to his short stature. Enano has a great social position and influence, borne out by the fact that the most important and prestigious men in the community are married to some of his six daughters. As his sons-in-law, Alfredo and Jacinto are therefore obliged to perform bride service duties for some years. Jacinto is married to one daughter and Alfredo to another; two other daughters became the wives of an auxiliary of simplified medicine, Vichato – a man of great prestige and material wealth who worked in the clinic for many years. At the time of my fieldwork he owned a boat with an outboard motor, a double-barrelled shotgun, an expensive stereo and a power generator for electricity in his house.

The Local History of the Mahekoto-theri

During the second half of the nineteenth century, the Mahekoto-theri forebears were living in Sierra Parima as part of the 'mother' community called Uhepëki from which, according to Lizot (1984), one of the three major clusters of communities later originated. At the turn of the twentieth century, they started to migrate, slowly descending towards the lowlands and eventually settling at the headwaters of the Puutha kë u (Putaco) River where they built a large shapono next to a hill called Husirawë. From there, they moved in a southwesterly direction, making a series of gardens along the way, before settling around 1920 at a place called Kunawë at the foothills of Parima Massif. There they entered into conflict with some neighbouring communities and consequently moved further south, eventually reaching the area of the Upper Manaviche River – a right tributary of the Orinoco – and settled at Kaomawë around 1930. From there they made frequent visits to communities on the other side of the Orinoco, namely Hasupiwei-theri and Namowei-theri to trade with them and strengthen alliances. Due to internal quarrels, the community in Kaomawë split up into various groups. During the 1930s one group, the Shitoya-theri, which later became the Mahekoto-theri, moved southwards and established themselves on the other side of Manaviche, closer to the Orinoco River. They obtained material goods through trade with Yanomami groups from Padamo, who had regular contact with the Yekwana (Ferguson 1995). A decade later, they established direct contact with some rubber tappers from whom they obtained Western goods (see Chapter Eight).

According to Okoshiwë, who was very young around the time when they encountered the white people for the first time, the Mahekoto-theri (then called the Shitoya-theri) were still located somewhere in the area around the Upper Manaviche River. The Yanomami greatly feared the newcomers and the only one who could approach them without fear was Okoshiwë's father, who was their leader. The newcomers offered him machetes, saucepans and various other gifts, which he eagerly accepted. Upon returning to Shitoya, Okoshiwë's father told his people that the foreigners were good and generous and did not want to harm the Yanomami. Encouraged by these words, the Yanomami came to meet the foreigners and received a substantial amount of gifts from them. Not long after this event, they decided to abandon their shapono and move closer to the Orinoco. Around the mid 1940s they crossed the river and established a large garden with lots of plantains and erected their shapono at the place where the Orinoco River bends in the shape of a knee (maheko) and thus they became the Mahekoto-theri (Biocca 1971; Valero 1984).

Jacinto recalled the original Mahekoto-theri shapono as being a large, open-type communal house with numerous inhabitants. It remained intact until the 1970s when it grew so large that it bifurcated into two groups known as the downriver (*koro*) Mahekoto of which Okoshiwë was a leader and the upriver (*ora*) Mahekoto of which his brother was a headman. The two communities lived relatively close to each other in peace until one day Alfredo killed a young man from the upriver Mahekoto. As a result of this incident, a fraction of this community left and established the separate community Guakamaya-theri, situated further up river where they are still located today. At some point in time, one family left Guakamaya-theri to build their own house, which became the Yoipana-theri community, while a second family left to establish the community of Payara. In 1989, Makowë's father lost his life in a club fight. Consequently, Jacinto and Alfredo turned against each other. Jacinto and Makowë disappeared for a while. Makowë went with his family to his natal community of Arimawei-theri near the Manaviche River. Jacinto and his family went to his natal community of Sheroana-theri where they stayed for the next three months. After this he came back to Manaviche to join Makowë. They eventually returned to Mahekoto-theri where they made a temporary shapono on the opposite bank of the Orinoco River. After some intense negotiations, they resettled near the missionary residence where they are still located today.

Sheroana-theri: Past and Present

The original Sheroana-theri (Patanowë) community where Jacinto was born was made up of two big shaponos consisting of three lineages, which eventually split up and became three separate communities: the Toritha-theri, Sheroana-theri and Hapokashita-theri. The Sheroana-theri shapono is nowadays situated near the Shanishani River – Orinoco's left tributary, approximately eight hours on foot from its confluence with the Orinoco, some distance below the Goaharibo rapids, where the forest trails begin. The name Sheroana derives from a nearby mountain called Sheroroi Këkɨ (Painted Mountain), as the side facing the community is black. In the year 2000, the Sheroana-theri numbered 29 living in a small-sized, traditional Yanomami shapono with an unbroken angled roof. Sheroana-theri belongs to the area of influence of the Platanal health clinic, but during my stay between 1999 and 2000 no doctors or missionaries visited the community.

The ancestors of the present-day Sheroana-theri were once part of a larger group called the Namowei, who at the turn of the twentieth century lived on the slopes of Sierra Parima at a place called Konata to the north of the Peñascal rapids (Chagnon 1968a; Ferguson 1995). Frequent conflicts with local communities forced them to abandon the site and move south, crossing the Orinoco River and settling around 1910 at a place called Wareta. New wars compelled them to abandon Wareta and relocate to Namowei on the other side of the Orinoco. From there, they migrated westwards to Hahoyaoba but as the soil quality at that location was poor, they crossed the Orinoco yet again and established themselves at Patanowë sometime between 1925 and 1930. During that time, the Namowei grew in size with two enormous gardens and many inhabitants. Helena Valero recounts that it consisted of four separate groups or lineages: the Namowei-theri, the Patanowë-theri, the Yaminawë-theri and the Pishaasi-theri (Biocca 1971). The leaders of all four lineages were shapori, as were their fathers from whom they inherited the leadership and their hekura spirits. Helena's husband Fusiwë was a leader of the dominant Namowei-theri lineage, and his uncle was a leader of the Patanowë-theri, the most numerous of the four lineages. The antecedents of contemporary Sheroana-theri formed a part of Patanowë-theri lineage.

Helena Valero comments how on one occasion, around the late 1930s, the Namowei-theri invited the Shitoya (Mahekoto-theri) and some other groups for a feast. After the feast, some Yanomami from the Namowei-theri quietly abducted seven Shitoya women (Biocca 1971). Members of the Patanowë-theri lineage did not approve of this act, and, knowing that the Shitoya-theri were friends with white people, thought it likely that they were going to return with guns and retaliate. It is important to note that the Yanomami from Shitoya by that time had developed a superior position over other communities because of their possession of Western goods through contacts with both white people passing by the river and the Yanomami groups from Padamo, who traded with Yekwana. Patanowë-theri left the Namowei in protest, or, according to Fusiwë, the headman of the Namowei-theri, out of fear and became a separate community, migrating south-westerly to settle at a place called Karepa. From there, they migrated westwards and made a new, larger shapono and changed their name to Ahiwei-theri. Finally, they moved again, northwards, and settled near the Sheroroi Mountain where they changed their name again to Sheroana-theri.

The further fission of the Namowei occurred in the early 1940s when Yaminawë-theri decided to leave after a serious club fight. Only thirty people from Fusiwë's once dominant lineage remained with him as Namowei-theri. Finally, after a series of confrontations, Fusiwë was killed and the Pishaasi-theri with their leader Rashawë split up and migrated westwards near the mouth of the Mavaca River (Chagnon 1968a). The shapori Ruweweriwë, Jacinto's older brother, told me that it was the Patanowë-theri who experienced the first encounters with white people, albeit they had heard about them before they met them face-to-face. At that time, they had very few machetes, which they had to acquire through trade with the Mahekoto-theri, but, according to Ruweweriwë, they had a large number of shapori. One of them – probably Fusiwë (see Chapter Eight) – saw white people in a dream before the actual encounter. Upon waking, he told others, describing the white people as ghost-like and having the second skin or *iro sikɨ* ('skin of a red howler monkey'), which is the term that the Yanomami use for T-shirts. When the Patanowë-theri met the foreigners they received machetes and metal saucepans as gifts. 'Those first napë [non-Yanomami][5] were much more generous than today's napë', commented Ruweweriwë with smile on his face, but he quickly added that once the napë refused to give more trade goods, the initial peaceful encounters between the newcomers and the Yanomami quickly deteriorated. Back then, both the napë and the Yanomami were much more valiant than today and not averse to killing each other. When the newcomers refused to give their goods, the Yanomami attacked them with their arrows and the napë quickly retaliated, killing Yanomami with their shotguns, which Ruweweriwë called *wakeshipɨ wayu* ('deadly smoke or smoke that harms').[6] He said that those guns were different from present-day rifles, explaining how napë were not shooting at Yanomami directly. In his own words: 'They were shooting towards the sky. This produced a smoke containing deadly *shawara* (epidemic disease), which fell down on them, and later they died together with their dogs'.

According to Jacinto, the first fission of the original Sheroana-theri community (the Patanowë-theri) occurred in 1987 after their confrontation with the Tayari-theri, a community that was once located on the banks of the Orinoco River between Platanal and Mavaca, but who no longer exists. The Tayari-theri visited the Sheroana and asked for a good hunting dog. They received what they requested, but this created some friction when some of the Yanomami protested and formed a small group to go to the Tayari-theri and bring the dog back. When the Tayari-theri refused to surrender the dog, open confrontation erupted in which one Tayari-theri Yanomami was killed. Fearing reprisals, the Tayari-theri, who were less numerous than the Sheroana-theri, allied themselves with the Mahekoto-theri, seeking their help and protection. Back in Sheroana-theri, the killing sparked further tensions within the community, which eventually culminated in another open, bloody confrontation. As a consequence, one section of the community left and migrated further inland to the upper reaches of the Shanishani River. They became the Toritha-theri. Further fission of the remaining Sheroana-theri occurred after a club fight when one section of the group decided to leave. They eventually settled near the Orinoco River and became the Hapokashita-theri, who changed their name in the year 2000 to Koyeta-theri. The remaining Sheroana-theri fused with the now extinct Wanapiwei-theri and they jointly erected a new, much smaller shapono.

Ruweweriwë eventually passed on the leadership of the new Sheroana-theri (now reduced in size) to a younger man, Maruwë; however, Ruweweriwë remains the most influential and prestigious man in the community. Up until the year 2000, when I came to live with the Sheroana-theri, Ruweweriwë was the only shapori in the community. In that year, his nephew Arawë, whose deceased father was an eminent shapori, approached him with the desire to become a shaman and inherit his father's hekura spirits. In the following chapters we will examine the entire process of his initiation and his ensuing progress. Before his initiation, Arawë was a quiet and rather shy young man, but after his initiation, where he transformed into a hekura, he evidently became more assertive, outspoken and confident in dealing with others. His new status conferred on him new social responsibilities and duties towards his kin. Maruwë, who inherited the official leadership of Sheroana-theri, is outwardly calm and reserved and has gained a reputation for being brave, responsible and generous, as well as a skilled hunter – all the desired attributes of a traditional Yanomami leader.

During my fieldwork, I developed a strong friendship with a man who called himself Wanapiwei-theri (who I named Neboisa) and his wife Preyoma from Toritha-theri. Neboisa claimed to be the only surviving Yanomami from the Wanapiwei-theri. Their youngest son, who was three years of age, sadly died during my fieldwork, an event that I will describe later on. Jacinto's father-in-law from Platanal, the shapori Makowë, and another shapori, Taramawë, from the Toritha-theri, who assisted Ruweweriwë in Arawë's initiation, are Neboisa's brothers. The oldest and most respected woman in the community was Neboisa's ex-wife Mahekosi, who has a reputation for being *waitheri* (strong and brave).

Notes

1. Kamakari, a supernatural being associated with death, has putrid breath and a face covered with white maggots (Lizot 2004: 146).
2. According to Lizot (1984), this group was the Warokoawë-theri, camping in the area at the time when Rice reached the Goaharibo rapids.
3. Before they arrived in Ocamo, this group lived near a small stream of a bright red colour and adopted the name Iyëwei-theri ('people of the colour of blood'). When they settled at the mouth of the Ocamo they retained their new name (Steinvorth-Goetz 1969).

4. Cejal is situated near Tama Tama and stems from the original, mother community of Moshata that between 1940 and 1950 was situated somewhere in the headwaters of the Mavaca River.
5. Napë is every non-Yanomami person, whether from another Indian group or a non-indigenous person.
6. *Wakeshi* is the smoke and the term *wayu* can refer to a warring party (*wayumou*), a disease or the efficiency of a substance, sentiment or an object that provokes physical or psychic reactions, such as strong, freshly made tobacco (Lizot 2004: 477).

Chapter 2

INSIDE THE BOA'S ABDOMEN

The Yanomami Cosmos

༺◦༻

The concept of cosmology derives from the Greek *kosmos*, which in its most general sense means 'order of the world'. Cosmology, as an object of study in itself, is an investigative quest for the ultimate principles of the world as a totality and the human place in it. But, in a conceptual framework, it is a given state of affairs embedded in any lifeworld with its cultural practices under investigation and as such serves as a matrix of understanding. In his introduction to the study of Maori cosmology, Gregory Schrempp (1992) points out that the analysis of any cosmology implies a twofold concern for the integral wholeness of the present order and the search for its grounds or origins. In the first instance, according to Schrempp, the quest for wholeness becomes a search for closure or a search for the ultimate boundaries as a condition for that wholeness. But, a search for the origin of the cosmic whole implicates that one thing rests on another, thus it is also a regression from any given state of bounded wholeness.

The starting point for understanding the Yanomami lived reality of their cosmos, especially as articulated in shamanistic initiation, is depicted in the transformative cosmogonic process or passage from prime matter of the primordial, pre-cosmic sphere to the multiplicity of beings and cosmic strata constituting the world as a whole. In this chapter we will examine the origins of the world and the establishment of ontological order through Yanomami accounts of multiple creations. The Yanomami cosmos is not a metastructure that exists outside of human consciousness, nor is cosmology a fixed set of ideas equally shared by everyone, forming a uniform belief system akin to what was long thought to be the monolithic concept of 'culture'. On the intersubjective level, different cosmological conceptions exist among different individuals. The distinctive feature of Yanomami cosmology is its dynamism and openness to innovation whereby the existing concepts, which are primarily determined by the shamans' knowledge gained through their personal experiences, are continually open to modifications. Later in the book, we will see how the concept of cosmogenesis is essentially related to the process of embodiment of the cosmos through shamanistic initiation. Hence, the cosmogonic act of creation and re-creation is a process that is dynamic and open-ended whereby the cosmos is being constantly generated and restructured.

Holographic Totality of the Yanomami Cosmos

The Yanomami conceive their entire cosmos as one multilayered totality enclosed within the abdomen of a giant cosmic boa (*hetu mɨsi*). This primal image of a cosmic snake, widespread in Amazonian cosmologies throughout the continent, contains in itself the whole of existence. Nothing exists outside of it. Yanomami refer to the celestial vault (sky) as *hetu mɨsi* but on a broader scale it is in fact the whole of the cosmos. This fragmented, holographic whole is structurally subdivided into five interrelated discs or cosmic levels existing in their own right and positioned on top of each other along a vertical cosmic axis. They are directly interconnected, so the bottom surface of each disc is the top surface of the one below. Each stratum is concurrently a certain kind of whole, a world in itself with its proper name and its own horizontal dimensionality, occupied by its proper denizens. The suffix *mɨsi*, attached to the name of each cosmic stratum, signifies 'abdomen' or 'abdominal wall in animals', in this case of the boa constrictor (hetu). The abdominal wall of the cosmic boa is a membrane, which sets the limits of the Yanomami known universe.

Each cosmic layer replicates this fragmented totality as a state of the cosmos or condition of the cosmic boa's abdomen. Each fraction corresponds to a different structural part or changing conditions of the overall cosmic whole or cosmic boa as a set of stages from new to old and from male to female. This is reflected in the names of each respective disc. In his analysis of the nature of the fractal, holographic structure of New Guinea lifeworlds, Roy Wagner comments, 'When a whole is subdivided, it is split into holographs of itself' (Wagner 1991: 167). Hence, the uppermost layer of the Yanomami known universe is cosmos in its genesis or making, known as *oshetiwë mɨsi* or the new, young abdomen – the child or new born animal, while the farthest down is described as an old woman (*hetu mɨsi suwë pata*). Both the celestial and terrestrial realms are mirroring each other. However, sky is not simply a mirror image of the earth. As Viveiros de Castro (1992: 71) commented in his analysis of the social and religious life of the Araweté – a Tupi-Guarani people of Eastern Amazonia – 'Heaven is neither a reflection nor an inversion of the earth; it is something other than an "image"'. Souls of the dead that live in the sky are mirroring the life of their living counterparts. They sleep in hammocks, hunt, grow gardens and practise shamanism. The only difference is that they are all decorated and painted to perfection and their celestial forest is abundant with forest fruits and game animals. Terrestrial and celestial realms together constitute the primal totality of the cosmic boa, which I call the 'world body' or the 'cosmic body'. These are alternative terms for the classical idea of the macrocosm. In summary, the primordial image of a cosmic snake is an image of an enclosed universe, a bounded whole encapsulating the totality of existence in the past, present and future. We will later see how this mythic image of the cosmic boa fully manifests itself during shamanistic initiation, through the medium of the shaman's body as a microcosmic totality bounded by the shaman's skin, which is accordingly dotted in the manner that resembles the pattern on the snake.

The Yanomami cosmos is a dynamic place where things tend to move downwards due to ever-changing metamorphic processes produced by the greater weight of the lower cosmic strata. Dry and gaseous superior cosmic planes, profuse in light and heat, are unstable and still in formation (Chiappino 1995; Lizot 2007). The quantity and availability of light and heat decreases downwards as it diffuses towards the lower cosmic strata. As a result of these changing conditions, the primal cosmic matter cools down and develops into a solid crust of the terrestrial disc, characterised by high humidity content due to the presence of tropical forests. The age of the cosmos increases in a downward direction from being young and still in a process of formation to becoming the lowest and the oldest cosmic strata, assuming the form of an old woman or an ancient boa's abdomen of female sex. Male and female cosmic principles converge on the earth plane, which is a central component where human beings or the Yanomami live and where a cosmic order is manifested at the moment of regeneration, transformation, death and rebirth of the universe.

The uppermost, embryonic part of the Yanomami cosmos, known as oshetiwë mɨsi (a new boa's abdomen) is a luminous, elementary world-in-the-making and in constant flux. It is where many things originated, including the cosmos itself, in a very distant past. This far-off region of the universe was accessible only to a few shapori, who revealed its existence to the rest of the Yanomami. Apparently, nowadays it does not play any active role in practising shaporimou and accompanying mythological lore. The shapori Ruweweriwë from Sheroana-theri told me once that he had never visited this place but his personal hekura had told him about it. He attempted to come close to it but it was just unbearably hot, making him very dizzy, so he gave up. Located directly underneath the topmost layer is the spherical celestial disc called hetu mɨsi or the boa's abdomen, whose inner wall surface is the actual visible sky covered with stars. As we saw in Chapter One, the highest, central part of the sky or zenith is ãmo mɨsi. Sky realm is inhabited by a number of celestial ancestral beings including Mothokariwë[1] (Sun), Periporiwë (Moon), Yãru (Thunder), Watawatariwë (Thunder's son-in-law) and Yãmirãyoma (Lightning), Yãru's ex-spouse, who is now married incestuously to her own son Tãhirawë (Beam of light). Watawatariwë is responsible for receiving souls of the dead. His father-in-law Yãru (Thunder), akin to all other ancestors, is an anthropomorphic being, described as 'a hunchback with red hair and a yellowish, corpse-like appearance' (Lizot 2004: 472). He is known as master of snakes, which he sometimes sends down to the Yanomami. One myth recollected in the community of Kakashiwë-theri recounts how Thunder was a tapir (ibid.: 1989: 106). One day, the older brother of Feifeiyomi (Cotinga Bird Ancestor) shot the tapir with an arrow and threw his liver high up into the air. The liver transformed into Yãru (Thunder), who sounded the very first thunder blast. Within the overall cosmological scheme, Yãru is the custodian of a large celestial, communal 'house of souls' where Yanomami migrate after their deaths and continue a posthumous existence, having first been transformed into souls (no porepɨ). This happens after cremation, when disembodied soul essences (pei mɨ ãmo) ascend into the sky along the path of the souls by means of smoke released from the fire. In this case, the shapori acts as a psychopomp and is responsible for supervising this process, ensuring that the departing soul's passage is clear. This transformative process is of vital importance for cosmic continuity, because only through the proper cremation ceremony can souls of the deceased reunite in the afterlife with their relatives in the sky shapono.

Apparently not all deceased Yanomami end up in the house of souls. The ones who were stingy during their lifetime do not join their dead relatives, but instead undergo an existential annihilation in the eternal flames of shopari wakë that devours their posthumous soul essences in the same manner the funeral pyre consumes their material bodies. To be stingy (*shiimi*) is a very negative Yanomami cultural trait that is considered to be the worst possible breach of good interpersonal relationships for its potential to jeopardise group interests and threaten its survival. In this situation, a shapori will still assist departing souls but without escorting them to the sky shapono; he will negotiate the soul's safe passage only to Watawatariwë – Thunder's son-in-law – who waits for them on top of the mountain where the path of the souls bifurcates before reaching the sky. One path is ugly, while the other is beautiful but deceptively so, for this is the path that descends into the burning fire of shopari wakë. At the end of the beautiful path, the earth is covered with leaves that mask the entrance to shopari wakë. People who were stingy choose the deceptive path, and Watawatariwë escorts these souls to the shopari wakë where they will be devoured by fire. Other souls Watawatariwë will take to the sky where they will join their relatives in the house of souls (Biocca 1971: 137; Lizot 2007: 272). In 2012, I discussed this subject with a young Yanomami student of medicine called Ishmael, whose deceased grandfather was a well-known grand shapori from Ocamo. His grandfather told him that before the missionaries arrived, shopari wakë did not form a part of the Yanomami cosmos. Ishmael thinks that the missionaries invented this place and likened it to hell in order to exercise a certain degree of control among the local indigenous population.

Celestial vault envelops the vast and flat terrestrial world or the actual boa's abdomen (*hei kë misi*), where the contemporary Yanomami live. Earth disc is an old sky or 'the boa's abdomen of an old man' (*hetu misi wãro pata*). But some Yanomami also refer to it as 'earth old woman' (*pitha suwë pata*) (Lizot 2004: 314). This is in no way contradictory because when the old masculine sky collapsed in the archaic past, it displaced the ancient earth disc and became a feminine earth but, at the same time, being an old sky it also retained its masculine epithet. By analogy, when a certain Yanomami group decides to change the name of their community, which happens very often, they continue using the old as well as the new name for some time. Earth cosmic plane or the present boa's abdomen unfolds along the east-west axis where the east side is considered to be both the higher part of the boa's abdominal wall (*ora misi*) and a higher part of the sky. The west side (*koro misi*) is the lower part of the abdominal wall and therefore the lower part of the sky, the place where the sun goes down and the moon comes up as day is replaced by night (Lizot 2007). All major waterways across the Yanomami geographical region correspondingly tend to flow from their mountain sources in the east (*ora hami*) towards the west (*koro hami*). In addition to describing horizontal space in terms of easterly and westerly directions, Yanomami use these two linguistic terms to characterise vertical spatial dimensionality whereby ora hami also means 'up' and koro hamɨ 'down'. The Yanomami conception of space is vital for understanding the patterns of shaporimou practices and mythical logic, like, for example, in the myth of the twins, which I will discuss later in this chapter (see also Chapter Eight). This understanding is critical to a wider comprehension of the Yanomami perceptions of introduced diseases, as will become clearer later in the book. Yanomami identify the vast tropical rainforests that cover their lifeworld by the term *urihi*. For them, the forest is a perilous place, frequented by jaguars, snakes, merciless biting ants and stinging bees, all of which cross the path of humans. It is where the Yanomami hunt, gather forest fruits and find building materials for their houses. Urihi, however, is not just an ecosystem; it is home to a number of dangerous and malevolent discarnate beings, such as ɨrariwë (Ancestral Jaguar), *pore* and *yawari*, among many others. Pore or ghosts are existential manifestations of people who died violently and whose bodies were not cremated and therefore did not transform into posthumous souls (no porepɨ) and ascend to a celestial cosmic level by means of the funeral pyre. They are a constant peril to the living. Yawari is a class of sub-aquatic spirit beings considered to be experts in the use of certain magical plants against humans. On one occasion I visited the community of Toritha-theri, the principal shapori Shawarawë told me that yawari look like Yanomami and live in their shaponos at the bottom of rivers and streams. They come out at night and search for potential victims to enchant before luring them underwater where they transform into one of them. Yawari trick people by appearing as their relatives; they are very appealing and can be of either sex. The female yawari search for male victims and vice versa. Shawarawë told me about his close encounter with such a being:

> I was once in the forest at night, looking for game. I sat on the tree trunk to have a rest and spotted a beautiful woman standing nearby. She was calling me to come closer and I couldn't resist. I got up and moved towards her. I felt the sweet smell that dazzled me. Everything around me turned yellow and I nearly lost consciousness. I then realised that the woman was not human but yawari. I called my personal hekura to cut the effects of the enchantment, swiftly came back to my senses and ran away. If it were to be another man instead of me who was not a shapori, she would have had certainly taken him underwater and he would have transformed into yawari.

Vast tropical rainforest regions of the terrestrial layer are criss-crossed with numerous trails linking Yanomami communities that can be anything from a few hours to a few days away on foot from each other. Shaponos are generally situated close to a mountain; for example, Mahekoto peak near Mahekoto-theri or Sheroroi Këki Mountain near Sheroana-theri. Yanomami refer to mountains as homes of hekura. Mountaintops are the highest cosmo-geographical points on the earth's surface and, as such, are closest to the sky vault.

The terrestrial world extends downwards into a subterranean stratum. Shapori Ruweweriwë from Sheroana-theri referred to it as boa's abdomen of an old woman (hetu misi suwë pata), albeit it is also denoted as being male (cf. Lizot 2007). The inhabitants of this underground cosmic layer are known as the Amahiri, who once lived above on the terrestrial level just like contemporary Yanomami, but the old fragile sky above them collapsed and was crushed into the earth. As a result of this cataclysmic collision, the terrestrial disc was shattered. A large broken part descended and crushed the Amahiri together with their shapono into the earth, which became the underground level. The fallen sky replaced the earth, while another, new sky emerged above this new earth or old sky. The contemporary Yanomami call the actual earth 'an old man' and underground levels 'an old woman'. The collapse of the old sky was a transformative moment – the end of one cosmic cycle and concurrently the beginning of a new one. The image of the fallen sky indicates the motif of the reversal of two disparate conditions of being through the interplay of complementary opposite cosmic forces – masculine and feminine. Burridge (1969: 50) explains this idea as 'the reversal of a previous mode of being … the cosmos turning over so that the sky, now above, was once below'. In Yanomami case, it is the opposite: the sky that is now below was once above. When the old sky collapsed and became earth from the topmost layer of the young boa's abdomen in the making, it emerged as the actual masculine sky (hetu misi); the earth is now an old man when previously it was an old woman. The reversal of the mode of being from female to male is a process of harmonisation of opposites through the abrupt clash of male and female cosmic principles, which is arguably a violent version of the archaic cosmological motif of the sky and earth conjunction. For the Amahiri, the present terrestrial layer became their actual sky or hetu misi; earth to them is transparent (Lizot 1985). What to the Yanomami is the solid earth is the airy sky to the Amahiri below. Likewise, what to the Yanomami is the airy sky above is a solid ground for dead souls and other inhabitants of the celestial level. Together with the old sky, the old moon, which Yanomami call *peripo hupëpi*, also went under the surface and became blind. Occasionally the moon comes up and contaminates the Yanomami with shawara illnesses. Indeed, at one point during the initiation in Sheroana-theri, which I will describe later, the shapori Ruweweriwë embodied this 'old moon'. In a crouching position with his eyes closed (he was blind) he was waving his arms and spitting shawara.

Ancestors that transformed into Amahiri are bold, immortal beings[2] living in a shapono just like the Yanomami; they practise shamanism but their gardens are empty. There is a system of negative exchange and competition between the Amahiri shapori and their living counterparts. The latter send shawara to Amahiri but Amahiri shapori retaliate in the same manner or even steal souls of the living. Underneath the subterranean stratum of the Amahiri lies the lowest and oldest fifth cosmic layer. It retains male characteristics, but, again, Yanomami also refer to it as an old woman (hetu mɨsi suwë pata). Cold, humid and in a state of decay, the only inhabitants are giant maggots (shirimo mamo) (Lizot 2004). By this stage, metaphorically speaking, the abdominal wall of a cosmic boa slowly starts to rot just like the shed skin of a snake. But, being an ouroboric[3] totality, a cosmic boa is in a constant mode of self-generation; it is constantly generating through and out of itself. To be sure, throughout Amazonia, the shedding of the anaconda (and other snakes) is a sign of its immortality; while one part is in a state of decay another part comes into being. Things become anew as soon as they end. The whole cosmos folds over on itself in a way that the youngest cosmic layer in the making or the new abdomen (oshe mɨsi) is at the same time the oldest part of the cosmos, close to the source of its self-generation. Cosmic layers exist separately but are implicitly holographic in a sense that each of them replicates the same fragmented whole of the cosmic boa.

No Patapɨ tëhë: The Ever-present Mythical Time of Creation

How did this cosmic boa come into being? What conditions prompted its genesis and how is this related to shamanism? In Yanomami cosmogony the concept of the earliest beginnings are unknown. There is no creation ex nihilo: things always transform from something else. In Yanomami myths, the world has been there from the beginning, created but incomplete. In fact, most Amazonian cosmogonies begin with some a priori substance or already given state of affairs that then undergo transformation into a new type of being. Every new appearance, whether it is animal, plant or some geographical feature, presupposes the existence of some prior state of being. The common basis from which everything in the Yanomami cosmos unfolded and came into being is the mythical realm known as the epoch of the ancestors (no patapɨ tëhë). It is but one manifestation of the omnipresent Amerindian concept of the all-embracing, primordial dimension of the world in its raw, pre-cosmic state of undifferentiation or 'undifference'[4] between humans, animal and plant species that are yet to be actualised (Viveiros de Castro 1998: 472, 2012: 55). Primordium is not yet cosmos but a condition of the possibility for any cosmos. The primordial situation is a totalising non-condition without determinations: it is neither static nor dynamic; it was then and it is also now. It is the atemporal flow of cosmic time, which allows the cosmos to regenerate itself through the process of decay and rebirth. When the Yanomami talk about events surrounding their ancestors they use the expression *yëtu hami*, which means something that happened in the very distant past, or in some other time – in the epoch of the ancestors (no patapɨ tëhë).

The primordial matrix is a non-cosmic ontological dimension in continuous flux and universal metamorphosis, where everything is possible and happens rapidly. Immediacy and directness are expressed in instant transformations of being from one form into another (human, animal, vegetable and mineral) in omniphagy (eating anything) and in deviant sexual practices, including incest (Sullivan 1988). In the myth of the primordial twins, for example, children mature overnight. In the myth of the arrival of the first night, plants grow instantly and things come into being by the mere act of naming them. The ancestors were engaged in deviant and nowadays unimaginable and culturally unacceptable practices and behaviours, such as (auto) cannibalism, as in the myth of Periporiwë, or uninhibited and indiscriminate sexual relations across different species, which is evident in a series of myths involving the Ancestral Jaguar, or eating crude food as in the myth of the origin of fire. They are anthropomorphic, multiform beings with mixed human and other-than-human attributes, akin to the present-day shapori and their auxiliary hekura spirits. They all appear to each other as humans but with characteristics associated with later developed species of animals and plants. The original humans have inherent sexual dualities not yet concretised (Viveiros de Castro 2012). They communicate akin to present-day Yanomami and eat, drink, dwell in villages, live in conjugal relations, copulate and produce offspring. For example, Iwariwë (Caiman), the original 'custodian' of fire, is coupled with Prueheyoma (Frog woman), while Pore Poreawë, the custodian of plantains, lives with Thoothothoyoma (Liana (vine) woman). Moyenayoma (Thorned-vine woman) is the mother of Omawë and Yoawë – the primordial twins. Her mother is Mamokoroyoma (Poisoned-vine woman). Some primordial couples are of the same type; for example, Rahararithawë, the mythic aquatic snake monster, who is the owner of manioc, and his spouse Raharayoma. Their daughter Hokotoyoma (Boa woman)[5] is married to Omawë. Some ancestral beings, such as Periporiwë (Moon) and Kanaporiwë (Crested oropendola), appear distinctively male but are in fact androgynous, having some female characteristics. Kanaporiwë's calf muscle became pregnant and gave birth to the first woman while the Moon is like a mother, because from his blood one generation of Yanomami originated.

Therefore, Yanomami mythical episodes and a vast part of Amazonian mythologies describe partaking of the original ancestral beings in a generalised unstable primordial condition, which caused their irreversible transformations into a multiplicity of animal and plant species, geographical features, celestial bodies and human beings. They contain certain moral underlying currents that relate how distinctive features of the world emerged from the cosmogonic primordium and acquired their present forms. They also narrate how some components of the cosmos that are not directly perceptible, such as human souls and animal and hekura spirits, relate to their living counterparts (human, animal, plant). Development of the cosmos was thus a process of diversification of the primal substance. The end of primordial immanence and the dissolution of the pre-cosmic state of fluidity and undifferentiation resulted in the bifurcation of sky from earth, culture from nature and humans from animals and other species, including hekura spirits. Humans became finite beings while some components of the original ancestors retained their immortal status and continued to exist as hekura. Yet, this condition is reversible, as the ever-present primordial dimension of the myth unfolds as the horizon of consciousness within the ritual context of collective shamanistic sessions.

The notion of humanity as prime matter that precedes the primal cut of existence and the reversibility of the primordial condition through shamanism posits further philosophical concerns for the nature or essence of being posited, in philosophical terms, as the relationship between the one and the many. We have already established that the image of the Yanomami universe as a cosmic boa is implicitly and intrinsically a multiple universe or a fragmented holographic whole that proceeds from the clash of opposites – male and female cosmic principles. Yanomami myths essentially depict primordial events that contributed to the fragmentation of the pre-cosmic whole into a multiplicity of forms, separating humans from other species, masculine sky from feminine earth and material from non-material components. As we will see later, it is from the body of the original androgynous male that the first woman was born. Again, it is the same principle of a unitary being that split into two complementary opposites who are to be constantly reunited through the sexual act of procreation to re-establish primordial, androgynous unity. In philosophical terms, it is the process of multiplication of the original oneness. What was once a primordial whole has split into two separate but interconnected and interdependent cosmic spheres.

Within the primordial wholeness there is already an inherent sexual dualism of things (humans, animals, plants, etc.) and the sky and earth were conjoined from the beginning, albeit unified: it is the original 'one' but already dual from the beginning. Not a single Yanomami myth describes their separation as one abrupt event. Instead, ancestors from whom celestial bodies emerged ascended for various reasons to higher regions of the primordium and have remained there ever since. For example, during the process of primordial differentiation, the stars (*shitikari*) became the eyes of Shitikariyoma and other women who climbed the sky after being rejected by their potential in-laws (Eguíllor García 1984). The moon was a hekura living in the chest of a shaman prior to becoming a celestial body. Multiple transformations of primordial ancestors have marked in one way or another the end of the original state of undifferentiation, when primordial unity was permanently broken and the world determined by time and space emerged.

Shamanistic initiation or corporeal cosmogenesis is a process that is opposite from sky and earth separation or the interplay of various factors that contributed to the multiplication of the original oneness. The embodiment of the cosmos and its constitutive components through the medium of the shaman's body is the inverse progression of unification of the plural into the original oneness of the undivided ancestral beings, manifesting as all-embracing dimensionality of primordial consciousness. Thus, the two transitions – the multiplication of the one and unification of the plural – are two sides of the same coin, the two parts of a single transition (Schrempp 1992). In fact, we will see later in the book how the same concept of unity in multiplicity posited as the relation between the whole and its parts or between the one and the many is implicitly present not only in the shaman and his embodied hekura spirits but also in the concept of the primordial twins and the Yanomami notion of a multiple soul that constitutes a person.

Origin Myths

Arrival of the First Night

In Yanomami myths, the primordial world of unity and undifference is characterised as being in a state of uninterrupted light and eternal day, while among the Sanema a perpetual darkness is the original condition that changed into first light (Colchester 1981). The myth of Titiri (Lizot 1989, 2007) explains the origin of night and the establishment of a permanent cyclical order of day and night. The sun was eternally static at its highest point and the night did not yet exist. Ancestors led a peaceful and happy life without disputes and wars. They slept whenever they were tired and copulated in front of everyone. This condition permanently and irreversibly changed when Hõrõnami (a significant ancestral figure – a great hunter who introduced agriculture) killed Titiri – the harbinger of the night. Titiri in the guise of Paruriwë (Black Curassow Ancestor)[6] was advancing and rolling his burning eyes as the darkness unfolded behind him. He perched on a tree branch and started to sing, full of lament. Through his song he was naming certain mytho-geographical features, namely mountains and rivers that correspond to present-day geographical features of the Yanomami lifeworld. Titiri's lament irritated other ancestors and they decided to kill him. Hõrõnami's son launched a poisoned dart through his blowpipe, but it only scratched Titiri's wing. Titiri lost his vigour and the sky temporarily darkened; day sounds became replaced by night sounds for the very first time. Hõrõnami was more successful and his dart split Titiri's chest open. His blood spurted everywhere, transforming into a multiplicity of *weyari* or malevolent spirit beings of the type *yai thë*, while Titiri himself transformed into a multiplicity of Black Curassow and concurrently remained in an ethereal form as a hekura. Ever since then, he has traversed the sky on his dark path covered with thorns from east to west during the day and from west to east at night. He steals people's vital essences, and shapori in their rituals have to traverse his path and bring them back (Lizot 2007). The coming of the very first night marked the beginning of perpetual day and night cycles and from then on *no patapi* (ancestors) learned to sleep and copulate during the night only. In alternative versions of the same myth (see Lizot 1989, 2007), the arrival of darkness was a form of punishment for ancestors who were engaged in incest; they transformed into a multiplicity of sloths.

The Emergence of the Moon

In ancestral times Periporiwë (Moon) was a hekura living in the chest of a powerful shapori. When the shapori died, disembodied Periporiwë started roaming around. People were mourning the dead shapori and while they were cremating his body (just like they do nowadays) Periporiwë started eating the bones stripped of their flesh. The deceased shapori's son spotted the intruder and immediately recognised his father. Periporiwë ate all the bones and went up to the sky while the ancestors tried to spear him. He almost escaped when Suhirinariwë (Scorpion Ancestor), who was a good hunter, managed to pierce Periporiwë's chest. His blood dispersed in a southerly direction and each falling droplet transformed into a Shamathari Yanomami, who nowadays inhabit the Siapa region and are renowned for being brave and ferocious (*waitheri*). Suhirinariwë and his family transformed into scorpions (Lizot 1974, 1989). In another version of the same myth (Cocco 1972), Periporiwë wrapped his daughter's ovaries in leaves, roasted them and finally ate them, in the same manner Yanomami nowadays prepare fish, crabs, mushrooms and maggots. He soon fell sick with fever, became pale and lost strength. He ascended towards the sky and then started sinking slowly towards the edge of the earth where he died. His body petrified and transformed into a huge mountain called Peripori makɨ, while his no porepɨ or posthumous soul essence continued to live in his celestial shapono as the moon. Yanomami nowadays say that the contemporary moon (*peripo*) is not Periporiwë's body but his no porepɨ. He descends whenever a shapori calls him, or of his own accord, and devours children's soul essences.

When discarnate Periporiwë descended to the shapono's central area, the son of the deceased shapori recognised in him his father, who was in this instance eating his own bones. This primordial act is autocannibalistic because shapori and their personal hekura have a very intimate relationship; hekura are regarded as shaporis' children. In the following chapters, we will see how during contemporary shamanistic initiation and transformative experiences of death and rebirth, human beings metamorphose into shapori/hekura. After his biological death, all of a shapori's embodied hekura retain the characteristics of the deceased shapori. In the myth, prior to the shapori's death, Periporiwë was one of his personal hekura, who was caught eating his own body. Other no patapɨ condemned Periporiwë's behaviour and he was accordingly punished. Periporiwë is directly autocannibalistic, whereas the present practice is sufficiently allocannibalistic, because a person is eaten by 'others' (From Greek: állo 'other') – that is, by his or her kin. The corpse of the deceased is cremated on the pyre, and after the bones cool down they are pulverised, mixed with banana soup and ingested by family members. The rest of the ash is placed inside a gourd. One year later, the act is repeated. Yanomami consume the bones of their deceased just like Periporiwë did in the myth, but he commits the unacceptable act of eating his own bones in an inappropriate manner – by crunching them with his teeth without pulverising them into a fine powder and mixing them with banana soup as the Yanomami do nowadays. Just as with the death of a primordial ancestor in myths, the death of a person in the context of contemporary shamanistic initiation is a transformative act that causes an ontological shift whereby a segment of the world metamorphoses into a new entity. In order for transformation to occur, something has to recede, to die simultaneously, giving way to a new being, which emerges at the ontological transformative moment of death. Death becomes both a creative act of transformation and an instrument of creation. Death transforms reality inasmuch as enduring elements of the world come into existence (Sullivan 1988). Myths of the origin of night and the moon bear striking similarities. In both instances, ancestral beings were pierced with arrows and were not killed instantly but after several attempts. In both mythical dramas the prevailing motif is the creative act of metamorphosis from a bodily fluid; blood is the transformative substance. In the myth of Titiri, the original primordial condition was broken when darkness unfolded out of the displaced, uncontained blood spurting from the ancestor's open chest that gave origin to a multiplicity of Black Curassow and weyari spirit beings, while the death of Periporiwë resulted in the emergence of the moon as a celestial body, which parallelled the emergence of the first generation of human beings.

Periporiwë (Moon) is a pre-eminently masculine being, who adopts the feminine attributes of the mother. This androgynous state is equivalent to the state of perfect totality. Moon is simultaneously father and mother, creator and destroyer: 'It symbolises the universal becoming, the periodical destruction and creation' (Eliade 1960: 185). Moon is a destructively powerful cannibalistic being who devours human vital principles but is also an androgynous life-giver. He is associated with the procreation and fertility of women but also with death, wars and destruction. After a shamanistic initiation he starts to live in the shapori's chest, just like he did in the myth. Shapori can metamorphose into Periporiwë in order to take or to save lives. By its very nature, Moon participates in perpetual cycles of death, rebirth and regeneration of the cosmos. Together with the sun he forms a split unitary being. Yanomami use the term *peripo shii* (light of the moon) for both sunlight and moonlight (Lizot 2004: 312). Moon is also associated with the cyclical passage of time. Yanomami call the new moon *peripo oshe* (young) and, similarly, refer to the uppermost cosmic stratum as oshe mïsi ('recent or new boa's abdomen'). When the moon is full, the Yanomami say that he got fat (*prewë*) or has aged (*patarayoma* or *pata*), and when it disappears for three days, the Yanomami say that the moon he has died (*nomarayoma*), after which time he will be reborn and come back as young (*oshe*) in the same way as the cosmic boa continually regenerates and re-emerges as young.

Origin of the First Woman

The concept of primordial androgyny and another situation of incest is also evident in the myth of the origin of the first woman and the multiplication of the Yanomami. The first woman was born from the calf of Kanaporiwë[7] after another male ancestor had copulated with him by introducing his penis into a hole between his toes (Lizot 1974). In some versions (Cocco 1972) the hole was in Kanaporiwë's calf. As a result, the calf became pregnant and started growing. The muscle exploded and a baby girl was born. Kanaporiwë nurtured her as her father and later took her as his wife. She gave birth to another girl, who matured fast and was given to the man who had copulated the first time with Kanaporiwë. This primordial act is an example of what Dundes (1988: 170) calls 'reversal of biological reality', whereby a woman – a 'natural' procreator – was created from the male body. Another well-known example is the creation of Eve from Adam's rib:

> And the lord God caused a deep sleep to fall upon Adam, and he slept: and He took one of his ribs, and closed up the flesh instead thereof; And the rib, which the Lord God had taken from man, made he a woman, and brought her unto the man. And Adam said, "This is now bone of my bones, and flesh of my flesh: she shall be called Woman, because she was taken out of Man". (Holy Bible 1979, Genesis 2:21–23)

In the Yanomami myth, the original male ancestor bifurcated into male and female thus becoming mother and father, as well as a future husband, to the only existing female. It appears that the original incest was inevitable. Leach (1969: 15) comments that 'the logical basis of incest categories must occur in all mythologies', while Dundes (1988: 177) argues that 'the creation of the original man or even the original human couple cannot avoid the incest issue … although incest may be defined differently in various cultures, it does seem to be universal'.

Origin of Fire and Loss of Immortality

In the myth of the origin of fire (Lizot 1974; 1989) a whole generation of ancestors lost their immortal state due to the curse of Iwariwë (Caiman Ancestor) and became vulnerable to diseases as an expression of human imperfection. Iwariwë was the original, stingy, custodian of fire. The rest of the ancestors felt cold at night and ate their food raw. Iwariwë, who had been hiding fire inside his mouth, was soon discovered. He initially refused to share it with the others, but some small, young birds (Yorekiritami) – Hiyomarithawë (Colibri) and Kanaporiwë (Crested oropendola) – made him laugh and he lost the possession of fire. Kanaporiwë quickly grabbed the fire and left specks on trees so that the Yanomami could burn them in future. An analogous version of the same myth exists among the geographically distant Shipibo of the Peruvian Amazon (Roe 1982: 201). An angry caiman cursed the Yanomami, declaring that from then onwards they would lose their immortal state and fire would devour them at the moment of death. Iwariwë then went underwater, lost his original humanity and transformed into a caiman while simultaneously remaining an immortal hekura. The Yanomami nowadays explain that the caiman has a short tongue because it was burnt by the fire concealed in Iwariwë's mouth (Lizot 1989). Iwariwë's spouse Prueheyoma (Frog woman) announced that her husband's fire was eternal (pãrimi) and it was a grave mistake to take it out of his mouth because fire was going to make them suffer forever; all future descendants would be prone to burns. She also jumped into the water, and transformed into a frog. In this primordial drama, the caiman was selfish and was punished. His fellow ancestors wanted fire but lost their immortality and indestructibility. The everlasting fire, which was displaced by an ancestral act, turned into a symbol of human finitude and immanence of death. Their perishable bodies are nowadays consumed by fire during funeral practices.

Primordial Twins, the Great Flood and the Origins of Shawara Epidemics

One of the most important Yanomami mythical cycles relates to the primordial twin brothers, which is the most widespread Amazonian myth (Levi-Strauss 1996; Sullivan 1988; Velásquez 1987; Whitehead 2002: 98; Wright and Hill 1986). Omawë and Yoawë are the twins and great transformers that have had an important role in shaping the Yanomami cosmos. The twins are considered to be a split unitary being akin to the sun and moon. They epitomise two parts of one original ancestral being. When referring to Omawë, the Yanomami frequently couple his name with the adjective kë kɨpɨ, which signifies duality or two things together. In this instance, 'Omawë kë kɨpɨ' stands for both Omawë and Yoawë (Lizot 2004: 283). The twins were born out of Moyenayoma (Thorned-vine woman), who was a daughter of Mamokoroyoma (Poisoned-vine woman). Around the time of their birth, Ɨrariwë (Jaguar Ancestor) and his son lived together with the two vine women. He was a ruthless cannibal who relentlessly devoured children while their parents were away in the forest and at one point even threatened to exterminate all of the existing Yanomami. When Moyenayoma became pregnant, Ɨrariwë ate her as well but her mother saved the placenta with the unborn twins inside from being devoured.[8] Ɨrariwë did not eat Mamokoroyoma because her skin was bitter (from poison). She reared the unborn twins inside the placenta in a large saucepan, and the first to be born was the more disadvantaged and less attractive Yoawë. The younger twin Omawë, on the other hand, was handsome, intelligent and brave. In some parts of the Yanomami territory, namely among the Sanema and in Sierra Parima, Omawë appears as the older brother (Chiappino 1997; Colchester 1981). The symbolism of the twins does not imply that they are a personified dichotomy of good and evil; one of them is simply more advantaged than the other.[9] It is always Omawë who knows better and discovers things. Known as a great transformer, he was responsible for the creation of various cultural elements and mytho-geographical features of the Yanomami lifeworld. He also outwitted and killed Ɨrariwë, saving other ancestors from being devoured.

The existence of twins in Yanomami mythology is interrelated to the occurrence of the universal mythological motif of the great flood – a crucial event that broke the primordial unity and made human beings mortal. The myth of a deluge as a cosmic catastrophe is an 'essential moment in the history of the cosmos. It wiped out the primordial age of undifferentiated form, which seemed bent on its own destruction, and brought into being the world in which humans now live' (Berge, cited in Sullivan 1988: 102). In South America, myths of deluge are widespread among both pre-Colombian and contemporary peoples, from the Araucanians of Chile to the Chibcha of Colombia (Classen 1993; Osborne 1968). The common motif is of a group of survivors who take refuge on a high mountain and start a new generation of humans in a regenerated world. The great cosmic flood is thus associated with destruction and subsequent (re)creation that marks the end of one epoch in the cosmogonic act of creation and transformation of the cosmos and the beginning of a new era of humanity. 'The flood opened the way to a re-creation of the world and regeneration of humanity' (Eliade 1965: 55).

In the Yanomami myth, Omawë was (in)directly responsible for triggering the flood, which swept through the primordium and nearly wiped out all of the ancestors. The flood was a turning, transformative point: out of destruction a new cosmic cycle began and a new generation of Yanomami emerged from those who survived. The myth of the cosmic deluge not only explains the origin of contemporary Yanomami but also reveals the origin of white people as well as other neighbouring groups, namely Yekwana, also known as Makiritare in Brazil. In one version of the flood myth from Karohi-theri (Lizot 1974), the indirect cause of the flood was the rivalry and animosity between Omawë and his father-in-law Rahararithawë,[10] who became angry because Omawë stole his daughter Kamanaeyoma, also known as Hokotoyoma (Boa woman). Rahararithawë, like all the ancestors, was capable of manifesting his powers directly and instantly. On one occasion while Omawë was visiting him, Rahararithawë sniffed some yopo snuff and made the waters rise. His intention was to kill both twins by tricking them into entering his house and drowning them. But Omawë had his powers too. To save him and his brother, he transformed them into crickets and hid in a crack in the roof. In retaliation, they sniffed yopo too and ascended into the sky to ask Mothokariwë (Sun Ancestor) to create a severe drought and punish Rahararithawë. The cosmic drought was so fierce that almost all the waters dried up. This made Omawë's son very thirsty, and to relinquish his thirst, Omawë went with his family to the headwaters of the Shukumɨna kë u River (Siapa) to dig a hole with the help of Koromarithawë (Bird Ancestor) and access the great reservoir of underground water called *motu*. Koromarithawë pierced the ground with his beak, which caused it to bend. The underground water gushed out into the sky. Omawë rushed to close the hole with a rock, but to little avail. The first big spatter of water reached the sky and became the source of rain. The rest of the overflowing water flooded the earth. The water level rose dramatically, eroding the land and bringing down the trees, devouring the Yanomami on its way. The flood killed almost everyone except one small group, which escaped it by climbing Mãiyõ Mountain, which is an actual huge black rock, situated near the foothills of the Parima Mountains (between the Puutha and Heritha rivers). It rises approximately 1000 metres above sea level, and in its vicinity is the village formally known as Mãiyõ-theri, but now called Suwërope. Corresponding versions of the flood myth with related, local geographical features exist in other parts of the Yanomami territory; for example, the Pishaasi-theri (Mavaca) narrate how the flood survivors climbed the Homahewë, Koawë or Howashiwë Mountains (Lizot 1989; Chagnon 1968a).

Continuing with the representative myth from Karohi-theri, the survivors on top of Mãiyõ Mountain managed to preserve a few plantain and manioc plants. Water covered the visible landscape, gradually climbing up the mountainside. The rushing current carried the ancestors along with it; some of them converted into white people, some into *waika*[11] and some into other ethnic groups. At one point, only the top of Mãiyõ was visible when one shapori told a child to push his old mother into the rapidly advancing waters. The child obeyed and the water soon started to recede westwards and far away downstream (*koro hamɨ*) and became the sea. The floodwaters also carried the twins westwards where they transformed into malevolent beings, bent upon sending shawara sickness to the Yanomami (Lizot 1974: 35–36).

In another more elaborate version of the same myth from Ocamo (Cocco 1972), after the flood, Omawë was eating dead fish. He threw the bones and they transformed into various types of fish. Omawë robbed a daughter of Mãrõhãriwë (Big-mouthed Fish Ancestor) called Hauyakariyoma. Together with the rest of his family they returned to the headwaters of the Shukumɨna kë u (Siapa) River where he made a shapono and lived there for some time. One day, during a funeral feast (*reahumou*), Omawë's son Hiretoriwë heard a bird call and warned his father that enemies were approaching their shapono. Omawë escaped with his family and set out on a journey along the banks of the Siapa River. Other Yanomami who were invited to the feast ran in a northerly direction; nowadays they are called waika (see note 11). The rest of the myth describes Omawë's long, creative journey down the Siapa River. Along the way he shot a tapir that metamorphosed into a rock. Omawë and his family went far away, and from his offspring, who learned to make *matohi* or trade goods, white people originated.

The floodwaters stopped rising only after an old woman was sacrificed. Sacrifice is the 'cosmic necessity, which alone makes possible the passage from one mode of being to another and ensures the continual circulation of life in cosmos' (Eliade 1965: 189). The primordial flood was a transformative moment that symbolised the end of one epoch and the beginning of another. The sacrifice of an old woman was a reciprocal necessity that ensured a victory over chaos and the subsequently continuity of life in the cosmos. We can recall that in the case of the fallen sky, the universe reached a turning point at the end of another cosmic cycle of death and rebirth. The lower cosmic stratum becomes – through the interplay of male and female principles – an old woman, who is like an abandoned old garden no longer fertile (Chagnon 1992).

Notes

1. The suffix *-riwë* indicates 'ancestral being'. Another less commonly used variation is *rithawë* (as in Rahararithawë) (Cocco 1972; Lizot 1996).
2. Lizot (2004: 10) explains that the word *amahi* signifies firewood that never rots, which is a sign of its everlasting endurance or immortality, while the suffix *-ri* as in Amahiri indicates a community or people.
3. Ouroboros is the ancient symbol for continuity, the cyclical nature of the universe and creation out of destruction. It is most frequently depicted by the image of a serpent eating its own tail.
4. Viveiros de Castro (1998) points out that 'undifference' means 'of mixed qualities'; it is not the same as 'indifference' or 'sameness'.
5. *Hokoto* is a synonym of *hetu këki* (boa constrictor). Thus, Hokotoyoma is a female Boa Ancestor.
6. The black curassow (crax alector) is a nocturnal bird with black feathers and white down on its stomach, which symbolise day and night. Males make specific sounds as if 'crying' and in the dry season men go out at night to hunt them. Their meat is

much appreciated and their black and white feathers have various uses (Lizot 2004: 299; see also Levi-Strauss 1964: 302).

7. *Kanaporomi* (crested oropendola) (psarocolius decumanus) is a bird that lives in colonies; they have their nests suspended from the branches of the tallest trees (Lizot 1989). Kanaporiwë is an anthropomorphic ancestor of the kanaporomi bird.

8. By comparison, jaguars killed the mother of Waribi, a Barisana culture hero, because she became pregnant by her brother, the Moon. The girl's mother saved Waribi by allowing him to escape from his mother's womb into the river (Hugh-Jones 1988).

9. However, Helena Valero in her narrative said that her mother-in-law characterised Yoawë as an evildoer who wanted to kill everyone (Biocca 1971: 148).

10. Rahara is a mythical giant snake that controls the waterways, while Rahararithawë is the original mythological being and a precursor of Rahara and also the original owner of manioc – Yanomami staple food (Lizot 1996).

11. Waika is a relational term that one group uses to call other groups that live upstream (*ora hami*). It is also often used by more acculturated Yanomami to distinguish themselves from other remote groups (Lizot 2004: 456).

Chapter 3

HEKURA, THE BODY AND ILLNESS

The ancestral continuum of the primordial generative matrix, which started with the dawn of the world, remains the reference point for contemporary life among the Yanomami. The end of the primordial, pre-cosmic state of undifferentiation resulted in the onset of a cosmogonic process of separation of material from non-material cosmic components and permanently opened the cut of human existence. During the process of cosmic differentiation, the original ancestors underwent multiple metamorphoses and bifurcated into human beings on the one side and hekura on the other. Humans sprang out of the primordial sphere as finite beings with perishable bodies, albeit with enduring soul essences, while hekura continued to exist as ethereal, immortal (*pãrimi*) successors of the original archaic humanity, containing mixed human and extra-human qualities of species or things originating from them.

Shamans and Hekura

Hekura are the intangible and immortal nuclei of all material components of the Yanomami cosmos, such as animals, plants, fire, atmospheric and celestial components (sun, moon, wind, thunder), among others. They do not constitute a class of distinct beings but belong to a broad category of *yai thëpë* or 'invisible non-human beings', albeit with human qualities, that also includes *pore* (ghosts), *yawari* and others (Viveiros de Castro 2004 citing Kopenawa and Albert). Hekura can be male or female, terrestrial or celestial, discarnate or embodied. Some hekura are predominantly male, some are distinctively female, and some can be both male and female, as the two principles of a single ancestral being; for example, Ocelot Ancestor Yaoriwë and his female counterpart Yaoriyoma.[1] In their free, discarnate state of existence, outside of the context of a micro corporeal union with their host shaman, hekura take on the forms of tiny, anthropomorphic, vigorous and radiant beings. Celestial hekura, such as Mothokariwë and Periporiwë (Sun and Moon Ancestors), Yãru (Thunder) and Yãmirãyõma (Lightning), among others, reside on top of the sky vault. Terrestrial hekura live in their communities located on top of mountains and hills, in rivers and rapids, in very high trees and inside small rocks.

A German ethnologist Otto Zerries (1964) wrote that etymologically the term hekura derives from *he* ('head' or 'up') and *kure* ('to be or exist' or 'to collect'), hence the broad meaning of hekura as that which exists above (on top of mountains and in the superior parts of the cosmos) and can be collected or made to come down from those areas. Indeed, we will see in Chapter Four how during the course of shamanistic initiation, the master shapori repeatedly collects the incoming hekura from the shapono's central area and transfers them to the candidate seated under the high part of the roof, which is, in effect, on a large, macrocosmic scale, the boundary between the celestial and terrestrial stratum. In this way, the discarnate hekura are changing their mode of existence by migrating from their natural habitats into the future shapori's body and becoming 'domesticated'. When they answer the neophyte's call, glowing hekura arrive in innumerable multiplicities, dancing along their shining paths and moving to the rhythm of a shapori's songs. Each hekura is a unique being with proper name and combined human and extra-human attributes. One of the salient features that characterise the phenomenology of hekura is their abundance of light. Luminosity is not only their primordial quality but also a striking attribute of the epena-induced state of consciousness unfolding experientially in shamanistic rituals under the luminous intensity of the surroundings. Hekura appear to humans as both intensely terrifying and magnificent – beings of elevated beauty with immaculate body paint and ornaments. They have halos identical to those that shamans acquire during their initiations; they are a form of identification and when hekura see them they recognise the shapori as one of their kind. Shapori can perceive otherwise invisible hekura because they are able to transform into them under the influence of epena snuff. During the hekura metamorphosis, the shaman acts like the manifested hekura or more precisely they act through him. The shaman's transformation into hekura is the complete fusion of human and other-than-human attributes and a full manifestation of the primordial ancestors 'in the flesh'. When they summon hekura in their rituals, shapori wear monkey tails around their heads, armlets with feathers and necklaces that are the mirror image of those worn by hekura. Using ochre, they also paint their bodies with the same patterns that hekura have on theirs. Ordinary human beings (non-shamans) appear to hekura as grey and lifeless, akin to ghosts (Viveiros de Castro 2004 [citing Kopenawa and Albert]).

In Yanomami myths we find frequent references to both shapori and hekura. Shapori is a shaman while hekura implies a spirit. However, these two terms are synonymous. In the Yanomami language, the common root 'shapo-' as in shapori and shapono refers to its character of domesticity. A shapono or Yanomami communal dwelling is the domesticated, cultured human domain and a prototype of living for all other beings, including the ancestral hekura. Shapori is an aggregate of his embodied and thus domesticated hekura. He is a cultural type with the generic ability to transfigure into any human and other-than-human form. Hekura are the shapori's personal assistants – components of the shapori's self-enclosed corporeal microcosm. Notwithstanding this obvious distinction, when someone becomes a shapori through initiation he also transforms into hekura or, to say it better, assumes a new identity as a living hekura-in-flesh and simultaneously becomes a 'father' of all of his incarnated hekura. The term hekura designates shamans as well as their auxiliary hekura spirits. All hekura are shamans and all shamans have hekura powers. Both shamans and hekura are of the same nature. The new shapori candidates inherit hekura directly from their living fathers when they decide to discontinue their practice due to old age or sickness. As he transfers them to his son, the latter in turn becomes father to his own (hekura) children. If a shapori dies before he gets to pass on his hekura to his sons, the transference of father's auxiliary spirits can still be accomplished posthumously with the help of an initiated male relative or another competent shapori. This was the case with the young candidate Arawë, whose initiation I recorded in Sheroana-theri during my fieldwork. His father was a well-known shapori who died suddenly from a snake bite. It had been a few years since his father's death when Arawë said to his shapori uncle Ruweweriwë that he would like to become shapori and inherit his deceased father's hekura. Ruweweriwë agreed and performed a three week long initiation. During this time Ruweweriwë gathered all of his brother's hekura living on the nearby Sheroroi mountaintop and passed them onto Arawë, who eventually transformed into hekura. During the course of the initiation, Arawë repeatedly recognised his deceased father in the faces of incoming hekura. The reader will recall from Chapter Two that in the myth about the origin of the moon, the deceased shapori's son likewise recognised his father in Periporiwë, who was one of his father's hekura eating his own bones.

A shapori is a unified multiplicity of all of his embodied spirits and also one of the spirits. He is a total but divided being: a fractal multiple 'one'. Simultaneously he is one and many, a part of the whole but also the whole in itself containing other wholes – all other incarnated hekura. This is determined on the basis of the prevailing evidence of the nature of the shaman's 'postmortem' consciousness. In the course of the initiatory death and rebirth experience, the candidate's self is destroyed by hekura and reconstituted as a multiplicity of various hekura selves. These embodied hekura mature and grow old together with the shapori, whose body they inhabit. While a shapori will eventually die (in his body), his hekura remain immortal. After the shaman's biological death, his soul essence does not join others in the celestial house of dead souls. Instead, when he dies, his soul multiplies as each of his personal hekura become temporarily disembodied again, dispersing into various directions before eventually returning to the surrounding mountaintops and places in the forest where they lived before becoming part of the shaman's bodily hekura system. Each hekura retains an imprint of the shapori's persona thus becoming a carrier of his soul image. In their free state they have the ability to rejuvenate while waiting for other hekura aspirants to call them to descend from their mountaintops and become reincarnated. All hekura are the original ancestors (or *no patapɨ*), which is the term that designates the archaic humanity. But no patapɨ are also all recently deceased men of influence (*pata*), usually shapori, who continue to have an influence on the living. Through shamanistic initiations, shapori candidates receive knowledge and abilities from their no patapɨ ancestors – their embodied hekura. Only by surrendering their bodies and souls to their ancestors can they become one of them – the 'living ancestors' so to speak, and thus enter the cosmic circuitry of other hekura ancestors or no patapɨ that once lived. Continual initiatory transformations of humans into immortal hekura assure cosmic continuity between the primordial dimension of the world and human existence and the fusion of human beings with their ancestors. Each shamanistic initiation becomes a repetition of the cosmogonic process and is a direct route to the manifestation of the primordial unity of the cosmos through the shapori's body and his all-embracing mode of consciousness. Only competent shapori can become direct participants in the unstable realm of primordial flux and transformation and enable others to directly share their experiences within the intersubjective field of shared consciousness during shamanistic sessions.

Epena: A Transformative Substance
and an Aliment for Hekura

The unity of original ancestral beings was a state characterised by epena-free transformations. Within the context of a fluxing primordial sphere, the ancestors had explicit and instant powers of free transformation and influence. After the 'schism in primordium' (Sullivan 1988), this ability was afforded only to properly initiated shapori, who must resort to epena as a medium of transformation. Since the legacy of the primordial condition is accessible solely through initiation, the only way to regain and retain this unity of fluid, all-embracing primordial consciousness is by means of psychotropic, consciousness-expanding substances. The epena snuff is an indispensable component for a shapori's multiple metamorphoses into hekura, but it is also considered a form of nourishment for hekura, who enjoy getting intoxicated together with their master. Epena not only enables the shaman to access and directly participate in primordial mythical plenum but is also a powerful collective medium for the direct, 'live' transmission of mythical episodes articulated by the performing shapori to the other co-participants. The non-initiated Yanomami are not only passive receptors of mythic discourses but active participants in various mythological episodes. This ancestral knowledge is thus further, indirectly diffused to the rest of community – mainly the elderly, women and children.

The Yanomami nowadays use three distinct types of consciousness-altering snuff substances known as epena. Yopo was assimilated into the Yanomami language from local Arawakan groups and is now widely used alongside epena. However, epena is a general term assigned to any of the three sniffing concoctions while yopo specifically refers to *hisiõmɨ*, which is one of the three types. Yopo or hisiõmɨ,[2] also known by the Shamathari word *pararo*, is the principal, highly praised mind-altering snuff made from roasted and pulverised button-like kernels from the fruit of the yopo tree (anadanthera peregrina), which belongs to the bean family. Green kernels are dried in the sun or above a fire and then squeezed like plasticine until it coalesces into a soft dark brown mass that is then roasted on a fire and mixed with some ash from the bark of the ama ahi tree (elizabetha princeps). The bark in itself does not contain any psychotropic properties but serves as a spice to lessen the harshness of the principal snuff. It is then heated on a metal barrel lid and pounded with a flat rock into a fine brown powder. The Yanomami from Ocamo say that Ihamariwë (Sloth Ancestor) taught other fellow ancestors – the ancestral shapori – how to prepare and use hisiõmɨ in primordial times (Cocco 1972). Ocamo is nowadays the main centre for the production and distribution of ready-made hisiõmɨ due to the abundance of yopo trees in the area. Yopo is always in demand, especially in the Platanal area where yopo trees are not widespread.

Yakõana, also known as *ayukuma*, is the second consciousness-altering snuff substance made from the inner bark of a tree belonging to the virola family (virola calofiloidea or elongata), which is similarly dried, pulverised and spiced with ash from the ama ahi tree. According to the Ocamo Yanomami, Hõrãmariwë[3] (Ancestor of a Small Bush Hen) introduced yakõana to the Yanomami (ibid.). In other myths, the older primordial twin and great shapori Yoawë was known to be the first to inhale yakõana and he received many hekura into his chest in the same manner they come to present day candidates. However, being the more imperfect of the twins, his hekura left him and he lost his powers as a consequence of the vaginal scent on his body having had sexual intercourse (Lizot 1974). For that reason the senior shapori nowadays instruct young candidates to abstain from sexual intercourse or being in close proximity to a woman both during the initiation and for some time after. In a Sanema myth, it was Hayariwë (Deer Ancestor) who chanted and inhaled yakõana for the very first time and taught other ancestors how to use it before transforming into hekura Hayariwë and a multiplicity of deer (Colchester 1981).

Moshohara, the third snuff, is made from the dried leaves of two plant varieties belonging to the justicia pectoralis family. Myths from the Ocamo region narrate how Moshoharayoma – the original custodian of the snuff – introduced moshohara to the Yanomami but it was the subaquatic yawari who taught them how to prepare it (Cocco 1972). During my fieldwork, on two occasions, the shaman Ruweweriwë taught me how to prepare moshohara snuff. Both times we went to Ruweweriwë's section of the garden to collect the necessary plants. The first plant was a medium-sized bush with reddish leaves, called *rahara hena*, or 'leaf of a giant mythological snake'. The second one, planted right next to it, was a small ground shrub with thin dark green leaves called *pore hena* or 'leaf of a ghost'. Back in the shapono, we dried the leaves in the sun before grinding them with a small flat rock called *po* until they turned into a very fine green powder ready for use.

I noticed that throughout the whole shamanistic initiation the neophyte Arawë only took yakõana snuff while his master, shapori Ruweweriwë, took all three varieties according to the specific task at hand. For example, he would take hisiõmɨ when he was carrying out some key embodiments of the main microcosmic bodily structural components, such as the hekura path, their shapono and Pei Makɨ or Hekura Mountain. This is because Ihamariwë (Sloth Ancestor), whose task it is to incorporate those key components into the candidate's body, prefers hisiõmɨ to other substances. ɨrariwë (Jaguar Ancestor), whose role is to dismember the neophyte, also prefers hisiõmɨ. Other hekura like the other substances better: Moshoharayoma is drawn to moshohara whereas the subaquatic spirit beings (yawari) are fond of yakõana. During initiations, shapori candidates only inhale yakõana and receive hekura children. Later on, when they start inhaling hisiõmɨ, a more powerful set of hekura enters their bodies.

Outside of the context of shamanistic practices, Yanomami men like to inhale epena, especially hisiõmɨ snuff, almost on a daily basis. Quietly in pairs or in the context of group *epenamou* snuff-taking sessions, men gather and spend afternoons together, blowing epena into each other's nostrils, joking and remembering old times. Epena snuff promotes social gatherings and interactions. All important decisions and issues are debated under its effects, as it lowers inter-personal inhibitions, thus increasing the amount of talk. Men inhale epena during intercommunal visits and trading activities or in political meetings when they have to make important collective decisions about going to war or negotiating peace deals. Epena-sniffing plays a central role in the lives of Yanomami men and is a vital part of their masculine identity. It is the pillar of Yanomami collective cultural knowledge. Regarding the experiential effects of epena, snuff taking, especially in the early stages, is always a very intense and turbulent experience for shamans and non-shamans alike. Given that I was an outsider and an anthropologist, on a personal level, I found the experience to be very profound and peculiar. For those who are not used to it, the initial effects of epena, particularly of hisiõmɨ, can be very unpleasant and frightening. On the level of conscious experience, the first noticeable change in visual perception is that everything develops an aura of vibrant, multi-coloured neon light. Almost immediately, the snuff taker experiences side effects of red and teary eyes, a runny nose, excessive sweating, increased heartbeat and copious vomiting. This is accompanied by the sensation of twitching skin, muscle spasms, convulsions and the inability to coordinate body movements. The first few times I took hisiõmɨ, I used to faint at this point before regaining consciousness a few minutes later. The Yanomami were watching me seated in the middle on the floor all covered in dirt and hysterically laughing, teasing me that I was wrestling with hekura. Gradually, I got used to the effects and stop fainting. Once the initial storm-like, turbulent, psychophysiological effects start to abate early in the session, one enters a perceptual mode whereby everything within the field of vision suddenly becomes brighter and more vibrant. The surrounding noise and people's voices sound as if amplified through a microphone and their gestures and body movements appear distorted. After some time, the snuff taker enters a highly talkative and uplifting period. Experienced snuff takers pass through the first stage much more quickly and may on occasion enter a talkative mode almost immediately after the infusion.

Epena taking and hekuramou practices are predominantly male activities. Yanomami men generally hold the view that only men can become shapori. The Sanema, for example, assume that women cannot become shamans because of their inability to control themselves under the epena influence and are too weak to deal with *hikola* (hekura) spirits. Apparently, some Sanema women can incorporate a number of minor spirits and sing, without engaging in healing activities (Colchester 1982). Lizot (1985) wrote that Yanomami women cannot become shapori, but some do take snuff occasionally, chant to the hekura and even search for missing souls. In 1979 the missionary and ethnographer María Isabel Eguíllor García (1984) reported that there was one female practising shapori at the Ocamo mission post. Another missionary, Father Luis Cocco (1972), wrote that women generally dislike inhaling yopo, but he knew of one practising female shapori from the community of Yorexiana-theri. Helena Valero described in her narrative a female shapori from the community of Aramamisi-theri; she was a tall, strong woman, painted and decorated akin to male shapori when dancing with hekura spirits. She was allegedly capable of curing the sick and could even steal children's souls from enemy villages. During my fieldwork I did not encounter any female shapori or witness any women taking epena. I asked various women about this and they responded that epena taking is 'men's stuff' and that women are afraid of its effects and of hekura in particular. But in 2008, while I was visiting a large community of Yaritha from the sector Haximú near the Brazilian border with the health team, I encountered an elderly female shapori in action. She was singing to her hekura and curing a child. The Yanomami told me that she is not only a genuine hekura but well known and respected among her male colleagues on both sides of the border.

Shamanism in Myths and in the Contemporary Context

The pattern of shamanistic activities depicted in certain myths resembles the contemporary situation of exchanges of hekura attacks and reprisals between shapori from communities situated along the Orinoco River and their traditional Shamathari enemies living in the Siapa River Valley. Shapori from the same community or from neighbouring, allied communities maintain good interpersonal relationships and relative harmony without attempting harmful acts of destructive magic or aggressive shamanism against each other. They know that if they commit such offences other shapori would expose them and the whole community would punish them. The long myth of Nerõriwë (Opossum Ancestor) and his destiny (Colchester 1981; Lizot 1989) embodies precisely this type of primordial situation and has an underlying warning against some of the things that are considered a breach of interpersonal rules and conduct. It also explains how some bird ancestors transformed into hekura and continued living inside rocks and mountains. The main culprit Opossum was the ancestral shaman who developed spiteful and destructive thoughts against one of his fellow cohabitants and decided to kill him with his hekura. The victim suddenly became ill with a fever and chills and quickly passed away. Another shapori found him out and publically announced the wrongdoer's identity; Opossum was castigated and kicked out of the community. An angry mob went after him so he hid inside the crack of a big rock suspended from a branch of a tall tree with liana (vines); he was nevertheless tracked down and Ihamariwë (Sloth Ancestor) climbed the liana and cut it off with his teeth. The hanging rock fell to the ground and Mayepɨriwë (Big-beaked Toucan Ancestor) tried to reach the Opossum through a crack without success; his beak has remained bent ever since. The Opossum was smashed and his blood splashed everywhere. Various bird ancestors, including red and yellow-blue Ara macaws, smeared his blood all over their bodies and transformed into hekura birds and continued living inside rocks and mountains. Mayepɨriwë became the chief of all hekura birds and he allocated places for them to live inside each rock, though some stayed in trees. He then transformed into a multiplicity of toucan hekura. A tall tree coupled with giant hanging liana in this myth is one variation of a widespread symbolic motif of a cosmic axis connecting different cosmic spheres and preserving the unity of sky and earth. Different myths narrate how this unstable, fragile union broke up a few times, for various reasons, causing multiple transformations of primordial ancestors. In one such myth (Lizot 1974), a group of ancestors climbed the hanging liana all the way to the sky where they have remained ever since. Another group reached the tree canopy when the liana snapped and they transformed into monkeys, while a third group plunged from lower down and transformed into peccaries.

Shapori and Jaguar

The jaguar is an important symbol of power in South American mythology and shamanism (Cooper 1992; Reichel-Dolmatoff 1975). In primordial times, the original jaguar Ɨrariwë was a cannibal and a great threat to the population. Omawë, the younger of the primordial twins, decided to kill him. When Ɨrariwë died, he transformed into both animal and hekura forms and has remained on the earthly level ever since. Hekura Ɨrariwë nowadays roams the forest freely, searching for victims. He does not have a home because in primordial times ancestral shapori banished him to unknown parts; he became disoriented and lost. He is one of the most powerful allies of the shapori, who consider him to be chief of all terrestrial hekura. In shamanistic initiations Ɨrariwë maintains one important function – that of eating humans. In this regard, the master shapori has to go outside of the shapono and call the jaguar hekura to come to him. He then returns to the shapono as Ɨrariwë and devours the candidate's body. From then on, the jaguar hekura becomes the future shapori's personal ally. The jaguar animal has an ambiguous status, being somewhat more than an animal, and the Yanomami perceive it as animal-hekura. Along with the snake, the jaguar is the only animal with dual aspects: a dangerous carnivorous predator and an incarnated hekura. Shapori are able to use jaguars or poisonous snakes as 'vessels' to kill someone. First they must locate the jaguar (or snake) animal in the forest with the help of their hekura. Next, they summon their Jaguar (Ɨrariwë) ally and enter the jaguar's body. Now completely fused with the animal, they can 'guide' it to their targeted victim and kill him. For that reason, the Yanomami always suspect an enemy shapori whenever someone is attacked by a jaguar or bitten by a snake.

While in contemporary shamanistic initiation Jaguar Ancestor kills the candidate, in the primordial drama a shapori kills the jaguar. In this way the prey becomes predator; the hunted becomes the hunter. In Yanomami myths Jaguar is a trickster. Tricksters, who commonly feature in mythic and epic traditions, are involved in skulduggery and deception. They are depicted as selfish, lustful and greedy masters of deceit with a tendency to wander (Basso 1987a; Radin 1972 [1956]). Jaguar is a cunning cannibal: he tempts the Yanomami by telling them lies and then kills them to satisfy his craving for human flesh. But he is also a boorish imbecile who is always, in the end, outwitted and killed by shapori. In one myth from Karohi-theri (Lizot 1989), envious shapori decided to kill a hunting dog belonging to another community with the help of Jaguar hekura. The dog's owner, who was also a shapori, quickly detected the killers and managed to bring the dog back to life. On one occasion during my stay in Platanal, I was observing the shapori Makowë assuming the identity of Jaguar Hekura Ɨrariwë and apparently killing a hunting dog in a distant Shamathari community of Yehiopë-theri. He was hitting the ground violently while simultaneously impersonating a dog, whining and growling. Another myth (Lizot 1974) narrates how one shapori created Jaguar from dried frog skin and the plant called ɨra kë nakɨ ('the jaguar's tooth'). Jaguar was craving human flesh and his creator banished him far away, telling him not to return. Jaguar was menacingly roaming a nearby community when the village shapori detected his presence after inhaling some epena snuff. The shapori summoned his Turtle hekura assistant to fight Jaguar, telling it to aim for Jaguar's neck. Frightened village inhabitants had left the shapono and hid nearby. Other hekura had grouped around him ready to assist. After a long battle, the turtle and shapori finally killed Jaguar, but later the shapori died too, tormented by the spirit of the dead Jaguar. This myth portrays a typical situation that is also common nowadays: a hekura, in this instance Jaguar, threatens a community; a shapori inhales epena snuff and detects the intruder; then an ensuing battle unfolds while the shapori is in an altered state of consciousness.

Yanomami Conception of a Person and Causes of Illness

For the Yanomami, illness and instances of abrupt death are not just random occurrences but the outcome of an intentional act by a certain agency, such as a specialist in harmful magic, an enemy hekura or a ghost (pore). When a person is sick they are said to go from *temi* (a state of good health) to *hariri* (being sick). The triggers could be, for example, shawara, a magic thorn or an arrow sent by a hostile shapori, which invades his or her corporeal interiority and provokes fever, pain or general weakness. In this instance, the shapori's task is to expel the intruding agent from the sufferer's body, and from the community at large, to re-establish his or her corporeal equilibrium and socio-cosmic harmony. Alternatively, illness can occur when a person's soul component is stolen, damaged or consumed by an enemy soul-eating hekura or a ghost. These two conditions and causes of illness or death go hand in hand, as a body intrusion by a pathogenic agent commonly damages a person's 'spiritual tissue' or the soul component. In this second instance, a shapori first has to locate and then, if necessary, repair the damaged or missing soul component or vital principle with the help of his assisting hekura before reinstalling it. Each instance of an illness is distinctive, despite the fact that they share clearly discernible symptoms. The resulting illness causes temporary disruption of the sufferer's bodily equilibrium and the suspension of their everyday activities. Concurrently, each case of illness causes the transitory disharmony of the whole group whose security is temporarily suspended until the shapori re-establishes socio-cosmic equilibrium whether the affected person recuperates or dies.

Yanomami knowledge of the human self-constitution, as revealed through shamanism, is the key element in understanding the process of illness and cure. The myth of the origin of fire (Chapter Two) tells us how the original ancestors lost their immortality through the curse of the Caiman Ancestor and became subjected to aging and death. Consequently, human beings emerged from the primordium with finite, physical bodies that are consumed by fire at the moment of death. In the Yanomami language, *pei ya* refers to 'my body' and *pei a* to 'his or her body'. 'Pei' is a generic base term or lexeme that links the names of different body parts and organs, as well as their functions, to the body as a whole; for example, *pei he* (head), *pei amoku* (liver) *pei niaasi* (urine), *pei iyepe* (blood). Pei also links things that imply direct human contact and physical activity, such as *pei mayo* (footprints) or a *pei yo* (path) (Lizot 1996).

Together with body parts and internal organs there are immaterial components of the Yanomami multiple soul. Jointly they constitute the totality of a human being. These soul essences are vulnerable to various afflictions and manipulations that can threaten a person's health or even their life. Only shapori are capable of perceiving and manipulating these soul essences to inflict sickness upon a person or to cure them. The first soul element is called *puhi*, which is a moving cosmic substance that saturates all of existence. It is a life-giving cosmic force that provides vitality to all living beings and material objects in the universe, including human bodies in which case it becomes *pei puhi*. On the one level, puhi is a mental capacity associated with will power, thought and emotion and does not have a bodily coefficient (Albert 1985; Lizot 2004). In this instance puhi is used in conjunction with personal pronouns; for example, to describe certain subjective, psychological states or emotions such as *Ya puhi* (I want), *Ya puhi toprarou* (I am happy), *Wa te puhii?* (Do you like it?) *Ya puhi kuu* (I think). The first example is an expression of demand while the second is an emotional state. The third instance is the question of liking, again as a mental capacity. In the last example, the subject expresses an agreement or opinion on something, as a thinking process.

Puhi, in conjunction with the base-word pei, becomes pei puhi – which is the existential, constitutive bodily soul component of a person, with each bodily organ having its own amount of puhi. For the shapori, pei puhi exists in a tangible form. It is not simply a function of the psyche but the essential part of a person's embodiment. As a manipulable substance, it is prone to various afflictions and is vital for life. Ruweweriwë likened it to a breath resembling the white down (*horoi*) of the curassow bird. It has an anthropomorphic form. The starting point in a healing session is to assess the condition of a person's pei puhi. In one such session in Platanal, I observed Makowë assuming the identity of the Spider Monkey hekura, Pashoriwë, and 'taking a sample' of pei puhi from the body of a sick child to determine the nature of the affliction. With monkey-like movements he scooped up an amount of pei puhi with his hands and was holding it, watching it, smelling it, listening to it, examining it and tasting it before gazing into the distance. The hekura was attempting to identify the pei puhi's content. The information thus gathered revealed to the curing hekura the type of affliction and the perpetrator's identity. If pei puhi is damaged, the shapori will attempt to repair it. If it is gravely affected, he will bring a new amount of external puhi to replace the old quantity. Pei puhi can be damaged when an enemy shapori launches spirit darts, arrows or thorns, which can generate sharp pain, illness and sometimes death. Ruweweriwë said that pain produced by the tearing of pei puhi commonly occurs in the solar plexus area, above the kidney, right through the forehead or sometimes in the leg or foot. In this last instance, the swelling and pain in ankles (haye hërï) is an outcome of a harmful action of a subterranean Amahiri shapori, shooting a spirit dart or sending a magical thorn upwards. The shapori must engage his hekura helpers to extract the pathogenic object from the foot through suction and vomiting to despatch it back to where it came from. Ruweweriwë customarily sends extracted spirit darts or shawara sickness southwards to a distant Shamathari community, or in the direction of Mavaca or Sejal. Once the pathogenic object is expelled from the body the shapori completes his treatment by 'repairing' the damaged pei puhi with the help of his hekura.

Pei mï ãmo ('the centre' or 'core') is the second anthropomorphic constitutive soul component of a person. Mï ãmo, without the base word 'pei', is the central part or core of anything. On one occasion, a young Yanomami man asked if I would share my wad of tobacco, which is for men habitually made from two large tobacco leaves. The man actually asked if I could give him the mï ãmo or inner leaf of my share of tobacco wad. Within the context of a human body, pei mï ãmo is the essence of a person, with each body part and inner organ having its own amount of mï ãmo. For example, pei he (head) has its own pei he mï ãmo. The whole body (pei ya) is the total sum of pei mï ãmo or the person's anthropomorphic essence. This vital principle is open to hekura attacks. To capture someone's essence (pei mï ãmo), a shapori summons cannibalistic Moon Ancestor Periporiwë, Ancestral Jaguar Ïrariwë or Sun Ancestor Mothokariwë to be able to reach into another's body, take out their soul essences and consume them. A ghost (pore) also feeds on people's mï ãmos. A shapori's main task is to attempt to locate the lost mï ãmo with the help of his personal hekura assistants and reinstall it into the body.

Thus the base word pei in the given context is fundamental to the human body. Pei in conjunction with names of body parts and inner organs indicates that it is a part of the whole. The essence of a whole person (his or her pei puhi and pei mɨ ãmo) is contained within each body part and internal organ. Each body component thus contains a quantity of its own pei puhi and pei mɨ ãmo. The body as a whole is a sum of its constitutive parts and internal organs. The relationship between the parts and the whole of multiple soul components is implicitly holographic in nature. Each individual mɨ ãmo is part of the whole but concurrently it is in itself whole, in a sense that both part and the whole share the same substance just like a drop of ocean and the whole ocean. In the aforementioned example of Makowë treating a sick child, his hekura helpers in action were repeatedly taking 'the sample' of the child's overall pei puhi to determine which part of the puhi was affected. The shapori then proceeded to restore the damaged part, working on the whole body simultaneously.

When a deceased person's body is cremated their pei mɨ ãmo becomes liberated. Ascending to the sky, it eventually transforms into a no porepɨ posthumous soul and joins other souls of their dead kin in the celestial shapono. In the case of a violent or sudden death, when a body will be left to decompose without being cremated, the metamorphosis of the soul still takes place but it transforms into a ghost – no uhutɨpɨ (pore). Trapped in this earthly plane of existence, a pore will spend time wandering through the forest or hang around near the location where they died. Pore can be of either sex. Yanomami describe them as white skinned – timid yet dangerous beings. This is the reason why the Yanomami during their initial contacts with whites likened them to dead people or their own ancestors. Pore hang around shaponos at dusk near forest paths that lead to and from the shapono, aiming at stealing souls of careless persons to make them ill. Apparently, there was one such spectre of a man who died long ago living near the Sheroana-theri shapono. Ruweweriwë often warned people to abstain from going out of the shapono at night because the pore comes out of the ground at dusk and preys upon the shapono's inhabitants. A few witnesses described him as a large, solid built Yanomami-like male, painted with red ochre and carrying a bow and arrows. Ruweweriwë's son Mirko told me that he saw him once standing in the garden in the middle of the day. Every day at dusk, Ruweweriwë would block all forest paths with the dry branches. He told me that pore walk on paths just like the Yanomami and tree branches prevent him from entering the shapono at night.

During shamanistic initiation, pore also get incorporated into a shapori's body. Joining a shaman's arsenal of personal hekura helpers, pore become a beneficial ally whose main role is to guard the entrance into the shapori's corporeal shapono where hekura rest in their hammock just like the Yanomami. A shapono's entrance where the pore dwells is located just above the navel, which is the place where earth meets the underworld on the microcosmic scale. When Ruweweriwë embodied a pore to transfer him into the candidate Arawë, he first covered his entire body with dust. Transformed into a pore, the shapori was waving his arms as if trying to strangle someone. He appeared to be disoriented and his eyes were full of fear. He looked at me intensely for a brief moment, then took a few small steps and came close to my face but then quickly withdrew. Ruweweriwë later told me that this pore was particularly afraid of me because he had never seen a white man before.

The final constitutive soul component of a person is *pei noreshi*. On the one hand, pei is an indication of being part of an embodiment. On the other hand, noreshi is a generic term associated with an extracorporeal image of a person's animal double. More recently, noreshi have become associated with photographic images, drawings, or a TV screen. Yanomami dislike photographs because they believe that a person's soul essence is captured together with an image and therefore it becomes prone to various manipulations. '… Taking a picture of a person is akin to capturing his shadow soul (noreshi)' (Steinvorth-Goetz 1969: 42). This belief is still prevalent in remote communities where I was not allowed to take photos of children. They were clear and firm about this restriction; however, the Yanomami living around mission centres did not believe such things and I was generally allowed to take photos of my choice.

Within the context of a human embodiment, the noreshi is quite a unique constitutive soul component of a person with a dual, bilocal manifestation. It is part of the human embodied soul and simultaneously a corresponding extracorporeal animal double located in the forest. The two components are directly linked and inseparable to such an extent that they mirror each other's actions. When a person sleeps, their noreshi also sleeps; when they wake up, so does their noreshi animal. According to Ruweweriwë, it is not only the Yanomami who have noreshi but foreigners too. Each noreshi animal bears certain characteristics of the person with whom it forms the union. Ruweweriwë said that my noreshi animal double is a spotted eagle (*mohomɨ*), whose body is very long just like mine. Howard, the missionary from Platanal has a monkey noreshi that has big ears just like him.

Every morning during the wet season (from April until October), the forest surrounding the Sheroana-theri shapono would be completely covered with thick morning mist (*ihirashi*). Everyone would be quietly sitting around the fire, munching on something or lying in hammocks, waiting patiently for the mist to lift. They told me to stay quiet because then my noreshi animal would also remain in its place, feeling warmth from the fire during the wet and cold early morning hours. If a Yanomami moves about the shapono or leaves its confines during morning mist, their noreshi animal would mirror their action. If someone makes loud noises, noreshi would do the same. This undesirable behaviour, known as *noreshimou*, increases the probability of hunters detecting and killing their animal double. In this instance, a person would die instantly in the shapono. If a person dies first, their noreshi animals would also die. On one occasion, the candidate Arawë had to skip his usual morning round of hekura embodiments and wait for the mist to lift up, otherwise, as Ruweweriwë explained, his own noreshi would have come to him attracted by his calling, which would have increased the chance of some hunter detecting movements of his noreshi and ultimately killing it. A corporeal person's noreshi can be lost or stolen, which could provoke an illness or death. Small children are particularly prone to losing their not yet fully formed noreshi, especially in cases where they suddenly get frightened of something. This so-called 'sudden fright syndrome', commonly known as *susto* (Spanish: fear), is a common cause of illness or death in many other parts of Latin America (Anderson 1996). When a Yanomami child experiences sudden fright, his or her noreshi could leave their bodies and become lost in the forest. The child becomes unwell with fever and weakness and his or her mother must go into the forest to search for and bring back their lost noreshi. Once the noreshi is reinstalled, the child's health will start improving (Lizot 2007).

Another way to inflict sickness or death is through sorcery techniques, mainly *mayo hëri* and *ōkã*. To inflict harm, the malefactor, in the first instance, carefully collects earth bearing someone's footprint (*mayo*), mixes it with potent magic herbs (*hëri*) and heats the concoction over hot flames while chanting. By that time, the owner of the footprint should develop a burning fever that sometimes leads to death. The Yanomami say that a footprint left on the ground has an inseparable union with the person it belongs to. It contains the essence of a person as a means to influence the person as a whole – that is, to make them ill. The same principle applies to aforementioned soul essences; the part stands for the whole. Manipulation of a part affects the whole. The conscious intention of a sorcerer is projected onto intended objects with the aim of contaminating the bearer of the footprint through his or her own essence. Snow, drawing on Sir James Frazer, describes contagious magic as being '… based on the premise that things that were once joined together can never be fully put asunder: the part stands for the whole. A lock of hair or a fingernail clipping thus represents the individual from which it was taken' (Frazer 1979 [1922]: 346; see also Levy-Bruhl 1965 [1928]: 114–16). The same principle seems to be at work in Yanomami footprint sorcery.

Õkã is another common type of harmful sorcery practice, involving the use of a pulverised poisonous *aroari këki* herb (cyperus articulates) coupled with the invocation of specific spells. This plant grows in abundance in the Siapa Valley and the Shamathari, the arch-enemies of the Yanomami from the Orinoco region, have a reputation for being skilful and efficient õkã practitioners. A specialist in õkã sorcery will hide near a forest path and blow the herb powder through a blowpipe or from the palm of their hand in the direction of a passer-by, who will directly inhale it. Õkã is one of the Yanomami's most feared activities; they are convinced that those who are attacked will almost certainly die and even shapori have trouble saving their lives. My host from Platanal, Jacinto, apparently survived one such attack. He said that many years ago after attending an important meeting in his native community of Toritha-theri, he was on his way back to Platanal when he suddenly experienced chills, dizziness and weakness. He became extremely thirsty and could hardly walk. With great difficulty he finally reached his boat anchored on the Shanishani River bank and immediately fell unconscious. His boatman took him to Platanal where Makowë, Jacinto's father-in-law, swiftly diagnosed his condition as an õkã attack. Makowë managed to save his life by 'squeezing' the venom out of his body until he finally recuperated.

While shapori and õkã practitioners are predominantly men, women do have their own skills, including the ability to manipulate various situations to have a direct effect on others. They accomplish this through the use of hëri or certain magical substances and herbs, coupled with the recitation of spells to inflict harm, provoke a cure or prevent events or the actions of others. To cure the sick, women use herbal remedies, massage and simple manipulations, which they consider to be their domain or 'women's knowledge'. Elderly women are the most experienced and influential in this type of healing practice. They treat mostly children, who may be suffering from diarrhoea (*krii*), fever (*yopri*), various pains (*nini*) or eye infections (*mamo wayu*), with various herbal concoctions but also with massage, accompanied by singing or chanting. During my stay in Sheroana-theri, I was fortunate to see women treating the eye infections of their children on two occasions. The first time, a mother extracted juice from the leaf of a plant called *yama* and used it in the manner of eye drops to alleviate the redness caused by inflammation (*mamo wayu*). The second time, another mother treated her son's red and swollen eyelids by soaking in water a small stem with round green leaves from the *thori* (tick) plant and rubbing the liquid around the boy's eyes. On yet another occasion during an outbreak of a contagious epidemic of a disease that caused painfully enlarged and inflamed groin glands (*pei moshiki nini*) accompanied by a general lethargy, Mahekosi, the oldest and most influential woman, treated her cousin by applying pressure to the glands with her thumb while chanting:

kuye, kuye, kuye,
ho pepi, ho pepi,
si komi asi naki ho pepi,
kuye, kuye ... ('Go away! Disappear! Go back to normal, Go away!')

Notes

1. The suffix -yoma indicates the female gender; Hekura of animals can be both male and female while Hekura representatives of plants are exclusively female (Shamakoroyoma, Mamokoriyoma).
2. Hisiōmɨ is a tree belonging to the bean family (anadanthera peregrina). Consciousness-altering snuff is prepared from the seed. The main hallucinogenic properties include: N, N-dimethyltryptamine; NMT (monomethyl-tryptamine); 4-Hydroxy-5-methoxydimethyltryptamine (Schultes 1976: 86).
3. This grey and black coloured bird explores the rainforest floor for food. Its call indicates a threat, such as the approach of people or the proximity of large bush pigs (*warë*) (Lizot 1989).

Chapter 4

HEKURAPRAɨ

Corporeal Cosmogenesis

Summary of the Initiatory Ordeal

In shamanistic initiations, certain hekura, by virtue of being attracted to the sound of the candidate's calling and lip vibration, leave their natural habitats – the shaponos located on the mountaintops or in forests – and move into the candidate's body, which becomes their new abode. Hekuraprai literally means, 'to transform into hekura'. Throughout the initiatory ordeal, the neophyte undergoes a series of rebirth experiences through various forms of dying: from being slashed by a hekura with a machete or shot by an arrow, to being dismembered by the Jaguar or consumed alive by fire. After receiving the mountain of hekura into his chest, the candidate eventually reaches the ultimate death experience after which he fully undertakes his new identity as hekura and a multiplicity of hekura selves. Joining the cosmic circuitry of ancestral hekura and ultimately becoming one of them requires personal sacrifice of one's own soul essence and humanness to hekura to be reborn as a living hekura and a sum of other hekura. A shaman's corporeal hekura become his personal allies and sources of knowledge and power. They multiply a shapori's post-mortem ego and his sense of self into a holographic range of hekura selves.

The process of initiation involves not only the incarnation of numerous hekura and the candidate's transformation into a new hekura but also involves the metamorphosis of his human body into a cosmic body or corporeal cosmogenesis. To turn the candidate into hekura, the incoming hekura bring into his body certain hekura implements, namely two head crowns called *watoshe* and a pair of toucan wings called *hoko*. The toucan is considered to be chief of all bird hekura and the candidate receives a pair of wings from Hekura representative of the smaller species of toucans Mayepɨrithawë, and a pair of wings from Hekura representative of larger toucans Piremarithawë. The wings are made from palm branches and later implanted by hekura – one pair of wings is placed horizontally on each side of the candidate's body, which will enable the new shapori to fly like a toucan. The two glowing watoshe head crowns or halos of light are representative of the Anaconda Ancestor Wãikõyãriwë and the Ancestral Jaguar Ɨrariwë, which they respectively place on the candidate's head. The master shapori places the two crowns made of woven palm leaves and covered with white curassow feathers on the candidate's head. On a deeper level they become a part of the candidate's permanent embodiment. Shaporis' luminous head crowns are exactly the same as those that all other hekura wear around their heads. Interestingly, Yanomami shapori are not unique in having halos around their heads. Shamans from other indigenous groups, such as the Jivaro that live in the headwaters of the Marañon River and its tributaries in northern Peru and eastern Ecuador, also have auras of radiating light around their heads, which other shamans can see (Harner 1972). When enemy hekura approach the Yanomami village, they flee when they see the glow of light around the shapori's head. But, for the shapori, watoshe is not only a form of identity or recognition of other hekura. The light crown also enables the shapori to detect other hekura nearby or to look by means of watoshe at distant places, which is impossible for an ordinary human being to accomplish.

Throughout the initiation the candidate undergoes a personal hekura metamorphosis but also becomes a sum of all the embodied hekura. To transform the candidate's body into a cosmic body, the incoming hekura must also bring and install the three main structural body components in order to form a complete microcosm of hekura and their living habitat. They are: the Hekura Path (*Pei Yo*), which is embodied between the candidate's legs; Hekura Shapono, embodied in the candidate's chest and Hekura Mountain (*Pei Makɨ*),[1] situated next to corporeal shapono near the base of the neck. These three iconic features of the shapori's corporeal microcosm are also the features of the Yanomami macrocosmic lifeworld. Shaponos are commonly situated nearby mountain peaks, as this is where hekura live in their shaponos, and there are always paths that lead to and from a Yanomami communal house just as the embodied hekura paths lead to and from the corporeal shapono where embodied hekura rest and sleep in their hammocks, just like the Yanomami. Thus, the shapori's body becomes both a corporeal microcosmic imago mundi and a matrix for macrocosmic manifestation of the candidate's ego consciousness. In other words, the candidate's self-perception vis-à-vis his body undergoes a radical transformation as it slips out of its usual self/body boundaries and expands into a cosmic, all-encompassing open mode of being, thus becoming unified with the external dimensionality of the macrocosm.

All throughout the initiatory ordeal, with his legs outstretched and open, and his chest exposed to the influx of hekura, the candidate has to cope with and conquer his own fear and pain. The literal invasion of the interiority of his body by the exteriority of the world through the continual hekura embodiment stretches the candidate's stream of ego-bound consciousness until reaching a final point of rupture and ego dissolution, posterior to the embodiment of Hekura Mountain. Following the disintegration of self through this death experience, the post-mortem stage of initiation involves the ego's reconstitution through rebirth and the emergence of a new sense of self in a hekura mode. During this period the candidate undergoes a series of direct revelatory experiences of various hekura abilities and modes of manifestation. For example, he cognises the role of embodied crowns of light and toucan wings through direct experience. As he calls hekura through hekura-calling chants (*tutomou*) and experiences the further influx of incoming hekura, the candidate eventually re-experiences himself dying; and this is the moment when he enters his first trance. From that moment onwards he stops the tutomou chanting and commences the first independent steps of shaporimou. The new mode of cosmic consciousness in fact remains open for continual expansion through further incorporation of new hekura and hekura songs that will come to the shapori in dreams and shaporimou sessions.

The candidate's metamorphosis into hekura during the shamanistic initiation involves not only the creation of a cosmic body as a template for the manifestation of the larger structures of the Yanomami macrocosm; it also provides shapori with access to the primordial condition of pre-cosmic undifferentiation. Initiation, in this sense, becomes a return or regressive movement towards the a priori state of original wholeness of the world or mythopoeic dimension in constant flux. As such, this movement is a direct reversal of creation. More precisely, the fission of the original being and the multiple transformations of the original ancestors generated the diversification of species and the bifurcation of human beings and hekura. Initiation is a process diametrically opposite to the process of primordial fission of the original ancestors into human beings and hekura. It is a process of recreation through regression to the original condition of the undivided ancestral beings. The original ancestor is brought into existence as the body and the world merge into one all-embracing modality of consciousness.

The two week initiatory ordeal in Sheroana-theri unfolded under one section of the shapono's roof in front of Ruweweriwë's house. Yanomami shamanistic initiation is not a secluded event but customarily takes place in the midst of the ebb and flow of everyday village life. The candidate is constantly surrounded by kinfolk and yet isolated from them and exempt from his daily activities and obligations. When the time came for Arawë to be initiated he temporarily left his family and put up his hammock in Ruweweriwë's house. Throughout the whole initiation no one was allowed to come close to him apart from Ruweweriwë, his assistant shapori, Taramawë, and me. During the initiation, Arawë repeatedly received large quantities of epena snuff and called in the hekura to come. There were about four to five daily rounds, each one lasting approximately an hour. The first round would follow the sunrise, after the morning mist had lifted, and the last one would be terminated in the moments when the sun was lowest in the sky. Upon the completion of each round, Arawë would crawl back slowly to his hammock – still facing the shapono's central area – where he would lie down on his back looking upwards. He rested in this position until the next round and did not talk to anyone. In this way, the candidate was 'cut off' from his immediate surroundings and fully immersed in his continual transformative experience. During these periods of rest in between the rounds – or at night – he was not allowed to scratch himself with his fingernails but could only gently touch the itchy spot with a thin wooden stick. He was forbidden to leave the shapono under any circumstances, not even to go to the toilet; instead, he would relieve himself into a prepared hole in the ground next to his hammock, moving about in a crouched position. During the night, he rested in his hammock, lying on his back. Makowë, the shapori from Platanal, told me about his periods of rest and sleep when he was initiated; he used to hear the sound of Pora Hekura or White Water Ancestor everywhere around him, in the ground and in the sky above.

The shapori's new cosmic body-in-the-making is a delicate structure, the maintenance of which requires compliance to a strict set of rules. To attract hekura and make them permanent within the structure of the fragile body microcosm, both during initiation and for a certain period after, the candidate must abstain from washing himself and from having sexual intercourse; he must also stop eating and drinking water during the period his cosmic body is being built. The first food he receives is a few sips of banana soup on the sixth day, after Hekura Mountain is embodied.

He must take the soup with a wooden spoon that only he is allowed to touch and which he hangs on his hammock after the meal. His only indulgence during this time is a wad of tobacco, and he only uses weak tobacco, because hekura dislike the strength of freshly made tobacco. Due to a lack of food and water his body eventually stops producing fluids and is reduced to the minimum of flesh. As he becomes weaker every day, his voice also loses its tonality. After the crucial first week of the initiatory ordeal, following the death experience, he starts eating small quantities of boiled plantains and sugar cane. In time, he can slowly increase the quantity and variety of food he eats by eating a piece of fish or red meat, but it will be months before his diet returns to normal.

Transformation into Hekura: Day-by-day Process

Beginnings: Setting up a Network of Protection

Early in the morning, a day before Arawë's initiation officially began, he went into the forest and brought back a big bunch of bark strips from the yakõana tree (virola elongata) as well as a pile of leaves from the moshohara plants in his garden. He dried the barks and leaves on the fire and then prepared large quantities of yakõana and moshohara snuff, enough to last through the entire initiation. In the meantime, Ruweweriwë and his assistant Taramawë prepared their own epena, which included hisiõmɨ that Taramawë had recently brought back from Ocamo. At noon, Ruweweriwë stood up and traced a foot-wide trail on the ground with his feet, starting just under the roof's edge of his house and terminating at the shapono's centre. He then sat on a log and called Arawë and Taramawë to come. They all took turns inhaling epena. Arawë and Taramawë remained seated while Ruweweriwë repeatedly circled around the shapono's central area, fetching hekura from multiple directions to domesticate them and turn them into guardians of the shapono against potential unwelcome intruders. He placed these hekura strategically in various places under the roof and near the shapono's entrances (Figure 4.1); for example, he positioned the Hekura Peripo wakë (No. 15), who is a small red-coloured version of the moon (*peripo*), on top of the left post of his house so it could jump down and squash any potential unwelcome intruders. Ruweweriwë also called upon Piyawanamoriwë (No. 7) the Hekura Ancestor of Violaceous Jay (cyanocorax violaceus) from the crow family, who is very boisterous and known for mobbing predators, and Iroriwë, also known as Shoshorithawë (No. 8), the Hekura of Red Howler Monkey (alouatta seniculus), who was placed near one of the

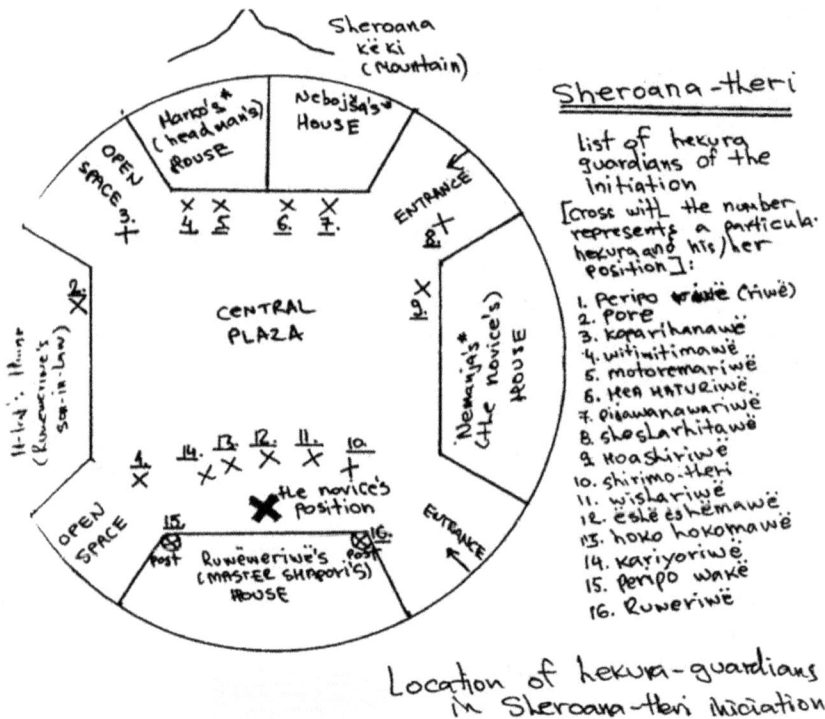

Figure 4.1 Hekura guardians of the shapono strategically positioned by Ruweweriwë at the beginning of Arawë's initiation.

main entrances into the shapono. This hekura consumes its own faeces and when Ruweweriwë was embodying him, he was alternately sticking his finger into his anus and then into his mouth. He then went to the shapono's entrance and 'relieved himself' there, later telling me that the strong smell of his excrement repels hekura intruders. On the other side of the shapono, in front of the candidate, Ruweweriwë positioned two hekura associated with air movement: Motoremariwë (No. 5) and Heãhãturiwë (No. 6). The first one has the ability to make other hekura spin and then slings them towards the candidate to facilitate the whole process of hekura embodiment. The other is the hekura of whirlwinds, who likewise assists the movement of hekura, sending spinning columns of air towards the candidate's body.

Day One

The thick morning mist has just lifted up and the sun is shining bright. Arawë's body is speckled with dots. While Arawë is anointing his face and chest with red ochre he is evidently nervous. A few days ago he admitted that he was anxious but determined to go ahead with the initiation: 'I want to become shapori to protect and cure my family just like my father did. I want to be just like my father. His hekura will come to me!'[2] He puts on a pair of feathered armlets made from the skin of the curassow bird and sprinkles white down over his freshly cut hair. He takes a seat under the raised part of the roof, assuming a typical initiatory body posture by widely opening his legs and leaning on both fully stretched arms. Meanwhile, Ruweweriwë and Taramawë have decorated themselves and they are now blowing some hisiõmɨ through a long inhaling tube into each other's nostrils. Taramawë gets up and blows great quantities of yakõana into Arawë's nostrils, which makes him wobble (Figure 4.2).

After a few moments Arawë collects himself, looks straight ahead and starts making a lip-vibrating sound. He is calling hekura to come. Ruweweriwë is singing and walking along the marked path to the centre of the shapono to fetch incoming hekura and transfer them from his into Arawë's body. The master shapori is commenting through his song how he can see hekura coming from all directions, announcing their presence

Figure 4.2 The shapori assistant Taramawë blows yakõana snuff into Arawë's nostrils.

moments before embodying them one by one. If a hekura descends from above, the shapori embodies them in a specific manner, by lifting his arm up and moving his hand in a circle. If they ascend from the lower cosmic stratum, Ruweweriwë bends down and stretches his arm towards the ground thus allowing hekura to enter his body. To bring in the terrestrial hekura, such as Ɨrariwë (Jaguar) and Yaoriwë (Ocelot), the shapori goes outside of the shapono to fetch them. Upon capturing and temporarily incarnating each hekura, Ruweweriwë traverses the path back towards the seated Arawë and passes the hekura on to him. After each hekura transfer, he walks back along the path to the centre of the shapono and, by announcing the next hekura's arrival, repeats the whole process. On the level of immediate perception, the hekura transfer is a horizontal movement, as the master continuously traverses the path stretching from Arawë to the shapono's centre. But, we can remember that the shapono's open central space is simultaneously a celestial sphere (hetu mɨsi), which joins the earth right where Arawë is seated – under the elevated part of the shapono's roof. The migration of hekura thus becomes an exclusively vertical movement, as they ascend from below the ground or descend from their shaponos located on top of the surrounding Sheroroi mountain peak, the place cosmo-geographically closest to the sky. For the candidate, the horizontal and vertical movements of incoming hekura experientially merge into one single path (Pei Yo), which terminates in his body. He is continually calling hekura to come, vibrating his lips and repeating after Ruweweriwë, thus confirming from direct experience that which the master shapori has just announced. In fact, the whole initiation unfolds as a form of dialogue between the master shapori, the candidate and the incoming hekura. It develops indiscriminately as the initiation progresses.

At the very beginning, Ruweweriwë announces through song that Yãwãriyõma (a female subaquatic spirit being) is the first hekura to arrive and that her face has already appeared. She has brought with her hërɨ (a magical substance) to offer to the candidate. The master shapori walks back towards Arawë saying that Yãwãriyõma will now give him hërɨ and that it will make him feel sick.[3] The shapori then announces the approaching arrival of paushi këkɨ[4] (feathers and animal skins) with the whirlwind, saying that the candidate will feel them very soon and that the hekura of feathers will make him feel weak. Ruweweriwë grabs two green feathers, runs towards the central area, lifts his arms up and starts dancing back towards Arawë, who is responding: 'Feathers have arrived with the wind and I feel them right now!' Ruweweriwë inserts plugs adorned with feathers through Arawë's pierced earlobes, where they will remain until the end of the initiation, but concurrently they will become embodied as pieces of his more permanent hekura attire. The next moment the master shapori proclaims: 'The shining Hutukara Mountain is coming into view and you will get frightened when it comes. Here it is, take it! Enter, enter!'[the embodiment takes place]. Ruweweriwë continues with a series of consecutive embodiments by singing and dancing as hekura and then transferring them to the seated candidate.

The master is now proclaiming that the whirlwind carrying shining feathers is descending and exclaims: 'Angry feathers are poking their tongues out; take them, trust me, they are yours!' Arawë confirms that the wind has really brought the feathers and that he recognises them as truly belonging to him. A variety of feathers are coming down: of red and blue macaw (ara); of a dark grey hawk (wi himi) (cooper's hawk); of a parrot called krau kraumi; a cotinga bird (ushuemi); heron (conori); small toucan (kata katami); currasow (paruri); royal parrot (kurikaya) and many more are arriving with singing mouths facing down. 'They are truly my father's feathers', recognises Arawë through his song and continues chanting:

> Shiny feathers of kuhararomi parrot are coming
> and they look very happy.
> Koromari parrot feathers are coming from the immortal river
> where hekura are preparing many flutes [exclaims Ruweweriwë].
> The fluttering feathers of Kanaporiwë are coming!
> Feathers of Titiri (night)[5] are coming dancing.

Arawë is complaining through the chant about the hekura feathers making him dizzy and weak. Their heat makes him sweat and his mouth is dry. To ease Arawë's suffering Ruweweriwë brings in two hekura associated with liquids: Ãmoã u ('liquid song'), whose task it is to facilitate Arawë's singing by quenching his thirst and a tree sap called Hōshō Hekura nou[6] that spreads all over Arawë's body to refresh him.

> Yes, these are my father's proper hekura. I recognise them.
> Please hand them over to me they truly belong to me now.
> I want to become hekura just like my father was [announces Arawë].
> These hekura will make you feel sad because they will remind you of your father.
> I will bring not only your father's hekura but others as well [says Ruweweriwë].

Arawë responds:

> Right now I feel happy.[7]
> The oncoming hekura are also happy to come to me.

He then continues announcing:

> Tiger Skin Mountain (*Yaomi këki*) is approaching.
> It is all covered with white down.
> *Sharapi* [type of large basket] full of down is coming with the whirlwind.
> They are the spirits of my father.
> *Shori*,[8] [brother-in-law or friend] hand them over to me!

Hekura of the Leaf shaped like the Machete (*Sipara pei hena*) is singing through Ruweweriwë how he is coming to cut Arawë, who repeats the song after him. 'Take them', exclaims the master and embodies them with his arm saying: 'Enter, enter' (into Arawë's body). He then continues commenting:

> Hekura are coming from all over the place.
> Over there other hekura are happily preparing lots of flutes.
> They will play them when they arrive.
> It is true. They are coming indeed!
> These shouts and applauses are theirs [confirms Taramawë].
> The immortal hekura of bush turkey (*mãrãshi*) are coming!
> They are carried by the sounds of hekura's flutes.[9]

Arawë then comments how he is sad (they are all feeling sad) and that he alone is feeling poor.[10] The master continues singing and announcing how the hekura of feathers are sweating from the heat; Arawë replies that feathers are jumping towards him. 'You are my brother (*apawë*)', speaks the ancestor through Ruweweriwë. 'They, the immortals (*pãrimi*) accept you as their true brother,' exclaims the master shapori. Evidently elated, Arawë responds to the hekura: 'I will accept you and become one of you'. Ruweweriwë announces that Yãpisi-theri ('community of Grey-winged trumpeters') are coming, facing backwards. They don't want the candidate to look at their faces, as he would recognise his father in them and start crying. Arawë tells them to recognise and accept him and he will take them or incorporate them into his body.[11]

At the end of the day Taramawë says to Arawë: 'Tonight you'll feel sad and angry and may ask yourself why you are doing this. Don't worry because later you'll feel good about it I promise!' 'Hekura were coming to your father [when he had his own initiation], in the same way they are coming to you now,' adds Ruweweriwë.

Day Two

Embodiment of the Hekura Path (Pei Yo)

Today, Arawë will receive from hekura the first major structural component of the new embodiment – the path of hekura. For this occasion, both Ruweweriwë and Taramawë inhale some hisiõmї and then move to the centre of the shapono where they spread a long, thin piece of red loincloth on the ground to represent the path; they then put a folded blanket on top of it and cover it with a pile of dry twigs. Ruweweriwë then takes his machete and crouches. He drives the tip of the machete into the ground and twists it, at first very slowly, before abruptly pulling it out. He and Taramawë then start shouting and violently hitting the ground with machetes. After a few moments they lift their machetes high in the air and hop back towards the loincloth. Next, Ruweweriwë crouches again and slowly removes the twigs then lifts up the blanket with the tip of his machete before placing it aside. Transformed into hekura, both shapori break the Hekura Mountain (blanket) with their machetes and then remove it to retrieve the path of the hekura within. They pick up the path (loincloth), raise it cautiously above their heads and start hopping towards Arawë. The candidate suddenly panics, and yells as Ruweweriwe's son-in-law, Kiawë, approaches him from behind, grabs both of his shoulders and pushes his knee against Arawë's back to keep him straight. At that moment Ruweweriwë places the red cloth on the ground between Arawë's legs, summons the Sloth Ancestor Ihamariwë, kneels down and starts pushing the hekura path with his fingers up one leg and then the other; Arawë is screaming – his body is twisting and shaking while the path is being embodied.[12] After a few moments he collects himself and recommences vibrating his lips and calling hekura while Ruweweriwë is announcing the arrival of the blue golondrina parrot (*shorori*). This hekura asks Arawë to close his eyes so as to not look at his face. Arawë heeds the hekura's command and closes his eyes, saying how he feels week because the hekura descending on him are big and heavy. 'Keep calling them and tell them that you are feeling sad and poor, [without hekura powers, see Note 10] says Ruweweriwë.

Ruweweriwë announces the arrival of more glittering feather hekura, who are poking their tongues out. 'They are coming to spear our brother-in-law [referring to Arawë]', comments Taramawë. Arawë is announcing the arrival of the hekura of a Pointed Mountain (*Shimorei këkї*) covered with shiny white down, followed by a glowing mountain of skin from the blue parrot (*ushuwemi siki këkї*) (from the Tangara genus). They are falling down and shining. 'Big and heavy, Mountain of Whirlwinds (*Heãhãtu*

këki pata) is heading towards me with many hekura of whirlwind' 'Ma!
Peheti ai', confirms Ruweweriwë.[13] Taramawë warns that some strange
and terrifying sounds are coming from the Hekura of Clothing (*watota
peshiyë*),[14] who brings shawara, which will make the candidate feel sick.
Arawë responds that he is afraid but continues singing:

> Hekura of feathers are coming with their bloodshot eyes.
> Their dry tongues are sticking out.[15]
> The immortal Moon Children (*peripo ihirupi*) are also coming!
> They are going to dry out ['cook'] the saliva in my mouth.[16]

'Don't worry about that, you'll be all right', Taramawë reassures the
candidate. The master shapori tells Arawë that these strange hekura
belong to him and that their eyes are red from the fire within them.

> Yes, they are not just any hekura.
> They are my proper hekura
> that once belonged to my father [responds Arawë].

The master announces (and Arawë repeats after him) that the Mountain
of Halos (*Watoshe këki*) is where there are lots of luminous crowns to be
found. 'Take this house of watoshe crowns, enter, enter!' Ruweweriwë
passes on the Mountain of Halos to the candidate. 'It is so big and green',
comments Arawë and quickly continues chanting:

> I can now hear the sounds of the tails of *mãrõha*.[17]
> They are carried by the wind towards me.
> Many whirlwinds are coming towards me from various directions.

Taramawë comments that once this is over, Arawë will be a true shapori,
able to cure his people from diseases and defend them from other hekura.

Day Three

*Deaths by Black Bee Hekura and Boa Constrictor
and the Shapono Embodiment*

Early in the morning Arawë is undergoing a trial involving fire.
Ruweweriwë summons Õiriwë or Black Bee Hekura; he puts a basket over
his head and starts walking in a crouched position towards the candidate.
Arawë is screaming and panicking, as he is hearing a loud, ubiquitous
buzzing sound. Right behind the hekura, the 'fire front' is advancing
towards him from all sides; slowly engulfing him while the hekura is

hugging him. He feels the unbearable heat (as he later told me) and then blacks out.

In the midday round, the master summons Heturemariwë or Boa Ancestor (Boa Constrictor) to slay the candidate with a machete. The mighty Boa is slowly approaching and the intensity of Arawë's singing increases (Figure 4.3); it is only interrupted by sporadic screams. The hekura swings the machete inches from Arawë's face and the candidate drops down instantly. He remains motionless for some time, with arms and legs outstretched. The shapori then heals his body and lifts him into a seating position. Arawë continues chanting for a little while and then it is over. Afterwards, I went up to him and asked about his experience of being hit by the machete and he replied:

> It felt like I was hit by a lightning. When I dropped to the ground, I was still conscious but unable to move because my body was heavy. It felt as if ants were entering my body through my toes and travelling slowly up my legs. The earth was moving under me. It felt like many fingers were stabbing me from below. I started to sink down and opened my eyes.

In the afternoon, Arawë is receiving another major structural component of his bodily microcosm-in-the-making – a shapono from the respective hekura. This procedure is identical to yesterday's embodiment of the path, albeit this time Ihamariwë (Sloth Ancestor) has to bring a

Figure 4.3 Ancestor of Boa Constrictor approaching Arawë.

shapono in a square-shaped red cloth and install it directly into Arawë's chest. The shapono embodiment is about to commence. Taramawë is seen abruptly pressing his palms against his abdomen and sliding them upwards, passing his neck and head and finally releasing them 'out through his hair' in the same manner as shapori when extracting the agent of sickness from other bodies. He does the same to Ruweweriwë, who is standing next to him and murmuring something. I ask what is happening. Ruweweriwë grins and responds light-heartedly: 'It was some enemy hekura shooting arrows into us. Taramawë squeezed an arrow out of his body first before doing the same to me. It's not a big problem so I let him continue.'

The initiatory procedure for the shapono embodiment commences with Ruweweriwë announcing that the shapono (to be embodied) is guarded by other shapori inside the mountain. With the hekuras' help he must break the mountain to retrieve the shapono. The master shapori continues singing:

Beautiful House of Boas (*Shapono Wathapera*)[18] with tall edges comes shining with twisted boas moving about in a crouching manner (*hãmorimou*).
There are lots of immortals [hekura ancestors] over there [where the shapono is].
The shapori ancestors were observing yesterday how the path (Pei Yo) was taken out of the mountain and embodied.
They are all preparing to come together with the shapono that will also be retrieved from the mountain and embodied.

Ruweweriwë conveys through the song that waika Shorowë – (an enemy Shamathari shapori) – is nearby and taking a keen interest in the initiation. Shorowë was also observing them yesterday while Ruweweriwë and Taramawë were retrieving the hekura path. Ruweweriwë announces loudly that he is watching him closely (so that he does not interfere with the initiation). He asks Arawë to stay alert and to keep calling hekura while he and Taramawë are fetching the shapono. Both shapori move to the central area while Arawë is chanting about the shapono that is truly his will arrive at any moment. He can already see the fire coming out of Closed Mountain (*Tari këki*). At that very moment, the two shapori start breaking up the Tari Mountain by hitting the ground with machetes and then take out the shapono (in the same way they uncovered the hekura path the day before). They approach Arawë with the square-shaped cloth, which they hold in front of his chest. The candidate is now screaming and gasping for air while his upper torso is twitching in agony.[19] Taramawë quickly grabs Arawë from behind and stretches his shoulders while Ruweweriwë transforms into Ihamariwë and slowly starts pushing the shapono with both hands towards Arawë's chest. 'Hold him tightly, do not let him move and lift up his head', Ruweweriwë instructs his helper while pressing Arawë's chest with his hands and making one final 'O tuuum!' sound. The shapono is now embodied. Arawë is still gasping for air. The master shapori quickly normalises his breathing but Arawë continues to make gurgling sounds. Upon hearing this, most of the people in the shapono start to cry. The next moment hekura speaks through Ruweweriwë: 'You know me well, I personally broke the burning Tari Mountain and retrieved the shapono from it'. 'Father!' Arawë exclaims, but quickly loses control by entering what seems to be a state of disorientation and 'drunkenness' (*shi wãri*). Ruweweriwë continues singing and announcing the presence of immortal animals (*yãã henari*) with their heads moving like leaves. 'Brother-in-law [referring to Arawë], call them with your lips, answer them!' However, Arawë fails to respond; he is having a personal crisis, evidently experiencing a turbulent part of the initiation. His mouth is wide open and he is making deep gurgling sounds that appear to be coming from his innermost depths. He vomits a lot of saliva. Suddenly, he opens his eyes and continues vibrating his lips and singing to his newly embodied House of Boas (Figure 4.4).

Arawë's first words attest to his disbelief. 'Are they my proper hekura that belong to me?' 'Yes they are truly yours', Taramawë assures him. 'You

Figure 4.4 Arawë singing to his embodied House of Boas.

are lying!' 'But look at their faces and recognise them.' Arawë suddenly bursts out crying when he recognises the multiplicity of his father in the faces of the hekura:

> It is true! They are my fathers!
> Yes, your proper hekura are coming to you and they always belonged to you. From now on, they will be with you because they like you very much!
> I want them to like me the way I like them.
> This comes with time. They have to get use to you and your body as their new home. Be patient and respect the rules and they will stay with you forever.
> [Taramawë instructs the candidate.]

Arawë continues vibrating his lips and chanting about the presence of a beautiful Mountain of the Snake Image (*Oru Noreshi këkɨ*) together with the shapono and a blood red path twisting like a snake in front of it. 'That is your House of Boas (Shapono Wathapera),' explains Taramawë and continues saying:

> It was situated within the Tarɨ Mountain when my father-in-law
> [hekura of Arawë's father] broke the mountain and retrieved your shapono.
> I know. I personally saw the shapono surrounded by fire
> coming out of the broken mountain. It is so big, beautiful and shiny.
> I am very happy to have my shapono.
> It looks better than mine [Taramawë is giggling].
> I wish I could have a shapono like yours.

The shapono is now successfully embodied – mission accomplished! Ruweweriwë and Taramawë are both looking at Arawë's chest from a distance and smiling, evidently overwhelmed with satisfaction and commenting on the size and beauty of the embodied shapono.[20] People around us, especially Arawë's wife and their two children, have stopped crying and everyone seems to be happy and relieved. Ruweweriwë continues bringing new sets of hekura to the candidate in the usual manner. Arawë announces the arrival of many different multitudes of radiating halos (watoshe) singing happily with their mouths wide open. 'Watoshe of the parrot krau kraumi are coming with the wind.' 'Watoshe krau, krau! [sound of the parrot].' 'Take it. It is yours, enter, enter!' Then comes Shapono Hayapɨ (Deer). With this house of deer come lots of deer hekura. 'Deer hekura are so beautiful!' Shapono Yaopɨ (Ocelots) arrives with lots of ocelot hekura. 'Strange hekura and various lights are approaching me now!' 'You are doing well. Keep calling them. You will be a good shapori,' Taramawë assures him. Arawë continues chanting:

Shapono *Kuu kuumi* [the house of the nocturnal monkey] has arrived
with lots of monkeys, followed by the Shapono *Krukupi mari*
[house of the parrot krukupi mari], which shines like the moon.
It is full of bad parrots with big eyes,
which are moving up and down and shining like moonlight.
Beautiful Shapono *Makoayo* [type of parrot],
covered with glittering white down (*horoi*) is moving up and down
and landing in my chest full of hekura parrots makoayo.
A liquid blue ochre *Kashi pina* is flowing towards me,
which makes me feel dizzy.
Do not worry about it! [exclaims Ruweweriwë].
My hekura are beautiful. I will be just like my father.
Ma! Wa horemou,[21] [confirms Ruweweriwë].
Many sounds of different flutes are coming to my ear.
They are increasing and decreasing in volume.
I can hear beautiful sounds of the *hetehia* flutes … eee … eee …
The glowing flutes made from a ghost's bone (*pore matono*)[22]
with fire coming out of their eyes are playing
their own beautiful tune … uuuu … pore kë a matono!

Next, a hekura brings a song to Arawë, who immediately starts singing,
repeating the words after Ruweweriwë:

Look over there, many bees are watching.
My brother-in-law broke the mountain
so that he can deliver my song to me.
Brother-in-law, look over there.
They brought you a song.

'You will later sing along the same way we are teaching you now.'
Ruweweriwë embodies the song by singing it literally into Arawë's body
then at the end repeats several times the phrase *amoami yamaki*[23] while
simultaneously making a spiral-like movement with his index finger
around the candidate's chest.

The last round of today's embodiments has finished. It is dark. I am
lying in my hammock awake and immersed in my thoughts, reliving the
intense moments of the day. Arawë is resting in his hammock next to
me. It is silent and peaceful. Suddenly, Arawë gets up and starts shaking
his head while touching his chest. Something is not right. He opens his
mouth widely with his tongue sticking out and has vomiting convulsions.
Ruweweriwë quickly leaps out of his hammock, sniffs a pinch of yopo and
blows some into Arawë's nostrils. Arawë looks terrified. He is screaming
and spitting but then starts vibrating his lips. Ruweweriwë presses his right
palm against Arawë's chest, slides it upward and then pulls something

out of Arawë's mouth with his fingers. Next, Arawë sits on the ground in the classic initiatory position and Ruweweriwë does the usual hekura embodiment for approximately the next fifteen minutes. Then it all stops. It is quiet again as if nothing has happened. Ruweweriwë returns to his hammock and I ask him quietly what just happened. He replies that an enemy hekura launched an arrow into Arawe's chest (just like they did to him and Taramawë yesterday). The following morning, I asked Arawë about his night troubles. He replied in a low voice, almost whispering: 'While I was lying in my hammock, I suddenly experienced breathing difficulties and had a sharp pain in my chest. I woke up this morning with body aches'.

Day Four

Death by Wãikõyãriwë (Anaconda Ancestor)

Arawë is ready for another day. He is sitting on the ground and calling hekura. Ruweweriwë summons Anaconda Hekura Wãikõyãriwë to slay the candidate (just like the Boa Hekura Heturemariwë did yesterday). Shapori is announcing that Wãikõyãriwë got ready in his house located inside Anaconda Mountain (Wãikõyã këkï) and is now on his way. When he arrives, his brother-in-law (Arawë) will die. Taramawë confirms that the mighty Wãikõyãriwë is coming and Arawë says that he is really worried and scared. 'Wãikõyãriwë will cut me into pieces with his machete.' 'Yes! He will cut you open with his machete any moment', confirms Taramawë. 'He is bringing a big machete and is truly coming now!' responds a terrified Arawë with an ascending tone of voice. The hekura is now right in front of him. He swings his machete; Arawë screams and drops to the ground. Ruweweriwë immediately prompts the candidate to listen to his voice and not be afraid. He kneels beside his motionless body, attempting to 'open it up' with his hands: one leg first, then the other, then the stomach, arms and neck. The shapori then walks back to the centre of the shapono and incorporates Thora Hekura (yopo inhaling tube), whose task is to heal the candidate's body by welding it back together. Holding a yopo tube in his hands, he approaches Arawë and with the receiving end pointing towards him starts to slide the tube along his skin, retracing the line of the previous cut. Another hekura starts to sing into Arawë's body via the cut (Figure 4.5).

Finally, yet another (bird) hekura Yarapï Yamï grabs the prostrate body of Arawë by the hands and lifts him back into a sitting position. The candidate opens his eyes and starts to vibrate his lips and sing: 'I like it this way brother-in-law, they are not doing any harm to me now!'

Figure 4.5 Hekura healing Arawë's body after it had been slashed by the machete of Anaconda Ancestor.

Figure 4.6 Arawë receives the glowing Anaconda head crown.

'That's right! Keep calling them', exclaims Ruweweriwë, and running towards the central area announces the arrival of the anaconda's shining crown (Wãikõyãriwë watoshe). The shapori grabs the crown made of palm leaves and white down. He then places the crown on Arawë's head (Figure 4.6). At the same time, the bird hekura is implanting the crown into the new structural stratum of the shapori's bodily mode of being as hekura.

'Inside the crown there is a light which is moving like a fire', comments Arawë. The hekura starts to sing and Arawë repeats:

Nai fruit smells beautiful.
Smell comes from the mouth of yopo tube.
Nai Fruit Mountain is covered with white down
It [the Mountain] extends high up to where the sky is.

The hekura embodies the song. At that moment, a curious spectre (pore) suddenly appears nearby. He is observing the initiation with anticipation and saying through Ruweweriwë how it is all good and how he feels very happy about the work. Ruweweriwë, however, advises him to stay away and not look in his direction, otherwise he will hit him. Ruweweriwë, who obviously distrusts him, calls him a liar and deceiver.

The usual hekura embodiment continues until the end of the round with Ruweweriwë singing and Arawë repeating after him:

Shitipori fruit tree has beautiful flowers that release sweet smell.
Palm tree of the troupial bird (*Hoko Ãyãkõrãmɨ*)!
That is where many immortals are gathered to arrive
[at the Sheroana-theri initiatory place].
Mountain of Ushuwemɨ [bird] is beautiful.
Mountain of *Rorokona* fruit (*Rorokonakɨ Parɨkɨ*)
stands tall and red [like fire].
On the other side,
Honeybee Mountain (*Shaponakɨ kë kɨ*) is humid and pretty.
Inside the skin of a peach palm (*hoko*) comes Hehuriyoma.[24]
She comes together with her children lined up behind her.
They all shake (*prisɨprisɨmou*) happily together.
These hekura leave me breathless and thirsty.

Both Ruweweriwë and Taramawë alert Arawë that his mouth will be dry and his voice shaky thus he should breathe slowly and deeply. 'But do not worry! Here comes the liquid of a Leafbird Hekura (*Shopa Henariyoma u*). She'll moisten your mouth so that you can sing well', says Ruweweriwë and transfers the hekura.

Day Five

Death by Wathaperariwë (Rainbow Boa Ancestor) and Yaoriwë (Ocelot Ancestor)

The following morning Ruweweriwë summons Wathaperariwë or Hekura Ancestor of the Rainbow Boa and pierces the candidate with an arrow. He is announcing through his song that earlier the shapori Warishana (the other name for Wathaperariwë) gathered numerous hekura around his house in Boa Mountain (Wathapera këki) and gave them ochre to decorate their bodies. Boa Hekura asks if everyone is ready to go and sets off on his way to kill Arawë with his arrow but has to stop half way down the path to have a rest and wait for others to catch up. In the meantime, 'Mountain of Sun (Mothokari këki) has arrived, glowing red like fire. The immortals from the Mountain of Moon (Peripori këki) are swinging in the air'. Arawë is commenting how the Mountain of Hammocks (Yïi këki) looks very odd from the front. 'Wathaperariwë is now asleep half way down the path but will be here soon to kill you with his bow and arrow', Ruweweriwë reminds the candidate. Arawë sings, announcing the arrival of Mayepïriyoma (female Toucan Ancestor), followed by Kiya kiya-theri (people from the community of the kiya kiya parrot) dancing happily on the path. Thoriana-theri (tick people) are also coming and yelling

Figure 4.7 Wathaperariwë – Hekura Ancestor of Rainbow Boa pierces Arawë with an arrow.

happily. The master shapori announces that Warishana has just woken up and is on his way again. The Boa Hekura arrives and Arawë comments on how beautiful he is but immediately screams and drops to the ground after Wathaperariwë launches an arrow into his body (Figure 4.7).

While Arawë is lying motionless, Ruweweriwë starts singing the following song: 'Come down, come down. Liquid of sun with face painted with ochre'. 'You will now sing like this'. He quickly summons Yarapɨ Yamɨ Hekura, who grabs Arawë's arms and lifts his upper torso back into a seating position. Arawë opens his eyes and starts singing his new song again: 'Come down, come down ...'. Ruweweriwë complains how hot it is and comments how brother-in-law (referring to Wathaperariwë) has brought lots of hekura with painted faces. Arawë continues chanting:

> Mountain of the Singing Ant-eating Parrot (*Ikekeamɨ këkɨ*) is coming, covered with feathers.
> Bee Mountain (*Romo romo këkɨ*) looks strange from the front with its shining light.
> Many hekura with their beautifully painted faces are dancing towards me and making me dizzy.
> Do not worry about that [exclaims Ruweweriwë]. Once you stop feeling dizzy you will feel happy. I felt exactly the same when I was initiated. Once it was all over I felt very satisfied.

Ruweweriwë continues singing and Arawë repeats after him:

> Hapa pano-theri [Flower People] are coming!
> Their arms are full of adornments.
> Teshoriwë [Colibri Ancestor] is coming with flowers.
> His legs are covered with shiny white down.
> Many colibries are coming with him.
> The wind brings lots of hekura of *witiwitimɨ* parrot.
> They are covered with glistening feathers.

At the very end of this cycle of embodiments Arawë comments how all these hekura entered the shapono in his chest.

During the afternoon round of embodiments, Ruweweriwë summons Yaoriwë (Ocelot Ancestor), whose main task is to devour the candidate and thus become his ally. Prior to the embodiment, Ruweweriwë encircles his face with a long piece of cotton and speckles his whole body with black lines and dots to resemble the pattern on the ocelot's fur. He then exclaims: 'Yaoriwë is coming!' 'He is coming indeed and he is not coming alone. He is bringing lots of hekura lined up behind him,' chants Arawë. Ruweweriwë confirms again through his song that Yaoriwë is

Figure 4.8 Ocelot Hekura Yaoriwë is arriving!

coming together with numerous other hekura and all their possessions: hammocks, bows and arrows, feathers. These hekura are migrating from their shaponos – primordial habitats located on tops of the mountains – and moving into the corporeal shapono, traversing the recently embodied hekura path. They bring all of their possessions in the same way the Yanomami do when they move from one shapono to another. Incarnated Yaoriwë (Ruweweriwë) is slowly approaching the candidate, making cat-like movements and wriggling his tongue (Figure 4.8).

Petrified Arawë is screaming and shouting in panic:

It's me! Here I am. I am here!
[this way announcing his presence to the advancing hekura]
Yaoriwë is really beautiful but I know he is here to eat me.
It's me, my brother-in-law! Do you recognise me?
Look closely at my face [says Ocelot Hekura].

Ruweweriwë instructs him to have faith and maintain positive thoughts; to be calm and strong or else the hekura will hasten away. The incarnated Yaoriwë stands up in front of Arawë then leaps and knocks him to the ground. Some mucus starts bubbling from Arawë's mouth, while the shapori transformed into Ocelot Ancestor enacts movements resembling an ocelot devouring the candidate (Figure 4.9).

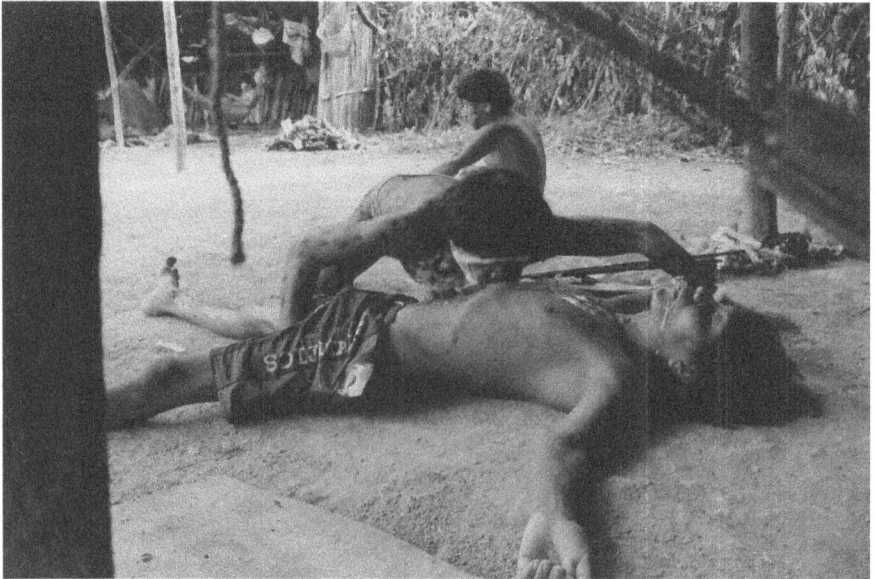

Figure 4.9 Ocelot Ancestor consuming the candidate's body.

The hekura swiftly dismembers Arawë's lifeless body and scatters his limbs in all four directions of the cosmos, licking up the remaining blood. Ruweweriwë then summons another hekura, whose task is to reassemble Arawë's bones and ultimately his whole skeleton. After that, the Thora Hekura (yopo inhaling tube) welds Arawë's flesh back together as Ruweweriwë passes the tip of the tube along Arawë's body. 'Hekura will start to sing now,' announces Taramawë. Indeed, the hekura manifested by Ruweweriwë starts to sing the following song:

> White down (horoi) is ready for decoration.
> My brother-in-law was searching for shapono of boas.
> He saw the shapono in his dreams. He found it.
> Shapono was well protected inside the Tarɨ Mountain.
> My brother-in-law broke the mountain.
> He then brought back with him shapono of anacondas.
> Hekura killed the person [Arawë] and he came back to life again.

Yarapɨ Yamɨ Hekura lifts the candidate back into a seating position, telling him to keep his head high up and stop looking down.[25] The song is repeated about the brother-in-law who broke Tarɨ Mountain and so on. 'When the shapono was released, fire shot out of the mountain, which then started to bleed. The Yanomami do not think that this is all truly happening but they are wrong', exclaims Taramawë and Ruweweriwë subsequently confirms this. The latter then tells Arawë to pay attention to the song and to repeat the words after him:

> White down is all over the head.
> Song of Hekura of Guama Fruit with red skin! (*Tosha amoa wakë sikɨ*)
> White down is shining.
> Hekura of Guama Fruit with red skin.

'Mountain of Guama Skin is painted red. When you sing, you can explain this in your song,' Ruweweriwë instructs Arawë, while the latter continues singing the song. 'Louder!' commands Ruweweriwë and transfers the song directly by circling his index finger around Arawë's solar plexus. 'While I was singing, the earth was trembling', comments Arawë. 'Yes it is true!' confirms Ruweweriwë. Arawë continues singing:

> Hekura Toucan of Peach Palm [*Hoko Piremari*] is hopping towards me.
> He is beautiful with his black chest emanating light round its edges.
> Hekura People of Tree Trunks [*Hii hikɨri*] are coming!
> Their faces are painted with ochre.
> They can see me, albeit they are not looking at me.

Lots of hekura are coming together with this tree hekura.
The earth is shaking! [comments Ruweweriwë and Arawë confirms].
Skin of a ghost (*Pore pore sikɨ*)!
The whole earth is painted like the skin of a ghost [chants Arawë].
This is my proper father-in-law [referring to the arriving hekura ancestor].

In continuation, Ruweweriwë announces that Hutukaramɨ parrot
(guilded barbet – capito auratus [Ramphastidae]) painted with golden
ochre is coming, looking ferocious.

Hutukaramɨ [parrot] Hekura is angry.
He is angry because whenever he paints his body with this ochre,
he sweats a lot [Arawë answers].
It does not matter keep calling them to come! [urges Ruweweriwë].
I will keep calling them, more of them.
You can say that because they are your hekura [says Ruweweriwë].
I would like you to stay this way [focused].
Do not get confused [insists Taramawë].
[Ruweweriwë exclaims]: Moyerimi[26] is here and it is dangerous!
Moye, moye, moye [voice of hekura].
Moyerimi will hurt me and make me faint.
He will turn me upside down [Arawë is complaining].
Do not worry about it and keep calling him [Taramawë reassures him].

'Tei, tei, tei,' [voice of hekura]. 'Day is waning, night is coming Titiriwë
[Hekura of Darkness] is here!' Arawë acknowledges the ancestor's
presence and complains of having a sharp pain (*haye hëri*) in his chest.
Ruweweriwë embodies the Hekura of Darkness and announces that the
night has come and Periporiwë (Moon Ancestor) is awakening.

Moon is looking from above.
He is so big and blind with his teeth bleeding.[27]
Periporiwë's presence generates intense heat.
It makes me sweat a lot [comments Arawë].
Peripo, peripo, peripo [voice of hekura].
Come to me Periporiwë quickly and rest within me.
I am personally calling you to come,
[affirms Arawë and then announces
that Periporiwë spat saliva all over his face].
Do not worry about that. Keep calling him [instructs Taramawë].
Father-in-law [referring to Periporiwë]!
I keep calling you because
I want to get to know you and want you [inside me].[28]

Periporiwë grabs the candidate with both arms and presses him against his body: 'ootuumm!!!' Periporiwë is now embodied. Ruweweriwë later told me that Periporiwë's saliva contains shawara sickness. By spitting, he spreads shawara and makes the Yanomami sick. In the context of initiation, Arawë has to take in shawara brought by the hekura and experience its effects so that in future healing sessions his personal hekura helpers can recognise it and treat it accordingly.

Ruweweriwë comments that some unknown hekura have suddenly appeared from nowhere. Taramawë observes how Fish Hekura (*Mashapɨri*) are black and wide-eyed. 'I can't see them clearly. Tell them to come to me', complains Arawë. 'What's that strange looking bird hekura? He's got the same nose as me,' Ruweweriwë is wandering and continues: 'I don't recognise these hekura but they are here, take them and make them your own'. They are coming towards me, here they are!' [there is a sense of panic in Arawë's voice]. Ruweweriwë transfers hekura from his body into Arawë's. 'Take them they are all yours. When you get sick in the future they'll help you.' At the very end of this round, forest beings known as *urihiri* arrive and start to sing Arawë's new song: 'Deer hekura painted ocelot's fur'. Urihiri via Ruweweriwë embodies the song and installs it into the candidate's chest.

Day Six

Death by Ɨrariwë (Ancestral Jaguar) and Embodiment of Hekura Mountain (Pei Makɨ)

Today the candidate will receive the Hekura Mountain into his body. This requires a suitable *mõrã mahi* tree (burseraceae) from which a ceremonial pole will be crafted. It is early morning and while Arawë is resting in his hammock, Ruweweriwë, his son-in-law Kiawë, Taramawë and I are fetching the tree. After about half an hour's walk we spot one that appears suitable, and Ruweweriwë immediately instructs us to clear the leaves and undergrowth surrounding it. The two shapori take a few pinches of epena snuff, place their hands on the trunk, and, looking up, start shaking the tree. Ruweweriwë then chops the tree and strips the bark. I ask why they had to shake the tree before cutting it down. 'To loosen it up first before embodying the hekura custodian of the Pei Makɨ' replies the master shapori. We walk back to the shapono where a few men and women are ready to decorate the pole. First they paint the pole with red ochre and criss-cross it with thin black lines. To get a dark ochre colour, they mix red ochre with pulverised charcoal. The women attach a crown made of small black and white feathers from the curassow bird to the top of the pole. They also affix another ring of green parrot feathers around the middle part of the pole. The whole ceremonial mast was eventually covered with white down. Next, they make three crowns from peach palm leaves (bactris gasipaes) all speckled with black dots and covered with white down – one each for Arawë, Ruweweriwë and Taramawë, who are decorating their machetes with red and black ochre and attaching white down along the blade. Finally, the two peach palm branches are prepared and decorated with ochre and white down.

The most vital part of the ceremony is ready to commence. However, before Arawë can finally receive the Hekura Mountain into his body, he must undergo the experience of being consumed by ɫrariwë (Jaguar Hekura) that lives in the forest; an experience similar to that of being devoured by the Ocelot. To devour the candidate, Ruweweriwë must fetch ɫrariwë outside the shapono. The shapori decorates his body with big black dots – larger than those painted the day before for Yaoriwë – and encircles his face with a white cotton ring, resembling the facial contours of a jaguar. Taramawë blows some epena into his nostrils and Ruweweriwë goes out of the shapono to summon Jaguar Ancestor. A few moments later, the incarnated ɫrariwë enters the village, growling and pacing towards Arawë, who understands that he is about to be eaten. 'It's me, here I am!' exclaims the candidate, and screams in panic while shivering with fear. The jaguar is licking his cheeks (Figure 4.10). Arawë

Figure 4.10 Ancestral Jaguar ɫrariwë is coming to eat the candidate.

is in trouble. He screams for help, asking for his bow and arrow to defend himself. Yet he is vibrating his lips, chanting and letting out loud screams. Evidently, he is experiencing an inner struggle between his fears and his determination to continue with the ordeal.

Watching Arawë suffer, his wife, their children and other Yanomami are crying again. 'He will finish me off! Where is my bow and arrow?' shouts Arawë again and then releases a final agonising scream. Ɨrariwë leaps towards Arawë, sweeping him to the ground (Figure 4.11). At that moment, epena mixed with saliva literally bursts out of Arawë's mouth and nose. In front of us onlookers the shapori (transformed into Jaguar Ancestor) is enacting movements with his mouth and hands that resemble a jaguar tearing off big chunks of flesh piece by piece and then licking the blood. He dismembers the candidate's body and scatters his head and extremities. 'My son! He killed you, I am worried about my son, why did he do that?' Taramawë is weeping. Ruweweriwë joins his assistant's lament and confirms that Ɨrariwë has finished Arawë off.

The grieving abruptly stops and Ruweweriwë quickly summons the Hekura Yopo Tube (Thora Hekura) to begin his repair work by singing through the tube into the candidate's unresponsive body, starting from his toes, then moving up his legs to his chest, arms, neck and finally his head. In the customary manner, Yarapɨ Yamɨ hekura grabs Arawë by his

Figure 4.11 Jaguar Hekura attacking Arawë.

arms and lifts him back in to a seating position. Arawë opens his eyes and immediately starts to vibrate his lips, chant and call hekura to come:

Jaguar's glowing head crown (*Watoshe Mashaema*)
is descending towards me.
My brother-in-law [referring to Irariwë] has brought with him
his beautiful Jaguar Crown as a gift to you,
[says Ruweweriwë to Arawë].

The master shapori (still embodying Irariwë) grabs the pre-made peach palm rings; he gives one to Taramawë, puts one on his own head and holds the third one in his hand. Arawë is weeping and asking the shapori not to do him any harm. 'Shut up and take a good look at the face and recognise it!' Taramawë yells as the hekura puts his crown on Arawë's head. 'My father!' exclaims Arawë, still crying. He continues singing and looking towards the sky (Figure 4.12). The physical crown is simultaneously implanted into the candidate's ethereal body and becomes a halo of white light, a constitutive component of the new hekura mode of being. Irariwë informs the candidate that the crown of light will equip him with the ability to see far into the distance and detect the presence of other hekura (the halo is akin to radar]. All hekura have the same watoshe crowns on their heads. They can see the glowing halo from a distance and recognise that it is a hekura who wears it.

Figure 4.12 Arawë with Jaguar's crown of light singing to the hekura spirits.

Taramawë warns Ruweweriwë to be careful because he has spotted some enemy Shamathari shapori from far away Siapa, who are trying to sabotage the initiation by mixing in their hekura. 'I am not worried about that. I will pacify them as well!' responds Ruweweriwë assertively. But Arawë is not very convinced: 'Don't lie to me. Shamathari hekura are coming and my chest feels hot like fire'. Ruweweriwë transfers the Shamathari hekura from his body to Arawë's body. In continuation, the master shapori consecutively transforms into the two toucan hekura ancestors Mayepɨrithawë and Piremarithawë and grabs the premade pair of peach palm branches (the toucan wings) and places them on either side of Arawë's body. In future, these hekura wings will enable the new shapori to fly like a toucan. The process of hekura embodiment continues:

> The community of singing hekura is here!'
> ['Amoana-theri këpë!'] [announces Taramawë].
> I can see them. They are my proper people.
> When [I and] they[29] dance and sing together
> the lightning sparks under their feet [comments Arawë].
> Children of the moon with sleepy eyes are also here!
> They are releasing the moonlight around them.
> Right behind them comes the Jaguar's ochre and it looks quite scary.
> They ['children of the moon'] will use this jaguar's ochre
> to paint their bodies when they arrive.
> They also eat jaguar's faeces [responds Taramawë].

Arawë continues chanting:

> When they arrive, my [hekura] people will recognise me and I will recognise them. When that happens I will be very sad.[30]
> They are coming with their heads covered with white down (horoi) and ears decorated with earrings that shine like stars (puriwa shitikari).[31]
> Shinariyoma [Female Cotton Hekura] and her children are passing by. They are all my [hekura] people!
> The immortal sky (Pārimi hetu pata) is high above but it is slowly descending towards me.

Incoming hekura are saying to Arawë:

> We are intoxicated with epena just like you are now.
> We are coming with the wind.
> He is also shi wāri [under the influence of epena snuff].
> Sing the hekura song with us.
> We smear our bodies with star ochre.
> We come to you embraced with each other, dancing and glowing like stars.

Arawë continues announcing the hekuras' presence:

> The [parrot] hekura Kiya kiyamawë comes with the wind
> [and demonstrates how he can split *nowari* or 'disease' with his beak].
> Take them, my brother-in-law [referring to Arawë].
> This is how you will attack diseases in the future [say the incoming hekura].
> Children of Tãrãkãõmɨ (manakin bird) are crossing the path
> [that leads towards Arawë's chest].
> They are coming with the whirlwind in circling movements.
> The wind is blowing towards me [the candidate].
> It is bringing the Jaguar's dart (*puriwa mashaema*) that is flying towards me
> and the earth is trembling.

Upon completing the round of hekura embodiments, Arawë slowly crawls back to his hammock to rest. It is noon now and he is ready to receive Hekura Mountain into his body. Ruweweriwë beckons him with his hand to come. Arawë is instantly on his feet and then assumes his initiatory posture on the ground. Taramawë grabs his machete and makes a hole in the ground between Arawë's outstretched legs where the ceremonial mast is to be implanted. Ruweweriwë starts to sing, referring to the Pei Makɨ pole, which rests against the wall on the opposite side of the shapono as the glowing House of Boas. Next, he runs towards the centre of the shapono then turns and looks back at Arawë, admiring through song how he can see many hekura paths converging and extending all the way into Arawë's body.

> The path ultimately leads to the House of Boas [Shapono Wathapera], which my father-in-law [referring to the hekura of Arawë's father] personally retrieved for you by breaking Tarɨ Mountain and implanting it into your chest. It is so big and beautiful. Now, my brother-in-law [referring to Arawë], you need to have Hekura Mountain implanted into your body.

Both shapori then take machetes into their hands and start waving them high in the air. Assuming the crouching position and yelling, they then waddle to the pole, lift it up and lumber back towards the candidate. Concurrently, Arawë is vibrating his lips and commenting:

> Hekura Mountain (Pei Makɨ) is House of Boas (*Yahi Hetupera*). It is beautiful indeed but it feels very heavy and is already affecting my breathing. I want to receive it. This Hekura House belongs to me! But I am afraid because I cannot breathe anymore.

Figure 4.13 The candidate singing to his Hekura Mountain with ceremonial mast rammed between his legs.

The two hekura are now standing nearby and the tone of Arawë's voice intensifies. At that moment, Ruweweriwe's son-in-law, Kiawë, approaches Arawë from behind and supports his upper torso with his arms. The hekura then ram the pole into the hole in the ground between his legs and Arawë screams piercingly. He then screeches again but in a less intense manner. The lingering sound of his cries gradually dissolves into the air. After a few long moments of silence, Arawë looks up towards the top of the pole, starts to vibrate his lips and says: 'This House of Boas is so big and beautiful and it is truly mine. It's glowing. I am delighted' (Figure 4.13). With the ceremonial mast firmly lodged in the ground in front of him and the Hekura Mountain successfully implanted into his body, Arawë's corporeal microcosm is now complete.

Later, Arawë spoke about the moment of Pei Makɨ embodiment:

My throat was so tight that I could hardly breathe. It felt as if my breath [had] sank into my abdomen. The shapori quickly restored my breathing by lifting up my breath back into the chest area. When Pei Makɨ was fixed into the ground and I lifted my head up, I saw the mountain that looked just like [the nearby] Sheroroi Mountain.

The Author's Personal Experience and Comments

Before continuing with Arawë's initiation, I will describe my personal experience of the Pei Makɨ mast after it was fixed into the ground between my legs. Experientially, there was no sense of separation or distance between the pole and myself. 'I' as subject and pole as the object merged into one experiential dimension of consciousness. The pole was there in front of me and it seemed endless, stretching infinitely from one extreme of the cosmos to the other. Although I was immersed in my experience, a part of me was thinking that this must be the axis mundi that connects all spheres of the universe. In the middle section of the pole there was a bunch of green parrot feathers, symbolising the forest on this earthly level of existence over which the Ancestral Jaguar Ɨrariwë reigns. After the pole was embodied, my consciousness entered a state of flux and became 'alive'; suddenly, the forest opened up and I transformed into a jaguar. At that moment, the green feathers spectacularly transformed into green forest foliage, moving in flux and producing a profound sense of the forest and its dangers. I looked up towards the top of the pole and saw the mountaintop extending all the way up to the sky. A crown made of black and white bird feathers suddenly started expanding and pulsating, emitting alternate bright light and dark shade. As I looked downwards, the pole extended deeply into the subterranean levels, a cold place of rotten matter and humidity; the home of the Amahiri – Yanomami mythological ancestors. I felt the whip of cool air passing through my entire being, and experientially the entire pole appeared to turn into an opening that was stretching horizontally. The white down glued to the pole was fluttering and turning into a multiplicity of tiny, radiant beings. At that moment the pole became the equivalent of the mountain full of hekura, which was now located inside my chest. When Arawë received his Hekura Mountain he told me about his own experience:

> With Pei Maki, many, many hekura arrived. When the pole was fixed into the ground, the hekura started pouring directly into my body from the top of Sheroroi Mountain. They were entering through the top of the pole and then sank down along its axis before entering my body directly through my big toes. The hekura looked like a long thread of children, no bigger than the tip of the finger, lined up behind each other.

Continuation of Arawë's Initiation

Now, let us return to Arawë's initiation. In continuation, he received two more songs to accompany his first independent steps of hekuramou practice and by means of which he would be able to evoke and mobilise his incarnated hekura in the future.

> I seized Toucan Yopo Tube (*Thora piremari*).
> My saliva has dried out.
> Today is the day.
> This tube is from the toucan.
> Many immortals are coming now together with the Toucan Tube.
> I cannot breathe from their weight.
> Many adornments are sticking out of their mouths.
> Lots of them are arriving and the earth is trembling.

> Mouth of the Bamboo (*Hete hiki*) is singing.
> My brother-in-law [referring to this particular hekura]
> has white down around his [bamboo's] mouth.
> When he plays this bamboo tube, the down is moving.
> My [hekura] people are coming with saliva hanging from their mouths.
> When they arrive the tears will fall.
> When my older brother [hekura] comes, he will be sad.
> He will cry when he sees his younger brother [referring to himself] seated.

Arawë keeps repeating both songs until they become embodied. Up to the end of this crucial round of embodiments, Ruweweriwë continues bringing various hekura, announcing their presence and directing them towards the pole:

> The Woodpecker (*Eshami*) is coming!
> He will touch the [embodied] house with his beak;
> you will hear this sound!
> Bird-Dog Hekura Wiwimawë is here!
> Owl Ancestor Krukumariwë is angry and is moving his big eyes.
> What is that beautiful sound that I can now hear? [asks Arawë].
> It is the song of Falcon Hekura Kãõmãrithawë.
> He is happy to be here and unite with you [responds Ruweweriwë].
> [Female] Toad Hekura Hãsupïriyoma is bringing some water with her.
> She will throw this water on you and refresh you! [comments Taramawë].
> Yes, she is truly magnificent![32]
> Another toad hekura is coming right behind her.
> She is also approaching my [corporeal] house [announces Arawë].
> It is Mamakokoriwë [responds Taramawë].
> Community of Yopo Tube Hekura (*Thora-theri*) are also here!
> They are entering [my] head crown (watoshe) and will remain there.
> They are very clever and skilful.
> They have fire coming out of their mouths.
> Inside your head crown there is a hekura mirror.
> This mirror will help you see far away.
> This house [referring to Arawë's embodied Hekura Mountain]
> is very well ingrained [comments Ruweweriwë].

Post-Pei Maki Stage of Initiation: The New Cosmic Alignment

Now that Hekura Mountain is located inside Arawë's body he is henceforth able to invite and take incoming hekura alone, without the shapori's assistance. Ruweweriwë is no longer needed as a link between the cosmos and the candidate; however, he will continue supervising Arawë's progress and will remain alert to any possible unwanted hekura interference. Arawë's hekura ancestors continue to migrate in their masses from their mountain habitats, singing and dancing happily along their hekura paths before entering the ceremonial mast and then flowing into his embodied Hekura Mountain. The migratory movement of hekura is now a direct channel that opens up through the alignment of a geographical mountain (Sheroroi këkï) and Arawë's corporeal Hekura Mountain, which takes on the symbolic meaning and practical manifestation of the centre of the universe.

Concomitant with the cessation of Ruweweriwë's direct involvement in the initiatory process, the dialogue between him, incoming hekura and Arawë gives way to a chanting monologue called *tutomou*, which the candidate has to recite up to five times a day, seated under the Pei Makɨ mast. Tutomou derives from *tute*, which means something recent or new – in this case, the new shapori calling hekura to come. Looking at up at the pole firmly rooted between his legs, Arawë is chanting:

> This morning a whirlwind (*heāhātu*) has arrived, moving towards me.
> When hekura start coming I will feel exhausted.
> This is my own house [referring to the embodied mountain].
> Moyerimi [forest being] and her children poured into me and made me feel sick.
> Yawari Dart (*Puriwa yawari*) is flying towards me.
> This [embodied] House of Boas (*Yahi Hetupera*) is beautiful and glows with brilliant light.
> Moon has also arrived now.
> Do not deceive me and come to me!
> I see a beautiful Fish people (Mārõha-theri) arriving at my house.
> Children of the moon are painted with moon ochre.
> [Female] Toad Hekura Hāsupɨriyoma is beautiful and arrives singing happily.
> Children of Hekura of Thirst (*Amishi-theri pë ihirupɨ*) are coming! When they arrive I will be thirsty.
> A large whirlwind is approaching and bringing lots of embraced hekura.
> Today all of us [hekura] got together to come [to the candidate].
> Harpy Eagle (*Mohõmɨ*) is coming with the wind.
> We [hekura and the candidate] are happy together.

Between the hekura calling rounds of tutomou, Arawë rests in his hammock. When it is time to sing again, he gets up very slowly and crouches. He then sits under the pole, looks up and starts chanting. Upon finishing each round of chanting he crouches and walks backwards towards his hammock, still facing the pole. In times of rest, Arawë is unable to talk with his normal voice intensity but rather he whispers. His voice temporarily regains its force and full tonality only when he is chanting under the pole. His whole body is weak; he can hardly move any extremities, even while resting in his hammock. I ask him why he is feeling like this. 'Hekura that are inside my body are making me ill.' He often complains of feeling nauseous, having a headache, experiencing sharp pain in his chest or of having shivers from an 'inner chill' (*si sãihõu*). Sometimes his whole body aches. His mouth and throat are often bone dry and after taking a few sips of water he instantly vomits. I am worried about him but Ruweweriwë keeps reassuring me that it is all part of the initiation: 'He is feeling ill because the embodied hekura brought shawara sickness with them'. The frequency and intensity of the manifested symptoms of his 'initiatory sickness' have been progressively increasing, particularly with the embodiment of Hekura Mountain when hekura rushed into his body without Ruweweriwë's assistance. Arawë has been gradually recuperating after the major death experience, two days after Hekura Mountain was embodied.

Day Eight

At the Threshold of Death

Since the beginning of initiation, Arawë has undergone various quasi-death experiences at the hands of hekura. He was eaten and dismembered twice by feline ancestors, scorched by fire, sliced with a machete and shot with an arrow. In all these instances, death came about through an agent. Today the time came for Arawë to surrender himself to a major death experience, which happened without any warning. After he completed his midday round of tutomou chanting, he went to lie down in his hammock; I was on the other side of the shapono when he suddenly lifted his hand and called to me. I sat next to him and asked him what had happened. With a mixed expression of terror and happiness he said: 'I have just died and visited the house of souls in the sky'. I asked him to describe his experience and he replied:

> I was [lying] in my hammock when suddenly I felt as if I was [being] thrown into a whirlwind, spinning in circles without any control. I got really scared because I did not know what was happening. I was short of breath and [it was] as if falling asleep. I quickly realised that I was about to die and then lost my senses. But next, I saw a very large shapono below me with many Yanomami inside. It looked like a picture [noreshi]. They were all painted with red ochre. When I spotted my dead relative standing among them I got frightened because I thought that I was dead. But then I came back to my senses and called you.

At that moment I remembered Makowë telling me in Platanal about his experience of dying. He said that he also journeyed to the sky where he saw the shapono of dead souls. But the way he had described his experience was more like the sky had descended on him rather than him ascending to the sky. He had put both of his palms in front of his eyes to demonstrate how close the sky had been to him at that moment.

The following morning, Arawë's ceremonial mast is removed and taken into the forest where it is affixed to the trunk of a big tree together with his watoshe crowns. He does not need them anymore because the

Hekura Mountain and the crowns of light are obviously now part of his embodiment. He is now sitting on the log, and continues to chant and call hekura while looking straight ahead towards the nearby Sheroroi Mountain. Hekura continue to arrive along their hekura path that has become a direct channel between the actual geographical mountain and Arawë's corporeal mountain.

The Author's Personal Experience of Death and Post-mortem Consciousness in Transformation

Like Arawë, two days after I had sat with the Pei Makɨ mast between my legs (and inside my chest) I experienced myself dying. Upon completing my habitual morning round of tutomou chanting, I slowly crawled back to my hammock and lay down on my back, contemplating the shapono's roof. All of a sudden, I was overwhelmed with the sensation of imminent death. Gripped by great panic and fear, I knew I was about to pass away. I lifted my head to look for Ruweweriwë or Arawë but they were absent. There was nobody around. Dreadful thoughts crossed my mind at that moment that something had gone terribly wrong with the initiation and that I was dying. A few moments later I lost all my senses and my self-consciousness dissolved into nothingness. Moments later my visual perception gradually started to come back and I became aware of myself again. I lifted my head and looked around the shapono wondering if I was dead or alive. When I saw familiar faces around me I thought to myself that I must still be alive and I felt immensely happy, but this feeling was short lived; I suddenly felt that my body was melting like ice and saturating into the earth below. In fact, at that moment there was no 'below' – what until then had been 'I' became the earth itself. Almost simultaneously, I journeyed to the sky, but the resulting out-of-body experience was not the type commonly described as a 'flight of the soul' (Eliade 1989 [1951]). In fact, I did not experience leaving my physical body behind on my way up to the sky; rather, the sky was directly experienced in its full dimensionality at the moment of death – the moment at which I became the sky, inasmuch as my consciousness embraced the full dimensionality of an open sky space. I felt the lightness of the air as opposed to the formerly experienced heaviness of the earth. At this moment of 'dying', my usual sense of self vanished or rather transformed into a new sense of being: there was no distinction between self and surroundings. During those moments, as my ego consciousness survived the threshold of death, I became self-reflective, contemplating my own death. I knew that I was dead, albeit still conscious. All the panic disappeared as there was no longer anything to fear. The ultimate victory over death as the main aim of the initiation had been accomplished. In fact, it was a narcissistic experience of the sense of my own immortality and the totalising cosmic unity of the ego and the cosmos. The ego was 'one and all' at the same time.

My disembodied consciousness had taken the identity of earth and air. In continuation, I turned into the wind that saturates the forest, zigzagging between the trees. At the same time, my self-image started undergoing certain structural transformations. As the old self died, sacrificed to hekura, the new bodily self-sense was gradually taking its place. In the first instance, I experienced a sensation of 'opening', the unfolding of my ears in a funnel-like manner, which became a supersensory auditory perception; I could hear the distant sounds of the forest. Following this, I felt my whole facial structure changing its shape; notably, my eyes felt as if they were sinking deep down into their sockets before expanding outward in the opposite direction. At that moment I experienced an extrasensory 'vision': a jaguar roared and literally jumped out of my chest but it was actually myself; it started running through the forest with me looking through its eyes. My own eyes were actually open, not closed during this time. Then I assumed the identity of a snake, slithering along the forest floor and looking around me from the snake's eye view. Finally, I turned into a bird and was looking down at the forest from above, through the eyes of a bird. Next, I experienced my jaws 'sinking' into my throat, shrinking and then expanding again. My neck, arms and legs were stretching and growing longer. Concurrently, I felt that my toes and fingers were turning into paws.

During this period, I also experienced some direct revelations of various truths, abilities and modes of manifestation of hekura. Thus, parallel to the experience of various fluid transformations of bodily self-consciousness, revelatory knowledge about the hekura mode of being was synchronistically unfolding through the mental act of self-reflection and direct experience. In other words, the hekura knowledge was revealed to me by directing my mental focus to various questions. For example, when I thought about the role of the watoshe crowns, the answer came in the form of direct experience of 'looking through' the watoshe, seeing far into the distance, not unlike looking through a pair of binoculars. My visual experience, in this instance, was directly associated with the acquisition of knowledge; seeing was thus a form of immediate understanding. This extrasensory vision, although accomplished through the watoshe crown, seemed to be processed internally in the chest area, in the same way that a camera image is recorded internally – on the back of the camera's box – when light enters the lens. Watoshe in this sense can be metaphorically likened to a camera lens. The viewed image in the distance is 'filtered' through the head crown. I perceived an image directly inside the body and not through my eyes.

Ego death

The shapori has to get to know and overcome death during his lifetime to be reborn and to continue living as hekura. Death in the context of shamanistic initiation is a culminating moment of consciousness being ruptured within the overall process of the radical modification of the candidate's egoic self. The subsequent rebirth represents the reconstitution of a new sense of a hekura self, which encapsulates the world as a totality of the cosmos. The experience of death and rebirth – in one way or another – is not unique to shamanistic initiations but to human beings in general. All over the world during puberty rites, boys and girls transform into responsible adults through an ordeal that involves agony, pain and suffering. All rites of initiation of various secret societies and ritual groups involve in one way or another the enactment of death and the sacrifice of an old personality to become something bigger than him (or her) – to be reborn as a new being that can access and participate in a group's mysteries. Stanislav Grof described 'dying' in the context of LSD-induced psychotherapeutic seances as 'an experience of total annihilation on all levels – physical, emotional, intellectual, moral, and transcendental … it [ego death] seems to involve instantaneous destruction of all the previous reference points of the individual' (Grof and Halifax 1977: 51).

The influx of hekura into the candidate's body during shamanistic initiation can be characterised as a movement of 'saturation towards the centre' (of the universe) that can be metaphorically compared to air entering and inflating a balloon. Hekura invade the interiority of the candidate's body and cause expansion of his self-consciousness in the same way that air enters a balloon and causes its expansion. The tension in a shapori's consciousness produced by the inflow of hekura gradually rises until reaching its maximum point of expansion before rupturing. At that precise peak moment when the interiority of the psychic realm of the body is fully externalised and the world as macrocosm internalised, the shapori undergoes the death experience and consciousness reaches its cosmic, all-embracing mode of manifestation. During this process, the candidate's ego is totalised in the continuity of metamorphoses. In other words, there is no separation between the sense of the egoic self as 'I-in-my-body', as 'mine', and the world as something existing outside of me. The inside and outside dimensionality is neutralised and ego ceases to be a limited embodiment. The distinction between the ego and the world vanishes as they fuse into a one world continuum of consciousness, which is the cosmic body. If we additionally liken the air inside our metaphorical balloon to the content of the candidate's consciousness or sphere of his subjective experience, we could say that the air outside of the balloon is analogous to the exteriority of the cosmos that lies beyond the candidate's subjectivity. In other words, during the initiation, not all hekura enter into the candidate's field of consciousness and his body, but only the ones that he calls and that belong to his father. The others remain outside of him. All hekura who contribute to the rupture of the candidate's consciousness will become embodied and involved in the constitution of his new totalised and totalising modality of consciousness and the cosmic egoity. All embodied hekura form together the basis of the new shapori's all-encompassing egoic consciousness. He will start addressing them using kinship terms such as his 'children', 'brothers' and 'sisters'. Each shapori becomes a hekura and a separate cosmic system of personal hekura. Each individual hekura within the embodied set is concurrently the whole or a single site for the cosmic manifestation.

We can compare the shapori's overall post-mortem state of consciousness to the estimated experience of what psychiatrists call the ego boundaries of an infant and its relation to the world around him or her:

> From what we can ascertain by indirect evidence, it appears that the newborn infant during the first few months of its life does not distinguish between itself and the rest of the universe. When it moves its arms and legs, the world is moving. When it is hungry, the world is hungry. When it sees its mother move, it is as if it is moving. When its mother sings, the baby does not know that it is itself not making the sound. It cannot distinguish itself from the crib, the room and its parents. The animate and the inanimate are the same. There is no distinction yet between I and thou. It and the world are one. There are no boundaries, no separations. There is no identity. (Peck 1978: 85)

From a baby's perspective (if we allow a baby without a defined identity through self-consciousness to have a perspective), there is no distinction between it and the rest of the world. Likewise, after the candidate crosses the threshold of death his new sense of self emerges as a state of all-encompassing world embodiment. The analogy between the transformation of the egoic self during the shamanistic initiation and a child's early perceptions of the world implies that the shaman at the moment of reaching the threshold of death has no stable perception of having a body, of being inside it or belonging to it. In other words, the fluid boundary between the body and the world ceases to exist. During a short few moments, while the candidate is experientially crossing the threshold of death, stimulus is no longer perceptible. The shapori cannot sustain a stable differentiation between himself, others around him, the shapono and the rest of the universe, in the same way that a baby has no lucid and structured self-consciousness of being located 'inside' the cradle, or being surrounded 'by' the room. For the shaman and the baby, the inside and outside dimensionality is dominated by a sense of oneness and unity, but after the shaman crosses the threshold of death, his sense of self comes back, as his embodiment is structured by a fully developed adult body image. Certainly, the candidate's ensuing shape shifting is due to the disintegration of his body image, something the infant does not experience. It has yet to be constructed.[33] By becoming hekura through a transformative experience of death and rebirth, a human being is raised to the state of a primordial being. A human being is born into the world of human limitations, while the shaman is reborn into the immortal cosmos. The future shaman is born into the world and on a grand scale the whole world is also reborn. It is the dynamism of the ouroboric universe – a cosmic cycle of death and decay, birth and growth. Subsequently, when the shaman enters his first trance he is in fact re-experiencing himself dying but this time it is less turbulent. The same 'raw' trance (death) state of consciousness coincides with the fluid, pre-cosmic mythical dimension of the primordial ancestors as a state of free transformation. The shaman is embodying the experiential reality to which the myth bears testimony. In this state of free transformation, the shaman can turn into any form: the whole can manifest itself through its parts.

Day Ten

Embodiment of Warëriwë, Posheriwë and Tëpëriwë

It is early in the morning and the darkness of the night is progressively fading away. The initiation is far from over. Ruweweriwë must carry out three consecutive embodiments of the following hekura: Warëriwë or the Ancestor of White-lipped Peccary, Posheriwë or the Ancestor of Collared Peccary and Tëpëriwë (Anteater Ancestor). The white-lipped peccary (warë) is a very mobile animal that leaves behind well-trodden, wide paths. In its wanderings from place to place in search of food, a peccary will break up large amounts of debris and soil in the same way that the hekura of this animal, Warëriwë, breaks up a fever when healing the sick – with its hooves (the shapori's hands) and nose. In shamanistic initiations, his special task is to extinguish 'the Eternal Fire' (Pãrimi wakë) with his hooves smeared with a special liquid to equip the new shapori with the necessary protection against any future damage caused by harmful magical actions relating to fire. 'This is Warëriwë's gift to everyone who becomes hekura,' explains Ruweweriwë.

Ruweweriwë's son blows epena into his father's nostrils and Ruweweriwë quickly disappears into the early morning darkness towards the other end of the shapono. Meanwhile, Arawë also sniffs some epena and sits on the ground, then starts to vibrate his lips and call Warëriwë. Indeed, White-lipped Peccary Ancestor embodied by Ruweweriwë is now slowly approaching him in a crouched position, making pig grunts while sniffing and touching the ground in front of him. In between grunts the shapori is revealing through his song:

> Warëriwë is on his way!
> He has just crossed the immortal River of the Stars.
> He is leaving his footprints behind that smell just like him.
> This is the path of Warëriwë!
> Posheriwë is following in his footsteps and Tëpëriwë is right behind them!
> Numerous other hekura are coming in their footsteps.

Next, Ruweweriwë embodies Hõrãmariwë or Bush Hen Ancestor, whose distinctive sound announces the hekuras' arrival in the same way it announces in the forest the proximity of human beings or big game animals, such as tapirs or anteaters (Lizot 1989). The shapori is approaching while Arawë is chanting:

> Meat-hungry Yanomami (porepore)[34] are following hekura footprints but the animals [three incoming hekura] are advancing quickly. Warëriwë is close by and I can already feel his breath and sense his strong body odour. Warëriwë is leaving earth behind him damaged.

Bush Hen Ancestor Hõrãmariwë again calls through Ruweweriwë to announce the arrival of White-lipped Peccary Ancestor: 'The everlasting hekura is here to extinguish the eternal flame. When he puts his wet hands on it, the "shhh!!!" sound will be heard'. Warëriwë is now circling around the seated Arawë, waddling in a crouched position and scraping up the ground in front of him with his hooves (the shapori's feet) in the same way peccary removes the earth when searching for food. Next, the shapori as Warëriwë takes Arawë to the nearest hearth, extinguishes the flames by sprinkling some water, then takes the burning logs out and levels the hot ash with his hands. Then it is all over. The eternal fire is now extinguished and the new shapori is protected against any possible damaging hekura activities associated with fire. Ruweweriwë transfers the ancestral Hekura of White-lipped Peccary from his body into Arawë's.

He then quickly announces that Warëriwë's hekura cousin the Collared Peccary Posheriwë has also arrived and embodies him as well. 'Take them both they are with you now!' In continuation, Ruweweriwë swiftly transforms into Wayahanamawë (also known as Wayahororiwë) or hekura of a nightjar (caprimulgidae). This particular sort of bird is known to alert Yanomami hunters through its song when an anteater is nearby. Anteater Ancestor Tëpëriwë is the last major hekura in this series of embodiments.

> Wayahanamawë is singing and making pendulum-like movements with his body. Tëpëriwë is coming for sure! [announces Arawë]. Tëpëriwë is coming now together with his house – the Mountain of Bachacos [ants] (*Osheriki pariki*) and these ants are his food [responds Ruweweriwë].

Ruweweriwë incarnates the ancestral anteater, and with one arm bent in front of his face – to resemble the anteater's long nose – he approaches the candidate: 'I am Tëpëriwë and who are you?' Arawë quickly responds: 'It's me! Don't you recognise me?' 'Yes of course I do!' Ruweweriwë transfers this hekura to Arawë, and then lies down on the ground in front of him before standing up again to tell Arawë straight in his face: 'You must remember the words of the following song. It is very important. This song that hekura will now bring to you is your personal song. Repeat now after me and sing it whenever you want to obtain more songs from the hekura song tree in the future without my help':

> A huge song tree (*Amoahiki*) has flowers that move like lips and sing like tanager bird (thraupidae).[35]
> The tiny bird hekura will prepare juice from the fruits of this tree and drink it.
> This tree with shining blue and green leaves is their house.
> Brilliant blue and green leaves are falling off a hekura song tree.
> My brother-in-law [referring to the hekura] has brought you this song from the song tree.

At the end, the two Yanomami helpers approach an exhausted Arawë and carefully wash his body with lukewarm water for the first time since the beginning of the initiation. They skip the chest area where the thick film of mucous mixed with epena is formed.[36] Finally, they speck Arawë's body with dark brown dots (Figure 4.14).

Figure 4.14 Arawë's body is carefully washed and speckled with dots resembling Boa's skin.

Day Eleven

Embodiment of Hekura Hammocks

Today, Ruweweriwë is set to carry out the final series of embodiments to complete the whole initiation; namely, he must now implant into Arawë's body a number of individual hekura hammocks (*yɨ kë kɨ*), which will provide rest to all incarnated hekura. More specifically, he has to pair each embodied hekura with their matching hammock all over Arawë's body starting from his feet and moving slowly up his legs, stomach, chest and finally his head. Arawë is standing in front of Ruweweriwë with his arms outstretched. The master shapori is carrying out embodiments of hammocks and coupling them with their corresponding hekura by making a zigzag with his index finger across the entire surface of Arawë's body. Finally, he makes circular finger movements on each side of Arawë's head, starting just behind the ears and extending vertically downwards until reaching his shoulders. According to Ruweweriwë, the purpose of this last act was to fasten two large hammocks for Boa Hekura (sky or boa's abdomen – hetu mɨsi).

To finalise the initiation, Ruweweriwë has to make all embodied hekura lie down in their hammocks and then transfer them collectively into their

House of Boas, deeply rooted and standing erect inside Arawë's chest. Thus he repeats the whole procedure, but this time instead of making a zigzag with his index finger he is waving the palm of his right hand across the surface of Arawë's body. With each hand movement, the shapori makes a different sound. Ruweweriwë later explained that it is the actual sound that the hammock itself is making at the moment when its hekura owner lies in it. The hammock mimics the sound of that particular hekura. All hekura are now happily resting in their hammocks. Next, Ruweweriwë slides his hands about two inches above the entire surface of Arawë's body one last time, in a manner that resembles shaping of a clay figure before pressing his palms firmly against Arawë's chest to make one final long 'ootuuummm!!!!' (sound of embodiment) to deposit all the embodied hekura together with their hammocks into their new House of Boas. A corporeal shapono is henceforth their dwelling where they sleep from dawn until midday while shapori perform their daily rituals. He wakes them up by singing his personal songs that call them to sing and dance with him. Upon finishing his hekuramou session, for the rest of the day and night the hekura can move freely around the shapori's entire body and beyond. Ruweweriwë is now looking at Arawë's body from a distance; he looks at him from the front, then from the left side and finally from the right. Evidently satisfied with his work, Ruweweriwë comes close to Arawë, and with his thumbs and index fingers joined to make circles he makes two impressions around Arawë's eyes. Finally, he looks straight at Arawë, emits a loud, high-pitched sound and places his fingers on top of Arawë's eyelids, saying 'Peripo! Mothoka!' (Sun! Moon!) to place the hekura of the Sun and the Moon into each of Arawë's eye sockets.

The Cosmic Body and its Dynamism

With the completion of this final act of pairing all embodied hekura with their respective hammocks and placing them collectively inside their new hekura house, the initiation had come to an end. After two intense weeks, Arawë had finally become hekura. His body had correspondingly been transformed into a cosmic body – a microcosm of other hekura and a matrix for the full manifestation of the Yanomami macrocosm and any of its constitutive components. The upper part of the shapori's body (head and shoulders) is equivalent to the superior cosmic stratum – the domain of celestial hekura. The two sky hammocks that support the sky (day and night) are fastened on either side of the shapori's head, extending from the bottom of each ear down towards his shoulders. The Sun and Moon hekura are positioned inside the shapori's eye sockets. His torso is the earth stratum where the cosmic mountain or Hekura Mountain (Pei Maki) is implanted. The top of the Hekura Mountain terminates at the base of the shapori's neck – the low part of the sky or boa's abdomen (hetu misi). The base of the cosmic mountain is situated in the lower ribcage area of the shapori's torso. The Hekura house or shapono is positioned inside the shapori's chest near Hekura Mountain. Hekura Path (Pei Yo) is a twofold path, with each side beginning in the shapori's big toes, which, in this case, serve as 'gates' for hekura. The paths extend alongside each leg before merging in the navel area and terminating at the chest, in front of the corporeal shapono. The navel is a kind of border region in the bodily image of the world, a frontier between terrestrial and subterranean cosmic strata and ultimately the point where earth (torso) and underworld (lower abdomen and legs) meet, which is diametrically opposite from the base of the neck where sky and earth conjoin. 'Pore [ghost] lives here!' once commented Ruweweriwë while pointing his index finger at the spot just under his navel. A ghost's role, within the shapori's overall microcosmic bodily image, is to guard the shapono's entrance and alert its hekura inhabitants if an outside intruder is nearby. Let us recall how a day before the initiation commenced, Ruweweriwë was distributing guardians of the shapono, which included a pore. The beneficial behaviour of the embodied pore is inverted and diametrically opposite to their otherwise dangerous reputation when they are in their extracorporeal state of existence; as mentioned previously, they tend to hang around forest paths near a shapono's entrance in order to steal the souls of careless inhabitants and make them sick. Only through initiation does a pore's status become inverted for beneficial purposes.

The shapori's cosmic body as an integrated and dynamic whole is a homomorphic model that resembles the integrated and dynamic totality of the Yanomami stratified cosmos. The main characteristic of the shapori's cosmic body is its capacity to disclose a unified structure of human consciousness corresponding to the structure of the world. In other words, consciousness is rooted in the organic body and has its own integrity just like the cosmos. The horizon of the cosmic body opens up as an experiential realm during initiation and the subsequent hekuramou practices. Explicit knowledge of representations of the cosmos is generated implicitly through the lived experience of the initiation and the creation of the shapori's corporeal microcosm or cosmic body, which itself is a replica of the Yanomami macrocosm and a site of the manifestation of cosmic dynamism, as explained earlier in this chapter. Inside the shapono, embodied hekura rest and sleep in their hammocks just as the Yanomami do. When they are awake, they are free to move around the whole body and Arawë once told me that he can physically feel this happening.

Symbolism of the 'Centre'

The embodied Hekura Mountain is a symbolic manifestation of an ancient concept of a 'Cosmic Mountain as Centre of the World' (Eliade 1989 [1951]) – a cosmic pillar or axis mundi that connects different cosmic spheres. The shaman becomes the centre of the universe and a site of its full manifestation. By attracting hekura from other (geographical) mountains towards itself, the shapori's embodied Hekura Mountain serves as a point where hekura converge. It is one symbolic manifestation of the absolute 'centre', which draws the universe towards itself and towards which hekura – the building blocks of the Yanomami cosmos – will inevitably gravitate. Not only will the shaman's body through the initiation become the 'centre of the universe' but also the symbolism of axis mundi is attested in the very structure of the Yanomami dwelling. The whole shapono is a site of the shapori's actions where the cosmos manifests itself and upon which at any given moment the universe is centred. The multiplicity of shaponos across the Yanomami territory also represents the multiplicity of centres of shaporis' activities, just as each one of them is an individual site of cosmic manifestation.

The inflow of hekura from the outer cosmic spheres towards and into the candidate's body is by its nature intrinsically centripetal. The shaman's expanding field of consciousness draws the cosmos and its components towards itself while the body becomes a receptor and a centre of cosmic convergence, integration, accumulation, saturation and unfolding of the world. Through the shapori's body, these constitutive elements of the Yanomami cosmos are integrated and made structurally permanent. On the other hand, the expansion of the candidate's consciousness that involves the integration of the unconscious or not-yet-conscious elements into the field of his ego sphere is intrinsically centrifugal in its nature. In other words, the centripetal movement of hekura towards the candidate causes a centrifugal reaction as his consciousness extends outwards to incorporate those arriving hekura.

The concentration of hekura within the body induces its metamorphosis, with consciousness emerging as a cosmic sphere. The transformed body becomes a nucleus of a new consciousness in its expanded, cosmic modality. At the moment of death, when the interiority of the body equalises and fuses with the exteriority of the world through the major rupture of consciousness, my body ceases to exist as mine; consciousness slips out of its natural body boundaries and disperses outwards. Human consciousness is rooted in the organic body, while the constitutive components of the shapori's new being are rooted in the cosmos. In fact, they have been rooted in the cosmos all along, since for the Yanomami, hekura come from the 'outside'. In this manner, the extension of the body as 'my own body' corresponds with the dimensionality of the universe. By means of shamanistic initiation, polarities between body as an egoic self and world as cosmos are integrated and consciousness reaches its cosmic self-totalisation as a cosmic body. The ontological dimension of the concept of the cosmic body is articulated as a holographic relationship between the embodied self and the world, which, through the initiation, become one. As the body becomes equal to the cosmos, the new emerging sense of self as hekura fuses with the world (air, earth, jaguar, and snake, for example).

First Trance: Re-experiencing Death and the Beginning of Hekuramou

Continual repetition of tutomou chants as a method of ego inflation and subsequent transformations of the self eventually lead to further expansion and 'stretching' of the candidate's consciousness until it reaches another point of rupture or 'bursting' of our aforementioned metaphorical balloon. At that moment, the candidate effectively enters his first trance state of consciousness, which he would have felt when he experienced himself dying, but this time it is less turbulent. Entrance into a trance state, and the subsequent re-entrance into the 'death state', is an all-important moment because it marks the end of tutomou and the beginning of hekuramou – the mobilising of the embodied personal hekura into action.

When Arawë reached the point of his first trance/death state of consciousness the Yanomami assistants carefully rewashed his body with lukewarm water and speckled it again with brown dots to resemble a boa's markings. By means of initiation his body became a microcosmic container of a cosmic boa, or, more precisely, her abdomen (hetu mɨsi). But the new shapori also emerged as a hekura and to commemorate this the helpers clipped his hair with scissors and removed a circular patch from the top of his head, which is called *pei he mono* shapono ('he mono' being a superior part of the cranium). Arawë said that the head shapono has no specific meaning in relation to hekura but in a way symbolises the new beginning. The crown of the head is shorn of hair in the same way that the site of a new shapono is cleared of undergrowth. At the end, the Yanomami helpers sprinkled white down all over Arawë's head so it looked as it did at the beginning of the initiation and placed a pair of feathered armlets made from the chest portion of a curassow bird around his upper arms. For the past two weeks Arawë was crouching, sitting or lying in his hammock. The time had now come for him to stand up and take his first independent steps within shamanistic practice. It was Ruweweriwë who grabbed him by the wrists and gently pulled him up and took him for his first walk (Figure 4.15).

Arawë's first shaky few steps resembled a baby's initial toddles, but with each new step he grew more confident. While they were walking hand in hand, the master shapori sang the following four songs in a row, asking Arawë to repeat each one after him before embodying them:

In the Mountain of the Curare [plant] (*Aroaripiwei këkï*)
Toucans (*Mayepiri aroari thari*) are the owners of curare.
Curare dart sings like a toucan.
When they sing, darts disperse to all sides.

Honey Hekura (*Puu Yanomami*) lived like the Yanomami once.
He transformed into [Honey] hekura.
After an ugly man poisoned him.
All honeybees went up into the sky
They [have] stayed up there ever since.

Deer painted like ocelot;
It's a Deer Hekura that looks like ocelot
Once they were separate

Figure 4.15 Ruweweriwë and his disciple walking together.

Ocelot was hunting the deer
When he attacked and killed the deer
The deer became painted like ocelot.

Flowers from the naɨ tree.
My yopo tube smells like flower[s] from [the] naɨ tree.
My brother-in-law [referring to hekura],
He has brought this yopo tube that smells so nice and sweet.
The Mountain of Naɨ trees is white and smells nice.
It is white from numerous naɨ trees.
Everything is covered with white naɨ flowers.

'With these songs you will be able to call up your hekura', Ruweweriwë told Arawë. Evidently exhausted from the intensity of the experience, Arawë was wobbly on his feet. 'Don't worry and take it easy.' 'Grab this bow with your hands. Bow Hekura Hãtõnahiriwë is here to help you!' instructed Ruweweriwë while pointing his bow at the new shapori. 'Keep walking slowly!' 'This is your own hekura path from now on that you will traverse each day at noon.' Both shapori looked at Arawë and commented on his embodied hekura path and shapono. Ruweweriwë sang:

My-brother-in-law [referring to hekura]
He has brought this gleaming path [of boas] to you from the sky.
Your shapono is very big and beautiful.
Your House of Boas is all covered with shiny white down.
It is full of your own hekura.
Their heads are also covered with down.
They have watoshe [halos] around their heads just like you.
They painted shapono's edges and seem settled down and happy.
Behind the shapono is your hekura rock.
It will attract new hekura to come to you in the future.

Initially, Arawë lumbered up and down his hekura path and sang, lifting his arms higher and higher each time. He was becoming more confident and his voice grew stronger by the day. He practised only at noon when the sun was at its highest point; Ruweweriwë had repeatedly warned him that when the sun sets low more experienced shapori could turn into predators and harm him or even kill him. One day, however, Arawë did do his hekuramou when the sun was low in the sky and at that moment, apparently, a shapori from the Yanomami community of Sejal, situated hundreds of kilometres down the Orinoco, carried out a magic assault on Arawë that nearly killed him. I will return to this episode later on in the book.

The Dynamism of Hekuramou

The fluid flow of consciousness within the overall dynamism of the hekuramou practice involves a combination of push and pull factors or the interplay between centrifugal and centripetal forces operating in the world. Every time a shapori takes epena snuff and becomes intoxicated (shi wãri) his personal hekura jump out of their hammocks and also become intoxicated; when he starts to sing his personal songs, hekura also sing with him. They dance with him a dance of hekura with his arms rising and falling rhythmically. This mobilisation of a shapori's personal hekura and the intensity of their combined singing and dancing causes his chest to expand. Concurrently, such action produces a continuous mounting of tension in his consciousness until reaching a peak moment of rupture, culminating in a trance (death) modality of consciousness of multiple, fluid transformations. At the point of maximum surge, the shapori stops singing and dancing, having run out of breath, and bursts into a euphoric state of consciousness, accompanied by extreme outbursts of laughter and happiness, heightened activity and general liveliness. By that time, his almost contagious euphoria is directly transmitted to other participants in the ritual with whom his experiences are intersubjectively shared.

Ecstatic rupture of consciousness is the moment that precedes (but also permeates) a trance state. It is an experience of short temporal duration. Although the ecstatic moment is a gateway to a trance state, it does not stop once the trance has been entered; it fuses and permeates the trance state. In fact, a trance is intrinsically ecstatic in its nature; it is fuelled by ecstasy. A trance state is a state of consciousness in which shapori can remain for some time, transforming and shape-shifting in exercises of control and taking in cosmic affairs. In other words, entranced shapori can transform into any form and shape. The intensity of a trance diminishes quickly so that after some time the shapori has to go through the whole cycle of singing and dancing again, albeit much quicker than the first time; sometimes he takes extra doses of epena snuff. The Yanomami do not have a specific word for 'trance' but they do recognise it as a state of being dead (nomai̶). Each time when a shapori performs hekuramou he 'dies' anew through trance and ecstasy and directly re-enters the original primordial condition. In this peculiar state of consciousness, the shapori becomes the vessel for the manifestation of a variety of hekura beings that constitute the totality of the Yanomami cosmos. The trance state as an arena of free transformations metaphorically resembles a cloud – a body of condensed vapour in a constant state of flux and fluid transition from one form and shape to another.

Notes

1. Pei Makɨ is a polymorphic symbol signifying simultaneously a ceremonial wooden pole and a cosmic or corporeal mountain (the abode of embodied hekura). 'Makɨ' without the incorporating word 'pei' stands for a geographical mountain or a rock face (abode of discarnate hekura). Pei Makɨ is one manifestation of a central axis, which connects different cosmic spheres (axis mundi).
2. Arawë's deceased father was a grand shapori. All hekura that come to him are his father's hekura, which he now reincarnates and thus directly inherits. At the same time, Arawë transforms into a hekura.
3. This way, the future shapori via his hekura assistants will be able to recognise directly if someone has been the victim of yawari's magical substance.
4. Paushi këkɨ are all sorts of body adornments – mainly feathers and animal skins – that the Yanomami as well as hekura wear. They are one of the first things to become embodied. In our example, paushi are two green feathers that Arawë receives from his father's hekura.
5. We shall remember that in the myth, the ancestor of night is a black curassow bird called Titiriwë.
6. Lizot (2004) writes that hõshõ noupë is a tree sap from the tree hõshõ nouhi from the protium family that is mixed with ochre to give it a sweet smell.
7. Instead of the personal pronoun 'I' he uses yamakɨ meaning 'I and others', in this instance he and other hekura (see Lizot 1996: 54).
8. Shori means brother-in-law but it is also a term that can loosely be interpreted as 'a friend'. Shapori generally call each other shori. But they often refer to each other during the initiation as father and son, even if they are not biologically, as was the case in Sheroana-theri (Ruweweriwë is Arawë's uncle). Another initiation, which took place earlier in Mahekoto-theri, was with a candidate from the Karohi-theri and his uncle the shapori Enano.
9. Arawë told me that he could only hear the sounds that they produce.
10. 'Poor' here does not mean poor in a material sense, but poor as in powerless or still a human being and not (yet) shapori with hekura powers.
11. Here he uses the term koaɨ, which literally means 'to drink'. Thus he is saying that he will 'drink them' (together with the epena snuff).
12. Later on, I asked him for the reason he was screaming at the moment of embodiment and he replied: 'The path was very heavy and shiny, dispersing into all colours of the rainbow along which the file of hekura were dancing and fluttering towards me. It left me almost breathless'.
13. He was literary saying 'No!' (Ma!) When hekura speak, they often use inverse language whereby 'no' really means 'yes'.
14. Watota peshiyë is hekura of an immortal textile or clothing and for this occasion the master shapori Ruweweriwë was holding in his hands a piece of red loincloth and dancing towards the candidate.
15. The arrival and presence of hekura is generally accompanied by heat and dryness; as a consequence of their migratory movement from the mountaintops to lower atmospheric levels they heat up and sweat just like the candidate.
16. The heat and dryness is thus passed on to Arawë.
17. Mãrõha is a type of fish (tambaqui).
18. Wathapera (rainbow boa) closely resembles the Hetupera (boa constrictor).

19. I asked him afterwards about his experience and he said that the shapono in his chest was very heavy, like a rock, and it left him almost breathless.
20. Here, again, the shapori use inverse language to express their aesthetic appreciation of the shapono, which they refer to as being *wayu* (beautiful). Wayu, as discussed in the notes of Chapter One, is a polysemic word referring to disease, a warring party (*wayumou*) and very strong freshly made tobacco.
21. This is yet another example of inverse language. In this instance, Ruweweriwë literally says: 'No! You are lying' but really means: 'Yes! It is true'.
22. Matono is a polysemic word that can also mean either a 'voice box' or a 'bottle'.
23. Ruweweriwë here instructs all of the thus far embodied hekura to sing the new song together with him and remember it. When they hear Arawë singing it in the future, they will recognise it and start singing and dancing together with their master.
24. Hehuriyoma is a hekura associated with the mountains (*hehu* is a synonym for mountain).
25. This is to maintain the flow of incoming hekura, which would otherwise be disturbed if Arawë lowered his head. In one of my experiences, after the hekura song was embodied, my head tilted backwards slightly and then dropped onto my chest for a brief moment. At that moment it felt as if my whole interiority had started to spill out of me before someone quickly lifted my head up. Arawë in his chants describes his experience of hekura embodiment by using, again, the word koai ('to drink'). So to embody hekura is literally 'to drink them'.
26. Although Lizot in his dictionary (2004: 242) refers to Moyerimi as a female hekura, Ruweweriwë said it is not hekura but a wild and dangerous forest being (yaithë) who is also referred to directly in the transcribed text of the initiation.
27. In the myth, Periporiwë is portrayed as a cannibal.
28. Arawë used the negation *mai kë të* but it is meant as a confirmation or an agreement. So while Arawë openly rejects having anything to do with Periporiwë, he is in fact calling him to come and unite with him.
29. Arawë again uses *yamakɨ* (see also note 7) hence 'I and they' (hekura).
30. He will be sad because he will recognise his father in them.
31. Puriwa is a polysemic word that can variously mean a 'star', a 'dart' and also an 'adornment' (a specific type of earring).
32. Again the inverse meaning of the word 'wayu' (see note 20) is used, in this instance to describe the toad.
33. On this topic see: Merleau-Ponty (1964b); Lacan (1977); Schilder (1956); Wallon (1984).
34. Porepore or *poreri* is not the same as pore (ghost). From the point of view of hekura, human beings appear as grey and lifeless, akin to ghosts; therefore, they call them poreri (Lizot 2004).
35. These small birds are vibrantly colourful – mainly a mixture of turquoise blue and green and Yanomami use their shiny skins to make ear ornaments (Lizot 2004).
36. Epena is considered food for hekura and the crust on the shapori's chest is their excrement; therefore it must not be washed away (Lizot 1985).

Chapter 5

ONEIRIC ENCOUNTERS

꘎꘎꘎꘎꘎ ● ꘎꘎꘎꘎꘎

Having acquired a set of personal hekura and transformed into a hekura himself, Arawë can now carry out hekuramou practices. However, the overall quantity of hekura embodied during the initiation is by no means finite. Throughout his lifetime, the new shapori will continue to expand his personal powers and skills by incorporating more hekura into his existing personal collection (but will sometimes lose hekura too). Hence we could say that the initiation, in a way, never really terminates; it is an ongoing, open-ended process of acquisition of more hekura and their powers. A shapori is, in effect, a constant 'hekura-in-the-making'. In time, Arawë will acquire from hekura an additional celestial light crown (*watoshe hetu mïsi*), which will facilitate him in the task of seeing and contacting celestial hekura. Through his commitment to hekuramou practice, a shapori's personal powers and expertise in handling the craft will continually grow together with his social prestige and people's trust in him as he becomes more skilful at hunting, healing, conducting ceremonial dialogue[1] and managing political affairs.

Hekuramou and Expansion of Shamanistic Powers

The shapori's relationship with his recently embodied hekura is fragile. Hekura can be very fastidious in the beginning until they get used to their new condition. To preserve the integrity of his bodily microcosm of incarnated hekura, the new shapori at the outset of his vocation has to adhere to a prescribed set of rules and restrictions for some time. Some of his hekura can become rebellious and turn against their new master or even abandon his body. The new shapori's main obligation is to take epena snuff almost on a daily basis when the sun is at the zenith and to sing and dance with his hekura. Rules include not to practise while the sun is low in the sky to avoid potential attacks from more experienced and powerful shapori, which Ruweweriwë repeatedly warned Arawë about. Ruweweriwë also advised Arawë to take epena regularly because it is hekura food: 'Each time when you take epena, they [hekura] also drink it! If you stop taking epena, your hekura will become hungry and will abandon you'. Sometimes, in the middle of his shaporimou seances, Ruweweriwë would unexpectedly stop singing, expel brown mucus from his nose or burp and excitedly exclaim: '*Pë pëtiwë! Pë puhi toprarou!*' ('They [referring to his hekura] are full [with food-epena] and satisfied!'). Interestingly, the shapori Makowë from Platanal told me that hekura also like alcohol, or anything that can make shapori feel dizzy or drunk (*shi wãri*). If a shapori stopped practising and taking epena, his hekura would leave his body and return to their mountaintops. In this instance, the structure of his corporeal microcosm (hekura path, house and mountain) would normally remain intact, albeit resemble an abandoned shapono or 'ghost town'. In some instances, however, a shapori can even lose some structural components from his corporeal microcosm, which is precisely what happened to Arawë when he broke the rule of practice and performed his hekuramou later in the afternoon. As a result of a near-fatal blow from an enemy shapori, Arawë was almost killed and temporarily lost his bodily shapono, one of the watoshe crowns and the bulk of his hekura (see Chapter Six).

From sunrise until midday hekura sleep in their hammocks inside the shapori's corporeal shapono where it is night-time, while the shapori goes about their normal daily activities, such as gardening, hunting, making new arrows, repairing the old ones or doing some other work around the house. At noon when the shapori takes epena snuff and starts calling his hekura to join him, they wake up and start singing and dancing together with their master. They can recognise his songs. Let us recall from Chapter Four when Ruweweriwë embodied the songs together with their hekura by making a spiral movement with his index finger around Arawë's chest while saying: '*Amoami yamaki!*' ('We are singing!'). In this way, he was telling hekura to 'remember' the song so that they would recognise it and respond to it in the future. Throughout the rest of the day and at night, after the completion of the hekuramou session, hekura remain awake and active, moving freely around the shapori's body or simply resting in their hammocks just like the Yanomami. Nevertheless, they are on constant alert for approaching danger and always ready to warn their shapori master if a foreign hekura is nearby. The shapori for his part will still feel the effects of epena long after the session and so his radar-like awareness remains 'sensitive' to the presence of other, intruding hekura. For this reason, it is difficult to clearly differentiate between the shapori's consciousness as modified by epena and his consciousness in its wakeful, everyday modality; they clearly overlap sometimes in the same manner that the dream and waking mode of consciousness can blend into a waking dream modality. This echoes Tart's (1969) observation that what constitutes 'normality' of consciousness varies across cultures. We cannot simply assume that what for us is normal, wakeful consciousness is the same for everyone. During the night, hekura remain awake because it is still day time in their actuality. They are alert and guard the shaman during his sleep, ready to wake him up in cases of danger. Sometimes, hekura slip outside of a shapori's body while he is asleep and wander off to nearby mountaintops, returning just before the dawn to sleep until noon. Various shapori told me that when they dream they actually leave their sleeping bodies behind and take on the form of their temporarily disembodied hekura; they journey to various places where they encounter other disembodied beings. Temporary nocturnal absence of embodied hekura is more common with a recently initiated shapori because his hekura are still not used to being with him. With time, and if he follows the rules of conduct, their symbiotic relationship will become stronger and his hekura will eventually stop wandering off at night.

Ruweweriwë also asked Arawë to stay calm and to avoid quarrels and arguments, which could also upset hekura and make them leave.[2] A few days after he finished his initiation and 'officially' started practising hekuramou, Arawë did have one such experience of runaway hekura. While resting in his hammock one afternoon, Ruweweriwë's son-in-law, Kiawë, suddenly got into a heated argument with one of his wives that slowly turned into a physical confrontation. Arawë shouted at them and shook his head in disbelief. Ruweweriwë had been out all day and when he returned late in the afternoon Arawë called to him. They exchanged a few words and took epena before Ruweweriwë carried out a short session of hekura embodiments in the same manner he did during the last two weeks of initiation. Arawë sat on the ground and started to vibrate his lips. Meanwhile, Ruweweriwë ran around the centre of the shapono and shouted (to hekura as I was later told): 'Hapo!' ('Come!'). Towards the end, Ruweweriwë made movements with his hands that looked like he was placing a big box on top of Arawë's head and boxes all around the outside of his body. Later, Arawë explained that the confrontation made him distressed, which caused ten of his overwhelmed hekura to run away. When I asked Arawë about the final act, he responded that Ruweweriwë had been arranging for some of his own, more mature, hekura to stay with him for some time to keep his hekura in place. If, in the future, some of them attempted to escape, Ruweweriwë's hekura guardians would quickly catch them and bring them back. One ex-shapori from Platanal told me that his hekura left him after his mother died due to his lengthy and intense period of mourning.

With regards to food consumption when becoming a shapori, we saw with Arawë that it can take months for a shapori's diet to return to normal, albeit with the exception of salt, which hekura strongly dislike. Ruweweriwë allowed the new shapori to have sexual intercourse only between sunrise and high noon, when hekura are asleep, and only with his wife, who the hekura gradually learnt to accept. If a shapori were to copulate outside of the permissible time or with another woman his hekura may get angry and make him sick or may even leave him. Let us recall how Yoawë – the older primordial twin – lost his powers when his hekura left him due to the scent on his body after he had intercourse with a woman. In Helena Valero's story, she mentions a recently initiated shapori whose hekura left him simply because a woman had passed by (Valero 1984). I was curious about shapori who do not have a wife. Ruweweriwë smiled at me and replied that any shapori could satisfy his sexual cravings by calling Hehuriyoma – an attractive female hekura associated with mountains – who would sometimes descend from nearby peaks at night and copulate with shapori. Hehuriyoma is able to respond to Arawë's call for sexual intimacy because during the initiation when Ruweweriwë embodied her, she rubbed the inside of her vagina with her finger, then smeared vaginal fluid around and inside Arawë's mouth.

One critical personal task for the shaman is to continue incorporating additional hekura into his existing arsenal of embodied hekura, which can be accomplished in various ways. As discussed earlier, different hekura like different types of snuff. All the shapori with whom I conversed said that during the principal shamanistic initiation when hekura children are embodied all candidates exclusively use yakõana snuff. When a recently initiated shapori starts using hisiõmɨ he will attract more powerful hekura, who like this type of snuff, and consequently augment his powers and abilities. Arawë received such hekura approximately one month after being initiated; prior to this Ruweweriwë had gradually been preparing him for it by giving him small doses of hisiõmɨ so that he could get used to its effects. Arawë had consumed hisiõmɨ before he became shapori, as the majority of Yanomami men do – whether they are initiated or not – but this time it was different because he was now a hekura. At first, he would sit quietly while his body wobbled like jelly but he was soon ready to receive more powerful hekura. He took the usual dose of hisiõmɨ then suddenly sat down on the ground and started calling *pararo* to come. Pararo is a synonym (Shamathari term) for hisiõmɨ but also the hekura custodian of this snuff; he is incarnated first among other hekura who like hisiõmɨ. Yet again, Ruweweriwë assisted Arawë and eventually incorporated twelve additional hekura into Arawë's body, along with two new songs. Since then, Arawë has been using hisiõmɨ in his hekuramou sessions, progressively increasing the amount taken and concurrently working with a new set of embodied hekura.

Sometimes a shapori can augment his personal powers by receiving an additional hekura or songs as a gift from another shapori. In this case, hekura are transferred directly from one shaman to another. In some instances one shaman's hekura can fall in love with another shaman's hekura. My host from Platanal, Jacinto, told me that this happened to him once in his youth when he was a practising shapori living in Sheroana-theri. He had come to Platanal for a visit and met up with his deceased wife's grandfather – a grand shapori who was also visiting from another community. After one hekuramou session, the grandfather approached Jacinto telling him that one of his male hekura had fallen in love with one of Jacinto's female hekura and that he wanted to pass the hekura onto him as a gift. Jacinto accepted the offering because the old shapori was a trusted friend; Jacinto's father, Okoshiwë, who was also an active shapori, had warned him that some shapori could deliberately introduce a bad hekura – something which had then happened to Jacinto: 'The experience of having them [bad hekura] inside my body was like a whirlwind that opened up the ground underneath and nearly swallowed me'.

Dreams and Shamanism

The main source of acquisition of additional hekura and by extension the expansion of the shaman's personal powers by far comes from dreams and dream-related activities. Spirit beings interact with humans both in dreams and during hekuramou rituals in the same mode of experience. Phenomenologically speaking, the shared feature of both modalities of consciousness is the same unbroken flux of imagery and fluid transformation from one form to another; however, for the Yanomami, dreams do not have an ontological monopoly. Dreams are subjective experiences that only take place during sleep, albeit they can have the same experiential qualities as mythical dimensions of consciousness or trance states manifested in shamanistic rituals.

As discussed in Chapter Four, Yanomami identify the alternating states of consciousness produced by entheogenic substances with dying (*nomai*), but to them it differs from dreaming. The dream imagery may contain the death motif, or they may see dead people or spirits, but dreams are distinguished from other modalities of modified conscious experiences. The main difference between dreams and shamanistic, epena-induced rituals is that dreams are private experiences while the experiential dimension of trance states of consciousness in rituals have a social, intersubjective dimension and they are visible to the whole community. However, as we will shortly see, when shamans incorporate hekura that come to them in their dreams, they are capable of summoning these dream entities later on in their rituals. The rest of this chapter will hence deal with the phenomenon of shaporis' ritual enactment of their dream components that assume a social dimension. I will mainly focus on some specific instrumental aspects of dreaming practices associated with shamans. These dream images are not symbolic representations but real visits of spirit entities that bring help, healing and power, not unlike other spirit beings, which populate the Yanomami cosmos.

Thapimou: Capturing Dream Content

When the Yanomami talk about their dreams they use the term *mahari*, which means 'in dreams' or 'dream-content'. In addition, 'to dream' is to do maharimou, and to dream specifically about distant (and often unknown) places, people and spirits is to do *thapimou* (Lizot 2004: 434). During my fieldwork I found out that thapimou also denotes a particular method of dream control through chanting that a shapori carries out during the night but more commonly in the early morning. It is a specific technique of consciousness associated with dream retrieval. It relates to the lucid dreaming and the transitory period between being awake and asleep experienced immediately upon waking up, which is referred to in the science on dreams as a hypnopompic state of consciousness. In other words, a shapori is capable of seizing a lucid dream component (e.g., a spirit being or song) that enters his field of dream consciousness, hence it becomes an integral part of his arsenal of personal powers. Thapimou chanting resembles the hekura-calling technique of tutomou, which the shapori candidate employs during shamanistic initiation, as discussed in Chapter Four. Although the respective contents of chants are different, in both instances the shapori aims at incorporating hekura into his body thus augmenting his personal powers. By means of tutomou the candidate calls hekura to come and stay with him. In thapimou, the objective is the same but, in this instance, a shapori calls upon the dream component or a song to remain within him and become his personal ally and 'power tool'. Immediately upon waking, a shapori will sniff some epena and while remaining in the same supine position, with his eyes open, will start intoning thapimou chants, thus calling upon the dream component or song to stay with him. When all thapimou chants are exhausted, the shapori will continue singing his personal hekura songs that he received from hekura during initiation.

The most common dream components are various hekura or other types of spirit beings and images from the Yanomami immediate lifeworld. The most common images include various animals and plants, a house (mountain), river, waterfall, forest, rapids, tree(s), sky, moon, sun, and stars. Apart from these common features, which constitute the Yanomami lived reality, shapori sometimes encounter in their dreams some unknown (to them) beings or dream images that are external to the Yanomami cosmological circuitry. In addition, shapori regularly hear the matching songs in their dreams that are associated with hekura previously 'captured' and embodied by means of thapimou chanting to be sung in the future to summon hekura that appeared in dreams. For instance, if a shapori encountered a jaguar in his dreams he would try to seize it and make it stay in his body through thapimou chanting. The corresponding jaguar song would then come to the shapori in one of his dreams and likewise be embodied. With this song, the shapori will be able to evoke the same jaguar that originated in the dream and put it into service as his personal hekura assistant. Sometimes a song may come into a shapori's dreams first, before the matching hekura dream component. When a shapori hears a new song in his dream, he immediately proceeds with the thapimou chanting before repeating the words of the new dream song and all other previously embodied songs. The newly embodied dream hekura together with all other corporeal hekura will start to sing with the shapori and thus he will remember the new song. Later on when hekura hear this or any other of the shapori's personal songs during a hekuramou seance, they will recognise it and start singing together with the shapori, who is then able to transform into the animal that appeared in his dream. The greater the variety of spirit beings embodied, the greater the variety of afflictions the shapori is able to treat. While the mechanism of dream recall is the same for both images and songs, the common theme in the following dream accounts, as told by my shapori informants, is that their dream images and spirit beings were unknown to them and do not belong to the Yanomami cosmic circuitry.

Arawë frequently shared his dreams with me, especially around the time of his initiation. Once he told me that he had dreamed about a Red Mountain (*Wakë këkɨ*) that was shooting red, thread-like lines towards him. He was alarmed as he was unable to catch the red lines with his hands. When he woke up and realised that the dream image was still in front of him, he quickly sniffed some epena and commenced chanting to 'capture' the dream mountain before it disappeared. The following night, he heard the matching song about the hekura of Red Mountain, which he also embodied in the same manner:

Wakë kë kɨ, Wakë kë kɨ
Hekurapë, Hekurapë
Wakë kë kɨ, Wakë kë kɨ
[Red Mountain, Red Mountain, Hekura of Red Mountain]

He referred to Red Mountain as a house for other potential foreign hekura that may come to him in future dreams and stay in his body. Recall that discarnate hekura live in their shaponos located in big rocks and mountaintops. During the initiation, the candidate embodies all hekura together with their shaponos and mountaintop habitats. Arawë had never seen anything like Red Mountain and likened it to an abode for foreign hekura. For the Yanomami, all hekura live in their houses, just like Yanomami live in their shaponos. 'Even God of white people lives in his house. He came to me last night in my dreams,' the shapori Makowë told me one morning, evidently excited about his dream encounter with a foreign entity.

In another dream, Arawë felt the effects (shi wãri) from a reddish coloured Ghost Smoke (*Pore wakeshi*) coming from an unknown plant with hand-shaped leaves, which he called *hena wayu*.[3] He also heard the song related to Ghost Smoke. When he woke up, he was still dizzy from the dream smoke and commenced the thapimou chanting immediately, without having to resort to epena. When he commenced chanting and capturing the dream image of a plant, its smoke and the matching dream song, the effect of his altered state of dream consciousness was experientially 'carried over' into its wakeful modality. While he was chanting, he felt his chest and mouth expanding and his body trembling. In fact, as he put it, 'the whole earth was trembling'. During the noon session while he was singing his newly embodied dream song about Ghost Smoke, he said he experienced the same bodily sensations as during his dream-catching exercise. A few days later he shared another dream with me:

Last night when I fell asleep, I felt woozy from the red Ghost Smoke that came to me before. The smoke carried me far away to a strange place where I saw lots of napë [foreigners, white people]. They were like ants and looked strange. Their bodies were emitting red smoke as they were inhaling burning sticks. Their houses were tall and touching the sky.[4] There was also a huge mountain that looked just like Sheroroi Mountain [near Sheroana-theri shapono] but much, much bigger. I think it was Caracas.[5]

'But how do you know about Caracas?' I was intrigued. He responded that he never travelled beyond La Esmeralda but had heard incredible stories about distant places such as Caracas and Puerto Ayacucho. When he woke up he embodied the new mountain, together with 'houses that touch the sky'. Yanomami shapori are not unique in having these types of dreams. In the State of Apure, Sumabila-Tachon (1999) recorded the dream journeys of Cuiva shamans, who travelled to big towns with cars and white people, when they had never in fact travelled beyond their native territory.

Ruweweriwë told me that he had dreamt about a foreign bird hekura with big eyes, together with its house, by the name of *Shoro Henaki* ('Swift Bird Plant'). This hekura bird was made of the unknown plant's smoke from which he felt dizzy. While still feeling the effects of the smoke upon waking up, Ruweweriwë sniffed some epena, carried out the thapimou chanting and embodied the dream entity together with its house. The next night he heard in his dream the following matching song, which he also embodied:

Shoro kë Henaki,
Shoro kë Henaki,
Purimayoma hei,
Shoro kë Henaki

This oneiric spirit being and his dwelling thus became part of Ruweweriwë's permanent embodiment. Soon after this event, in one of his hekuramou performances, he summoned this bird hekura by singing the newly embodied song, and the dream entity promptly manifested itself. On another occasion in Platanal, the shapori Makowë woke me up before dawn and excitedly said that he had encountered napë (non-Yanomami) hekura Diosi (from the Spanish '*Dios*', God).[6] The dream entity was hovering above his head and sprinkling water over him with his hand. Makowë portrayed him as powerful and good-natured with 'hair on his face' just like me; he was pointing his index finger at my unshaved face. Diosi arrived together with his house, which Makowë compared to the nearby clinic building. When he woke up he sniffed epena and carried out the thapimou in order to embody this oneiric being and his house. From then onwards, Makowë (Diosi) could heal people with his hands. The true identity of Diosi remained obscure, as we will shortly see; however, it was certain that he was external to the Yanomami cosmos. Not long after Makowë's dream, I had a chance to see his newly embodied foreign hekura in action with an old sick man in one of Makowë's shaporimou sessions; he suddenly came up to me and whispered in my ear: 'Diosi hekura, pay attention!' Next, he wrapped a piece of cloth around his head with both ends falling on his shoulders (which reminded me of an Egyptian pharaoh) and started hopping from one foot to the other. Then a dramatic dialogue commenced – relayed through Makowë – alternating between Diosi with a strong, explosive voice and someone else that appeared submissive and noticeably afraid of him. Suddenly, Makowë started slashing the old man's sickness with his hands, as with a machete, then closed his eyes and placed both hands on the man's shoulders. After the session, Makowë confirmed that Diosi had slashed *no wãri* sickness with his machete and repaired the old man's damaged soul essence (*pei puhi*). A few days later while I was resting in my hammock and flipping through the pages of a book, Makowë squatted next to me and looked curiously at the various photographs. Suddenly he pointed his finger at one of the pictures showing a water house on stilts and commented that the old man's no wãri sickness looked exactly like the house.

My shapori informants claimed that they were not familiar with the experienced dream imagery, but, most likely, their dream images are in a Freudian sense 'day residues', originating from our daily conversations, which make an impression on us and influence our manifest dream content. For example, I remember telling Arawë once prior to his dream that in my part of the world (Australia) there is a red mountain called Uluru – a home for many foreign hekura – which may have had an impact on his consciousness, influencing his dream imagery. Similarly, the presence of a consciousness-altering smoke in the dreams of both Arawë and Ruweweriwë could have been the result of our conversations about the existence of epena in my country; I told them that there are many types of epena, the most common being a plant (cannabis sativa) whose leaves people burn and inhale. I made a drawing in my notebook to show them what the leaf looks like. They listened attentively and were amazed to hear that people could swallow smoke; for them it was something incomprehensible. Arawë, however, commented that he had already heard stories before about white people inhaling smoke. An interesting and important detail of Arawë's dream experience was that he felt the effects of the smoke, not only while dreaming but also upon waking. He did not have to take epena but immediately commenced the thapimou chanting. Regarding his dream journey to the 'city of foreigners', which he referred to as Caracas, this oneiric experience could have been influenced by stories about distant cities that he had heard about, which may have had a strong impact on his imagination and dreams. But for Arawë, his dream experience was a real journey not a symbolic representation or a product of his nocturnal brain activity; hence, the possibility cannot be excluded that his dream ego may have literally journeyed to a distant city in which case his manifest dream was a literal description of events that happened on a still unknown level of consciousness. Similarly, Makowë's dream encounter with an entity he identified as the God of white people could have been influenced by stories he heard from his son-in-law, Jacinto, who collaborated with the missionaries for many years and who is somewhat familiar with Christian teachings. In Platanal, I never noticed Makowë or any other shapori showing interest in Christian practices and beliefs or attending the Sunday Mass. He identified his new hekura helper as God of white people (Jesus), but when this hekura manifested himself during one of Makowë's hekuramou sessions, his exact identity was not revealed and remains a mystery. It is only certain that he is external to Yanomami cosmology.

The nature and the origin of the aforementioned dream imagery are subject to interpretation; however, whatever they are, they are not 'cerebral ghosts in the mind' but autonomous images whereby 'the imager does not have the sense that he is making up these productions, but feels that he is getting involved in an already created process' (Price-Williams 1987: 248). For the shapori, they are real dream visitation by autonomous entities that can become embodied, actualised and appropriated in their own way through rituals and the use of epena snuff. Specifically, these dream entities become instrumental tools for healing or doing harm, just like any other of the shapori's personal corporeal hekura.

A direct correspondence and overlap between the horizons of dream consciousness and the spirit facet of the world, including seeing dead people, is widespread among many other Amerindian groups. Spirits are said to frequently appear in dreams and grant the dreamer spirit powers, which they fully manifest in future healing ceremonies, with the application of these spirit powers in ritual context benefiting the whole community (Tedlock 1999). Basso (1987b) talks about dreams among the Carib-speaking Kalapalo of central Brazil, where knowledge and power is said to come from dreams in which the dreamer is visited by a powerful being, who can also appear in waking life. Roy D'Andrade in his (1961) study of dreams in hunter-gatherer societies claims that spirits who appear in dreams grant the shaman powers and knowledge. Shamans use these dreams in shamanistic session for curing, divination and soul retrieval. In his own words:

> There is a persistent association found between dreams and beliefs about supernaturals, including other souls. Dreams have been shown to be one of the chief means of communication with supernaturals, and supernaturals

have been found to have certain similarities to figures, which typically appear in dreams. (D'Andrade 1961: 298–99)

Tupi-speaking Kagwahiv of Brazil also view dreams as a means of communication between human and superhuman beings, who also appear in their myths (Kracke 1987). In ancient Mesopotamia, various deities were able to communicate important messages to the dreamer (Kilborne 1987), while in Greco-Roman antiquity, 'the dream was considered a sphere of communication shared by the god and the dreamer' (Walde 1999: 121).

Dream Lucidity and the Transitional States of Dream Consciousness

The aforementioned examples of dream activities of the Yanomami shapori reveal a close link between lucidity associated with the hypnopompic state of consciousness between dreaming and waking and the ritual re-enactment of revealed dream components in the epena-induced states of consciousness. The mastery of the lucid dream dimension by means of thapimou allows shapori to continually augment their powers and knowledge, which they use for healing or harming.

In sleep research, the transitional states associated with the intermediary borderline between sleep and wakefulness are known as hypnagogic and hypnopompic states of consciousness. The term 'hypnagogic' (Greek: *hypnos* 'sleep'; *agogos* 'leading'), which was originally coined by Alfred Maury in 1848, describes the state of consciousness during the onset of sleep, while, as discussed, the term 'hypnopompic' (Greek: *pomp* 'sending away'), coined by Frederic Myers (1903), refers to the partially conscious state that precedes complete awakening from sleep experiences. Control of these transitional states of consciousness, especially the hypnopompic state combined with lucid dream control, is critical to the practice of thapimou, through which the initiated shapori continually boosts his personal powers during the course of his lifetime. 'Lucid dream' is a term that was coined by Dutch psychiatrist Frederic van Eeden ([1913] 1969). It suggests that the dreamer is aware that he or she is dreaming. The difference between a lucid dream and the initial dream is that the former generally occurs between five and eight in the morning. The main characteristic of dream lucidity is that it involves a kind of 'mental awakening within the dream' (Rechtschaffen, cited in Hunt 1989: 118), or the dreamer's awareness within the dream that he [or she] is dreaming (Shulman and Stroumsa 1999; Van Eden 1969).

La Berge (1985) writes that the (lucid) dreaming subject is trained to maintain conscious awareness during the transition from waking to sleeping. In relation to shamanism and lucidity, Hunt (1989: 82) states that the shaman is often said to be awake during the dream, entering it either from sleep and lucidity or from a waking trance. In other words, what is present here is metacognition or maintaining self-awareness and self-reflection while dreaming, which was thought for a long time by many dream researchers, and especially psychologists, to be absent in dreaming (Bulkeley 2008; Kahan 2001). The main characteristic of the hypnopompic state of consciousness between sleep and wakefulness is the persistent presence of dream images in the first moments of waking up (Myers 1903). In other words, when a sleeper wakes up, they may open their eyes while a dream is still running its course. At that precise moment, the two modalities of consciousness – dream and a wakeful state – fuse into the hypnopompic state during which the dreamer consciously experiences the revealed hypnopompic imagery. One variation of the hypnopompic state is when the dreamer briefly wakes up and then returns to sleep but with waking consciousness preserved (Mavromatis 1987). In this instance the sleeper continues dreaming in a lucid mode. Swedish mystic and theologian Emanuel Swedenborg described in his diary his own hypnopompic experience during which the 'vision comes … when the man is waking up, and has not yet shaken off sleep from his eyes' (cited in Mavromatis 1987: 100). Peter D. Ouspensky, a famous Russian esotericist and explorer of the nature of dreams, described his personal experiences of early morning hypnopompic 'half-dream states':

> After waking I again closed my eyes and began to doze, at the same time keeping my mind on some definite image, or some thought. And furthermore, … in 'half-dream' [hypnopompic] state I was having all the dreams I usually had. But I was fully conscious, I could see and understand how these dreams were created … I had a certain control over dreams. (Ouspensky, cited in Mavromatis 1987: 100)

In addition to visual imagery, hypnopompic and hypnagogic experiences can also include the less frequently reported experiences of hearing sounds. For example, Jane Sherwood describes trying to retain the words of a beautifully ecstatic poem upon waking:

> I have sometimes come back to consciousness with great reluctance, still exhilarated with an inspired poem I am reading, the last strains of which are still ringing in my ears. The lines are too lovely and important to be

lost and I make frantic efforts to retain them through the mists of returning consciousness. (Sherwood 1965: 90)

Bodily sensations of flying, floating or spinning are also common to hypnagogic sleep onset (Hunt 1989: 182). Many researchers on dreams (Hunt 1989; Mavromatis 1987; Shafton 1995; Tart 1969; Vogel, Foulkes and Trosman 1966) have recognised that hypnagogic and hypnopompic dream images exist in their own right, independently from dream images that occur during deep REM[7] sleep, although hypnagogic and hypnopompic dreams are phenomenologically identical to REM dreams.

With the Yanomami shapori, the majority of nocturnal spirit visitations take place in the early morning hours, while shapori are still asleep. However, it is hard to determine precisely if the reported dream images originated during deep sleep (REM) or during the actual transitional hypnopompic state. Evidently there is an overlap between the imagery revealed during dreaming and the hypnopompic transition from dreaming into wakefulness. It appears that the revealed dream images enter the dreamer's consciousness during the REM stages of dreaming but persist during the hypnopompic awakening before finally fusing with the epena-induced state of consciousness. In other words, there is a continual flow of dream imagery from deep sleep via the hypnopompic period into the drug-induced state of consciousness.

In their study of ego functions and dreaming during sleep onset, Vogel and his colleagues (Vogel, Foulkes and Trosman 1966) outlined three phases between waking consciousness and falling asleep. The first phase is pre-sleep, during which the ego remains relatively intact as reality content weakens and imagery increases. As the ego further descends into the hypnagogic period associated with the first stage of sleep, it becomes 'destructuralised' in the process of transition from waking consciousness into sleep. Consequently, during the second stage there is a complete loss of contact with the external world. The final step involves stage two (NREM) (non-rapid eye movement) sleep, during which the ego becomes restructuralised and dream content more plausible. But there is no reported contact with exteriority. In continuation of the ego's descent towards deep sleep, it passes through stages three and four of NREM sleep before finally entering REM deep sleep.

If we now apply this model of falling asleep to the dreaming activities of the Yanomami shapori but in reverse, we could outline the three upward steps of the waking up pattern. The first stage is a deep sleep (REM) stage, during which a segment of a shapori's self that dreams is fully immersed in his dreaming activity and contact with waking reality is absent. During this period of deep sleep, a dream image emerges. As the shapori's dream ego reaches the threshold of waking, it starts ascending from deep sleep to the second stage of hypnopompic waking. The first moments of awaking are characterised by the encroachment of waking consciousness into dream modality, as the dream the ego gets a hold of the external world. During this transitory period at the onset of wakeful consciousness, when it starts emerging from its dream mode, there is a brief moment during which the two modalities fuse with each other. During this hypnopompic period of juxtaposition of the two ego modalities – of being neither asleep nor fully awake – the dreamer becomes more lucid vis-à-vis his dreaming. This is, however, a precarious moment because during the intrusion of waking consciousness the ego's contact with external reality strengthens as the intensity of imagery simultaneously decreases. In other words, at the onset of rapidly returning waking consciousness, the ego starts losing control over manifest dream content while concurrently trying to retain its presence in consciousness. For the shapori, at this precise moment, he will sniff some epena and start to chant as his ego consciousness undergoes its modal metamorphosis from hypnopompic waking to an epena-induced state of consciousness. In this way, the shapori manages to 'capture' the dream hekura or song and thus fully establish an unbroken continuity and permanency of a revealed dream image. Both Ruweweriwë and Makowë pointed out that the period between waking and sniffing epena must be as brief as possible, otherwise the hekura or related dream images will quickly vanish or words of the dream song will quickly be forgotten.

Dreaming and Drug-induced States of Consciousness

Arawë's and Ruweweriwë's experiences of modified dream consciousness described above could be compared to other examples in different contexts. A renowned researcher on the nature of consciousness Charles Tart (1969: 169) described a distinct type of dreaming activity, which he labelled 'high dream'. It involves a peculiar state of egoic dream consciousness – experientially similar to the one induced by psychedelic chemicals – which persists after the dreamer completes the transition from sleep into waking consciousness. Tart gives an example of a young woman who dreamt of taking the drug LSD after which her dream ego's perception changed from ordinary dream consciousness to perceptual changes associated with taking LSD. Towards the end of the dream she was elevated to what she described as a 'state of ecstasy', a sensation that persisted for a few minutes upon waking up. In another example, a male subject experienced altered bodily sensations and an expanded sense of space while dreaming of taking an LSD-like gaseous substance. Upon waking, he reported that the same 'high' state of consciousness and perception of space experienced in his dream was carried over into a wakeful state of consciousness. This sensation lasted a few minutes before he drifted back to sleep.

Around the time of my own and Arawë's initiation, I had a series of lucid dreams and epena-like transformations of my egoic dream consciousness that resembled daily initiatory experiences. In my dreams, I experienced the effects of yakõana snuff as I did during rituals, with my mouth and chest expanding and my whole body pulsating. After a few moments, the intensity of epena would start to recede and my consciousness would assume a lucid dream modality. While dreaming, my breathing rapidly altered my consciousness, having the same effects as epena inhalations. After waking up, the same sensation lingered for a few moments. During the night on the fourth day of Arawë's initiation, I dreamed about Ruweweriwë singing and carrying out the hekura embodiment and experienced the same bodily sensations and egoic transformations produced by epena intake during the actual initiation. Upon waking up the experience was carried over into my wakeful consciousness so vividly that I thought it was really happening. However, I quickly realised that both Ruweweriwë and Arawë were sound asleep. On another occasion, the same experience occurred, albeit in a lucid mode of hypnagogic sleep onset – I was conscious that I was lying in my hammock, and simultaneously experiencing consciousness in flux produced by epena and Ruweweriwë's singing. This sensation was so authentic that when I 'snapped out of it' rather than awoke, I was looking around, touching my body and thinking that they had started another initiatory round but again found them sound asleep in their hammocks. Yet another time, while dreaming of firewood I suddenly felt a gust of wind coming from the direction of Arawë's hammock; the fire was lit by Arawë's lip vibrating 'brrrr!' sound. Upon waking up, I realised that Arawë was in fact chanting and vibrating his lips. In the first two instances, day residue affected my dream content, while in the last instance it was the external stimuli – Arawë's singing.

Let us recall how during Arawë's initiation the incoming hekura were progressively giving him shawara diseases; how the intensity of the manifesting symptoms greatly increased after he received the Hekura Mountain and hekura started entering his body directly without Ruweweriwë's help. During my own initiation, I similarly experienced fever, inner chills and nausea along with splitting headaches during the day as well as at night. This, in turn, greatly influenced the manifest content of my dreams. One night while resting in my hammock I could feel the waves of nausea in my solar plexus. Later in my dream I had the sensation of moving forward rapidly and experiencing some kind of inner turbulence in the form of vibrations. As I was accelerating, I was progressively experiencing the same changes in consciousness as when taking epena snuff. Suddenly, there was a kind of 'opening' ahead. As I ran out of breath I woke up still feeling the sensation of inner turbulence and flux. My head and chest were vibrating. I felt an overwhelming 'movement' in my abdomen and some awkward pressure in my ears. Then it all stopped and I fell asleep again.

There were dreams that did not necessarily involve changes in consciousness as when produced by a psychotropic drug but nevertheless involved experiences of spirit possession and subsequent self-transformation through shape shifting, identical to experiences of transformation into a hekura mode of being while in a trance. In one such dream I metamorphosed into a jaguar, growling and roaming the forest as I had done during my initiation (see Chapter Four), but in this dream there was another man standing next to me. I did not want him to notice what was happening, as I was concerned he would call a priest to exorcise the jaguar hekura from my body. This dream segment suggested the psychological influence of my own Christian heritage. In another dream, I was walking with Arawë through the forest and suddenly felt a pressure in my chest, which made my breathing difficult. I panicked and soon regained my waking consciousness. The pressure in my chest, accompanied by fast and shallow breathing, persisted for a few minutes. There was, however, no change in consciousness associated with epena intake either during or after the dream.

Dreams, Illness and Healing

For the Yanomami, dreaming generates risk, as their physical bodies and dream egos become open and vulnerable to the potential harmful acts of enemy shapori. The activities performed by or on the self in a dream mode of consciousness are instrumental and have crucial effects on waking reality. In other words, 'there is a continuity of dialectical conscious processes between waking and dreaming' (Rossi, cited in Kahan 2001: 342). In this final section I will examine the link between dreams, illness and healing, and how dreaming and wakeful realities mutually influence each other. For this purpose, I will focus on two interrelated phenomena associated with shamanism – dreaming and illness – which Yanomami identify respectively as *kuramaɨ* and *yashokaɨ*. In his earlier version of *Diccionario Yanomami-Español*, Jack Lizot defined the term kuramaɨ as 'to dream about distant places or people different from the ones that can be found at the site where the dreamer is located' (Lizot 1975: 43).

Yashokaɨ, on the other hand (and according to him), means 'to be above or to dominate' (ibid.: 98) or, in his more recent dictionary, 'to bow down under the influence of a weight' (Lizot 2004: 502). During my fieldwork, I learnt that 'kuramaɨ' also denotes a conscious and wilful, malignant shamanistic practice that involves introducing shawara sickness into victims' bodies through dreams while they are asleep.[8] *Kuramirema* is a state of being unwell on account of an act of kuramaɨ. A victim will have bad dreams and upon waking experience aches, a fever and weakness. This is a serious condition that can be fatal if the shapori does not expel shawara out of the victim's body through the rite of yashokaɨ. Thus, the abovementioned first definition of yashokaɨ could be translated as 'to dominate sickness or counteract the action of an enemy shaman and hence be above him (dominate him)'. During this act of purification, the shapori whips the affected person with a tree branch in an attempt to rid the body of shawara and thus the bad dreams caused by it, in turn preventing him or her from dying. In a comparative practice in New Mexico, the Zuni shaman wraps a blanket around the body of the person who had bad dreams and instructs him (or her) to inhale the smoke of a burning pine tree twig that is then placed in a glass of water. The shaman then removes the twig and orders the dreamer to drink the water. In more serious cases, a person is ceremonially whipped. Whipping is believed to remove traces of bad dreams and thoughts from a person's body and transform them into positive thoughts (Tedlock 1987). In their attempts to cure people from shawara, a Yanomami shapori will employ a similar method using a branch or his bare hands (and his assisting hekura) outside of the context of dreams. In both these instances, the shapori aims at re-establishing a person's bodily equilibrium.

I discovered these phenomena accidentally one morning while I was with the Sheroana-theri on a seasonal food-gathering expedition (*wãyumɨ*). Moments before waking up, I dreamt I was at an overcrowded train station. The trains kept arriving and crashing into other trains. As I was attempting to escape the incoming trains I saw Ruweweriwë, who was waving at me and instructing me to follow him. I felt indifferent towards the dream scene with a pervasive feeling that I was not responsible for these accidents. Upon waking up, I coughed feeling tightness and sharp pain in my chest. Ruweweriwë came up to me and started gently whipping my body with a leafy tree branch from head to toe for a few minutes. He then left without saying a word. I asked his son Mirko why Ruweweriwë had done this and he answered: '*Titiha shaporini wa kuramirema*' ('Last night you were made sick from shawara by the shapori' [He was referring here to his father]). He explained that during the night while I was asleep, Ruweweriwë introduced shawara into my body and then drove it out with the branch through the act of yashokaɨ. I was puzzled and decided to ask Ruweweriwë why he would do this. He said that while I was asleep an awkward tension in his chest was keeping him awake; his lungs were bad (parɨkɨ waritiwë), which affected his breathing and made him cough and thus unintentionally introduce the shawara sickness into my body. More precisely, as he described, during his interrupted sleep (maharishi waritiwë) his dream content (mahari) entered my body, thus contaminating it with shawara sickness. In the morning, he 'exorcised' his dream together with the sickness from my body with a branch. I thought about my dream the night before and how – in my own interpretation – my disturbed bodily condition had affected my dream content; the chaos at the train station reflected the bodily disorder that was caused by the onset of sickness. These events were a prelude to the waves of shawara epidemics that incurred the same flu-like symptoms of chest pain, headache and weakness, which at that time swept the entire region from the remote Siapa River all the way up to Platanal and Mavaca. As a consequence of Yanomami mobility and intercommunal visits, the epidemics were able to spread rapidly from community to community, including to the Sheroana-theri.

Though Ruweweriwë somewhat apologetically explained that he had inflicted me with shawara sickness through the dream unintentionally, some shapori do this on purpose to make others ill. He said that if some enemy shapori introduced the sickness or his hekura into my body intentionally while I was dreaming, my life would be endangered if he or some other shapori did not carry out the rite of yashokaɨ. According to Ruweweriwë, this is precisely what had happened to Neboisa's three-year-old-son, who suddenly became ill with abdominal pain and blood in his faeces. His condition progressively deteriorated and he died two days later. Ruweweriwë's diagnosis was that the Shamathari shapori from the community of Narimipiwei-theri introduced shawara in his sleep, which culminated in his death a few days later. I first heard from the boy's mother about her son's condition. The day before he died the amount of blood in his faeces had significantly increased. On the day of his death, as his mother was holding him in her arms, a red, jelly-like substance oozed from his anus. He did not suffer from diarrhoea. Lying on the ground were solid, dark red colour faeces and vomit. Moments before he died, the boy turned very pale. He screamed a few times and started looking around with his eyes full of fear. Someone mentioned hekura and upon hearing the bad news, people started to cry. To them he was already lost, for the situation had become extremely grave. As fate would have it, Ruweweriwë and his son were away on a fishing trip on the Shanishani River. Moments before passing away, the boy opened his mouth, gasping for air in panic as his little body was twisting. He was crying and calling for his mother and father. All of a sudden he went quiet; his frightened look changed and with eyes full of anger and hatred he proclaimed in a deep adult voice: '*Ya amishi*' ('I am thirsty'). Then within a few seconds the fear and desperation returned again into his eyes as he continued crying and his body continued twisting. He called his mother and father once more and then stopped breathing.

Ruweweriwë returned that same afternoon and his son told me that while they were camping on the riverbank the night before, Ruweweriwë had commented how his personal hekura told him in his dream that an enemy Shamathari hekura had committed a killing in Sheroana-theri. The following morning, the boy's body was cremated on the edge of the shapono's central area. As I watched the flames engulf the burning pile of wood, a wave of thick yellowish smoke spiralled into the air. Later, Arawë commented that the funerary smoke had expanded across the sky and turned it red (*hetu misi wakëmou*). According to him, this same smoke was a carrier of shawara that was inside the boy's body.

As mentioned, Ruweweriwë said that the boy had died due to the actions of a powerful hekura from a community belonging to their traditional Shamathari enemies from Siapa. I questioned him further on how the child could be killed from a single hekura attack when he had health problems for several days prior to his death. He responded that the enemy shapori first introduced shawara in the boy's dream and left some of his hekura assistants over a few nights to ensure the boy's health deteriorated before finally strangling him. According to Ruweweriwë, certain hekura, such as Periporiwë (Moon) and Ɨrariwë (Jaguar) kill their victims, mainly small children, instantly by strangling them or by eating their soul essences (*pei mɨ ãmo*), while other hekura do not necessarily strangle their victims immediately but may come into a person's dreams and remain in their bodies for some time, gradually damaging his or her well-being as was apparently the case with the boy who died. Sometimes, hekura may remain in a person's body to make him or her ill, but eventually leave without causing any grave harm.

When the sick boy was dying, Arawë attempted to save him, but then shortly after he gave up. He was evidently anxious, having only recently been initiated and with no prior experience in dealing with this kind of situation. Besides his fear of hekura, I noticed he lacked enthusiasm to try saving the boy's life. For quite some time before this tragic event, Arawë and his family felt a certain degree of covert animosity and ill will towards the boy's father, Neboisa, and his family, who belonged to a different lineage. Neboisa claimed to be the sole survivor from the now extinct community of Wanapiwei-theri. Together with his wife from Toritha-theri and their children, he joined the remnants of the original Patanowë-theri, which became known as Sheroana-theri. Only days before the boy died, Arawë made a repulsive comment: 'They are all *shami*', which literally means 'dirty', but in this context it implies 'bad in character' or 'bad, unworthy people'. This prompted me to think that Arawë perhaps only tried to save the boy because of his social responsibility as a shaman that obliged him to act appropriately. When I asked Arawë about the cause of the boy's death, he reiterated that an enemy shapori had introduced the sickness into the boy's body while he was asleep (kuramai). Arawë did not dare to confront the intruding hekura nor did he know how to expel sickness with a branch (yashokai). As Ruweweriwë was away that day he was unable to assist the boy. Consequently, the boy's health deteriorated and he passed away. Arawë said that when he came up to the boy and placed his hands on his body, he quickly identified the intruder but then abruptly pulled away and went back to his hammock because he was not feeling well. He was still weak and recovering from a near fatal hekura attack that had occurred about two months before the boy's death, which I will describe in Chapter Six. Arawë admitted that he was too scared to confront a much more powerful enemy and risk being injured again or killed in the process. This case is a point of departure for the following chapter where I will analyse in detail the offensive and defensive types of shaporimou activities as well as the techniques that shapori use to inflict sickness upon people or to heal them.

Notes

1. The Yanomami identify two forms of ceremonial dialogue. The first is called *himou*, which is performed by elderly men during the day in the context of a funeral rite, a feast or as a manner of expressing urgent requests and extending invitations. *Wayamou*, the second dialogue, takes place during the night and is practised primarily by younger men in the context of visits and feasts (Lizot 1994: 217).
2. This echoes the words of the master shapori in Helena Valero's narrative (Valero 1984), who warns the potential candidates for initiation not to fight otherwise their personal hekura will get frightened and run away from them.
3. Hena is 'leaf' or 'plant' and wayu, as mentioned previously, can be a generic term for illness that manifests with strong symptoms (a disease), or in this instance a strong plant like tobacco.
4. In order to demonstrate what the napë house from his dream looked like, Arawë grabbed a banana and placed it upwards.
5. There is indeed a mountain called Avila (2,800 m) situated near the city of Caracas.
6. Kelly (2011) similarly commented how an eminent shapori from Ocamo, who was a great friend of the missionary Luis Cocco, used to summon the hekura of God, which

he regarded as very powerful. Before he died, he passed this entity on to his younger brother.

7. Researchers on dreams (Aserinsky and Kleitman 1955; Dement and Kleitman 1957; Hobson 2001) assert that the normal sleep cycle consists of alternation between two different kinds of sleep: NREM and REM. The initial NREM stage lasts roughly an hour and a half followed by ten to fifteen minutes of REM sleep. There are a total of three to seven NREM/REM cycles, and as the night progresses, REM periods become longer and NREM periods shorter. The longest REM period occurs in the early morning hours. Their findings in relation to dream recall indicate that 80 to 90 per cent of their subjects were able to recall their dreams when awakened during an REM period and only 7 per cent during an NREM period.

8. Raramuri sorcerers of New Mexico similarly have 'access' to other's bodies at night: they can kill and eat the souls of their victims in dreams. They are also able to send (non-specific) illnesses (*nawiri*) in anthropomorphic form with the intention of harming the dreamer (Merrill 1987).

Chapter 6

SHAMANIC BATTLEFIELD

The Pendulum of Life and Death

Dreaming within the context of the Yanomami lifeworld can become perilous, since the dreamer's body may become exposed to hekura attacks through intentional, harmful acts of enemy shapori. Such acts are likely to be fatal if countermeasures are not taken by another shapori, who in this instance assumes the curative role. Continuing within the dialectics between offensive and defensive types of shamanistic activities – the dual role that any shapori can adopt – in this chapter we will explore the dynamics of shaporimou craft, from the micro-bodily to the interpersonal and trans-territorial, macro levels. I use the conceptual offensive-defensive dichotomy as an analytical tool, which does not necessarily reflect Yanomami views. Nevertheless, the pattern of disease infliction by one shaman and the reaction of another is embedded and widely recognised as being an integral part of Yanomami intercommunal relations.

This ethnographic research into shamanistic activities was carried out in the context of a number of communities situated along and near to the Orinoco River, including Sheroana-theri and Mahekoto-theri and their traditional enemies – southern Shamathari neighbours. In addition, there is a history of reciprocal malignant shamanistic activities and sorcery accusations between the Yanomami of Sheroana-theri and the Yanomami of Pishaasi-theri (situated at the Mavaca mission post). The ongoing hostility between the two communities stems from the past dispute when both present day Sheroana-theri and Pishaansi-theri were part of the same mother community of Namowei-theri before splitting up. Another threat for the residents of Sheroana-theri comes from the separatist and politically opposed people of Sejal, situated downriver from Mavaca. Thus, this whole area can be viewed as a shamanic battlefield of offensive types of shaporimou activities that generate an endless cycle of tit-for-tat revenge and hekura assaults. This region is a macro universe of principally repetitive activities carried out by shapori from different communities.

A Shapori's Identity and Social Obligation on the Intracommunal Level

Upon successfully completing the initiatory ordeal, Arawë, akin to all other new shapori, assumed a new, dual mode of existence as a living hekura. This new identity of an immortal being occupying a perishable physical body has conferred on him a new social status and a new set of duties and responsibilities towards his residential group. Each shapono is a micro universe, subject to principally curative and protective activities by the resident shapori. Hence, on the intracommunal level, Arawë's main duty is to heal the sick and defend his kin from offensive actions committed by enemy shapori, but he will also carry out offensive acts himself against members of unrelated communities and their shapori. As a hekura, he is guardian of the community, shielding its inhabitants from the intrusions of the outside hekura. But, he is also an aggressor; a predator, preying upon the young and weak from other distant communities. Within his own community, he will be praised for his protective actions but in other communities he will be blamed for using his hekura powers to inflict sickness or to kill. A shapori's reputation and his social position are thus decided by circumstance and the possibility of conflicting points of view of two or more communities. The shapori can save lives, but he can also take lives. He is responsible for maintaining socio-cosmic order but he can also create disorder. A shapori can either heal or harm, but each case of affliction implies both offensive and defensive types of activity. Each case in which a health disturbance is caused by shaporis' hostile activities involves, simultaneously, elements of both sickness infliction and hekura attack by one or more shapori and the follow-up treatment or rescue countermeasures employed by another shapori.

The pattern of a shapori's engagement in hekuramou activities generally depends on their personal skills and reputation, the time of the day and weather conditions. Midday sessions are habitually reserved for purely 'recreational purposes'. When the sun is at the zenith, shapori sing and dance together with their embodied hekura without necessarily becoming involved in healing. They undertake curative sessions on demand, day or night, while more experienced shapori often carry out various offensive acts in the late afternoon or during the night. For the duration of the hekuramou seance, the whole shapono – and for that matter the whole cosmos – becomes the 'shapori's playground' where he undergoes multiple transformations into hekura and performs various procedures or discloses various mythical episodes in front of community members, who either watch his performance or go about their normal daily routines.

Before each hekuramou session, the shapori sweeps the ground in front of his house to ensure there are no stones he could step on during his performance. He then paints his entire body with red ochre and puts on hekura adornments – feathers, armbands and a monkey tail around his head. Other co-participating shapori also adorn their bodies and sit around on logs chatting among themselves. During the session, they assist by commenting and confirming what the ancestors are revealing through the performing shapori. Other non-initiated co-participants sit quietly and watch the performance, each reacting to their own experience of it with awe, excitement and fear. Lasting up to an hour, each hekuramou session is unique, but display some repetitive patterns of various hekura manifestations and their mode of appearance. Upon inhaling epena snuff, the shapori sets in motion his performance by opening up 'the cosmic stage' in a specific manner to instigate an influx of imagery. Each shapori has his way of doing this. Ruweweriwë habitually commenced his sessions with slow and rhythmic body movements, accompanied by hekura sounds. To close each session, he terminates the flow of imagery by making a spiral movement with his index finger while uttering one final 'o tum!' sound, an act that resembles the song embodiment during initiation. I once observed several hekuramou sessions being carried out by a visiting shapori from Hapokashita-theri. Each time, he would finish his performance in a specific manner, by turning the palm of his hand toward the sky and making the final 'o tum!' sound.

Shapori carry out various types of defensive hekuramou activities within the confines of their shapono or in neighbouring and other allied shaponos. On such occasions, the visiting shapori often share skills with their host colleagues when they unite their hekura powers towards healing or harm doing or by simply displaying their hekura abilities. Shaporis' transformative capabilities combined with the remedial powers of their hekura helpers make their family members and the whole community dependant for protection and healing. On the intracommunal level, a shapori engages his personal hekura in different situations and for various tasks in both ritual and non-ritual contexts. A shapori has to face a wide array of duties and responsibilities towards his kin group, including: protecting people from intruding hekura during stormy weather, locating game during hunting activities, assisting during childbirth, giving names to children, recovering or repairing people's missing or damaged soul components, disseminating and preserving the ancestral knowledge through the enactment of various myths, executing various emergency types of operation on victims of hekura attacks, decontaminating sufferers' bodies from various poisonous substances and shawara sickness during epidemics or extracting magic thorns and arrows sent by hostile shapori.

A shapori frequently engages his hekura in 'detoxifying' activities by neutralising the effects of various poisonous substances introduced into an organism. On one occasion, a female visitor from Toritha-theri accidentally boiled and consumed the poisonous, bitter type of manioc known as *pei koko wayu*, which is almost indistinguishable from the more common, edible, sweet variety. She was vomiting and complaining of feeling sick and dizzy. Ruweweriwë quickly got up, sniffed some epena and summoned White-lipped Peccary Hekura Warëriwë. The hekura was attempting to stop the poison's effects and save the woman from dying by breaking up the poison, as the animal peccary would break up soil in search for food – with its tusks and feet. Next, the shapori transformed into Spider Monkey Hekura Pashoriwë and squeezed the poison out of the woman's body with his hands before throwing it far away in a southerly direction towards their Shamathari enemies. After about half an hour, the woman recovered. After the session, Arawë told me about his own unpleasant past experience of consuming the bitter manioc by accident. He sat down in his hammock watching the fire burning and suddenly felt very dizzy. The flame was circling in front of him and he felt short of breath. Ruweweriwë quickly intervened, the dizziness stopped and his breathing normalised. In another, similar example, in the early nineties, the shapori Makowë managed to save the eyesight of a young teacher, Juan Bosco, from Platanal after some soldiers from the Venezuelan National Guard – placed in the region for security reasons after Brazillian gold miners massacred sixteen Yanomami in the community of Hashimú – mixed ethyl alcohol with fermented fruit and gave it to some Yanomami men to drink. One Yanomami died and two went blind. Fortunately, Makowë managed to save Juan Bosco's eyesight by 'removing' the effects of the poison with his hands. Shapori sometimes carry out a similar kind of responsive action with their hands; they remove or 'cut' the effects of epena in cases where the snuff taker loses control. One of shaporis' roles is to provide assistance to women in labour. For the Yanomami, childbirth is a potentially risky undertaking, as it is fraught with the danger that some enemy shapori or wild forest spirit may attempt to cause harm to both mother and baby. In this instance, the shapori's role is to support and guide the baby's safe delivery with the help of his hekura. One night in Sheroana-theri, Ashi – the younger of the headman Maruwë's two wives – gave birth to a baby girl. She experienced an intensive and arduous labour until the early morning hours, often screaming out in pain and crying. During the delivery, Ruweweriwë was awake and attentive, lying in his hammock next to mine and quietly chanting. Whenever Ashi screamed the shapori's hekura reacted by making a zigzag with his index finger in the direction of Ashi's hammock, presumably in an attempt to ease her pain. Despite a difficult labour, the baby eventually arrived in the early morning hours without any complications.

In the existing Yanomami literature, there is a paucity of information on shapori involvement during childbirth. A Colombian missionary, Amparo Restrepo (1993: 36), recorded that in the case of a difficult childbirth, a Yanomami shapori intervenes by summoning a female tapir hekura, Shamariyoma, because this animal always bears its young without complication (see also Cocco 1972: 424). What the shapori actually does when there are complications during childbirth is not known, but an ethnographic example from Cuna in Panama may shed some light on this subject. In his famous essay 'The Effectiveness of Symbols', Levi-Strauss (1963: 186) re-examined a lengthy song of the Cuna shaman (originally published in 1947 by Wassen and Holmer) used to provide assistance to a woman in labour. The song describes the shaman's journey to the home of Muu, the power responsible for the creation and development of the foetus. The purpose of the journey is to retrieve the woman's vital principle or soul component, which has been captured by Muu in an action that has interfered with a normal delivery. 'The subject [of the song] is a dramatic struggle between [a shaman's] helpful and malevolent spirits for the reconquest of a soul' (ibid.: 192). The shaman's journey to find (and subsequently reinstall) the missing soul component is a common cosmological motif, and, in this case, the destination for the shaman is the pregnant woman's uterus. At the end of the song, after many obstacles and battles, the shaman manages to restore the woman's vital principle thus ensuring the successful delivery of her baby.

The loss of a vital principle is one of the most prevailing causes of illness among the Yanomami and other Amazonian ethnic groups. As mentioned previously, for the Yanomami, the main threat comes from *pore* (ghosts of the deceased) wandering around in the forest, or a soul-eating hekura, such as Ancestral Moon Periporiwë or Jaguar Hekura Ɨrariwë, among others. In Platanal, I once observed the shapori Makowë engaged in a long healing session to treat a three-month-old boy with a fever. The baby's mother was sitting on the ground holding the child in her arms. The house was full of people. All through the session, the shapori was singing and dancing vigorously, looking attentively in all directions and reacting to the smallest sound; he immediately reacted to my tape recorder clicking when it got to the end of the tape, despite the noise and being at quite a distance from me. His behaviour was inconsistent – one moment he was acting as hekura the next moment he seemed to be fully present and alert to the immediate surroundings. At one point, as one of his hekura was brushing the baby's body with his hands, Makowë's wife suddenly asked him if he could fetch some bananas from an elevated wooden platform. Makowë immediately stopped and climbed a ladder to grab a bunch of bananas before continuing with the healing session.

Not long into the séance, the shapori entered a trance and briefly observed the baby's body through the eyes of his assisting hekura before commencing the treatment. He grabbed the child's feet and slid both of his palms slowly up his body, passing the chest and head before moving them forward through the air and releasing a loud, explosive sound. He was now holding the invisible essence of the sickness in his hands and crouched down to release it into the ground. At that moment, Makowë announced that it was the ghost of an old woman (poreyoma) who had been responsible for making the boy sick by stealing his not yet fully formed soul component:

> It is pore!
> It [the child] is cold.
> It [the child] is turning red.
> Pore is doing bad things.
> She harmed the boy with her stick (shimo).

Evidently disturbed, the boy cried as his T-shirt was lifted off by the shapori, who then slowly squeezed it downwards with his hand. Makowë then summoned Hoashiriwë (White-faced Capuchin Monkey Hekura) and Spider Monkey Hekura Pashoriwë to attack the pore:

> I will break her [the pore] in half! [shouts Pashoriwë and tells another hekura in a high-pitched voice]: When she [pore] gets up, grab her by the arm.
> Pore, pore, yei, yei [the pore announces her presence].
> It is the pore of an old woman! [exclaims Makowë].
> Her house looks strange and ugly!
> Get her now, carefully [says hekura].

At that moment, Hoashiriwë grabbed the pore by her arm and Pashoriwë grabbed her by the waist. 'Uuhe, he ya eee!!!' the pore screamed in agony, and then dropped to the ground, crying and begging the two hekura for mercy: 'Older brother don't hurt me! Younger brother, it's me! Don't do anything bad to me!' The shapori then got up and declared: 'she will not steal people's souls any more! Kre, kre, kre ...' The hekura continued sliding his hands up and down the baby's body and the shapori declared: 'I can see the fire over there where Mothokariwë (Sun Hekura) lives!' He stopped for a few moments and took another large dose of hisiõmɨ snuff, commenting how he already felt its strong effects ('nomarayoma' lit. 'died'). Next, the shapori reapproached the boy to continue brushing and blowing into his tiny body before going into a corner of the house to vomit. He then lifted his head up and with a heavy, dramatic voice exclaimed: 'It is an old woman but she has got the Moon's fire (Peripo wakë). She looks strange and does a lot of damage!' At this point, the shapori recommenced dancing and singing the following song:

> An old woman remained alone.
> They [Hoashiriwë and Pashoriwë] left her.
> Where is she now?
> She has transformed into [a] termite nest.

Hekura continued treating the child: 'Kreee, shaaaa!!!' (sound of hekura while using the shapori's hand as a sword to slash the fever). 'Eeeee' (another hekura vomits). Makowë kept on brushing the child's body and blowing into it while the boy was crying. 'His liver is hot!' The shapori explained to the mother that the boy was sick because she had taken him with her into the forest where the ghost of the old woman had stolen the vital essence of his liver (pei ãmoku mɨ ãmo) and boiled it in water, which resulted in his body temperature rising. He also warned the mother that small children are an easy prey for pore or enemy hekura and, therefore, should stay inside the shapono. She did indeed admit that she had been to the forest to look for honey together with her baby. In continuation, Makowë transformed into Spider Monkey Hekura Pashoriwë and scooped with his hands a sample of pei puhi vital essence (as he later told me; see Chapter Three) from the baby's body and walked to the corner of the house where he examined it carefully. He was watching it, smelling it and listening to it, tasting it and trying to identify its content. He was quiet for a few seconds before his eyes lit up. With great confidence and a smile on his face, Makowë continued treating the child. He was apparently sucking the fever out of his body with his lips tightly sealed to the boy's skin. He was repeatedly walking over to the corner of the house to discharge the swallowed sickness substance by vomiting and coughing it up. At one point, he was moving his lips as if tasting something and then announced: 'Yes, it is true! It is something ripe. There is a fire circulating in the child's liver'. He now called the Hekura Õmãyãriwë,[1] who continued sucking the inner fire out of the child's body while complaining about the bitter taste of the fire smoke. At the very end, he victoriously announced that the bile (*pei ãmoku yori*) (later described as a bitter liquid) located in a small bag inside the boy's liver had finally ruptured.

The shapori's role as a defender of his kin group comes fully into play during stormy weather when the world is temporarily in a turbulent state and the affairs concerning hekura become rather chaotic. In good weather conditions shapori intentionally provoke and regulate the circulation of hekura through their ritual activities and during the initiation. On an experiential level, the movement of hekura in itself produces a current of air. Arawë frequently reported in his tutomou hekura-calling chants of feeling the breeze and swirls of air (*heãhãtu*) immediately before the arrival of a particular hekura. When a shapori evokes Wind Hekura Watoriwë, he has the ability to heal some ailments by blowing through or across the surface of a sick person's body. In turbulent weather conditions, the wind can cause an uncontrolled and dangerous movement of discarnate hekura by forcefully blowing them off their mountaintop habitats in which case they can often end up inside a shapono and cause havoc and panic among the inhabitants. But not all airflows are considered dangerous. Light wind is usually not deemed alarming. The most dangerous movements of air are considered to be the wind gusts that precede thunderstorms, which could transport hekura. These sudden, miniature whirlwinds that 'sneak into a shapono' lift the dust and dry leaves from the ground and slip furious hekura into a community. Many hostile shapori take advantage of this type of frenzied situation and send their hekura assistants with the wind to attack other communities. For this reason, whenever a storm is approaching and the wind starts to blow, inside a shapono there is a state of emergency, with shapori warning women and children to stay away from the central area and hide under the shapono's roof until the storm weakens. Meanwhile, the men – led by the shapori – form a circle around the central area, with each one standing in front of their respective hearth and shouting and waving a machete or wooden stick to scare off the possible intruding hekura. The non-initiated men assist the shapori by performing a mock battle with the invisible enemy, hoping that their actions will frighten and chase potential intruders away. During this display of bravery, they often become euphoric without any visible traces of fear. Throughout my fieldwork, especially during the wet season (from November to April) when storms take place on a daily basis, the Sheroana and Mahekoto-theri shapori battled face to face with invading hekura that had been blown by a strong wind from their abodes located on top of the nearby Sheroroi and Mahekoto peaks. During one such stormy episode, Ruweweriwë summoned some of his most powerful hekura and started swinging his machete in front of him while shouting at the trespassers, ordering them to stay away from the community and keep on flowing with the wind. To drive them out, he called Motoremariwë or Whirlwind Hekura for help by chanting the following song:

> Motoremariwë will launch me to another place.
> The immortal earth is trembling from the gale.
> Ha, motorere, motorere, motorere…
> Motoremariwë is coming from the Motorere Mountain.
> That is where his house is located.
> Motoremariwë is singing.
> When he comes, children of the trees will become afraid.
> When he comes, they will run away from him!

After assuming the identity of Motoremariwë, the shapori kept turning his right arm in circles to spin the intruders from the shapono and send them elsewhere.

The Dialectics between Defensive and Offensive Hekuramou

Sometimes the shapori has to engage in a direct battle with unwanted hekura intruders. At other times, despite the shapori's watchful eye, the invading hekura manage to attach themselves to children, which results in death if the shapori does not intervene. One afternoon, soon after a thunderstorm had passed, Arawë's little daughter suddenly rolled out of her hammock and walked towards the shapono's central area, seemingly frightened and confused. She was deathly pale and appeared unwell. When she began to cry, Arawë immediately jumped out of his hammock and went to brush her body with his hands. But her condition rapidly deteriorated and the situation reached a critical point when the girl started to struggle for breath. Her mother and other women were weeping while anxiously watching the little girl's struggle. At that moment Ruweweriwë intervened and joined Arawë's efforts, and for the next hour or so the two shapori fought to save the girl. In the middle of the session, Ruweweriwë announced that the shapori by the nickname Mamiki shihitima ('the one whose toes are itchy') from the community of Warapana-Nasikipiwei-theri near Mavaca was attempting to strangle the girl. During the storm, he had used the sound of thunder to bridge the distance between the two communities, then had quickly located his victim and invaded her body with the intention of strangling her with his hekura. At that precise moment, the girl showed the first signs of feeling unwell. Both Arawë and Ruweweriwë confronted the intruder directly. At first, Arawë attempted to do it alone but being recently initiated he did not have the required experience. Ruweweriwë quickly took over after realising what had been happening. He transformed into Sloth Ancestor Ihamariwë to loosen the hekura's grip and save the girl from suffocating. Later, he told me that this particular hekura uses his claws to grasp an intruder in the same way a sloth will grasp the tree trunk when climbing a tree. Referring to Chapter Three, in primordial times Sloth Ancestor killed the runaway Opossum culprit by climbing the liana and cutting it off with his teeth. Ihamariwë also embodied the hekura path and corporeal shapono into Arawë's body. When the intruding hekura's internal grip had finally loosened up, Ruweweriwë assumed the identity of Spider Monkey Hekura Pashoriwë in an attempt to literally squeeze the aggressor out with his strong hands. Meanwhile, Arawë was trying to make his daughter breathe more regularly by, as he put it, 'bringing it from the stomach upwards towards the mouth and then out through to the sky where the house of breath (mishiãki) is located'. He then summoned some of his hekura assistants to bring new breath from afar and restore the girl's breathing.

Children are the most frequent targets of hekura attacks committed by enemy shapori, but sometimes a more powerful practitioner can strike from a distance a less experienced shapori with the intention to hurt him or even kill him. This is allegedly what happened to Arawë three weeks after his daughter was hit by the hekura. According to Ruweweriwë, he was attacked from the distance by an enemy shapori from the community of Sejal. As a result of this nearly fatal hekura attack, Arawë almost stopped breathing and temporarily lost his corporeal shapono together with the watoshe crown and the bulk of his recently embodied hekura. At the end of this terrifying experience, Ruweweriwë managed to reinstall Arawë's missing hekura components and restore his breathing, thus saving his life.

On that particular day, Arawë had commenced his routine midday hekuramou practice somewhat later than usual. While singing and dancing, he suddenly stopped and touched his chest. Evidently disturbed, he sat on the ground. Ruweweriwë, who was watching him, leaped from his hammock and quickly scanned the horizon for enemy hekura. He then walked up to Arawë and brushed his body a few times with his hands. The new shapori felt instantly relieved and continued singing and dancing for a few moments, thereupon he started to complain of feeling unwell and not being able to breathe. Ruweweriwë took him inside the shapono and instructed him to sit in a hammock. For the next few moments, he carefully observed Arawë from head to toe and touched his chest. Suddenly, he announced that a shapori from the community of

Sejal had invaded Arawë's body. The situation was rapidly deteriorating. Terrified, Arawë's nostrils began to flare and he was screaming while anxiously tapping the ground with his foot. One moment he was complaining again of not being able to breathe, while the next moment he was making bird-like sounds, spitting and looking around with hatred in his eyes. Ruweweriwë and his son-in-law Kiawë quickly lifted Arawë's arms while he was gasping for air and screaming: 'Mɨshɨã a kuami! Aaaiiii! Ipa mɨshɨãkɨ horemou' ('My breath is gone! [I am dead], I can't breathe anymore!'). He shouted in panic that his Jaguar hekura crown (watoshe mashaema) had just flown away. Ruweweriwë sniffed more epena and went to the shapono's central area, singing and dancing to regenerate his hekura powers. In the meantime, Arawë had announced that his bodily shapono had flown away. Ruweweriwë quickly smeared a gluey liquid from green plantain peel around his face and attached some white cotton to it. Transformed into Ancestral Jaguar Ɨrariwë, he went to search for the missing crown and after finding it, placed it back on Arawë's head. Next, he summoned Sloth Hekura Ihamariwë, who managed to bring back the lost shapono and reinstall it in Arawë's chest. Finally, the master shapori brought back several hekura who had escaped from Arawë's body. I asked Arawë, later, to describe his experience and he said that his breath had literally moved from his chest into his upper arms, threatening to slip out through his hands. For that reason, Ruweweriwë and his son-in-law had been holding Arawë's arms high up in the air, thus trying to prevent the breath from leaving the body. 'I was so close to dying at that moment', Arawë whispered solemnly.

The impact of this hekura attack was so severe that it caused structural havoc in Arawë's recently formed cosmic body. Ruweweriwë told me that sometimes even the Hekura Mountain can shatter and lead to an exodus of hekura from their host's chest. After this incident, Arawë became very ill. He stopped taking epena and practising shaporimou for some time. Day after day he was resting in his hammock, looking pale and complaining of an excruciating body ache, especially in his chest, back and neck. His throat was very sore and each time he breathed in, he felt a sharp pain in his chest. He would often squat next to the fire to warm up because he was almost constantly trembling from an inner chill (si sãihõu).[2] Eventually, he started taking a pinch or two of epena every now and then whenever Ruweweriwë was performing and would just sit quietly. I asked him once why he did not attempt to do shaporimou, and he replied that he felt 'drunk from epena' just like all other non-initiated Yanomami. He temporarily lost the ability to transform into his hekura. Eventually, he started singing quietly his hekura songs, and slowly started getting up and walking up and down. It was approximately two months before he fully recovered and started practising shaporimou again.

Every so often during Arawë's recovery, Ruweweriwë engaged his hekura helpers in healing or 'repairing' Arawë's damaged body. Each time he would first carefully observe Arawë's upper torso and touch it with his hands before attempting a cure. Part of the shapori's treatment consisted of normalising Arawë's breathing by throwing away the damaged breath essence (*pei mɨshɨã*) and bringing in a new breath essence (in the same way Arawë did with his daughter). Additionally, Ruweweriwë had to replace Arawë's damaged throat essence (*pei matono mɨ ãmo*) with a new essence. He had instructed Arawë to sit on the ground just like during his initiation and then started dancing and singing about Arawë's 'broken throat' and how his hekura were bringing a new one. Soon, he embodied the throat essence and then took on the identity of Thora Hekura (yopo inhaling tube) to mend Arawë's overall corporeal vital essence (pei puhi), pointing the receiving end of an actual tube towards Arawë's big toes where during his initiation the bodily hekura path entrance had been opened. The hekura then slid the tube up both of Arawë's legs and across his upper torso before finishing up at his throat area. Let us recall how during the initiation this particular hekura was responsible for 'repairing' Arawë's shattered body after each episode of quasi-death by the incoming hekura. Arawë told me that afterwards he felt much better indeed. On one occasion, the visiting shapori Shawarawë from the neighbouring community of Toritha-theri also assisted in healing by sliding a blanket over Arawë's body and collecting the illness with it. Despite these efforts, weeks later the new shapori was still complaining of 'feeling weak' with a throbbing pain in his head.

These cases of hekura attacks that were aimed at Arawë and his daughter, from his point of view and Ruweweriwë's response, are examples of defensive shaporimou activities focusing on the victims of these assaults. This typical intercommunal situation also occurred with Neboisa's son, who died as a result of a hekura attack executed by the remote Shamathari shapori, which I described in Chapter Five. I will now present two ethnographic examples of assault shamanism or offensive shaporimou activity from the perspective of the predator shapori – that is, I will focus on the act of ritual killing. The first example is a retaliatory magical assault carried out by Ruweweriwë disguised as Moon Hekura Periporiwë on a boy purportedly from Narimipiwei-theri. It happened a week after the boy died in Sheroana-theri (see Chapter Five). After the session, Neboisa and his wife were weeping, evidently reliving the death of their own beloved son. For me, it was rather peculiar that Ruweweriwë carried out this ritual homicide while the boy's family was still mourning his death. From my own perspective it was insensitive but then again I thought: 'Hey this is their world!' Ruweweriwë commenced the session by taking large doses of hisiõmɨ snuff together with other co-participants sitting around in a semicircle. After a few moments, the shapori summoned Witiwitimiriwë or Hekura of Swallow-tailed Kite (elanoides forficatus) and started circling around the shapono's central area with his arms spread, stopping at intervals to look into the distance with his hand above his eyebrows to locate his victim; this bird is renowned for its excellent eyesight and tends to glide in circles high up in the sky in search of prey. Its hekura counterpart likewise has the ability to look far into the distance, thus facilitating the shapori to locate his victim. At one point, he crouched and leaned forwards, almost touching the ground with his forehead; his body was shaking and wobbling, losing all its firmness and natural stability. He then stood up, arms crossed and eyes rolling, and with a deep, hoarse voice he announced: 'Peripo, Peripo!' Now transformed into Periporiwë, the shapori was slowly encircling the shapono, preying on his victim. After making the full circle around the shapono's central area, he then stopped and spoke in a child's voice: 'Nape, nape ya amishi' ('Mother, I am thirsty'), while leaning against the house post. He then sat on the ground and repeated the same phrase a few more times. This entire act of embodying the victim – purportedly manifested through the shapori – indicated that the attacked boy was obviously scared and confused and with fast and shallow breathing. He was looking around, touching his body in discomfort and calling his mother. The shapori then made a movement as if ripping his own skin open with his hands. He placed around his neck what to us onlookers looked like an invisible rope and then strangled himself with one energetic pull upwards. His body dropped lifeless to the ground before he immediately got up and started weeping. A female voice spoke through him: 'pushika, pushika' ('my child'). Periporiwë had allegedly strangled the child, whose mother was now mourning his death. The boy's behaviour during his last moments – as it was revealed to us onlookers through the shapori – displayed striking resemblance to Neboisa's son, who had died one week earlier. Both victims were scared and confused, gasping for air; both were thirsty and calling their mothers. In both cases the mothers were crying, albeit in the second instance the lamenting mother was revealed through the shapori. In another similar example of assault shamanism, demonstrated in Chagnon's controversial documentary film *Magical Death* (1973), a group of Shamathari shapori from the community of Mishimishimapowei-theri allegedly carried out an act of collective ritual paedophagy of the Mahekoto-theri children. When they reached a state of trance they began to embody their child victims in order to 'eat their souls' akin to Ruweweriwë, who became the little boy in order to strangle him.

My second case of assault shamanism occurred in Platanal, where three shapori led by Enano combined their efforts to kill a person from a distant Shamathari community. This group hekuramou session took place one afternoon in Enano's house in front of numerous onlookers. The shapori first painted their faces with red ochre and took their turns inhaling epena snuff. Next, they crouched in a circle facing each other while singing and swaying their bodies rhythmically from side to side, resembling the movement of a pendulum. After a few moments, Enano got up and walked to the corner of the house. He fetched a wooden stick, one end of which was adorned with a white feather to which a specific ritual meaning was assigned, as I will clarify in continuation. Enano placed the stick on the ground next to the other two shapori. They all continued chanting for a little while before abruptly stopping. During a few tense moments of silence, Enano picked up the stick, drew it to his mouth, 'swallowed the feather' and instantly vomited. His shapori colleagues repeated the act. At that moment, Enano's son-in-law Jacinto whispered in my ear that the shapori were eating the victim's soul in a distant community; it was an act of reprisal for the Mahekoto-theri man who purportedly died from a shapori's attack from that same community. Only the three participating shapori knew the true identity of their victim, and the feather attached to the stick was a tangible manifestation of that person's soul. Jacinto was saying that at the beginning of the session, Enano journeyed in spirit to the community in question to locate their victim then returned and placed the stick with the feather on the ground. In continuation, all three shapori departed their bodies and arrived there in spirit in order to fetch and eat the victim's soul. Enano managed to capture the victim's soul essence and trap it inside the feather while the other two shapori were there to ensure the action went smoothly without any interference from other shapori. Jacinto said that they were consuming the victim's soul there while simultaneously 'eating' the feather in front of us. Thus, the feather, as indicated earlier, was the essential component in the ritual and served as a vessel for the captured soul. At the end, I asked him if he believed that the victim had really died. He nodded his head affirmatively and without any hesitation responded that there was no doubt about it. The main reason why he had come to the session was his curiosity– he wanted to see if the shapori were really going to perform the ritual killing. He admitted that in the beginning he had been sceptical about it. He also said that he was once initiated as shapori but stopped practising. Nevertheless, he had not lost the ability to experientially 'connect' and check if a ritual act was authentic. 'During the session, I felt a distinctive smell of flesh and blood in the room' said Jacinto and continued: 'It was so strong and disgusting that at one stage I felt nauseous to the extent that I nearly left the house'.

Body Intrusion and the Dynamics of the Cosmic Flow

The above examples of combative and curative aspects of Yanomami shamanism demonstrate that magical practices and the accompanying social experience of violence, sickness and death are first and foremost embodied practices (see Kapferer 1997, 2002) with the body being a locus of magical action, involving the victim and several shamans. The primary power of Yanomami shapori is their ability to access the interiority of the bodies of others with the help of their assisting hekura, whether for healing or harm-doing purposes. When the shapori's cosmic body is invoked during a trance, the interiority of a person's body 'opens up' and becomes externalised as it fuses with the intentionality of the shapori's consciousness. In other words, during a healing or harming session, the shapori is capable of accessing human bodies with the help of his personal hekura, by either occupying them directly, as in the aforementioned cases of hekura attacks, or by detecting and extracting – again via his hekura – shawara sickness, an object of witchcraft or other invading hekura. This way, the practising shapori discovers the 'body fault' or the intruder through the work of his hekura, or he becomes the intruder himself. As mentioned, in the case of predatory shamanism, shapori prefer babies and small children as their potential victims rather than adults, because children are easy targets, as their souls are unstable and not yet fully formed.

In the previously mentioned Cuna shaman's chant, the shaman through his spirit assistants is able to enter the pregnant woman's vagina and search out the lost soul component inside her uterus. He can accomplish this by means of his 'illuminating sight', granted by his tutelary spirits. During his mission, the presumed location of the interiority of the woman's body merges with the exteriority of the world as her pains 'assume cosmic proportions' (Levi-Strauss 1963: 193). Hence, the woman's uterus becomes equivalent to the cosmos and is depicted in the song as the world populated with threatening monsters, disease-bearing animals and numerous mountains and paths upon which the shaman's spirits march. Yanomami shapori acquire through initiations a hekura sight, which goes beyond human capabilities. This particular modality of consciousness allows them to access the interiority of other bodies and detect the cause of a malady in a manner similar to X-ray vision, or look into the distance to locate potential victims. A shapori is capable of accomplishing this only because he is 'already dead'; he can transform into a multiplicity of hekura spirits and look through their eyes. He is simultaneously one and many – a fractal multiple one with a dual modality of consciousness of himself and of a being, which he incarnates. But the embodied hekura also forms part of a multiplicity. When a shaman summons a particular spirit and fully becomes that spirit, the state of that being is already multiple so that the shaman in fact becomes part of that multiplicity rather than being possessed by a singular being (Gow 2001). In the context of a curative ritual, a multiplicity of alternating hekura work together as a team through a shapori. The detection of a particular affliction by the shapori's auxiliary hekura and their follow-up curative responses unfold automatically, and recently initiated shapori do not have much control over this process. In other words, practical knowledge about the nature of a malady and the appropriate remedial action to take comes to him in a direct, experiential manner through his hekura and he is not able to reflect upon and decide on what course of action to take, at least at the beginning of his 'career'. The flow of consciousness, in this instance, becomes one continuous, unbroken experiential movement of a fluid transformation of imagery as one hekura gives way to another, each armed with their special powers and abilities of the particular species that they represent. In due course, when a shapori has become more acquainted with his personal hekura and their abilities, he will gain mastery over his practice and will be capable of selectively summoning the assisting hekura most suitable for the task at hand.

In the aforementioned example of Makowë treating a sick boy whose soul essence was stolen by the ghost of an old woman, the shapori assumed the identity of Spider Monkey Hekura Pashoriwë, who was repeatedly taking a segment of the patient's vital essence (pei puhi) and examining it thoroughly. In this instance, the monkey hekura used his guiding senses in the same way that the animal uses his, thus he investigated its appearance, its hot and cold properties and examined its taste, smell and other qualities. The shapori received direct clues about the nature of the affliction in any trace of a bad smell or taste. At the beginning of the session, Makowë commented that the child felt cold while his hekura helpers were brushing his body. He explained that if the damaged corporeal puhi feels cold but the person's body temperature has increased, it is a sign that a ghost (pore) is involved. The conclusion was that the pore took the vital essence of the child's liver and cooked it in a pot. As a result, the boy's body temperature increased, giving rise to the imagery of a circling fire. At the same time, the ghost's action made the boy's overall vital inner body substance (pei puhi) cold. Makowë also commented that if the vital principle that permeates the physical body feels hot (with or without a fever) it is a sign that the person is contaminated with shawara. Besides the sufferer's body, his or her items of clothing (e.g., a T-shirt or a skirt) will also contain traces of illness. Makowë approached the boy's T-shirt in the same way he approached his body, by 'squeezing' the essence from it and examining its invisible properties. When Arawë got sick after the hekura attack, the visiting shapori Shawarawë used my blanket to brush Arawë's body and thus 'collect' the sickness. We shall see in Chapter Eight that during their initial contacts with 'the outside world', the Yanomami identified the foreigners' clothing with shawara diseases.

Once the shapori's assisting hekura successfully determine the cause of an affliction, they proceed with curing the malady. When Makowë's monkey hekura identified a ghost of an old woman as being responsible for the child's illness, other hekura proceeded immediately with the cure by 'squeezing out' the damaged vital essence in the same continuous manner as in the aforementioned case of Ruweweriwë and his intervention to save a woman's life after she ingested the poisonous, bitter manioc. Ruweweriwë, however, did not have to resort to finding the cause of her condition as it was already known. Instead, he proceeded immediately with the cure, assuming the identity of Warëriwë or Hekura of White-lipped Peccary. Once the poison was torn to pieces, another hekura automatically took over and continued the treatment by squeezing the poisonous residues out of the woman's body. Recall also when Arawë's little daughter was attacked by an enemy shapori after a thunderstorm; Ruweweriwë summoned the Sloth Hekura Ihamariwë in order to 'loosen' the grip of the intruding hekura; it was gripping the same way that an animal sloth does when it climbs a tree – by hooking onto the tree trunk with its long claws. Once the intruding hekura lost its 'inner grip', another hekura took over and proceeded to extract the aggressor out of the child's body.

Each hekura have specific abilities according to their nature and use distinct healing techniques. For example, Yaoriwë (Ocelot) and Ɨrariwë (Jaguar) 'tear' the sickness into pieces with their claws, akin to Warëriwë (White-lipped Peccary) when breaking the poison with his tusks and trotters. Others like Pashoriwë (Spider Monkey) and Krukuriwë (Black Cougar) act in the manner of a sonar device or radar when detecting sickness inside the body. Spider Monkey Hekura uses his strong sense of smell to 'sniff out' the affliction, while Black Cougar Hekura relies on his sensitive hearing ability to detect the sickness. Sometimes shapori summon Pashoriwë to extract foreign objects introduced into victims' bodies by the enemy shapori, because the monkey has a good grip, thus enabling shapori to grab the object and remove it. Dog Hekura, known as Hiima Yawari, is a good watchdog. He alerts the shapori to approaching danger, that is – enemy hekura, in the same manner that village dogs become disturbed when visitors from another shapono suddenly arrive. In Chapter Seven, we will see how in one of his healing sessions the shapori Enano from Platanal summoned Yarusheriwë or Hekura Ancestor of the South American Coati (nasua nasua solitaria) – which has the appearance of a fox crossed with a racoon – to help him track down a missing vital principle, because the coati animal has the ability to locate its prey by tracking it down. Shapori also employ this hekura for the treatment of snake bites (Cocco 1972: 404). Yet other hekura are specialised in soothing, for example, Watoriwë (Wind), who is engaged towards the end of the healing session to blow across the body's surface. On several occasions, I observed shapori treating people suffering from muscle cramps (*wayuhi*) or fever with Hetumisiriwë (Sky Hekura) by sending rain on various body parts to relieve them. Frog Hekura Preyoma similarly alleviates heightened body temperature by spraying cool water over the sick person (ibid.: 405).

Phenomenologically speaking, for shapori, various forms of illness consist of a spirit substance that has a certain existential 'weight' and as such, it can be manipulated, captured or inserted. As we have seen, shapori draw out sickness through their hekura helpers either with their hands or by sucking and vomiting it out. Ruweweriwë once compared the extraction of sickness with his hands to 'scooping water from the creek'. At the moment when shapori vis-à-vis his hekura detect the nature of a particular affliction, he in fact fully experiences the symptoms of that malady. For Ruweweriwë, shawara illness appears as a kind of mist that saturates the whole being, while fever takes on the form of a circulating fire. To cure someone, the shapori first has to transfer the sickness agent from the victim's body into his own before finally expelling it. In cases of possession by enemy hekura, a shapori is able to detect its presence inside a person's body and discover its identity by momentarily merging with him or her. In this instance, the successful expulsion of the intruding hekura would depend on the shapori's personal experience and his hekura powers; he may be killed in the process of casting out the invading hekura if the possessing entity is more powerful than him. Let us recall how Arawë gave up on treating the dying boy when he realised that the intruding hekura was more powerful than him.

Upon extracting the sickness agent from the affected body, a shapori customarily sends it to the subterranean Amahiri if not towards their Shamathari enemies. When the shapori 'catapults' the sickness agent, he follows its trajectory with his arm pointing in the direction of its ultimate 'landing' site. When the expelled sickness finally reaches its destination, the shapori utters one final 'tuummm!!!' – an onomatopoeic rendering of the sound of the sickness 'landing'. Freed from the burden of the extracted sickness, the shapori repeats the act until the affected body is utterly purged of sickness. In cases where the shapori swallows the malady and subsequently expels it through vomiting, he will summon, in most cases, Anaconda Ancestor Wãikõyãriwë, because this particular hekura swallows and vomits sickness in the same way that the snake regurgitates its prey. The act of vomiting becomes the vomiting of one's own incorporated contents. Finally, as our ethnographic examples demonstrate, sometimes shapori have to repair the damage caused to an affected soul component or replace it with a new one. Recall how Ruweweriwë managed to restore Arawë's breathing by bringing in 'new breath' from afar, before replacing the damaged vital essence of the victim's throat (*matono mɨ ãmo*) with the healthy essence. Arawë had to employ the same technique on his daughter, who suffered a hekura attack.

In the same manner that the defensive shamanistic activities involve the two phases of diagnosis and subsequent cure, assault shamanism generally consists of two subsequent steps: surveillance of the terrain to detect the potential victim, and the follow-up attack. In the aforementioned example, Ruweweriwë first journeyed in spirit to the intended destination to locate the chosen victim. Upon returning to the Sheroana-theri locale he assumed the identity of Periporiwë (Moon) – whose specialty is eating children's delicate souls – and then attacked a boy. When I asked him to describe his journey, he said it was like looking at a photo (noreshi). Likewise, when the three shapori from Platanal intended to kill the person from a distant community, Enano first journeyed to the location to pin down the victim and then together with his colleagues terminated him.

During the killing, the somatic space of other people's bodies is accessible to the predator shapori in the same way the interiority of the human body opens up to the shapori involved in the healing act. If the intruder is a hekura/shapori, when they are detected, the shapori who undertakes a countermeasure merges with the intruding shapori by assimilating his hekura with the intruding one, becoming him or her. What follows is a direct clash between the two shapori, and their experience and power determine if the victim will live or die. Spiritual battles between rival shamans are well-known and a widespread phenomenon across the world (e.g., Riboli and Torri 2013; Whitehead and Wright 2004). It is often assumed that during a hekura assault, the shapori always guides his hekura remotely to take action. However, in most cases, when the shapori 'sends' his hekura he is in fact that hekura. The ritual action thus takes place simultaneously in two different locations – which is one of those shadowy, unexplained areas that modern science still finds difficult to understand, articulate and accept. However, the phenomenon of bilocation or multilocation, whereby a person is situated in two different places at the same time is common not only in shamanism but in many other mystical and religious traditions (McGovern 2007). Rasmussen (1979), for example, writes that during one particular shamanistic seance, the Inuit shaman was simultaneously in his dwelling and at the bottom of the ocean as a female spirit of the sea. In our example, while Ruweweriwë was physically present in Sheroana-theri during his ritual hekura assault, upon reaching a state of trance he invaded the victim's body as cannibalistic Periporiwë, while simultaneously the victim was manifested through his own body. Not only was the frightened boy's death acted out in front of us but the victim's mother was crying through the shapori after the boy allegedly died. At the moment of the boy's death, Ruweweriwë, who was strangling himself in front of us, also died or experienced the victim's death as his body collapsed to the ground. In the same manner, from the point of view of bilocation, we can assume that in the case of Neboisa's son, an enemy shapori was inside his body while at the same time presumably executing a ritual in his own community. We could only speculate if at that very moment the onlookers in that community were witnessing a victim's death through their shapori just like we observed with Ruweweriwë's performance.

What motivates a shaman to commit an offensive act? The primary motif is vengeance for the previous attack or a competition with other shamans. Evidently, assault shamanism involves negative exchange and reciprocity. The shapori from the Upper Orinoco River region are engaged against their distant enemies in perpetual cycles of tit-for-tat revenge and magical assaults. In this sense, this 'supernatural warfare' involves not only individual fates but also broader community relations. While offensive acts of assault shamanism are clearly hostile and motivated primarily by vengeance and rivalry, in some instances these malignant activities are driven by meat-hungry (*naiki*), cannibalistic hekura spirits demanding human souls. Although shapori intentionally engage in bellicose activities, sometimes they must kill to appease the ancestral spirits, thus sparing the lives of the shapori's kin. This is reflected in shamans' songs. For example, on one occasion Ruweweriwë called Vulture Hekura Watupariwë, describing him through the song as being dangerous and meat hungry. That same night in the ritual he allegedly devoured a soul component (*pei mɨ ãmo*) of a girl in a distant community to appease this particular hekura. On another occasion in Platanal, Enano was telling his incorporated spirit helpers to get up from their hammocks, announcing through song that the meat-hungry Periporiwë (Moon) had arrived; he was angry, craving human flesh and refused to leave. To appease him and prevent him from snatching someone's soul, Enano had to seize a soul from a distant village in in the guise of the same Moon Hekura. To maintain a cosmic balance, the shapori has to satisfy their cravings; otherwise the spirits become a threat to his community. In a similar act of sacrifice Whitehead (2002) writes that *kanaimà* ritual killers of the Guyana highlands commit acts of murder to appease the Lord Jaguar and his cravings.

Shaporimou and Intersubjective Knowledge Diffusion

The Yanomami practice of shaporimou is a totalising system of knowledge and power[3] whereby shapori, through their personal experiences, continually contribute to the intensification of Yanomami collective imagery. This, in turn, generates and influences both directly and indirectly Yanomami cultural beliefs and defines their reality. Shapori are capable of accessing knowledge beyond the horizon of immediate human perception and this knowledge is shared with others intersubjectively and discursively within the context of group shaporimou sessions. As a system of intersubjective diffusion of practical knowledge and cultural lore, the practice of shaporimou unfolds simultaneously on various levels. First and foremost, knowledge dissemination occurs between the shapori and their knowledgeable personal hekura. The shapori's cosmic body is their headquarters. Each shapori constitutes a distinct microcosmic totality, coexisting alongside other shapori and their respective bodily systems of personal hekura. The second level thus involves the interaction between multitudes of shapori within the transpersonal field of intrapsychic horizons of shared self-consciousness. Each shapori participates through his hekuramou activities in the sphere of conscious intersubjective relations with other shapori, mediated by their hekura and the epena snuff. They affect each other in a sphere of shared or overlapping modes of consciousness. And finally, each shapori eventually becomes custodian of the mythological lore, which is passed on to them directly from their ancestral hekura. This ancestral knowledge continuously being generated out of the collective imagery, is revealed and transmitted via shapori to other co-participants and, indirectly, to the rest of the community during group myth-enacting shaporimou sessions. A shapori may also reenact a specific mythical episode for healing purposes. In Chapter Two I discussed how various mythical events are situated within the realm of original, pre-cosmic wholeness known as the epoch of the ancestors (no patapi tëhë). During myth-enacting shaporimou sessions this primordial condition becomes fully accessible through the shapori. The primal, mythical dimension unfolds within the ritual context of group shaporimou sessions and fully comes into being as an all-embracing horizon of consciousness. Myth in its living form is not simply a story but a lived experience of primeval reality. Nor is myth a mere symbolic representation of something other than itself but '... a direct expression of its subject matter' (Malinowski 1954: 101). Primordial reality runs parallel to present reality – it is always there, ready to be incarnated; to spring out of a primal flux of the original wholeness. The practical significance of the overall cyclical patterns of myth re-enactments is that they enable the recreation of a primordial event in the present day. We may say that linear time in the given context is temporarily altered to a 'timeless' pattern of primordial, ritual time. Cosmic forces are thus enabled to spill into the flow of time, saturating the present with primordial powers. 'Myth-time is a discontinuous time, a repeated "now", not a duration, but an actualisation which proceeds by leaps from one "now" to another "now"' (Dardel 1984: 231).This 'now' of the myth is a dynamic, ever-present modality of consciousness in flux manifested and fully actualised through hekuramou seances. Through song and dance, the acting shapori and his personal hekura open up the experiential realm of myth to other co-participants and, indirectly, to the rest of the community.

> Ritual brings the creative events of the beginning of time to life and enables them to be repeated here and now, in the present. The ordinary reality of everyday life recedes and is superseded by the reality of ritual drama. What was once possible and operative in the beginning of time becomes possible once more and can exert its influence anew. (Honko 1984: 51)

The humanity implicit in the original primordial condition suggests that the primal realm of myth is not a metastructure that existed and continues to exist outside of the human body and consciousness. Primordial ancestors or archaic humans are hekura and it is only through hekura of the living shapori and their subjective experiences that mythical narratives of the origin of things can be passed on from generation to generation. Recall that the moon was a hekura living in the shapori's chest before he transformed into the celestial body. Omawë inhaled epena and underwent transformations just like present day shapori. The knowledge of creation is revealed to others through shaporis' direct experiences. Thus, we may say that myths are a depository of a preserved collective memory of shaporis' subjective experiences passed down through generations. Events in mythical narratives describe ordinary situations mixed with extraordinary circumstances that can nowadays only be fully manifested and experienced during shamanistic rituals. In many myths, there is a reference to epena intake and shamanism, which implicitly indicates the ever-present fine line between the primordial and post-primordial condition of previous generations of Yanomami. Primordium is 'an absolute past ...which was never present, and which therefore never passes, just as the present never ceases to pass ...' (Viveiros de Castro 2004). Pre-cosmic runs parallel to cosmic; they are, in fact, two sides of the same coin. Similarly, Mythical events contain a blend of historical and mythical components. They are complementary and not antithetical; 'myth is not static: it consumes history and may be consumed by it' (Chernela 1988: 35).

Before each myth enactment, a shapori and his co-participants must take epena. Afterwards, the shapori starts singing and dancing with his arms raised high until eventually reaching a trance. At that moment, he becomes the focal point of a dramatic, stage-like performative spectacle during which he establishes a close rapport with the spectators. They make frequent comments; at times confirming the shapori's statements or engaging him in dialogue. The mythic narratives contain many comic situations, which provoke outbursts of laughter, exclamation and expressions of awe within the audience. There is a constant channelling of interpersonal communication and interchange between the co-participants and the shapori. But, myth in its living form is much more than just a mere communication. Others are more or less familiar with the mythic plot. They are not just passive receptors of the mythic narrative but active co-participants. A shapori does not enact various mythical episodes personally (by himself). During the myth-enacting performance, the shapori's body becomes a vessel for the manifestation of a multiplicity of hekura, who directly channel various mythical episodes through him to others. An otherwise concealed primordial mythical dimension unveils in front of the spectators; everything is vividly expressed through the shapori's voice and an array of gestures and facial expressions as he impersonates successive manifestations of primordial ancestors in various ordinary and extraordinary situations. His body is decorated with various hekura ornaments and ancestral designs. Throughout the spectacle, the shapori sweats copiously and repeatedly takes new doses of epena snuff. If a segment of a myth is related to killing or hunting, the shapori may take a machete or bow and arrow to demonstrate it.

As the participants' subjectivly open up to the field of action during the shapori's performance, various mythical happenings become the lived experiences of everyone present and the whole group eventually becomes actively engaged in a collective trance led by the acting shapori. Shirokogoroff described this phenomenon of collective trance among the Tungus people of central Siberia:

> [T]he spirit acts together with the audience and this is felt by everyone. The state of many participants is now near to that of the shaman himself, and only a strong belief that when the shaman is there the spirit may only enter him, restrains the participants from being possessed in mass by the spirit. (cited in Lewis 1988: 826)

The people in the audience eventually become attuned to one another and the shifting boundary between subjectivities and physical bodies experientially appear to diminish and merge into an all-encompassing modality of collective consciousness. Whatever the shapori is doing – with his body twisting and the rhythm of his breathing changing with the sensation of the unfolding of some mythical drama– everything is lived and directly experienced by others. Thus, everyone who participates in the hekura milieu has the opportunity to receive the ancestral knowledge directly from the hekura and grasp the message of the mythic narrative (Lizot 1974: 8). Excluding the performing shapori, the main difference between the shapori and non-shapori spectators is that the former are more relaxed because they are already accustomed to metamorphosis into various hekura. During the session, non-shapori generally respond to various situations with a mixture of thrill and disquietude, with a constant dose of mild to severe anxiety. By contrast, most shapori spectators take their experiences somewhat lightly because they have already overcome their fear of hekura during their initiation. In some cases even initiated shapori are afraid of hekura, which can lead a shapori to abandon hekura practices. One such example was Enano's (now deceased) brother, Waraima, from Platanal, who preferred to spectate.

Notes

1. The Yanomami generally associate disease and death with bitterness. Õmãyãriwë is the ancestral hekura representative of Õmãyãri beings, who are associated, amongst other things, with rainbows, bitterness and bile (Lizot 2004: 283–84).
2. The term *wahati* is used to signify feeling physically cold while si sãihõu is used when the cold is felt to come from within (an inner chill).
3. I use here the concept of 'power' first and foremost in reference to a shapori's practical powers manifested through his personal hekura, but also in relation to his social power, his prestige based on his experience and, lastly, his knowledge and influence over people.

Chapter 7

TWO PATHWAYS TO FINDING A CURE

Biomedical and Shamanic Treatment in the Life of
Yanomami

꧁ ❧ ꧂

Colonial invasion had a devastating impact on the indigenous peoples of
the South American continent. Besides wars and slavery, one of the key
factors that contributed to a demographic collapse was the introduction
and spread of certain microbes and previously unknown epidemic
diseases (Ashburn 1980 [1947]; Freire 2011; Heckenberger et al. 2003;
McEwan, Barreto and Neves 2001). Various ethnic groups – including
the Yanomami – inhabiting vast areas of lowland tropical forest, away
from coastal population centres, were initially spared of this pestilence.
However, when European colonisers began to penetrate further into the
continent, infectious diseases eventually reached them. Today, infectious
diseases, as well as parasitic and nutrition-related diseases, continue to
be the principal cause of high morbidity and mortality rates among the
Yanomami population.

All throughout my fieldwork, within the area of influence of the
Platanal health post, malaria and diarrhoea were the most frequent
health problems and causes of high mortality. Other less life threatening
but progressively debilitating health problems included viral epidemics of
acute infections of the upper respiratory tract and lungs, which Yanomami
identified as shawara. Such respiratory infections can become lethal

when combined with malaria or diarrhoea. Ever since the Venezuelan government established health posts and a sustained presence of medical personnel with permanent health programmes in the Upper Orinoco, the Yanomami have had to get used to a new type of relationship with doctors and new methods of treatment. While they accepted that certain aspects of Western medicine could effectively reduce symptoms and ease suffering as well as cure certain introduced diseases, they continued to rely heavily on their shapori for consultation and treatment. In most cases, the western aetiological disease categories and corresponding symptoms do not reflect the Yanomami understanding of these health disturbances. This chapter explores the relationship dynamics between shapori and doctors, as well as the differences between their respective methods of treatment and Yanomami attitudes towards Western medicine, including the ongoing problems associated with prolonged treatment. The chapter also examines the ways in which shapori conceptualise and deal with malaria, diarrhoea and respiratory infections, with a particular focus on the key aetiological category of shawara that has various forms of manifestation and which the Yanomami primarily identify with fever. In Chapter Eight we will see how the concept of shawara – especially among the Brazilian Yanomami – has developed from an historical context of cultural contact and has taken new forms of manifestation.

Shamanism and Biomedicine: Compatibility and Differences

At health posts along the Orinoco, including the one in Platanal, biomedical and conventional shamanistic cures coexist without any significant degree of syncretism between them. The Yanomami do not see biomedical therapies and conventional shamanistic healing methods as mutually exclusive but complementary practices. Should one method fail, the Yanomami will resort to the other method. They can additionally opt for herbal remedies and massages to help an ailment such as a fever, diarrhoea or an eye infection. For the bulk of patients who visit the Platanal clinic, the cognitive model of Western medicine remains largely obscure and without influencing any epistemological change in attitudes and beliefs regarding health and illness. At the same time, the conventional shamanistic method entrenched within their cosmological framework continues to provide a supportive structure and a coherent system of explanation that the Yanomami patients understand and readily accept. Instead of substituting one system of cure for another, the Yanomami incorporate biomedical practices into their existing cosmo-shamanistic system of understanding disease and the cures, interpreting them in light of their traditional knowledge.

> For the Yanomami do not accept the recently introduced tools of modern medicine, its goods and services, as individual methods distinct from their own medical system. The qualities of any new method are modelled according to their own pre-existing conceptual system, so that it fits into the internal logic of their system of curing. (Alès and Chiappino 1985: 84)

Rather than saying that in Platanal there is a plurality of therapeutic systems, it is more appropriate to say that the Yanomami maintain a pluralistic approach in using them.

Shamanistic and biomedical approaches to health and illness are incompatible and incommensurable in their respective worldviews and methodologies, but from the Yanomami perspective, doctors' biomedical means of curing are to some extent complementary rather than opposed to the healing activities of their shapori. For them, biomedicine and shamanism accomplish similar ends, namely to cure and care for the sick. In some aspects, both approaches bear more similarities than initially noticeable but they also contain certain fundamentally profound epistemological and ontological differences. Analysis of an extensive bibliography and field data compiled from various indigenous groups in Venezuela, including the Yanomami (Perrera and Rivas 1997), demonstrate that similarities between biomedicine and traditional healing practices are more prevalent than differences. In both approaches, illness is considered an abnormal transitory state of rupture of healthy equilibrium that can be corrected. Both doctors and shamans strive to identify the cause of an illness by means of their respective methods and apply relevant therapeutic procedures aimed at restoring health. In both instances the cure is not always successful. In both approaches, the patient is a passive recipient of treatment, although within the context of Yanomami shamanistic healing sessions an adult male patient may often take yopo together with the shapori. With regards to aetiology, from both shamanistic and biomedical viewpoints, illness generally occurs when something external invades or contaminates the body (or in the indigenous view also damages or takes away its vital essence) and causes corporeal disequilibrium. The biomedical explanatory model of illness is primarily based on the concept of germs and contagiosity and does not take into account a socio-cosmic dimension. From a biomedical perspective, the intruding agents of sickness are harmful, impersonal pathogens (bacteria, viruses or parasites) that provoke a physiological malfunction of the body, which is manifested through the onset of distinctive symptoms. Perceived through the eyes of scientific determinism, according to which all natural phenomena shows a strict causal connection, disease is thus decontextualised and viewed as an outcome of some biological body alteration, which can be detected through a scientific method.

> The [Western biomedical] theory holds itself to be exhaustive; that is, all diseases located in the tissues and organs of the body can only be diagnosed by examination of the body, and can only be cured by treatments which act on the body. (Carrier 1989: 167)

As a result of a pervading physical reductionism entrenched within the biomedical scientific paradigm, the physical body is treated in isolation. As part of the physical world, the body thus becomes 'knowable as a bounded material entity' (Rhodes 1996: 167) and the primary focus for the treatment of diseases, which are likewise perceived as physical entities occurring in specific bodily locations. From the shamanistic perspective, illness is not merely a bodily concern but also an outcome of temporary socio-cosmic disharmony. As discussed in Chapter Three, illness or death within the Yanomami cosmo-shamanistic framework is primarily but not exclusively an outcome of the deliberate, hostile acts of human and non-human agents, such as an õkã sorcerer – an enemy shapori sending shawara and spirit darts or invading bodies directly by means of his hekura – or else a ghost or some other intruding spirit denizen taking away a person's vital essence:

> In both systems of thought, misfortune, illness or symptoms are produced by an agent which has a characteristic way of acting. But to the Yanomami, this agent also has an origin and a will of its own. (Alès and Chiappino 1985: 86)

Thus, while illness is considered an abnormal state of corporeal disharmony on both sides, for shapori the primary cause of illness is not to be encountered inside but outside of the body.

Both doctors and shamans must first diagnose the nature of a particular ailment before applying the appropriate treatment. When Yanomami patients approach doctors for help, they expect their bodies to be examined on the outside as well as the inside and to be asked questions about their symptoms as well as their general well-being. Due to the language barrier between Yanomami patients and medical practitioners, clinical communication between them is minimal and basic. When doctors ask patients about their symptoms they use certain key words in the Yanomami language that point to fever, pain, diarrhoea, a cough, etc., and expect a positive or a negative response. If doctors wish to obtain more detailed information, which requires more complex descriptions, they request assistance from a Yanomami interpreter. They generally conduct check-ups of Yanomami patients as other medical practitioners do in other parts of the world – by examining the patient's overall appearance, and specific body parts if appropriate. Doctors also resort to various medical devices such as microscopes for detecting harmful malaria parasites in blood samples, stethoscopes, thermometers, spatulas etc. In Platanal, laboratory diagnostics are limited to blood analysis for malaria. In cases where additional analysis is needed – a urine or stool sample – samples are collected and sent to La Esmeralda or Puerto Ayacucho. In more serious or suspicious cases when patients require X-rays or doctors are unsure about their condition, they send them to these places for further examination, treatment or hospitalisation. Upon identifying the problem, doctors proceed with appropriate treatments by administering tablets, injections, cough syrups, eye drops, an intravenous infusion or by orally rehydrating them. Depending on the nature of the ailment, doctors resort either to causal or symptomatic biomedical therapeutic procedures or combine the two. In the first instance, they administer drugs such as antibiotics, antiparasitics or antimalarial tablets to eliminate microorganisms as the main cause of an illness. In the second instance, they give patients analgesics, eye drops or anti-inflammatory drugs to relieve the symptoms of the illness indicated by the patient but these do not eliminate the original cause. Doctors provide Yanomami patients with simple instructions in their language telling them which medicaments are for what and when to take them.

While doctors primarily draw on their own medical knowledge and expertise, shapori rely entirely on their hekura assistants to make a correct diagnosis and will engage them in follow-up treatment. Since a shapori and his patients share the same cultural and cosmological milieu, in the course of shamanistic healing they are able to communicate extensively. During his diagnostic procedure, a shapori carefully examines the patient's body via his hekura assistants and may ask him or her certain questions to find out if they broke a rule or taboo; for example, they may have eaten something poisonous by accident or been into the forest at the wrong time of day.

Later, in the course of healing, a shapori will tell patients what the cause of their malady is. Thus, shaporis' diagnostic procedures and follow-up treatments are rather different from those of doctors. What both type of practitioners have in common is their access to the body's interiority, albeit by different means and on different ontological levels (Kelly 2011). When making a diagnosis, a shapori will crouch in front of a patient, touch various parts of his or her body and look intensely into their chest. At first sight it may appear as if the shapori is only examining the patient's outward appearance when in fact his conscious intentionality is directed at the patient's interiority. He is able to penetrate the body with his gaze because he can transform into one of his assisting hekura and look through their eyes. A shapori, with his special sight, is able to reach different levels of perception and detect if a patient's vital essence is missing, if they are contaminated by shawara or if there is a pathogenic spirit dart or an enemy hekura inside their body. Eventually, through their hekura helpers they are also able to identify who is responsible for the affliction. As we have seen in earlier chapters, a shapori involved in healing mobilises his auxiliary hekura through song and dance, engaging them concurrently in fighting various forms of aggression, extracting intangible pathogenic objects or else expelling the intruding hekura. The hekura manipulate the patient's body using the shapori hands or by using the shapori to suck out and vomit the sickness agent.

The shapori's curative treatment often contains a degree of uncertainty with unpredictable outcomes that sometimes result in death. Akin to the doctor, the shapori first has to identify the cause of illness and then work towards restoring the somato-cosmic balance. In cases where a soul component is stolen by a ghost, once the perpetrator is identified and then defeated, the soul component is restored to its proper condition, which should reduce the fever and general malaise. The sufferer may experience temporary relief and the alleviation of symptoms, which indicates that the shapori's intervention was successful. If necessary, the shapori will repeat his treatment until the sufferer is cured, just like the doctor who will repeat medication. This brings us to a key point of perceived fundamental difference between doctors and shamans in their respective healing methods. The prevailing anthropological understanding of the main difference between shamanism and biomedicine, from an indigenous perspective, is that the former deals directly with causes of illness while the latter only tackles its effects or symptoms (Buchillet 1991; Kelly 2011). Whilst this distinction may at first seem entirely applicable and accurate, the matter, in my view, is more complex, at least with regards to the Yanomami. When a shapori expels the intruding hekura or pathogenic spirit dart or else fights and wins over the entity responsible for stealing a missing soul component, he certainly eliminates the cause of illness and restores the personal integrity of a patient. However, when they attempt to heal patients suffering from fever or pain with their hekura assistants they are also working directly on alleviating the symptoms of malaise, akin to doctors. Furthermore, apart from working on elimination of symptoms, doctors also work towards eliminating harmful pathogens, by administering relevant drugs. For them, pathogens are the cause of an illness while a fever or malaise is its effects or symptoms. In cases of malaria, for example, antimalarial tablets eliminate the cause of illness and antipyretics would tackle its symptoms – the fever. From the scientific perspective, the trajectory of sickness is linear. It progresses from the build-up phase, peaks at the critical phase and is followed by a period of improvement that culminates in restored health. The person is considered cured when the body is finally free of microorganisms. During this course, however, the fever may return, in which case the doctor will again prescribe anti-fever tablets. The tablets work on the cause of illness as well as on its symptoms.

For the shapori, hekura that intrude people's bodies or ghosts that snatch souls are real and they confront them with their auxiliary hekura. Biomedical method demonstrates that pathogenic microorganisms are equally real for which doctors administer the appropriate medicaments. Only the shapori is able to deal with the problem of the missing soul or an intruding hekura, and only doctors with their biomedical procedures are capable of eliminating the microorganisms. With regards to fever, both methods work equally well towards restoring bodily equilibrium by reducing the body temperature. While the shapori qua his assisting hekura clearly does not have any power over microbes, doctors are equally unable to employ the same means of healing that shapori do. The main difference thus between their respective approaches to illness and health is in the level of conscious perception and in an ontological sphere of action.

Dynamics of Doctor-Shapori-Patient Interaction

Doctors and medical students generally respect shaporis' healing methods without interfering, except in a critical, life-threatening situation when they either work with them side-by-side or insist on the primacy of their therapy. They consider shapori an important component in the overall healing process without actually understanding the Yanomami worldview or believing in shaporis' knowledge and effectiveness to effect a cure. Since their biomedical methods are fundamentally different to those of shapori, diagnostic and therapeutic procedures of shapori are viewed as 'mystical' by doctors, who are primarily guided by a mechanistic explanatory model of diseases with its aetiology grounded in biology and scientific reasoning. Since the late 1980s onwards, however, there has been a shift in attitude among academic circles of the School of Medicine of the Central University of Venezuela (UCV) and among the SACAICET medical personnel, who nowadays recognise the socio-cultural importance of illness among indigenous populations and primarily view health in a more holistic manner as 'a situation of general wellbeing – physical, psychological, emotional and social' (Jauregui 1993: 31). Nevertheless, the guiding principle for most of the doctors is the biomedical model with its focus on the physical body and a scientific understanding of sickness. Some doctors working among the Yanomami population believe that shapori play an important psychological, emotional and socially integrative role in healing by resolving personal and social conflicts among patients through catharsis. They liken shapori to psychotherapists and when a patient recovers after a shapori's healing treatment, doctors ascribe the outcome to a placebo effect (see also Kelly 2011: 147).

Akin to medical professionals, some anthropologists believe that shamans do not have the ability to eliminate organic disorders but primarily attempt to restore emotional and psychosocial disharmony (e.g., Lizot 1998; Peters 1979). They interpret shamanistic healing as having a positive effect on a person's psyche while the doctors treat the physical problem. 'In Western medicine a distinction is made between what is physical and what is psychological. The Yanomami however do not view the body as separated from the "soul"' (Alès and Chiappino 1985: 85). Such views, influenced by the Cartesian mind-body divide, fail to acknowledge that not all health problems that shamans confront are located in the psychosocial sphere and thus require social reintegration of a patient. As we have seen, shapori in their healing treatments also treat physical complaints such as fever, headache and body cramps. Mindful of the fact that a psychosomatic component may play an important role in ritual healing, I argue that most if not all illnesses, regardless of their underlying causes, have certain somatic manifestations through symptoms such as fever, headache and difficulty breathing, among others. They are primarily bodily experiences per se, which the shapori attempts to relieve. The following example of a shapori's successful treatment of an ulcer after many failed attempts by doctors is significant because it challenges the aforementioned assumptions that shapori are not capable of curing physical ailments. Lay missionary Howard from Platanal told me that he was once suffering from a severe leg ulcer for about six months. Several doctors attempted to cure it to no avail. Finally, the ulcer disappeared after a shapori's intervention. He showed me a round scar on his left leg where, according to him, there used to be a persistently infected hole. The doctor in charge of the clinic gave him some antibiotics and repeatedly sanitised the lesion without any curative success. The doctors in Caracas could not help him either. Finally, he approached several shapori, who all told him that the ulcer had been inflicted by the ghost (*pore*) of a man who drowned in the lagoon on the Orinoquito River – Orinoco's right tributary situated further up from Platanal. He lives in the lagoon in an underwater cave and is guardian of the nearby Orinoquito rapids. Howard was astonished because he recalled swimming once in a lagoon near the Orinoquito rapids, despite some words of advice from the Yanomami of Hasupiwei-theri that he should have first asked the ghost guardian for permission. He dismissed their warnings and went swimming anyway. Be that as it may, the shapori he approached could not help but recommended that he see a prominent shapori from Ocamo, who subsequently managed to cure his ulcer. I asked him about the likelihood that the ulcer disappeared as a result of his body's self-healing system, but he shook his head in negation. He was convinced that the shapori had cured him.

Shapori, for their part, generally appreciate a doctor's ability to treat various types of wounds and abscesses and reduce fever and pain. With their holistic approach to health and healing, shapori do not see biomedicine as serious competition. On the contrary, in some instances when shapori are unable to help patients they send them to see the doctor, which shows that over the years the Yanomami have developed a certain degree of trust in them. By and large, they value medicaments, especially antipyretic and analgesic drugs because they bring quick relief. The shapori Makowë once commented that tablets have the same effects as a shaporimou session as they break down pain or excessive body heat. In fact, he sometimes told patients who were not seriously ill to take tablets because of their effectiveness in reducing fever or pain and therefore generating less work for him. In cases of serious health problems associated with diseases such as malaria, tuberculosis or onchocerciasis, which require prolonged treatment with tablets, Yanomami attitudes and responses were rather difficult, which made things complicated for medical workers. With cases of malaria, for example, the treatment of a more dangerous p. falciparum strain lasts only a few days, but for the p. vivax strain, doctors have to distribute a combination of chloroquine and primaquine tablets according to the patient's body weight on a daily basis for about two weeks. The Yanomami initially comply with the doctor, but once they start feeling better they often refuse to continue taking the bitter-tasting tablets, breaking down the cycle of treatment and therefore its effectiveness. If their condition deteriorates after discontinuing the treatment they often blame doctors and complain that 'the medicine is useless'. Sumabila-Tachon (1999) reported similar problems among the Cuiva of the Guahibo linguistic family, who inhabit tropical savannas of the State of Apure and neighbouring Colombia. They believe that antimalarial tablets are the same as aspirin and that one is enough to reduce the severe fever – one of the principal manifestations of this illness – and therefore cure them. The main consequence of not finishing treatment, from a pharmaceutical perspective, is that a quantity of parasites inevitably survive due to low drug levels in the system and become more resistant to the existing medication. Thus, a new, stronger medication has to be taken in order for it to be effective, but it also becomes more toxic for the patient.

At the Platanal health post and others, doctors are able to supervise the treatment on a daily basis. However, for the communities situated along the Orinoco River it becomes a problem because the health personnel are unable to visit them every day due to their strenuous work commitments in Platanal and the chronic lack of fuel for motorboats in order to reach such areas. The best they can do when visiting adjacent communities is to take blood samples from persons suspected of having malaria and distribute tablets to confirmed cases by giving the patient simple instructions in Yanomami with the help of a bilingual Yanomami assistant. They frequently prepare the exact daily doses of tablets for each Yanomami; however, when they return to the village some time later, they often find the tablets untouched. In Platanal, patients who have had the most frequent contact with medical personnel have formed a fair understanding of such treatments and tend to follow the prescription. However, others who do not follow the treatment frequently return to the clinic feeling unwell. When Dr Helen asked them if they had taken their tablets as per her advice they would nod their heads affirmatively and complain that the medicine was bad and useless. Afterwards, she would go to their houses and often find the tablets untouched. When I mentioned this to one of my colleagues, Dr Daisy Barreto from the Central University of Venezuela, who worked among the Pumé in the state of Apure, she remarked that they were collecting, in a bag, all the tablets not taken, which they had been receiving from health workers for the past five years.

At the other extreme, there have also been some cases where the Yanomami have taken medicaments, albeit in an inappropriate and quite hazardous manner. On one occasion, Helen, with the help of a translator, was telling a woman to take antibiotics twice a day for five days and then asked her if she understood. The woman nodded affirmatively and walked off. The following morning she came back to the clinic feeling very sick and Helen soon found out that she had taken all ten tablets at once. Fortunately, the woman eventually recovered. In such instances, Helen would complain that the Yanomami did understand the given instructions but simply refused to follow them; furthermore she thought they were stubborn, unpredictable, uncooperative and generally difficult to deal with.[1] She believed that the Yanomami liked to receive medical attention and the tablets but disliked taking them; they would often come to her pretending to be sick in order to obtain tablets, which they later forgot to take, threw away or shared with their kin. On one occasion, I accompanied Helen and a medical student, Yawri, on a routine sanitary expedition to nearby communities. In one community called Guakamaya-theri, lots of Yanomami were lined up waiting for their turn to see the doctor. The majority complained of suffering from abdominal pain and headaches, and after receiving the tablets, they went back to their houses and started breaking them into small pieces, which they gave to their family members in the same way they share meat after a successful hunt. Helen was furious. One of the main reasons for keeping tablets or sharing them with others is because of their tendency to view them as commodities, just like all other exchange objects coming from napë. In Brazil, the Yanomami became increasingly dependent on Western medicine due to their perception of medicaments as exchange goods. For the Yanomami, the quantity of administered drugs is an indicator of their friendship level with the whites (Sanchez 1999).

I asked Helen how she is able to distinguish if someone is genuinely sick or just feigning illness. She replied that when someone complains of a cough or sore throat they usually start coughing in front of her but the sound of a cough or a healthy looking throat is an indication that they are pretending to be ill. She mentioned a woman that came to the clinic every day complaining of persistent headaches and asking for painkillers. Helen suspected that she was pretending and one day gave her a vitamin tablet instead of a painkiller. That afternoon Helen asked the woman how she felt and the woman replied that the pill was good and it had stopped the pain. Helen immediately stopped giving her more tablets. I also discussed this subject with the doctor in charge of the Ocamo health post and she remarked that on rainy days the Yanomami tend to stay indoors where it is warm and therefore those who do come to the clinic are genuinely unwell. Upon speaking to Elias – the Yanomami microscopist working at the Platanal clinic – he admitted that while some Yanomami indeed pretend to be sick, sometimes the doctors make mistakes and turn away patients who are genuinely sick. As a consequence, when they become sick again in the future they refuse to take the medicine.

Medical workers clearly go to great efforts to explain the treatment to the Yanomami patients with the help of translators and are generally convinced that the Yanomami do understand instructions but refuse to cooperate. I agree to some extent with doctors that understanding is certainly not the main issue here and may partially follow Kelly's (2011: 140) suggestion that the problem is not with content but form; doctor's verbal explanations are either not sufficiently convincing or Yanomami simply do not take them seriously. But there are also other factors at play. Concerning the long-term treatment of malaria, for example, the main reason why the Yanomami dislike and refuse to take antimalarial tablets is because they believe this type of medicine makes them more sick. Indeed, the chloroquine tablets given in the early stages of the treatment, apart from having a bitter taste, tend to produce intense and unpleasant side effects, thus augmenting the already unpleasant onset of the symptoms of the disease. It is important to bear in mind that the Yanomami generally associate bitterness with diseases. When Makowë treated the boy whose essence had been stolen from his liver (Chapter Six), his hekura detected a bitter taste associated with the boy's inner fire smoke. An Ocamo doctor told me that she once treated a baby girl with a cough; the mixture she prescribed was formulated to break down the accumulated mucus and unblock the respiratory passages by discharging the mucus from the lungs and upper respiratory tract; this, as she expected, would increase the child's cough. Next morning the father returned to the clinic complaining that his daughter's cough had worsened after taking the medicine. In my view, the main problem of misunderstanding between the doctors and Yanomami patients undergoing long-term treatment lies in conceptual incompatibility stemming from different worldviews and resulting cross-cultural misunderstanding. While Yanomami generally understand doctors' instructions, the idea of a prolonged treatment is incompatible with their understanding of sickness and cure. Once they feel better, they stop taking the medicine. Likewise, if they feel better after the shapori's treatment, they do not seek the shapori's help again unless their health deteriorates.

Most Yanomami from Platanal prefer going to a shapori first, before visiting the doctor. Dr Helen told me that mothers, who were the most frequent visitors to the Platanal clinic, initially take their sick children to shapori – a number of times if necessary. If the child's condition does not improve, mothers then take their babies to the clinic. By this point, the child's health has deteriorated to such a degree that little can be done to save their lives. Angry mothers then hold doctors responsible for the child's death, which places the doctor in a very delicate situation with the rest of the community.

In some critical, life-threatening situations, it was not uncommon to see the doctor and shapori working together to save lives. Helen, or one of medical students, would insert an intravenous drip into a patient's arm and then stand back to let the shapori carry out his own treatment. On one occasion, three shapori were involved in curing a woman called Nancy. She was lying in her hammock, semi-conscious and looking pale. Helen was carefully observing the shapori take their turn to squeeze the sickness out of Nancy's body and then vomit. Suddenly, Nancy screamed and rolled her eyes. Helen reacted swiftly and set up an intravenous drip without interrupting the shaporis' treatment. Helen revealed that Nancy was suffering from malaria combined with severe diarrhoea and that if she did not recover quickly she would have to be taken to the clinic. Fortunately, Nancy's condition stabilised and she eventually recovered. I asked Helen which treatment she thought had saved Nancy from dying; she smiled and replied: 'I don't know, but I was trained to think that it is medicine that saves lives!' I then approached one of the shapori who was involved in the healing session and asked him the same question. He said: 'Shapori, of course! Mothokariwë [Sun Hekura] took her vital essence and we had to put it back. Doctors cannot do this'. On this occasion, Helen felt that she did not have to cut short the shaporis' treatment, but on another occasion she had to terminate the healing session and take the critically ill man to the clinic. She did, however, invite the shapori to continue working inside the clinic while she was administering the treatment. Fortunately, the man's condition rapidly improved.

In both instances the patient recovered; however, sometimes a shapori's healing efforts fail to save lives in the same way that patients may die after medical intervention. In the latter instance, the doctors may reflect on the fact that survival depends somewhat on the body defence system, which is different for each individual. If a patient dies after the shapori's treatment he may say that the hekura who inflicted the death was too powerful for him.

One evening, a Yanomami microscopist, Elias, brought his little son to the clinic. Helen quickly realised that the child's condition was critical and that he urgently needed a blood transfusion. She called the health district headquarters in La Esmeralda by radio and requested an army plane to take the boy to Puerto Ayacucho hospital. Unfortunately, they were unable to send the plane before the following morning. She inserted an intravenous drip into the boy's arm while his father went out to ask the shapori Enano for help. Upon entering the clinic, Enano sniffed some epena and started singing and calling some of his most powerful hekura helpers. For hours they attempted to save the child's life by using all the hekura's healing techniques, including squeezing, brushing, massaging, sucking and vomiting. However, as the night progressed, the shapori was slowly losing his confidence. At one point he stopped and announced that there was nothing further he could do. He complained of having a headache and asked the doctor for a tablet. He then wandered off into the darkness of the night. The child was picked up the next morning but passed away during the flight on the way to hospital. I discussed this very subject once in Ocamo with a medical student named Zorelis. She said that when her patients are not seriously ill she lets shapori do their work before applying her own treatment. However, if they are in a critical condition she insists on the primacy of biomedical treatment. Zorelis also mentioned that on one occasion she attentively observed one shapori treating a gravely sick boy, who suddenly started rolling his eyes. She demanded the shapori to discontinue his healing session immediately because the child had to be taken to the clinic. The shapori did not object.

Yanomami Responses to Diarrhoea, Malaria and Respiratory Infections

Intestinal Infections

Intestinal infections are not strictly 'imported' diseases and it has been generally agreed that intestinal parasitosis and certain infections caused by retroviruses are autochthonous to the American continent (MSDS 2000: 20). However, with regards to the Yanomami, radical changes in their settlement pattern from a more mobile, semi-nomadic lifestyle to a sedentary one and resulting unhygienic and unhealthy living conditions has mainly caused the proliferation of infection (Colchester 1985). During my fieldwork, infections in the intestinal tract generated by various bacterial, viral or parasitic microorganisms were one of the major causes of high morbidity and mortality rates, especially among young children. Although they bathe daily, the Yanomami generally have no concept of proper self-cleanliness. Children would often eat off the ground or let a dog lick food from their plates. Poor hygiene, careless alimentary and toilet habits, especially among children, render the high risk of infection and reinfection thus making control of diarrhoea difficult (Yarzabal, cited in ibid.: 5). Intestinal infections generated through infested soil, contaminated drinking water and food can cause diarrhoea, vomiting, fever, abdominal pain and intestinal obstruction due to an accumulation of intestinal parasites. The swollen abdomen evident among many Yanomami children is indicative of a high parasite content that can produce nutritional disequilibrium, anaemia and may eventually lead to death. Helen said that many small children suffering from acute diarrhoea dehydrate quickly and may die, especially if the diarrhoea is accompanied by vomiting. This occurs mainly because mothers discontinue giving water to their children, believing that liquid intake only intensifies the diarrhoea. In Platanal and adjacent communities, health post personnel give children suffering from diarrhoea and/or vomiting antiparasitic syrups and electrolyte solutions to drink in order to replace lost fluids and minerals.

Shaporis' views on this matter are not uniform. Interestingly, the two shapori – Ruweweriwë and Shawarawë – from villages distant from Platanal indirectly share doctors' views that during a bout of diarrhoea it is good to drink water because it cleanses the stomach and helps flush out the worms (kõhõrõmɨ),[2] which they can both apparently detect inside the abdomen through the eyes of their hekura assistants. On the other hand, the shapori Makowë, who lives in close proximity of the Platanal clinic, was of the opinion that drinking water excessively while having diarrhoea would worsen it. However, he specifically mentioned 'salty tasting water' (mau sayu), probably referring to the saline electrolyte solution that doctors give children to drink. His views are consistent with the widespread Amerindian notion that drinking salty water results in an excess of 'cold', which can further aggravate a child's bodily equilibrium, already affected by diarrhoea (Butt Colson and de Armellada 1985; Chiappino 2002). Makowë also associates diarrhoea with dirtiness (ahi). When treating a child suffering from stomach cramps and diarrhoea he summons some napë (non-Yanomami) hekura capable of detecting dust-like particles of dirt and worms through 'a transparent membrane' lying across the surface of the stomach. His response bears a striking resemblance to some claims from Kelly's (2011: 160) informants from Ocamo, who told him about a new type of hekura associated with criollos called napëramɨ, who speak Spanish and use napë objects such as mirrors and glass. They said that shapori use glass akin to a microscope, through which they can see shawara. When I asked Ruweweriwë about his views on this subject, he took a lump of solidified and transparent tree sap (warapa)[3] and pointed at the trapped dust particles, small pieces of wood and preserved insects, comparing it to the stomach of a person suffering from diarrhoea. He then halved the sap and made a slicing movement with the side of his hand just below my navel to demonstrate how his hekura cut the interiority of the stomach and break down the worms, which, according to him, work their way out through the anal passage. Ruweweriwë also mentioned that the hekura Õmãyãriwë could sometimes cause diarrhoea and stomach ache in children, albeit more frequently he tries to strangle them, with diarrhoea often occurring as a kind of 'collateral damage', if they survive. Shawarawë, a now deceased shapori from Toritha-theri, once told me that when he took yopo he could also detect stomach worms. He treated diarrhoea by giving patients roasted plantains to eat so the stomach worms would feed on it and multiply; when there were many, it was easier for him to expel the worms and cleanse the body, which he did by sucking them out and vomiting, with the help of his hekura.

When children suffer from diarrhoea they frequently have a fever or more localised heat around the abdomen, which both Makowë and Ruweweriwë perceive as a circulating ring of fire – or what Lizot (2007) referred to as a ball of fire – that they identify as shawara. In this instance, the treatment consists of repeated attempts to reduce the stomach fever by breaking the burning shawara with their hekura assistants associated with water and 'cold', namely various types of toads; for example, Hãsupɨriyoma, and extract it out of the body through suction and subsequent vomiting. Makowë admitted that though his hekura are able to reduce fever and pain they cannot stop diarrhoea thus he often tells the mother afterwards to take their child to the doctor. Yanomami living in remote villages with no access to the clinic are reliant on shamanistic treatment or conventional herbal remedies. On one occasion, while I was visiting the Shamathari community of Kayurewë-theri (Hyomitha) situated three days on foot from Sheroana in a southerly direction, I saw a woman sitting on the ground and preparing the root of some plant. I asked her what she was doing and she said she was preparing a remedy for her baby girl, who was sick with diarrhoea. The plant was haro këkɨ (cyperus distans [cyperaceae]), which is also used to treat a high fever. Her husband, who was a shapori and the village headman, had attempted to cure the child without any success. The woman said that on the first day of treatment she peels the root and pulverises it. She then mixes the powder together with the child's watery faeces on the ground before scraping the mixture up and discarding it. The following day, she soaks the pulverised haro in water and inserts it into the child's rectum using her finger. Finally, on the third day, she mixes the haro powder with water and gives it to the child to drink. She indicated that the plant, although poisonous, can be beneficial if taken in small quantities. To treat the fever, she mixes the haro powder with red ochre, chews it for a while and then rubs the mixture onto the child's chest and back.

The aforementioned shapori responses and attitudes plainly indicate that they associate diarrhoea primarily with the presence of impersonal agents – namely abdominal worms and dirtiness – rather than perceiving it as the outcome of sorcery or the intervention of a spirit denizen.[4] We could thus say that their interpretation of diarrhoea belongs to the aetiological category of impersonal naturalistic infection, which Murdock (1980: 9) defined as an 'invasion of the victim's body by noxious microorganisms, with particular but not exclusive reference to the germ theory of disease'. Green (1999) commented that in societies in which this view prevails, the agents of infection are described as worms or small insects rather than germs. Bear in mind that, for the Yanomami shapori, the biomedical concept of infection and germs is alien to their worldview. Thus, I refer here to what Green (ibid.: 84), following Murdock, calls 'the ethnomedical theory of naturalistic infection', to distinguish it from biomedical germ theory. It is difficult to determine whether the shapori concept of stomach worms is the result of the diffusion of Western biomedical thinking or whether it has arisen independently. Due to the absence of medical personnel in the Yanomami communities where I conducted my field research, and a lack of exposure to biomedical ideas on the part of shapori, it is unlikely that their views on stomach worms and diarrhoea were directly influenced by biomedical concepts. Be that as it may, the responses from various shapori indicate that they are capable of perceiving and dealing with stomach worms independently of medical personnel. But worms for the shapori are no more 'natural' and 'personal' than the hekura themselves, who cannot be classified as 'supernatural' entities. For that reason, shamanistic concepts may appear similar to biomedical knowledge despite their different ontologies. The lack of this critical distinction in the literature can be explained by anthropologists' stereotyping of Yanomami by assuming that they all attribute diarrhoea to 'supernatural' and 'personalistic' entities and causes.

Malaria

From the biomedical perspective, malaria is an infectious disease caused by plasmodium[5] parasites, which are transmitted to a human host through female mosquitoes of the genus anopheles. Once in the bloodstream, the majority of parasites invade the liver cells where they start to grow and multiply through their reproductive process (Gillet 1971). As long as the parasites are contained within the limits of the cell membrane nothing happens to the human host. However, once the quantity of parasites within each cell reaches critical numbers, the cell membrane ruptures causing the release of parasites into the bloodstream where they start invading red blood cells (Butcher 1990). At that point, the body's auto-defence system detects the parasites as foreign objects and starts fighting them. This is also the moment when a person starts experiencing the initial outbreak of fever and chills, followed by headaches, muscle ache and general lethargy. After a period of continual exposure to parasites, malaria sufferers develop a higher reactivity of the immune system and continue living with malaria, experiencing occasional relapses of fever and chills. They become carriers of parasites and can contribute to the spread of malaria from person to person through mosquito bites. In one study (Marcano et al. 2004), 508 Yanomami from twenty-five villages in Platanal, Mavaca and Ocamo were examined. The results showed quite low parasite loads (16 per cent), a low frequency of severe malaria cases (9.2 per cent) and a high frequency of individuals with splenomegaly (72.4 per cent)[6] acting as carriers of parasites without experiencing any symptoms. These findings demonstrate that over the years of continuous exposure to malaria parasites, the Yanomami have developed a certain immunity to malaria.

It has been argued that malaria did not exist in the pre-Colombian era (Sherwood 1975) and that while the principal vector for transmission – the anopheles mosquito – is native to the American continent, the plasmodium parasite was introduced by the Spanish conquistadors and Portuguese explorers, as well as African slaves (Newson 1993, 2001). Yanomami predecessors experienced significant population losses for the first time on a large scale during eighteenth century clashes with Portuguese slave traders in the Rio Branco region when they also became exposed to various pathogenic agents, including the plasmodium parasites. Nevertheless, they managed to recover their population numbers and health equilibrium after retreating into the culturally and geographically isolated habitat of the Parima highlands. When they migrated towards the lowlands during the first half of the twentieth century and settled near rivers, the Yanomami were exposed to the anopheles mosquito infected with the plasmodium parasite, which breed in water. Sporadic contacts with rubber tappers and timber workers helped to intensify the spread of malaria, which continued into the 1950s onwards with the arrival of missionaries, scientists, tourists, government officials and soldiers, causing a significant population decrease. Another significant factor that intensified the transmission of malaria and other introduced diseases among the Yanomami was a radical disruption of their settlement pattern and semi-nomadic lifestyle living in small villages with a low population density spread throughout the forest to living in large, more permanent riverine settlements. Since the 1950s, there have also been recorded cases of malaria in Parima villages situated at over 400 m above sea level (Smole 1976), which have probably been brought there from visits to endemic lowland communities. While the anopheles darlingi is generally found at low altitude, riverine environments and is the main vector of malaria transmission in the Venezuelan State of Amazonas (Magris 2004: 39), some recent evidence shows that the anopheles species is gradually adapting to higher altitudes. For example, they have been collected at heights above 800 m in the border region with Brazil (Sinka et al. 2010).

Yanomami Perceptions of Malaria

The Yanomami do not have an equivalent word for malaria in their own language so they incorporated the Spanish word for malaria *paludismo* into their vocabulary. When I asked various Yanomami teachers and health auxiliaries in Platanal how they conceptualise paludismo, they vaguely responded that it is a criollo disease of the blood transmitted by mosquitoes. The rest of the population primarily associated paludismo with severe fever and weakness, which they called shawara. This type of shawara for them is much more severe than other types, causing not only splitting headaches (*heki nini*) and a high temperature (*yopri*), but shivers (*si sãihõu*) and yellow skin (*pei siki frãre*). Consider the following personal experience of a young man called Mario from Platanal:

> When you get paludismo, you become weak and cannot walk or eat. You only lie in your hammock and cannot do gardening or go hunting. Your body becomes very hot and hurts. You shiver from the cold even when the sun is shining. Your skin becomes yellow.

Mario, who was experiencing some of the aforementioned malaria-like symptoms, albeit unconfirmed by blood analysis, referred to his illness as *prisiprisi*, which is the local term that medical staff identify as the Yanomami word for paludismo. The term *prisiprisi* and its verbal form *prisiprisimou* in this instance signifies shivering from the feverish cold of the shawara illness. The Yanomami also use this expression in regard to shivering from the cold in the early morning hours or getting wet from the rain. On one occasion I was watching the tree leaves quivering in the breeze when one Yanomami commented that they were doing the *prisiprisimou*; hence, this term signifies the shaking of any object not just the human body. Another local term associated with malaria is *hurapi*, which primarily relates to pain in the spleen (*pei hurapi nini*) together with the aforementioned symptoms.

My two key shapori informants from Platanal – Makowë and Enano – both said that before the arrival of napë, paludismo did not exist. Pointing towards the north-northwest, they both agreed that napë brought with them smoke containing a new type of deadly shawara. Makowë added that paludismo also came from Brazil, pointing towards the south. When I asked them if they could heal paludismo they shook their heads negatively, saying that people suffering from paludismo should go and see a doctor and ask for tablets because only doctors can cure it. I then asked if they could cure a person suffering from fever, headache, cold chills and general lethargy, which are the common symptoms associated with malaria, and they both nodded their heads affirmatively. In the vast majority of cases, the shapori associate the illness with the absence of bodily vital essence (*pei mi ãmo*) that is caused by ghosts (pore) or enemy hekura.

Approximately three weeks after I arrived in Platanal, I suddenly came down with a fever. I felt lethargic and generally unwell, and in the afternoon went to see Dr Helen at the clinic. Suspecting malaria, she took a blood sample and said that it had to be dispatched to the Mavaca clinic for analysis because she was short of litmus paper and thus could not provide a diagnosis. She gave me some antipyretic tablets and I went back to lie down in my hammock. I hardly slept but avoided taking the tablets because I intended to see Enano the following morning to test his ability to reduce the fever and general malaise. That day, I described my symptoms to Enano and he asked me to sit down. The house was full of curious onlookers lying in hammocks. Other co-participants were seated around me in a semicircle. We all took doses of yopo snuff and Enano started to sing and dance with his arms high up in the air, calling his hekura helpers to assist him. Upon reaching a trance he transformed into Spider Monkey Hekura Pashoriwë, and started sniffing the surface of my body before carefully observing my face and chest. He commented on how pale and hot I was and that there was a fire circulating inside my head and chest. He told me to take off my T-shirt, which he put on the ground near the entrance and placed a metal barrel lid on top of it. Various hekura co-assisted with my treatment, which alternated between brushing my head and chest and making repetitive slashing movements using the shapori's hands from head to stomach. He then scooped 'something' out of my head and chest and immediately vomited, complaining about my *pei puhi* feeling cold and tasting bitter. At that moment the shapori, transformed into Hekura Watota,[7] triumphantly announced that an Amahiri hekura by the name of Wãrishewë (also known as Sloth Hekura Ihamariwë)[8] had emerged from the ground the day before in the afternoon (when I started feeling sick). He stole the vital essence of my head (*pei he mɨ ãmo*) and introduced shawara into my body, which increased my body temperature and made me weak. Alfredo, the Mahekoto-theri headman, who was sitting next to me, whispered that Enano had said it was not paludismo. In continuation, to find the perpetrator and retrieve my missing bodily essence, Enano summoned Yarusheriwë or Hekura Ancestor of the South American Coati (nasua nasua solitaria), an animal renowned for its excellent sense of smell and ability to track down its prey. Through his song, the shapori, now disguised as Yarusheriwë, revealed how he was already following the footprints that the hekura had left behind and said that they led towards the subterranean cosmic layer where Amahiri live. Enano then grabbed a canoe paddle and started to tap the ground. I asked Alfredo what the shapori was doing: 'He is searching for the entrance into the underworld so he can go there and recover your soul essence from the fugitive. Tapping the ground is like knocking to open the door of the underworld'.[9] In continuation, Enano walked slowly to the place where my T-shirt was lying underneath the metal lid. He tapped the lid with the paddle and then instructed me to hold the T-shirt up in front of me. He then stroked the T-shirt repeatedly with his hands in the same manner he had stroked my body before placing it back on the ground in front of me and announcing that he had encountered the hekura responsible for my illness. What followed was the fight between the subterranean hekura and Enano's hekura, akin to Makowë's contest with the woman ghost, who stole the soul essence of the little boy (see Chapter Six). After a few minutes of a dramatic battle, Enano's hekura eventually defeated their Amahiri counterparts and successfully restored my missing soul essence back into its proper place.

Having commented on how pale I looked at the beginning of the session, Enano now noticed that the colour was returning to my face and that my body temperature was decreasing. After he finished, the fever and lethargy had abated and I felt significantly better. As I was walking back home I was relieved but also astonished by the experience. On the one hand, I believed in the shapori's treatment but the analytical part of me was trying to account for the results. I pondered on various possibilities, including that the treatment had been a placebo. While deep down I was open to this theory, I was also sceptical. In the end the most important thing was that the treatment had been successful and I had felt significantly better. However, though I slept well that night, the next day my condition deteriorated and I was unwell again, so I took the antipyretic tablets. Two days later Helen informed me that my blood test result had arrived and confirmed p. vivax malaria. Thinking about Enano's diagnosis I was somewhat puzzled, so I went back to his house and told him that I had paludismo. He was not surprised and calmly responded that I should see the doctor and get some medication. When I told him that I had a recurring fever he replied that I should come back and see him, take yopo and get better. His response was an indication to me that he recognised malaria as something foreign, which only doctors can cure with tablets whereas the fever was something he felt confident he could help with because he and his hekura were familiar with it.

Enano's handling of my ailment corresponds to Makowë's treatment of the sick child, described in Chapter Six. In both instances, shapori via their hekura assistants detected the perpetrators responsible for the loss of vital essences, in my case from the head and in the boy's case from his liver, which provoked fever and general malaise. Both shapori encountered shawara circulating as fire inside the bodies, which was for them a tangible manifestation of fever. After taking samples of damaged pei puhi from the affected body parts, both shapori respectively complained about its bitterness as well as the smoke that they understand as being a by-product of inner fire or shawara. They also said the pei puhi sample was cold, a side effect of the missing vital essence (mɨ ãmo), which was for them was also an indication of the damage caused by the intruding pore and enemy hekura. In both cases the doctor's diagnosis was malaria. In Sheroana-theri, Ruweweriwë told me that when he treats a person suffering from hurapɨ (paludismo) he also encounters the bodily fire shawara. To extinguish the inner fire, he summons yawari aquatic beings or hekura associated with water; namely frogs, as we saw before in cases of a fever related to intestinal infections. After that, his helping hekura begins to cut the resilient shawara into pieces with the side of his hand, like a knife, and then he squeezes them out of the body. To demonstrate this, Ruweweriwë took a banana peel and placed it in a vertical position on the left side of my stomach (where the spleen is), commenting that this is what he encounters inside the body. He then split the peel in half and tossed the pieces on the ground, saying that the sickness had gone (*'hurapɨ quami!'*). He sends the extracted pieces of shawara to the underground Amahiri or dispatches them towards their distant Shamathari enemies.

According to the shamanistic explanatory model, a soul theft conducted by a conscious extracorporeal being provokes a corporeal disequilibrium by generating a steady build-up of body heat, phenomenologically manifested as an inner fire shawara, but it simultaneously damages a person's pei puhi, which shapori experience via their hekura as being cold. Similarly, the Carib-speaking Pemon of south-eastern Venezuela view soul loss as being 'cold'. The Pemon shaman attempts to restore the missing soul to the body by singing, which attracts the soul back and consequently heats up the body (Butt Colson and de Armellada 1983). The Yanomami shapori likewise indirectly attempts to even out hot and cold bodily properties and thus re-establish corporeal and cosmic equilibrium, albeit by confronting directly the extracorporeal entity responsible for the soul loss and then re-embodying the missing vital essence or expelling the intruding hekura, thus extinguishing the inner fire shawara and revitalising the damaged (and cold) pei puhi. For them, the proof of a successful treatment is when their hekura can no longer detect excessive heat or cold. The same is relevant for treatment of stomach infections accompanyed by fever.

The shapori method of shawara treatment is suggestive of the so-called 'principle of opposites', involving 'a cold remedy for a hot illness, and a hot remedy for a cold illness' (Foster 1994: 159). The shapori acts on a hot illness (shawara fire) with a cold remedy (a water hekura). The concept of opposing humoral properties is widespread among many indigenous groups of South America, especially in the areas north of the Amazon River, from French Guiana right through to the Andes (Butt Colson 1976). Some anthropologists have argued that the concept of opposite qualities already existed in various Latin American indigenous groups prior to the arrival of the Europeans (Bourget 2005; Butt Colson 1976;

Butt Colson and de Armellada 1983; Messer 1987; Ortiz de Montellano 1975). Others argue that the Spaniards introduced the humoral theory of health and illness to the original inhabitants of the new world in the sixteenth century (Foster 1987, 1994; Madsen 1955). Our examples indicate that the Yanomami shapori do indeed have basic knowledge of the principle of the opposites, namely hot and cold, but for them it is not the dominant model for curing illness. In the Yanomami lifeworld, hot and cold polarities related to good health and illness are not limited to the human body but, together with other opposing qualities (dry-wet), are embedded in the entire multilayered cosmos. Let us recall that the upper, younger cosmic strata are characterised by an abundance of light, heat and dryness, while older, subterranean layers are humid, cold and dark. The most powerful celestial hekura possess large amounts of heat while the terrestrial hekura associated with water and plants are perceived as cold. Several times during the initiation (see Chapter Four) both Ruweweriwë and Arawë were commenting through their songs how the descending hekura were sweating from the heat that they generate and had their dry tongues sticking out. Arawë felt the effects of this heat throughout his initiation. When he was experiencing the influx of hekura descending towards him, he was commenting through his chants that he was sweating and had a dry mouth from an intense heat produced by hekura. In one particular instance, he literally said that immortals were 'cooking his saliva'. On one occasion Ruweweriwë responded by summoning two hekura of liquids associated with 'cold' in order to ease Arawë's suffering. The first one was a tree sap Hõshõ Hekura ņou smeared all over Arawë's body to cool him down. Another one was Ãmoã u ('liquid song'), which refreshed his tongue and mouth so that he could continue singing. In another instance, the shapori helper Taramawë commented how a female Toad Hekura Hãsupɨriyoma had sprinkled water on the candidate to refresh him. As we saw, shapori also used this particular hekura when treating shawara manifesting as inner fire associated with fever.

Respiratory Infections

Besides diarrhoea and malaria, shawara epidemics of viral and bacterial infections of the upper respiratory tract and lungs continue to be one of the most frequent health disturbances, affecting large segments of the Yanomami population. Like any acute illness, respiratory infections tend to generate large-scale human suffering and discomfort, disrupting social activities and the economy of the group, which ultimately has an effect on children – increasing the risk of malnutrition and mortality. Respiratory infections can become lethal, particularly for children under a year old, if they pass the acute phase and more serious broncho-pneumonial complications arise (MSDS 2000: 24).

Influenza epidemics had an especially detrimental impact on the Yanomami population in the whole area around Platanal in the early 1970s when European tourists – not subjected to any health control by the authorities – arrived in small airplanes and contaminated entire communities (Colchester 1985; Lizot 1976b). The situation relatively improved after Venezuelan authorities attempted to limit tourism. In recent years the Yanomami from Platanal and other riverine settlements have become more mobile – travelling to La Esmeralda and Puerto Ayacucho where they often get infected and bring the infection back to their communities and contaminate others. Throughout my fieldwork, almost continual influenza epidemics were affecting the majority of Yanomami living in the region. In Platanal and other community settlements along the Orinoco, high population densities and more frequent contacts with outsiders facilitated the transmission of influenza, whereas in the intermediary community of Sheroana-theri, epidemics were triggered through frequent inter-communal visits. While I was living with the Sheroana-theri, visitors often reported the existence of shawara in various places, from Platanal and Mavaca to the distant Siapa River Valley in the south near the Brazilian border. During flu epidemics, all activities in the village were temporarily suspended and the affected Yanomami spent days lying in their hammocks and keeping themselves warm by the fire. They had chills (si sãihõu) and complained of general discomfort (pei ya washimi). Other symptoms included a fever (yopri), sometimes restricted to the head and neck only, a headache (heki nini), chest pain (pei pariki nini), sore throat (õrãmi nini), cough (thõkõ thõkõ), blocked ears and a runny nose. The shapori Ruweweriwë was continually engaging his hekura assistants to decontaminate the bodies of affected individuals, albeit with very little success. Sometimes his repetitive healing interventions would bring temporary relief from fever and chills but the symptoms of body ache, sore throat, cough and runny nose stubbornly persisted. Ruweweriwë described shawara as an all-embracing, hazy vapour that permeates people's bodies, making them sick. While his hekura assistants are trying to break shawara into pieces, they also feel sick from the shawara attempting to engulf and suffocate them. He commented how this new type of napë-related shawara is much more resilient than the shawara in the past. His hekura are not familiar with it and therefore are unable to cut it into pieces and extract it out of the body. On two occasions when he was sick, Ruweweriwë engaged some of his most powerful hekura in a series of self-curative acts; brushing his arms, chest and head with his hands, but the symptoms of shawara persisted for days. Filled with despair, he would come and ask me for tablets to ease his suffering. He was so ill that he could not hunt or do gardening and was just lying in his hammock. His family relied on food that his wife was collecting until he was fit enough to resume hunting.

For the Yanomami, ghosts, hekura and other types of spirit beings that populate their cosmos, whether unbound or directed by an enemy shapori, are potential conveyors of shawara illnesses. However, when they form a symbiotic relationship with the shaman they become beneficial. Under a shapori's guidance they use their diverse abilities to heal people from the same shawara illness they inflict in the first place. In this sense, we could say that they are both the source of the problem but also its solution. Let us recall from Chapter Four how during Arawë's initiation, especially after Hekura Mountain was positioned inside his chest, a multitude of hekura arrived and brought shawara with them. The candidate not only received the hekura but also the shawara that they inflict. Throughout the whole initiatory ordeal Arawë continuously experienced the effects of initiatory sickness, both during the influx of incoming hekura as well as between rounds or at night while he was resting in his hammock. During hekura embodiments, he frequently revealed through his singing how hekura made him feel weak. At the very beginning of initiation, Ruweweriwë was singing about Yãwãriyõma (a female subaquatic spirit being), who had brought a magical substance (hëri) to give to Arawë to feel its ill effects. Now his hekura will be able to detect it and recognise directly if someone has been the victim of the same substance. Thus, he will be able to neutralise its effects. Recall also another instance when Ruweweriwë assumed the identity of Moon Hekura Periporiwë; he approached Arawë and spat saliva containing shawara at his face. The candidate immediately felt ill, but the master shaman told him not to worry because in the future his personal hekura would be able to recognise it inside the body of a sick person and treat it accordingly. The effects of shawara illness lingered between the rounds of embodiments and during the night when he was constantly complaining of having fever (yopri), sharp pains (haye hëri) and generally feeling weak and unwell. He was also repeatedly warming himself up by the fire because he was shivering (prisiprisimou) from inner chills (si sãihõu). Evidently, the range of symptoms of the initiatory sickness that Arawë experienced during his progressive metamorphosis into hekura are also the most common symptoms that Yanomami generally experience when they are sick, even when they suffer from malaria and other introduced diseases. In this latter instance, shapori are capable of easing the patient's suffering, without being able to cure the disease, and in that respect they recognise doctors' competency in being able to cure people. Ruweweriwë's aforementioned responses regarding respiratory infections indicate that his hekura are ill-equipped to deal with this type of shawara because it originated outside of their cosmo-geographical ouroboric circuitry and as such it is alien. When I asked the shapori Makowë from Platanal about the same issue, he similarly replied that while his hekura assistants are familiar with fever (inner fire) and thus capable of reducing the shawara associated with it, they have little success when fighting the new, hazy type of shawara. In those situations he often sends people to see the doctor. The great transformer and cultural inventor Omawë, the demiurge, was frequently mentioned, by shapori and the majority of other Yanomami, as a bearer of shawara. For the non-initiated, he has a bad reputation because he makes people ill. On the other hand, shapori view Omawë as good and beneficial because he can also cure people from shawara.

We saw how shawara inflicted by hekura is a deeply engrained concept in theYanomami cosmos, so the candidates experience various symptoms during their initiatory ordeals. The same hekura who inflict shawara are able to cure it. But shawara, albeit in its new form, is also embedded in their mythology and paradoxically associated with the arrival of white people and deadly epidemics of previously unknown diseases, such as malaria, respiratory infections and measles, among others. The Yanomami shapori clearly recognise this new type of shawara as an external factor, which invaded and continues to invade their lifeworld. The explanation for this apparent paradox, as we saw in Chapter Two, lies in the particular logic present within their cosmological matrix, whereby the Yanomami at the time of their first contacts with white people, who brought manufactured goods and shawara illnesses, perceived them as their own returning ancestors or Omawë's offspring, who once upon a time disappeared downriver after the great flood. In the last chapter we will broaden the analysis of culture contacts with a particular emphasis on the dual meaning of manufactured objects as desirable but feared as a link to imported shawara epidemics.

Notes

1. See Kelly (2011, especially Chapter 6) for a detailed analysis of the difficulties that Ocamo doctors encounter in their dealings with the Yanomami.
2. Kõhõrõmɨ shikɨ are earthworms that the Yanomami use as fish bait, but in this context it means intestinal worms.
3. Warapa koko is a sap obtained from the tree *warapa kohi* (crepidospermum rhoifolium [Burseraceae]) (Lizot 2004: 465).

4. On the basis of his research in Mozambique, Green (1999) similarly argues that childhood diarrhoea is not interpreted in terms of witchcraft, sorcery and spirits but in terms of emic concepts of pollution and contamination. He refers to a number of other studies in other African countries that also indicate that the overwhelming majority of informants associated diarrhoea with natural rather than social or spiritual causes. However, what is considered 'natural' for these people is open to conjecture.

5. There are four different types of plasmodium parasite producing different strains of malaria. They include: p. falciparum; p. vivax; p. malariae and p. ovale. From these, the first three types – especially p. vivax – are the most lethal and p. falciparum are reported to be present in the Upper Orinoco (Magris et al. 2007; Torres et al. 1997).

6. Constant exposure to mosquito bites and an increase of parasites in the system can result in a painfully enlarged spleen, the so-called 'Hyper-reactive malarial splenomegaly syndrome' (HMSS). The results of one study (Torres et al. 1988) indicated that the Yanomami from the Upper Orinoco area are the only ethnic group in Venezuela with reported cases of this condition.

7. According to Lizot (2004: 474), this being takes the form of a feathered blanket that can wrap itself around people and suffocate them.

8. Wãrishewë is the nickname of Sloth Ancestor Ihamariwë; the two are one and the same being (ibid.: 468).

9. This counteracts some claims (Lizot 2007: 274) that the passageway between the terrestrial level and the underworld was only open in mythic times.

Chapter 8

RETURN OF THE ANCESTORS

The All-pervading Shawara, the End of the World and the Beginning of a New Epoch

The great flood (see Chapter Two) was one of the key cosmogonic turning points of destruction and regeneration of the Yanomami cosmos, marking the end of one cosmic cycle and the subsequent emergence of a new socio-cosmic order. The Yanomami associate the aftermath of the cosmic deluge with their own origins, but have also come to associate it with the origin of napë – namely, neighbouring ethnic groups as well as white people. This relational Yanomami-napë dichotomy is the theme of this chapter. The word 'Yanomami' is commonly characterised as an autonym meaning 'true human beings', which inevitably places others in a category of being less than human. However, as Viveiros de Castro explained, names of ethnic groups refer to social condition of personhood. Hence, it properly translates as 'we people' or 'us' as 'persons' and not as human beings as natural species (Viveiros de Castro 1998: 476). Self-designating themselves as 'Yanomami' (persons) indicates their relational position or attitude towards others and is not the proper name of the ethnic group. Ethnonyms are usually derogatory names given by others (ibid.). The neighbouring Yekwana, for example, used to call the Yanomami Goaharibos ('white howler monkeys'), implying their subordinate position and lower status on account of being on the margins of the Yekwana lifeworld. Similarly, napë for the Yanomami – who see themselves as being at the centre of creation – are quazi-humans coming from the fringes of their socio-cosmic world and are not the bearers of true humanity as a social condition.

The arrival of strange-looking, pale-skinned newcomers within the bounds of the Yanomami cosmo-geographical locale posited a challenge to their existing cosmogonic suppositions and understanding of the nature of creation. The Yanomami responded to this cosmological dilemma by interpreting the origin and capacities of white people and their relations to them in terms of the cataclysmic deluge that destroyed the world of their ancestors. They initially assimilated the arrival of foreigners into the a priori existing cosmological matrix and mythologised their activities and material possessions. The flood myth not only explains the origins of the contemporary Yanomami as direct descendants of the flood survivors, but also the origins of white people, whom they initially perceived as ghosts or as one of Omawë's creations. In their logic, without their creative inventor Omawë, neither they nor white people would exist and therefore neither would white people's material goods and lethal shawara illnesses that they brought with them.

The Origin of Shawara Epidemics

The Yanomami undoubtedly knew about the existence of white people before the actual face-to-face contacts were made, as news and rumours rapidly travel through the forest, spreading from community to community. We saw in Chapter One how the Yanomami, prior to their migration from the Parima Mountains towards the lowlands, obtained material goods from neighbouring Yekwana and Mácu groups, who traded directly with the Europeans. Drawing on Albert's analysis, during this period (1850–1920), the Brazilian Yanomami had little direct contact with white people. They heard rumours and stories about encounters in the forest (at the edge of the terrestrial disc) with bold, whitish ghosts, speaking unintelligibly, who came from the back of the sky and upriver to look for their own people. They did not have any toes (they were wearing shoes) and could take off their second skin (clothes) at will (Albert 1988). They reasoned that those 'creatures' were creations of their demiurge Remori,[1] who inhabits the sandy place at the edge of the earth and gave them metal tools. These narratives differ in some ways from the myths documented in the Venezuelan Upper Orinoco, as we will see. However, they share some common themes, namely the disappearance of a creative being and the subsequent arrival of foreigners. Another common feature to both regions is pathogenic smoke associated with the presence of white people and deadly epidemics.

Before the arrival of white people and unknown infectious diseases, the Yanomami associated shawara with the pathogenic smoke released through burning certain magical substances – an intentional act, aimed at affecting a multitude of persons and belonging to a general category of 'warrior sorcery' (ibid.) or else associated with the clandestine activity of õkã sorcerers blowing lethal dust from a pulverised poisonous plant (see Chapter Three). In Lizot's compilation of myths (1974, 1989), shawara originates from the epoch of the primordial twins. A myth from Tayari-theri (Lizot 1974: 43) narrates how the twins unleashed shawara illnesses unintentionally for the first time after attempting to contaminate a woman called Yoyoma (a type of a large toad) with the smoke released from the burning *oko shikɨ* plant. The lethal pathogenic smoke became windborne, diffusing uncontrollably. In this narrative, the woman is a victim of hostile activity on the part of male ancestors. Nowadays women use this powerful and toxic magical substance (hërɨ) exclusively against men; sometimes they burn pulverised oko shikɨ plant (literally – crab intestines)[2] inside a shapono and direct its smoke towards their unfaithful husbands or unwanted visitors in the hope of making them ill or killing them (Eguíllor García 1984: 197; Lizot 2004). More commonly, women accompany men on their warring expeditions and burn this substance close to enemy villages (Lizot 2004: 283).

In the early twentieth century, when the Yanomami started migrating from the Parima highlands towards the fluvial plains of present-day Venezuelan Amazonas in search of new habitats and metal tools, they encountered few white people; perhaps only rubber tappers or explorers, namely members of Dickey's expedition (Ferguson 1995: 208). With the arrival of white people and deadly new epidemics, the new variants of mythopoeic narratives concerning the twins emerged. Here we may take into account Gow's suggestion with regards to Kayapo myths about the origin of white people, that these new myths are not inversions but modifications of the existing myths (Gow 2001: 18). The prevailing theme of Yanomami myths dealing with the origins of white people, material goods and shawara epidemics is the withdrawal of the creative ancestral being – the great transformer Omawë and his twin brother Yoawë. For different reasons, the twins disappeared from the cosmo-geographical locale beyond the limits of the Yanomami known world where they transformed and became immortal. In one particular myth (Lizot in Wilbert and Simoneau 1990: 418–19), the twins heard the song of a warbling antbird (hypocnemis cantator): 'Ikekea, kea, kea…' (a tearing/ripping sound) and got scared, thinking that the malevolent being Yai wanted to rip their skin open. They fled downstream, reached the place where the Orinoco disappears underground, transformed into malevolent yaithë spirit beings and started sending shawara epidemics to the Yanomami. In other myths, shawara epidemics came from the õmãyãri malevolent beings[3] generated by the twins. In yet other variants of the myth (see Chapter Two), the twins either drifted away westwards, carried by the receding floodwaters and joined the world of 'whites' where they transformed into malevolent beings (Lizot 1974), or else, in a myth from Ocamo (Cocco 1972: 469–74), Omawë and his family undertook a long journey down the Shukumɨna River (Siapa) towards its mouth where they settled and Omawë created white people. In another narrative told to Helena Valero by her mother-in-law, Omawë was even capable of resurrecting dead people: 'When a Yanoáma died, Omawë took that dead body, shook it, pulled one of its arms or an ear, and the dead body returned to this world' (Biocca 1971: 148).

The people eventually turned against the twins. Yoawë intended to kill all ancestors with mamocori (curare poison), which is, as we may recall from Chapter Two, related to their grandmother Mamokoroyoma (Poisoned-vine woman). Omawë was against this and proposed to exterminate them with a flood. He prepared a raft for his brother and their sons then dug a hole in the ground with his bow causing water to sprout and inundate the entire forest. The twins drifted downstream and at one point the raft spun around and Yoawë's sons fell off and disappeared. Fusiwë's mother said that shapori are still singing about that event:

> The sons of Yoawë are going weeping towards the bottom. Their weeping is disappearing; already they are far away. Yoawë answers: 'My sons, my sons, do not weep. The sons of Yoawë are parimi [immortal], are eternal, are like the Hekura'. (Biocca 1971: 149)

The twins eventually reached the mouth of the river where the draft is still located. They reunited with their sons, grew old together and became immortal. 'They are always down there, singing with the hekura, where the great river ends' (ibid.).

To grasp the logic behind those mythical events, let us pause for a moment and recapitulate how the Yanomami perceive the space around them in directional terms. As discussed in Chapter Two, the image of the Yanomami cosmos is contained within the abdominal wall of a cosmic boa (hetu misi) unfolding along the east-west axis, the lower west side (koro misi) of which is the lower part of the sky where it meets the terrestrial disc (the horizon) (Lizot 2007). All major rivers in the central part of the Yanomami territory flow from their sources in the Parima

Mountains (*ora hamɨ* or 'upriver') westwards (*koro hamɨ* or 'downstream'), which is consistent with the direction of the receding floodwaters in the myth. Finally, Yanomami use the same terms to distinguish vertical space, whereby ora hamɨ (or ora) also means 'front part' or 'up' and koro hamɨ (or koro) 'back part' or 'down'. A comparative example of the symbolism involved in the shamanic complex of the Evenk people of the Central Siberian Plateau may shed some light on the subject. The shaman's tent consists of the tent proper (symbolising the middle world where humans live) and two galleries – one to the east near the tent's entrance, symbolising the celestial or upper world, and the other to the west or the subterranean world of the dead ancestors. During the ritual, the tent fully takes on the symbolic meaning and practical manifestation of the 'centre' of the universe as the shaman sits on a wooden raft, beats his drum and journeys to different cosmic levels on the cosmic river, which flows from its source in the upper world (east) towards the lower one in the west (Anisimov 1963). A cosmic river on a horizontal axis flows from east to west but simultaneously runs along a vertical axis from the upper to lower cosmic strata. In this instance, analogously to our Yanomami example, east is simultaneously up and west is down. Recall also from Chapter Four how during Arawë's initiation the migratory movement of hekura from geographical mountaintops towards his embodied corporeal mountain is simultaneously horizontal as well as vertical. Let us further analyse the myth about the twins and the first contact. In all variants, the twins travelled far away in a downriver direction either on foot (in Cocco's version) or by being carried along by water currents (Valero's version). They disappeared beyond the horizon (where the Orinoco disappears underground), while their sons sank to the bottom of the river. In the end, they were all reunited, transforming into immortals akin to the hekura. In each instance, it is one and the same direction – koro hamɨ (downstream and down) or towards the confines of the terrestrial disc where it meets the lower part of the sky vault. Regarding the aforementioned statement that the Yanomami initially perceived white people as ghosts from the sky, let us recall that within the overall cosmological schema, dead Yanomami transform into beautiful *no porepɨ* posthumous souls after transmigrating to the house of souls situated at the back of the sky. Let us also recall from Chapter One that the multiplicity of cosmic strata reproduces itself in the architectural structure of the Yanomami collective dwelling. Hence, the high part of the shapono's roof is simultaneously the lower part of the sky (koro mɨsi) and the meeting point of celestial and terrestrial strata. From the shamanistic perspective, the edge of the roof is equivalent to the horizon of the macrocosmic modality of their expanded consciousness. Under the roof's edge, shapori carry out their hekuramou activities, including myth enactments and cremation ceremonies to ensure that souls of the deceased find their way to the celestial house of souls by means of smoke. Others who die away from the shapono remain on earth and become white, bold ghosts (pore or *no uhutɨpɨ*). Recall from Chapter Three Ruweweriwë saying that one such pore near the Sheroana-theri shapono emerges from the ground at dusk in search of victims. When a pore becomes incorporated into the shapori's cosmic body his role is reversed. After the initiation, he guards the shapono's entrance near the navel – the microcosmic boundary area between the earth and underworld. The subterranean Amahiri ancestors (see Chapter Four) are also bold just like pore. In light of this, the assertion that the Yanomami initially perceived white people as (white and bold) ghosts or dead ancestors coming from the back of the sky becomes rather paradoxical (ghosts do not go to the sky). Instead, it is more plausible to say that they arrived from the lower, back part of the sky or from the far away horizon at the confines of the terrestrial disc. Take the above mentioned shapori's song as related by Fusiwë's mother, for example. Yoawë's sons sank towards the bottom of the river but simultaneously ended up downstream, which is the same direction (koro hamɨ: 'downstream' and 'down'). Another important detail in her account is Omawë's ability to bring the dead back to life. Hence, the Yanomami initially likened white people to ghosts or their own returning ancestors (Omawë's offspring) originating from him. However, the Yanomami eventually realised that the newcomers were not ghosts but human-like beings, similar to them albeit possessing a wealth of material goods and with extraordinary knowledge and the capacity to generate deadly epidemics.

Let us now move on to the subject of the development of shawara discourse. In Chapter One we spoke about the predecessors of the present-day Sheroana-theri (then forming a part of the Namowei population block) migrating from Parima towards the lowlands and, around the 1930s, settling close to the Orinoco River at a place called Hahoyaoba. According to Helena Valero, there they found some burned pieces of textile, broken glass and pieces of a mirror and soon fell victim of a deadly epidemic. They did not yet link illnesses to the presence of white people and immediately thought it was the harmful activity of enemy shapori, who must have stolen such items from white people and burned them to inflict napë-related illnesses by means of the smoke (Ferguson 1995: 209). Epidemics and threats from other groups forced them to cross the Orinoco and settle in Patanowë (ibid.). In the 1940s, the increased presence of westerners in the Upper Orinoco area meant that the Yanomami encountered them more frequently. In 1941, the Venezuelan boundary commission sent an airplane to fly over the area (Cocco 1972: 78; Valero 1984: 207), which made a profound impact on the Yanomami, who had never seen an airplane before. Helena Valero recalls the plane flying quite low over the Namowei-theri shapono and leaving a smoke trail behind. The Yanomami quickly extinguished their fires and hid in the nearby forest. They were convinced that pore (ghosts) were sending shawara smoke to make them ill, regardless of Helena's assurance that it was not ghosts but white people. That night, everyone accept Helena fell ill, trembling with fever and complaining of a headache. The next morning some Yanomami women told her that the reason why she did not get ill was because she was not human but an animal (Biocca 1971: 163). Around that time, Helena's son was born and had less hair than other Yanomami babies; his skin was also lighter. The women also said that he was not a human being and advised Helena to kill him. Evidently, at that time, the Yanomami still likened white people to non-human entities. Notwithstanding, Helena's husband, Fusiwë, responded angrily to the women:

> What are you saying? You want me to kill him, because he hasn't got a human face and because he has no hair. Why do you say this? Who has ever told you to kill your sons? As you love your own, so she loves hers. Let her bring him up, even if he has no hair! (ibid.: 162–63)

A few years later, the U.S. Army Corps sent a team of engineers to inspect a possible shipping route in the area. They brought large quantities of material goods and introduced gasoline-powered motorboats, which conveniently facilitated travel along the Orinoco. Up until then, the Namowei-theri had not yet had any face-to-face encounters with white people but were eager to obtain material goods from them (Ferguson 1995). The Namowei-theri headman, Fusiwë, had organised a few exploratory expeditions close to the Orinoco but had not encountered any foreigners. On one occasion, they discovered an abandoned camp – probably left by the U.S. Army Corps engineers – and found some machetes. Not long after they returned to their community a terrible epidemic started. People were falling ill with fever and many died (Valero 1984: 169–71). Helena's son was one of the first to become seriously ill. A group of shapori, led by Fusiwë, desperately tried to locate the child's missing vital essence. Fusiwë was familiar with the (spirit) paths leading to various hekura: to underground Amahiri (ancestors), to Sun Hekura Mothokariwë, to Moon Hekura Periporiwë, to Night Hekura Titiriwë and even the path that led to white people. He stood up and declared that the spirit path leading to white people was closed, with no footprints to be seen; therefore they were not to blame. He continued:

> This is the path, which leads to the Amahiri, but there are no tracks. On this road towards the Moon, the tracks are old. Here is the path of the Hekura of the Shamathari: was it they? See, here go their tracks; they climbed up onto the roof of the shapono, here they hid! Look, here are the signs of two Hekura. (Biocca 1971: 211)

Finally, he declared that the culprit who stole the child's vital essence was Sun Hekura. Evidently, the two Shamathari shapori (one of them disguised as Sun Hekura) stole the child's soul. Fusiwë heard the child, who had been imprisoned by the hekura, weeping on the edge of the shapono's roof (or the low part of the celestial vault). The shapori ascended along the Sun's path and snatched the missing soul from the Shamathari hekura. In continuation, he engaged various toad hekura (associated with water and cold) to reduce the child's fever and draw the sickness out of his body.

The child eventually got better, but other community members were also falling ill. Many of them died. People were rumouring that the real cause of their suffering was pathogenic shawara smoke (shawara wakeshi) that had contaminated their bodies; it could even kill hekura. Fusiwë heard a shout in the distance and warned Helena: 'Do not answer; it is the Mother of sickness, the fever, who is calling. She has seen men's footprints in different directions and does not know where to go' (Biocca 1971: 213). He told her about his dream of the origin of shawara:

> Last night I dreamed of so many white men, all clothed and with a cloak over them; when they shook the hood, smoke came out, and that smoke entered into us. When the whites undress, they leave the illness in their clothes. We die because of Shawara-wakeshi; it is the whites. White men cause illnesses; if the whites had never existed, diseases would never have existed either. (ibid.)

Helena contemplated how she never got seriously sick while living with them. Only after returning to live with the whites did she become ill. Fusiwë also got very sick, at one point collapsing and losing consciousness. An old shapori approached him and said that he had lost his senses because the shawara had scorched the throat of his main bird hekura assistant, Hererehiriwë. The shapori performed a long curative session and Fusiwë's condition eventually improved. However, later, during a hekuramou session, Fusiwë told the shapori that his bird hekura had vanished because of the illness. Fusiwë was mourning his lost companion and the shapori promised to give him one of his own hekura (ibid.: 214).

At the onset of an epidemic, the Yanomami abandoned their shapono and dispersed into the forest. Many people died. Their corpses were not cremated but wrapped up in leaves and left high up in trees to decompose. When the epidemic abated, they collected the bones and returned to their shapono to reduce them to ashes; they then consumed them in a customary manner. This malaria epidemic took a deadly toll and many people from Namowei-theri, Mahekoto-theri and other neighbouring groups passed away (Valero 1984: 287–300). As mentioned, at the time of the epidemic, the Namowei-theri, who had already split into various groups, had not yet experienced direct encounters with white people. Recall from Chapter One Ruweweriwë talking about one of his shapori predecessors who had dreamt about white people before the actual contact took place. He likened white people to ghosts and as having another, second skin (clothing) or *iro siki* ('skin of a red howler monkey'), which, as mentioned, is the actual Yanomami word for a T-shirt.[4] Ruweweriwë was possibly referring to Fusiwë or perhaps another shapori, considering that Ruweweriwe's predecessors come from Patanowë-theri, who split from Fusiwë's Namowei lineage. Regarding Yanomami perceptions of white people as having a second skin, let us bring to mind Viveiros de Castro's (1998) comments about the widespread Amazonian notion of a cover or 'clothing' as a manifest form of each species in the sense that, in myths, a true internal human form – the soul or consciousness – is hidden under the outer cloak of its animal appearance (bodily form). The Namowei-theri women were continuously trying to strip Helena of her humanity by likening her to an animal because of her long hair, white skin and inability to be affected by shawara. When her son was born, they also said that he was not human (being white-skinned and bold akin to a ghost) but Fusiwë decided that he should live, regardless of being different. Ruweweriwë told me that it was his Patanowë-theri lineage who experienced the first direct encounters with napë and received metal tools. These initial contacts were peaceful but things soon got out of control when the foreigners refused to give more goods. Ruweweriwë said that napë were firing shotguns above the Yanomami and that it was the lethal smoke (*wakeshipi wayu*) containing shawara that fell down and killed them. He said that those guns were much shorter than today's rifles (which he saw many times), and according to their size (which he demonstrated with his hands) most likely he was talking about pistols. He did not say that napë killed them directly but were shooting above them (perhaps to scare them away). What he actually said was that they fell ill from shawara and died, associating illnesses with shawara-containing smoke.

Around the same period (1942–43), a group of rubber tappers led by a half Yekwana man, Silverio Level, established a camp on the other side of the Orinoco in the area of Upper Manaviche where they encountered a group of Yanomami from Shitoya-theri (Cocco 1972: 74; Ferguson 1995:

224).[5] Let us recall from Chapter One that this group, which later became the Mahekoto-theri and gained a reputation for being 'friends of the white man' (Ferguson 1995: 214), had settled there sometime during the 1930s. They found the area convenient as it provided them with the opportunity to obtain metal tools from the Yanomami living in Padamo. In the following narrative describing this encounter (Lizot 1985: 3–5), an informant said that the whites arrived in boats and made a shelter on the riverbank. They were extracting latex from the rubber trees and boiling it in massive metal pots. The Yanomami were curiously watching them for days, hidden in the nearby bushes. The foreigners had big frightening dogs and large amounts of metal tools (axes, machetes and knives). Finally, one Yanomami was courageous enough to approach them. Others were squatting at a safe distance, watching smoke coming out of the boiling kettles; shapori had warned that the smoke contained dangerous shawara beings that could enter their bodies and make them ill or kill them and even their hekura assistants would be unable to expel them. Some children did die and people related their deaths to pathogenic smoke.

Those first encounters were tense but peaceful. The situation deteriorated when one Yanomami man pledged his son's help in exchange for one of the foreigner's dogs. The boy soon escaped and returned to the group. The foreigners no longer wanted to trade with them but the Yanomami desperately wanted their personal possessions and some leaders called for action. The next day they sneaked into the camp and stole some metal tools and clothes. The foreigners requested the stolen items to be returned but the Yanomami refused. One of the foreigners fired his gun and wounded a man's arm. The Yanomami retaliated and killed one foreigner while others quickly left. This narrative strongly resembles the account as told by Jacinto's father, Okoshiwë, in Platanal (see Chapter One) although I cannot ascertain that it is the same story. On that day, Okoshiwë came up to me and requested a saucepan or a machete. I agreed to give him a saucepan in exchange for telling me the story of the first encounter with white people. Jacinto had once said that Okoshiwë was the only person who knew the story (being very young at the time) but was not very keen to talk about it. Okoshiwë told me that the man who first approached the napë was his father, who was their leader. He then only commented that those napë were generous and gave them lots of material goods. He went quiet. I continued interrogating him further but he became irritated and immediately changed the topic. I stopped insisting and also gave him the machete. I was wondering if he only emphasised the napë's generosity and did not mention the killings because his intention in the first place was to provoke in me the same sense of generosity or perhaps make me feel guilty in order to give him what he wanted. Be that as it may, not long after Shitoya-theri encountered rubber tappers they changed their name into Mahekoto-theri and settled on the other side of Orinoco where they met Eduardo Noguera and his party of loggers, who founded Platanal. Afterwards, the missionaries, and then the medical workers, arrived and established themselves permanently in the Upper Orinoco. The contact with foreigners has been increasing ever since, as Yanomami from inland communities have intensified their visits to riverine settlements in search of manufactured objects, which in turn has contributed to the proliferation of deadly epidemics and a subsequent population decline.

Further Expansion of the Shawara Concept

Up until the 1940s, the Yanomami associated outbreaks of shawara epidemics with smoke and dust originating from burnt or pulverised substances produced by enemy sorcerers. But thenceforth, the shapori began announcing that deadly new diseases came from white people and their material possessions. Bruce Albert's informant from the Catrimani River in Brazil told him that when whites opened their boxes containing machetes wrapped in waxed paper, the Yanomami saw smoke, which had a strong odour, spiralling out of them. Upon inhaling this intense smell they immediately felt sick and vomited. Thinking that smoke came from machetes they washed them in the river and rubbed them with sand (Albert 1985: 166). We saw in the accounts above how the Yanomami associated lethal epidemics with gun smoke and burning latex. Recall how Fusiwë mentioned the path of white people when he was treating his sick son. These accounts indicate that, even before the Yanomami experienced first direct contacts with white people, their presence was already embedded into the Yanomami cosmo-shamanic space, alongside other denizens. Fusiwë mentioned shawara following people's footprints. He also described his dream revelation of pathogenic smoke coming out of white people's clothes and entering their bodies. Shawara not only kills people but it also destroys hekura. When Fusiwë fell ill, one of his key hekura assistants disappeared although it is not clear if he abandoned his host or if he was annihilated by an illness. We will see later how the hekura are incapable of defeating the all-pervading shawara and are obliterated by it.

When doctors and missionaries arrived, the Yanomami began to link shawara illnesses with smoke released from burnt rubbish and plastics or the strong smell of gasoline released from motorboats; in fact any product related to criollos was believed to cause illness, even the noise of an electric generator (see also Kelly 2011: 70). At the time of my fieldwork, the Yanomami still associated shawara illnesses with abnormal lights, such as a rainbow or a red twilight sky, as well as smoke from airplanes and fabric or clothing. Ruweweriwë frequently warned me against leaving my towel spread out to dry overnight because it could attract unknown hekura or shawara and make me (and others) sick. When Arawë was recovering from the hekura attack (see Chapter Six), the visiting Toritha-theri shapori, Shawarawë, repeatedly slid my blanket up and down his body to catch shawara and ease his suffering. We also saw how shapori frequently brushed and squeezed the shawara out of patients' garments (T-shirts). Finally, recall from Chapter Four when Ruweweriwë summoned the hekura of textiles or clothing called Watota peshiyë and was dancing towards Arawë holding a loincloth in his hands. The shapori assistant Taramawë warned Arawë that these hekura bring shawara and would make him ill.

The smoke released from burning firewood is not deemed a lethal transmitter of shawara illnesses unless something else is burned with it. One afternoon in Platanal, I opened a colourful sachet of soup and emptied its content into a pot of boiling water; I then threw the empty sachet into the fire. The packet was coated with a thin plastic film, which released thick smoke. One Yanomami, who was sitting next to me, immediately jumped up and screamed: 'Ma shori, wa tatihe! Shawara wakeshipi a waritiwë. Pëhëki ta haririprou, thōkō thōkō, hura' ('No! Don't do that! This smoke containing shawara is bad and it will make us sick with a cough and fever').

The smoke released during the incineration of a corpse may also contain shawara, especially if the deceased was sick prior to his or her death (Eguíllor García 1984). For that reason, during outbreaks of shawara epidemics, the Yanomami temporarily abandon their shaponos, disperse into the nearby forest and construct provisional shelters. For them, the reason for not cremating bodies of people who died from shawara is to prevent a spread of the contagion; therefore, they leave bodies suspended high up in trees. However, Ruweweriwë once told me that they did this to prevent the dead from turning into wandering ghosts; high trees and mountaintops are closer to the sky thus the souls whose bodies are suspended in trees (between the sky and the earth) are more likely to find their way to the celestial house of souls.

When Namowei-theri saw the smoke coming from behind the airplane in 1941, they thought shawara was descending upon them. During my fieldwork, their descendants from the Sheroana and Toritha-theri still perceived smoke trails left by airplanes as a conveyor of shawara, which falls to the ground and could make them sick. For that reason, whenever a plane passed by, they hid under the shapono's roof for some time. One morning while I was visiting Toritha-theri, an airplane left a long, white trail of smoke behind. The chief shapori Shawarawë reacted immediately by slashing the air with his arms in the direction of the smoke and shouting: 'shawara, shawara!' People hid under the shapono's roof. The Yanomami reacted the same way on three different occasions, once in Platanal and twice in Sheroana-theri, during the afternoon manifestation of a typical atmospheric phenomenon, which they identified as 'hetu misi wakëmou' (Lit. 'The sky has turned red') and likened it to the shawara containing smoke (shawara wakeshipi). Each time, it occurred during the seasonal transition from the dry to wet period (September–October) and each time it rained heavily the day after. To me, the spectacle resembled a huge red cloud mass, but the Yanomami clearly distinguish smoke (wakeshi) from the clouds (ihirashi) and they plainly identified it with the former rather than the latter. The Yanomami associate certain abnormal lights resulting from atmospheric phenomena – such as a rainbow, yellow light provoked by an eclipse, and an unusually intense yellow or red colour at dawn or dusk– with diseases and human suffering (Cocco 1972; Lizot 2007). But for the Sheroana-theri and the Mahekoto-theri Yanomami, the red sky smoke was evidently something different. At other times when the horizon was red at dusk they didn't react. During one such afternoon in Sheroana-theri, Ruweweriwë warned people that the sky smoke contained sickness-bearing shawara and was falling down.[6] He also said that the smoke had made the sun turn yellow (Yanomami normally perceive the sun to be white) and urged people to avoid exposing themselves to its exceptionally harmful rays as it could make them ill with fever. The phenomenon lasted approximately half an hour. During that time, a considerable central portion of the sky was covered with a red coloured cloud-like mass with grey edges that indeed resembled the smoke released from a massive bush fire. The peak of the spectacle only lasted for a few moments. The red colour of the clouds could soon be seen fading and turning to orange before gradually losing density and utterly evaporating. At the same time, the sky was saturated with a golden light, which was concurrently merging and rapidly vanishing with the bluish shades of the approaching evening. In the end, the night replaced the day and the last traces of red disappeared from the horizon. Meanwhile, as those moments were unfolding, the people in the shapono were anxious. Ruweweriwë was telling women and children to go quickly under the roof. Many were weeping. The shapori was allegedly slashing the falling shawara into pieces with his arms then thrusting them back towards the sky and away from shapono.

The following morning while it was still dark and before an early morning mist engulfed the surroundings, Ruweweriwë ordered everyone to wash themselves and their personal possessions, namely bows and arrows, baskets and even their dogs, in the nearby creek. Afterwards, we returned to shapono. As we lay in our hammocks and ate roasted plantains, the shapori explained to me that the sky smoke from the previous day contained shawara and that it was falling down on the earth. By taking shelter under the shapono's roof and later washing their bodies and personal possessions, people avoid getting contaminated by shawara.

We had to wash before the onset of the morning mist because otherwise people's noreshi animal double (see Chapter Three) could have become lost in the mist and started making sounds. Thus, it would have been vulnerable and exposed to potential hunters; if they detect and kill the animal double a Yanomami will also die simultaneously (Herzog-Schröder 1999: 47). That day, the morning sun dispersed the mist somewhat earlier than usual. It was scorching hot and it rained heavily in the afternoon. I was curious to hear what the Yanomami thought about the origin of the red sky smoke. Therefore, I began asking various individuals and they all told me different things. Ruweweriwë immediately pointed easterly, commenting about big fires raging in Brazil.[7] His son Mirko believed that the Sun Hekura Mothokariwë sent the shawara smoke to make the Yanomami sick. For the Sheroana-theri headman, Maruwë, the smoke accumulated from the increasingly frequent smoke trails left by airplanes.[8] Lastly, Arawë associated the sky smoke with cremation (see Chapter Five). He explained that the thick yellow, shawara-containing smoke was released at the moment when the boy's body started to burn from the heat. It then spread across the sky and turned it red. Three days later there was an outbreak of an epidemic (despite the ritual bath precaution). People were falling ill with fever and chills. Ruweweriwë and the headman Maruwë decided to abandon the shapono for a while and take people on a food-gathering expedition (wãyumɨ).

The End of the World and the Beginning of another Cosmic Cycle

In Venezuela, prolonged contact with criollos resulted in the proliferation of deadly epidemics and the ensuing decline of the Yanomami population, coupled with the gradual but nevertheless devastating impact of cultural change. However, their fate was not as tragic as that of their Brazilian counterparts on whom the impact was much more severe, especially from the 1970s onwards. In 1973, the Brazilian government collaborating with military personnel constructed a 235 km stretch of road called Perimetral Norte right through the middle of Yanomami territory in the

State of Roraima. This controversial geopolitical project subjected a large number of Yanomami to numerous and frequent contacts with outsiders, exposing them to various contagious and infectious diseases, such as malaria, influenza, and measles and they consequently experienced severe demographic losses (Rabben 1998). In 1987, the discovery of gold in the State of Roraima resulted in an influx of illegal gold prospectors (garimpeiros), which triggered new waves of epidemics among the Yanomami population. In the following few years, gold prospectors constructed numerous clandestine airstrips close to the Venezuelan border and conflicts with local Yanomami populations became frequent. The constant supply planes and the noise from generators and pumps used for mining operations had frightened away game animals – a key source of food for the Yanomami. Garimpeiros dug holes with bulldozers and used high-pressure hoses to wash away riverbanks, silting the rivers and thus destroying spawning grounds. To separate the gold from soil and rock they used highly toxic mercury, which entered the ecosystem and in turn infiltrated the food chain in the form of a neurotoxin, affecting – amongst other things – child development. Between 1988 and 1990 around 15 per cent of the Yanomami population was lost (MacMillan 1995). In 1993, a group of gold miners assassinated sixteen Yanomami, mainly women and children, in the community of Hashimú on Venezuelan territory and burned down their shapono. This incident drew worldwide attention and prompted the Venezuelan government to increase security measures by placing soldiers in the area (Chapter Six).

In the wake of scores of deaths and general crises brought about by the increased intrusion of garimpeiros into the Yanomami territory, the shapori Davi Kopenawa from the Toototobi region in Brazil emerged as a new charismatic leader, warning about a looming cosmic catastrophe articulated as the immediate threat of the falling sky and the imminent end of the world. In his youth, Davi was groomed by the New Tribes Mission (NTM) to become a pastor but he ended up working for FUNAI (National Indian Foundation), becoming an activist and fighting for the Yanomami cause on both the national and international level. Surrounded by an aura of care, righteousness and sincerity, his status grew quickly. Eventually, he became a political leader and a cultural mediator between the Yanomami and the government. Kopenawa initially aspired to unite all the Yanomami against the outside threat and create in them a sense of pan-Yanomami identity. He soon started advocating the rights of all indigenous peoples when he began travelling to other countries and gaining insights of the problems and struggles of other groups. Davi attended various international conferences and political meetings, including the 1992 UN Earth Summit in Rio de Janeiro. In 2009, in the wake of the UN Climate Change conference in Copenhagen, he travelled to Europe and expressed his views to the media and politicians. In his recent book *The Falling Sky: Words of a Yanomami Shaman* (Kopenawa and Albert 2013), written in collaboration with anthropologist Bruce Albert, Davi provides an insight into his thoughts, his life and his people.

A combination of his shamanistic knowledge and insights as well as familiarity with the Christian doctrine, especially the Book of Revelation, led him to develop a powerful, synthetic discourse, with strong environmentalist and moralistic undertones (Amazon forests are 'lungs of the world'). His main concern is the deadly shawara-containing smoke (shawara wakeshipɨ) released into the ground through the reckless extraction of gold, iron and oil. It was Omawë, according to Davi, who buried gold and other minerals together with shawara deep in the ground. While all this was buried there was no problem. But today, foreigners dig deep holes to extract these minerals, which release smoke-like dust that is then carried on the wind and makes people sick.

Davi recounts in his book that when white people first appeared, the no patapɨ ancestors did not understand what they were doing in the forest. The Yanomami were scared but curious and wanted to obtain their material goods. Soon, they started getting sick and dying in their masses. Nobody knew why. All of Davi's relatives passed away. Both his parents died in the outbreak of a measles epidemic that swept through the area in the 1960s. The people soon realised that they were getting ill from the lethal fumes coming from white people's personal possessions. These fumes were viewed as deadly for the malevolent *xawarari* (*shawarari*) epidemic beings they contained and which only shapori are able to detect. Note the strong resemblance of Davi's statement to the aforementioned warning of Fusiwë about the 'Mother of sickness' (shawara fever) following footprints, including white people's footprints.

While my shapori informants identified shawara primarily with fever, Davi's views are much more elaborate. He describes xawarari or shawarari beings as bloodsucking, flesh-eating cannibals with long canine teeth and covered in thick smoke. They also have the appearance of white people, wearing clothes like them. There are various types of xawarari beings: beings of the cough (*thokori*) that slice people's throats and chests, others that consume people's intestines and cause diarrhoea (*xuukari*) or provoke nausea (*tuhrenari*) or weakness (*hayakorari*) and yet others that make people waste away (*waitatori*). They are able to hear people's voices in the distance, then sneak into a shapono at night and prey upon women, children and elders. From Davi's perspective, when people get sick from respiratory infections and severe fever related to malaria, xawarari cut their throats with machetes, roast them like game and pile up their corpses:

She [shawara] is eating a bunch of children; she does away with them, eats them without stopping, kills them and grills them as if they were monkeys that she'd hunted. She piles up a bunch of grilled children. All the Yanomami it kills are grilled and piled up in this way by *xavara* [shawara]. It only stops when it has enough. It kills a load of children the first time and then, a while later, attacks another lot ... the *xavara* is very hungry for human meat ... (Albert, cited in Rabben 1998: 117)

Davi remembers how shocked he was while observing a group of garimpeiros for the first time close to his village. They were digging into the ground akin to a herd of wild peccaries in search of gold, leaving waterways as muddy bogs filled with oil, rubbish and deadly fumes containing shawara illnesses. In time, he learned about the toxic mercury used to obtain pure gold and that it poisons the water as well as fish, anacondas and caimans together with their immaterial spirit essences and decided to defend his people and fight to save their environment from destruction.

When Davi began travelling extensively beyond Yanomami territory and learning more about the world of white people, he started talking about the dangers of deforestation, of global pollution caused by smoke released from factories and the climate change affecting the whole planet. The lethal smoke and dust initially released from burning gold is, according to Davi, now spreading everywhere and the whole world is becoming sick and contaminated. Deadly smoke containing shawara beings is released out of heated iron and oil in factories causing global pollution. Even bombs and wars contribute to this universal sickness of pollution. In one interview with Terence Turner (Cultural Survival 1991), he expressed his concern about the smoke that was unleashed from the atomic bomb (in Hiroshima and Nagasaki) and the black smoke from the petroleum that was burned during the Gulf War. He blames white people for the current crisis; it is they who cause pollution everywhere and will make sky and earth terminally sick. The whole world is in danger, not just the Yanomami but also white people. His discourse eventually becomes a shamanistic critique of western capitalism and of white people's greed and ignorance. His ultimate message is truly apocalyptic – a fatalistic vision of a decaying universe. Due to the increasing smoke, the whole cosmos is deteriorating and everything is becoming sick and dying, including the sky, the earth, and even the everlasting hekura are ceasing to exist. Souls of the dead are no longer in their perfect state of posthumous existence. Now, according to Davi, when someone gets sick and dies from fever related to introduced diseases, his or her liberated no porepɨ soul essence is also contaminated with shawara smoke. The soul essence ascends to the sky shapono in a diseased state and sick with fever. The dead will keep on multiplying and the sky will eventually become very heavy and sick. Even Omawë – and Deosime God of white people – are getting sick. The killer smoke is spreading unstoppably through the forest and beyond, reaching the lands where white people live. If the shawara smoke continues to expand, it will engulf everything and cause cosmic havoc. The sky will finally crash into the earth and it will be the end of the world.

Davi repeatedly emphasises the supremacy of indigenous people in relation to white people. Shapori are bearers of true knowledge and wisdom and it is only they who are capable of holding the sky high up to prevent it from collapsing, with the help of their hekura. Only shapori can save the Yanomami and the whole of humankind because they know how to repair the sky eroded by shawara. These statements emerged against the backdrop of 1992 UN Earth Summit in Rio de Janeiro, which was a turning point for the redefinition of indigenous knowledge. Since then, shamans have become identified in global discourse as representatives of their people with exceptional knowledge and as such have become the icons of indigenous identity. Shamanism has been being redefined and stripped of its negative components. Shamans' traditional role as mediators between human and spirit worlds has been expanded to include their new role as guardians of nature and mediators between their people and the state (Conklin 2002).

Davi stresses the importance of shaporis' capabilities of preventing the looming catastrophe, but he also admits that they are slowly losing the battle. Their hekura are vanishing, unable to cut through the tough, wrinkled, elastic, rubber-like shawara with their machetes. He warns that if all shapori die the sky will inevitably collapse and kill all the Yanomami and everyone else. Together with the sky, the sun, the moon and the stars will all fall down and everything will turn to darkness. If xawarari continue to invade their lands, they will kill all shapori together with their hekura and everything will eventually turn into chaos. Spirit beings of nature (night, mist, earth) will all get angry and grieve for dead shamans. Dark clouds will cover the entire sky and the sun will disappear. Rains will not stop falling and gale force winds will continually blow. The rumble of thunder will be ceaseless and lightning beings will fall on earth in masses. This will cause the earth to open up and swallow the trees and buildings in the cities. Airplanes will be crushed. Xiwaripë (chaos beings) will be unleashed, and there will be no more shapori to chase away the night being Titiri – perpetual darkness and cold will come. Giant wasps will sting people and turn them into peccaries. Snakes will fall from the sky and fierce jaguars will appear from everywhere to devour human beings. Continual rain will erode all the soil and cause waters to rise and cover the entire earth and humans will become 'other', just like it happened before. (Here, Davi refers to the previous cosmic flood, which gave origin to contemporary humans.)

When a shapori dies, his personal hekura abandon their corporeal microcosmic dwelling and are scattered back to nearby mountains and rocks. The lament of grieving hekura can produce macrocosmic effects whereby dark clouds cover the sky, thunderbolts are unleashed and it rains heavily. It is then that the Yanomami say that some grand shapori has just died (Cocco 1972: 426; Lizot 1985: 97) and the whole group to which the shapori belongs will then customarily abandon their shapono and move elsewhere to make a new dwelling. Davi warns that if multiple shapori die, all their unleashed personal hekura will disperse everywhere and become fierce and dangerous. They will be grieving for their dead masters and taking revenge by slashing the sky to pieces with their axes and cutting all supports that hold the sky up, thus causing it to collapse.

Incarnated hekura of the living shapori will try to convince their angry, disembodied counterparts to hold on and wait to become re-embodied (through the initiation). For as long as the cosmic circuitry of hekura incarnation takes place, the vitality of the cosmos will be preserved and maintained through shaporis' bodies. If the number of initiated shapori continues to decline, more hekura will become discarnate thus causing chaos and the collapse of the cosmic order that only shapori can maintain. In this case, not a single shapori will remain to hold the sky up and prevent it from crashing down and killing everyone. When the sky collapses, the earth will also collapse and sink into the underworld together with all people, who will vanish and become no patapɨ ancestors (Kopenawa and Albert 2013). This image of the dislocation of cosmic discs caused by the sky falling will be familiar, since in the past this occurrence turned one generation of the ancestors into the subterranean Amahiri, as discussed in Chapter Two.

Although Davi blames white people for the looming disaster, in the end the act of co-op revenge by dead shapori will eventually cause the sky to break up. The underlying message is that if white people are responsible for Yanomami deaths, they will also pay the price and end up dying; it will be punishment for the act they committed in the first place (Berwick 1992: 96). Davi is urging all shapori to cease with any hostilities they have against each other and unite their hekura powers to fight against a common threat. He raises awareness directly by visiting other communities or by sending a messenger with a tape-recorded speech. The tape containing people's responses eventually comes back to him. In one such response, a shapori from a remote Brazilian community said:

I am not a nabë. I am a Yanomami. Real Yanomami ... A Yanomami all the time. My *ebene* [snuff] doesn't stop. It's Yanomami; the life of the Yanomami ... I am not going to leave the Yanomami [life]. (ibid.: 73)

Some newly emerging Yanomami leaders in Venezuela have also begun to use tape-recorded messages to raise awareness of the threat of deadly epidemics in more remote communities. Yanomami generally admire the tape recorder as a technical device (as opposed to the camera, which they dislike). On numerous occasions during my fieldwork, they were very keen to tape their own songs and speeches and endlessly laughed at the sound of their own voices. It also amused them to listen to songs from other communities, some of them being traditional enemies. On one occasion in the Sheroana-theri, a child got sick with fever while Ruweweriwë was away. Evidently distressed, his mother approached me and asked me to play Ruweweriwë's previously recorded songs while the boy's grandmother brushed the child's body akin to the shapori. When I asked her later if this had helped she answered affirmatively, saying that hekuras' songs had alleviated the child's fever. In 1997, Davi organised the Third Assembly of the Yanomami People in his village and invited some Yanomami leaders from Venezuela (including my main informant, Jacinto, from Platanal). His intention was to familiarise the Venezuelan Yanomami with the tragic fate of their Brazilian counterparts and raise awareness of the importance of preserving their cultural identity and continuing to practise shaporimou. All his main speeches were recorded on tape, which was then played in Platanal and other Upper Orinoco communities. Jacinto was very satisfied with the meeting and its objectives to promote unity and solidarity among all Yanomami people.

Decline of Shamanism and the Shrinking of the Primordial Sphere

Davi admits that shapori cannot effectively eradicate shawara, which destroys their hekura. Recall that when Fusiwë was sick one of his most prominent hekura helpers vanished as a result of his illness. Shapori see this as a very serious threat because their hekura are clearly losing their primordial quality of immortality. For them, the eradication of hekura 'heralds the end of the world' (MacMillan 1995: 51). Shapori are cosmic pillars effectively holding the sky up thus preventing it from falling. If they continue to die from deadly shawara the distance between sky and earth will collapse, as Davi implicitly suggests. If we follow this logic, I argue that another looming factor that could contribute to the eventual collapse of a cosmic order, especially in Venezuela, is a general decadence of shamanism. There is now a growing disinterest among new generations to preserve the continuity of shaporimou practice, with many young men no longer interested in inheriting their father's hekura. In fact, ever since cultural contact with outsiders became more frequent in the Venezuelan Upper Orinoco region, there has been a gradual decrease in the number of initiated shapori in comparison to the past. Helena Valero, who lived with the Yanomami long before the missionaries arrived in the Upper Orinoco, recalled in her narrative that all adult males in Namowei-theri were shapori and young men would eventually become initiated. The abundance of practitioners in a single settlement was the distinctive feature that set them apart from other groups in the region. Father Luis Cocco, who was in charge of the Salesian Mission in Ocamo at the time, commented that in more remote communities, most if not all adult males were shapori, able to induce collective trances through their sessions (Cocco 1972: 424). Father Berno, who was in charge of the Mavaca Mission, commented that in some nearby villages 25 out of 30 Yanomami men were shapori. John Peters, who lived with the Mucajai Yanomami in Brazil for eight years from 1958, wrote that every male bachelor was either a shaman or had some relationship with the spirits (Peters 1973: 89). While Chagnon (1968a: 52) in his early days of fieldwork also observed that in some villages half the male population practised shaporimou in one form or another. In the 1980s, among the Venezuelan Sanema – the Yanomami's northern neighbours – 80 per cent of the male population became sapuli (shapori) (Colchester 1982: 138).

Nowadays, there are very few grand shapori left. They are keen on preserving the continuity of shaporimou practice but are becoming increasingly frustrated and disappointed with young men and their lack of interest in becoming hekura. For that reason, they welcomed my interest in their practices, despite the fact that I was an outsider. They were astonished and endlessly amused by my efforts to gain practical knowledge of becoming a hekura, while concurrently complaining about their own sons' lack of interest in learning the craft. I was told that the contemporary initiatory ordeals are less severe than what they used to be and consequently the shapori are not as powerful as their predecessors. Platanal Yanomami quietly admitted that their traditional Shamathari enemies from the Siapa River Valley still carry out more rigorous initiations thus their shapori are renowned for their great skills and powers. The medical presence in this part of Amazonas State was literally non-existent until a few years ago when it was included in government-sponsored health programmes, which engaged medical teams as well as the army.

While adolescents from more remote communities still aspire to become hekura, others living in the vicinity of mission centres and health posts are increasingly losing interest. At the time of my fieldwork, all these young men – trained and employed as health workers or teachers – were sons of shapori, who were supposed to inherit their fathers' hekura. But they were becoming increasingly disengaged and alienated from their own culture; they were more concerned with earning money to buy wholesale goods and spent time in Puerto Ayacucho or Caracas, away from their communities. During their time off from work, however, they were still keen to participate in group epenamou sessions and shaporimou performances but without showing any enthusiasm for becoming shapori themselves. One of the common reasons, besides lack of enthusiasm, was their fear of hekura. But most of them told me they still liked taking epena for the sake of experience. Makowë's son, Xavier, said he did not have any desire to become a shapori but he liked taking epena. 'When we take epena, we sit, talk, laugh and get drunk just like napë who get together to have a few drinks,' he once told me. I also asked an ex-teacher, Enano's son Freddy, the same question and he replied that he is not interested in practising shaporimou but would like to find a job and earn money to buy a power generator for his house. Enano was very disappointed with his choices and keen to pass on his hekura to his nephew from Karohi-theri. The initiation took place while I was in Platanal, but it ended abruptly on the fifth day after the candidate refused to continue; he lost his focus and succumbed to an overwhelming fear of dying. Enano was furious. He slapped him in the face, kicked him in the bum and told him to go back to his community and never return. Brujo the son of another practising shapori, Ruawë, was once initiated but later lost interest and became addicted to snuff. Potai wanted his son, Hairo, an ex-teacher, to become shapori; however, a few days into the initiation Potai caught him secretly taking a bath. Potai was so angry that he cut Hairo's hammock to pieces and terminated the initiation. Cardoso is another failed shapori, who told me that after he had been initiated he lost his powers due to engaging in sexual intercourse. I jokingly replied to him: 'Just as Yoawë [the older primordial brother] did', and we both wholeheartedly laughed. My main informant, Jacinto, told me that he was initiated at a young age while still living in his native community of Sheroana-theri. His uncle was a great shapori, who wanted to pass his hekura to Jacinto and convinced him to pursue it. Jacinto wanted to give up after the second day of initiation, but his uncle did not allow it. When Jacinto moved to Platanal, he got involved with the mission's work and stopped practising. Consequently, his hekura left him and he lost his powers.

The negative side of cultural change is evidently taking its toll and new generations are caught between the demands of tradition and the ongoing processes of cultural transformation and encroaching modernity. Due to their lack of interest (and fear) in becoming shapori and inheriting their ancestral hekura, the resulting intergenerational gap is now threatening to seriously disrupt the transmission of mythical lore and practical hekura knowledge. This is occurring despite the fact that the vast majority of Yanomami still rely on, and choose to consult, their shapori before seeing doctors. Because introduced diseases are now a perpetual threat and shaporis' ability to control them is limited, the Yanomami are becoming increasingly dependent on biomedical treatments.

What are possible consequences of all this? As the number of initiations decline, so does the opportunity for ancestral hekura to incarnate themselves and unfold the primordial horizons of expanded consciousness. As discussed in Chapter Four, the shamanistic initiation not only represents the transformation of a human being into hekura but is also the repetition of a cosmogonic act or the sky and earth fusion into the all-encompassing dimensionality of primordial consciousness or the a priori state of the original wholeness in flux. Afterwards, in Chapter Six, we saw how this mythical, primordial modality of consciousness manifests itself in collective shamanistic rituals, which become the arena for intersubjective horizons of collective experience for all participants. Everyone has access to this primordial sphere of consciousness but it is only shapori who are capable of transmitting and diffusing the ancestral knowledge in summoning their forbears, thus maintaining the cosmic flow. By metamorphosing into hekura, the shapori simultaneously becomes the sum of all hekura; he is a unified multiplicity of hekura, concurrently one and many. His cosmic body is a microcosm for hekura but also a base for manifestation of the larger structure of the Yanomami macrocosm. The main role of shapori is to preserve and reinforce the integrity of the cosmic whole and thus sustain the overall cosmic equilibrium. However, efforts to sustain the vitality of the cosmos through shamanistic activity are not infinite, especially when faced with threats of cosmic proportions (Chiappino 1995: 193). Yanomami shapori nowadays face great challenges, for the vitality of their whole cosmos is in jeopardy. The very existence of the sky as separate from the earth means there is a distance between the ontological spheres of the two cosmic realms.

> Since the primordial sky is so often the object of the first real separation, it betokens the very possibility of distance between one kind of being and another; its continued transcendence [through shamans] guarantees the symbolic life it signifies. (Sullivan 1988: 45)

Only shapori are capable of maintaining the distance between the sky and the earth through their rituals. As long as there are living shamans, the sky will remain high above. Without shamans to hold the sky up, as Davi suggests, the sky will not be able to sustain itself and remain in its place. Its collapse would then result in the end of a differentiated cosmos. Death of a shaman in this sense is thus analogous to the death of the world. Degeneration of cosmos parallels the extinction of the multiplicity of shamans and the subsequent end of the world, which goes hand in hand with the decadence of shamanism, removing any opportunity for the new manifestation of the cosmos. 'The eschaton knocks out the props that undergird the symbolic order that imbues and surrounds the spaces of the human body and of human society' (ibid.: 563). The cataclysmic imagery of the crashing sky thus implies that any symbolic distance between the two realms is removed and consequently, 'the basis for life in this world as it is known no longer holds' (ibid.: 45).

The End of another Cosmic Cycle?

The Yanomami are by no means the only people threatened by the destruction. The Mehinaku people living in the Upper Xingu area of Brazil similarly talk of the increasing encroachment of white people on their lifeworld; how the building blocks of their universe are slowly disintegrating and that if this trend continues the world will soon be destroyed. Akin to Yanomami shapori warnings about the destruction of their hekura, Mehinaku shamans are also warning that their spirits are angry and are being eradicated (Stang 2010).

In these times of global crisis, we often contemplate what exactly 'the end of the world' means. Is it something that looms only before dominated small-scale societies, such as the Yanomami and the Mehinaku? Is it to do with their responses in times of crises that lead to cultural dissolution and death or is it something larger forthcoming? Are there signs and omens of a final global apocalypse or is it just the end of another cosmic cycle (which started with the arrival of white people) and the subsequent beginning of a new one? Davi Kopenawa's prediction is unambiguously pessimistic and fatalistic. He does not seem to hope for direct or immediate salvation. Metaphorically speaking, his is a vision of 'a winter of despair rather than of a spring of hope'. He presents a composite picture of a final apocalypse and a message of misery and doom rather than of millenarian hope for either a promised time to come or a 'golden age' to follow.[9] Nevertheless, he prefigures the current crisis of a looming end of the world in terms of earlier cataclysms, namely the great flood that transformed their ancestors into other beings and the previous sky collapse, which dislocated the earth and converted one generation of the Yanomami into subterranean Amahiri. His foresight provides a teleological insight into the cyclical nature of the Yanomami cosmos. It is dynamic and endures through the passage of its own organismic, macrocosmic time flaw. But it is also open to catastrophes and changes through the process of death, decay, sacrifice, subsequent renewal and the emergence of a new order. Bear in mind that this is not necessarily a reflection of Yanomami self-understanding. Sullivan (ibid.: 63) suggests that the Yanomami distinguish between successive primordial ages without having developed their own systematic theory of epochs. According to Davi, the previous sky tumbled because it was still fragile but the current sky has had time to mature and solidify (Berwick 1992). This time, the new menace comes from the all-pervading shawara smoke capturing and eradicating hekura as well as from sweeping cultural changes threatening to severe the ancestral links between living and dead shapori. Davi warns that angry hekura, liberated after shaporis' deaths, will seek revenge by cutting the sky into pieces, but others will try to convince them to wait as there are still living shapori left. In other words, as long as shapori live, initiations will take place. Disembodied hekura remain in their mountaintops waiting to hear the call of the new candidates in order to be reincarnated and thus contribute to the cosmogonic act once again. Hopefully they will have more human bodies to inhabit in the future.

In Davi's home village of Watorikɨ, ever since the late 1980s there have been no less than thirteen shapori (Albert and Le Tourneau 2007). He has directed all his efforts to promote the (re)education and preservation of traditional values and the Yanomami way of life. He has worked towards counteracting the damaging effects of cultural change and has tried to prevent adolescents from eating napë food and becoming attracted to a non-Yanomami way of life. In his village there is only a radio, machetes and cooking pots from the outside. And yet, ironically, it was in his village where the first health and education programmes gave origin to well-trained Yanomami teachers and health workers (ibid.). Davi is aware that his leadership alone is not enough to prevent a disaster falling upon his people. In 2004, he founded the Hutukara[10] Yanomami Association in Boa Vista. But education is a long-term process and the Yanomami, faced with immediate danger that threatens to destroy them, need a short-term solution. 'Unless he oversees a miracle, Davi Yanomami may be remembered as a lonely, tragic figure whose words were lost in the smoke of Shawara' (Rabben 1998: 120) (her italics).

Davi is very well acquainted with the current world situation and is also talking about the planetary crisis. We certainly live in critical times; we are surrounded by the reckless destruction of the planet – escalating devastation of animal and plant life, the loss of biodiversity, accumulation of pollutants in soils, rivers, lakes and seas, climate change, global warming and the degradation of the biosphere, wars, famine and the looming threat of new pandemics. Scientists are constantly warning about greenhouse gas emissions and the need to reduce them in order to avoid large-scale destruction. The real possibility of the impending end of the world is surely becoming a prevalent issue in both religious circles and in popular culture, as well as in academia. In a recent 'Anthropology and Ends of Worlds' symposium held at the University of Sydney in 2010, Sebastian Job talked about '... a modern human destructiveness of such proportions and rapidity that it seems to be breaking free of the regenerative circuits which hitherto brought new life from death' (Job 2010: 85). Another participant, Carla Stang, urged anthropologists to take their informants' claims seriously and use their knowledge of lived cosmologies constructively for the purpose of finding alternatives to a dominant Western worldview responsible for the current global crises that threaten us all (Stang 2010: 124).

The word apocalypse derives from the Greek *apokalupsis* a derivative of *apokaluptein*, which can literally mean 'to disclose something that has been hidden or contained'. Davi revealed that it was Omawë who buried gold, iron, and oil together with shawara smoke, and when white people started taking it out of the ground they not only unleashed shawara but revealed their ignorance, carelessness, greed and the destructive nature of consumer capitalism.

World affairs are becoming progressively more complex each day in every aspect of the word making it impossible to reach straightforward, simple or immediate solutions for the foreseeable future. Over the last few centuries, humans have developed an interconnected, worldwide system of dependency driven by excessive consumerism and material overconsumption. To keep itself alive, such a system strives for an endless economic growth, resulting in perpetual competition, the depletion of natural resources and ruthless wars in what is an extreme expression of human insanity. But these are just a few amongst many other factors contributing to current planetary crises. Yet hope remains that a miracle may bring human consciousness to such a level of understanding that it will inspire a sense of duty among us all to pull the world back from the edge of the abyss. Ultimately, with the care factor being strongly embedded in people, providing that it is not too late the destiny of humanity may be redirected towards a more promising future filled with faith and optimism. Are we to be lured into thinking that what is occurring to the Yanomami and numerous 'others' is somehow removed from us and that it is only happening somewhere far away in distant lifeworlds? Are these crises not, in fact, instances of the global manifesting itself through the local? Part is equal to the whole. Let us hope that reason will ultimately prevail and that the decision makers and others who are in a position of power take a deep look inside themselves and realise that they also live on this planet. Moreover, let us hope that they will take a true stand of leadership in environmental affairs and that all of us – as individual inhabitants of this planet – become responsible planetary citizens, and maybe, just maybe, a miracle will happen.

Notes

1. Remori derives from the word *remoremo* (hornet). He is said to have created white people. For the Brazilian Yanomami, foreign languages resemble the buzz of flies (Albert 1988).
2. To make this substance more potent, women mix the oko shiki plant with the jawbone of *hāhō* (pinktoe tarantula (avicularia avicularia)), small crabs, and fruits from the shrub called *yāri natha* (anaxagorea brevipes) (Lizot 2004: 283).
3. Nowadays Yanomami associate Õmãyãri with rainbows, which they call 'the path of Õmãyãri' (*õmãyãri kë no mayo*). Rainbows are considered to be dangerous and powerful beings that send shawara illnesses to the Yanomami (ibid.). Õmãyãriwe is a hekura that comes at night and brings shawara. However, as we saw in Chapter Six, when incorporated into a shapori's arsenal of personal hekura, he is benign and beneficial.
4. Red howler monkey was also a nickname given to me by the shapori Makowë from Platanal. When I asked him the reason for this he replied that all napë look like howler monkeys.
5. According to Lizot (1985: 5), it was another splinter group called Thorapë (the predecessors of the Karohi-theri) that together with the Shitoya formed the original community of Kunawë before bifurcating into two separate groups.
6. The Yamalero shamans from the Colombian grass plains also associate smoke with illnesses. Sumabila-Tachon's (1999) informants claimed that malaria came from the city of Bogota, carried by clouds of smoke moving in a south-easterly direction, from city to country and from mountains to plains.
7. In 1998, the unusually strong El Niño effect produced a severe, long-lasting drought contributing to massive forest fires in the northern Brazilian State of Roraima. As a result, a vast amount of dense smoke was released into the air and some 34,000 square km of dry savanna and around 10,000 square km of rainforest burned down. In addition, the drought made the water more stagnant, resulting in a dramatic increase in numbers of mosquitoes transmitting malaria and dengue fever, with particularly devastating consequences for the Yanomami population (Butler 2012; Church World Service 1998). Fires have often spread out of control when subsistence farmers and landowners have cleared vast tracts of jungle for pasture on the other side of the Venezuelan border. After nearly four months of the government's incapability to control the blazes, officials from FUNAI brought in two Kayapo shamans from central Brazil to the Yanomami reserve to perform an elaborate rain dance. A few hours later it rained heavily for the first time in nearly six months (Conklin 2002: 1056).
8. Airplanes were flying in a two-way direction from the capital Caracas to Manaus in Brazil and their flight path traversed directly above the Venezuelan Amazon Region.

In 1999, during my first visit to Sheroana-theri, there was only one flight every few days. However, when I returned the following year there were flights more or less daily.

9. The myth of the 'golden age' or the 'eternal return', according to Eliade (1965: 115), articulates the fundamental cyclical nature of the cosmos, which is destroyed and recreated anew. '... [t]he mythical visions of the "beginning" and the "end" of time are homologous – eschatology, at least in certain aspects becoming one with cosmogony ...' (ibid.: 73). Hence, each instance of destruction is simultaneously a new creation or repetition of cosmogony. 'Every creation repeats the pre-eminent cosmogonic act, the Creation of the World' (ibid.: 18). The myth of successive ages or a 'golden age' takes place at the beginning of the cycle 'close to the paradigmatic *illud tempus*' (ibid.: 112) (his italics).

10 Hutukara is the part of the sky from which the earth was born.

POSTSCRIPT

Recent Developments

Seven years after I left the Upper Orinoco, I returned to Puerto
Ayacucho (in October 2007) and joined a multidisciplinary team of the
Venezuelan National Programme for the Elimination of Onchocerciasis
– Southern Focus Amazonas (PNEO-FS). Dr Carlos Botto – head of the
ecoepidemiology unit of the Amazonian Centre for Investigation and
Control of Tropical Diseases 'Simon Bolivar' (SACAICET) – has been
coordinating this programme since its foundation in 1995. For the next
five years, I contributed to the team's efforts to eradicate onchocerciasis
(commonly known as river blindness),[1] which is endemic in many parts
of the Yanomami territory. Furthermore, I became a consultant for the
Onchocerciasis Elimination Programme for the Americas (OEPA). With
its headquarters in Guatemala, OEPA provides support in Venezuela and
five other endemic countries of the Americas in partnership with the
Pan-American Health Organization (PAHO), The Carter Center and
various academic institutions and independent organisations. The main
aim of this inter-American initiative, which began in 1992, is to eradicate
onchocerciasis from the American continent through the coordinated
regional action of the OEPA and the implementation of various effective
national programmes and strategies. To this end, each of the six member
countries assumed the responsibility to administer an anti-parasitic
medicament called Mectizan (Ivermectin) biannually to at least 85 per
cent of the affected population in all endemic communities, and four

times a year in areas of very high transmission, such as the Amazonian region of Venezuela and Chiapas in Mexico.

Ever since 1997, members of the PNEO-FS have been distributing the appropriate doses of Mectizan tablets to all affected Yanomami living in endemic communities of the Venezuelan Upper Orinoco region. The established strategy is aimed at breaking parasite transmission and finally eradicating onchocerciasis. Activities of the PNEO-FS are integrated within the overall regional strategy of the Sanitary District Upper Orinoco and the Yanomami Health Plan for the comprehensive healthcare of indigenous populations in Amazonas State. Over the years, the number of Yanomami affected with onchocerciasis has grown from around 1,700 in 1998 to more than 8,000 in 2007, living in 180 endemic communities and ten geographical regions. From 2010, the distribution of Mectizan amplified from two to four times a year to all hyperendemic areas. However, due to numerous obstacles and challenging working conditions, it was not until 2006 that the PNEO-FS exceeded 85 per cent coverage of the affected population for the first time. They have been maintaining this high level of coverage ever since, and, as a result, the prevalence of cases has significantly diminished while in some areas parasite transmission has been completely interrupted. Notwithstanding the enormous ongoing achievements of the programme towards preventing parasite transmission, the battle to eliminate onchocerciasis from the Upper Orinoco continues to the present day. Currently, out of thirteen foci or endemic areas in six countries, the so-called Yanomami Focus, which comprises both Venezuelan and Brazilian Yanomami territories, is the only area left on the whole continent where there is active parasite transmission.

The main challenge for both countries and, for that matter, the entire American continent (Central and South America) is the hard to reach frontier region. In those remote mountainous areas along the Venezuelan-Brazilian border, there are still Yanomami communities that have not yet been identified or visited by the health system and as such are outside the scope of the PNEO-FS for treatment. This is particularly relevant on the Venezuelan side, where the infrastructure is very limited and the availability of helicopters to reach such remote communities is irregular. Consequently, one of the main priorities for the PNEO-FS in recent years has been to locate those unknown communities, obtain demographic and epidemiological data and treat the inhabitants with Mectizan. In my capacity as anthropologist-investigator within the PNEO-FS, I led the scientific-medical teams to various frontier areas of difficult access to reach the Yanomami communities whose existence was known about but they had not yet been reached. In each new community, I gathered socio-demographic data, including information about their origin, past migratory movements and their relations with other communities (alliances and conflicts). Over the years, I visited various remote geographical regions from the Sierra de Unturán and Siapa Valley to the south of the Orinoco to border areas around the upper reaches of the Ocamo, Cuntinamo and Metacuni rivers, north of Sierra Parima. All in all, with the support of the OEPA, twenty-seven previously unknown hyperendemic communities were located with a total population of more than 1,000 inhabitants.

In the course of my involvement with the PNEO-FS, I have had the opportunity to briefly revisit Platanal three times in 2008, 2009 and 2012, and the Sheroana-theri once in April 2012. I noted some significant changes within the pertinent areas of my fieldwork, which I had conducted between 1999 and 2000. Back then, medical personnel from the Platanal health clinic were only visiting close and intermediate upriver communities (those up to five hours by boat). They lacked personnel, willpower and logistics to undertake the long and strenuous hikes necessary to reach inland communities to the south of the Orinoco. Over the past few years, however, this has changed as a result of an increase in the number of PNEO-FS personnel, who are also better equipped for long walks. They are distributing Mectizan on a regular basis (every three months) to a total of twenty communities belonging to the area of influence of the Platanal health clinic. These include riverine communities all the way up to the Peñascal rapids as well as a cluster of five communities situated in the so-called sub area of Unturán, south of the Orinoco, which includes the Sheroana and Toritha-theri. Doctors from Platanal have been taking advantage of their activities, accompanying them in order to provide medical assistance. As a result, Sheroana-theri and other neighbouring communities now have much more contact with non-Yanomami than they did during in time of my fieldwork, when visits by health workers were virtually non-existent.

Another significant development in recent years, which has greatly improved health services in the whole Upper Orinoco region and elsewhere in the country, was the influx of medical professionals from Venezuela and other Latin American countries, who had graduated from the Latin American School of Medicine (ELAM) – a major international medical school in Cuba. Following an agreement between then Venezuelan president Hugo Chavez Frías and Fidel Castro in 2005, they return every year to Venezuela to provide medical services throughout the country, including the Amazonas State. Known as 'Batallon 51',[2] the first generation of doctors were coordinated by María Eugenia Sader, who went on to become the Venezuelan Health Minister between 2010 and 2013.

In Platanal and other communities along the Orinoco, the government recently began replacing Yanomami huts with concrete blockhouses and introduced electricity. The SUYAO cooperative is still active but lots of Yanomami now earn a salary and buy manufactured goods directly in La Esmeralda or Puerto Ayacucho instead of obtaining them through the SUYAO exchange. Jacinto Serowë still lives with his kinfolk outside of the mainstream Mahekoto-theri community. His own community of thirty inhabitants is now officially called Poriporimapiwei-theri. Jacinto knew Helena Valero very well and during one of my recent visits to Platanal, I inquired about her. She died in 2002 in the community of Lechosa near Ocamo. I had met her only once, briefly, on my way to La Esmeralda in Lechosa in 2000. Jacinto spoke about her futile attempts to reunite with her family in Brazil; when she finally went back, she found out that her mother had passed away and that her father (who was away during her visit) had married another woman. Helena's sister rejected her, saying how she had lived for too many years with the Yanomami and therefore should go back to them. Heartbroken, Helena returned to the Upper Orinoco and spent the rest of her life in Lechosa. When she died, the Yanomami cremated her body and consumed her ashes. Jacinto's brother Alfredo Aherowë, then headman of the Mahekoto-theri, tragically lost his life in 2011; he was the victim of an act of revenge carried out by some old enemies from the area of Koyowë near Sierra Parima. Apparently they had passed one night through Platanal on their way back from a meeting in Mavaca and shot Alfredo near his house. Jacinto swiftly retaliated, killing two men. The situation was very tense and threatened to escalate into all-out war before the dust eventually settled. Alfredo's son Keiro became the new Mahekoto-theri headman. The health post microscopist Elias Yakirahiwë founded his own community of thirty individuals in the vicinity of Jacinto's and named it Koshikapiwei-theri. He is still working in the clinic and recently undertook study in Puerto Ayacucho to complete his high school diploma. The Yanomami nurse Julio Vichato passed away in 2011 in his natal community of Lechosa near Ocamo. The real cause of his death remained unclear. According to medical workers, he died from pneumonia but the Yanomami from Platanal were rumouring that the real cause of his death was poisoning through sorcery. My dear old friend Makowë – Jacinto's father-in-law – is still practising shaporimou and so is Enano. However, Enano's older brother, the shapori Potai, passed away in 2007. There are now two new, recently initiated shapori in the Mahekoto-theri.

In April 2012, Pedro Rondón, a member of the PNEO-FS, together with Dr Mónica Díaz from Platanal and I went on a three-week semicircular hike through Unturán and eventually reached two communities in the remote Siapa Valley that had not been incorporated into the PNEO-FS. On our way back towards the Orinoco, we passed through a number of communities, including the Toritha and Sheroana-theri. For me, it was the first time I had visited those communities since the year 2000. In Toritha-theri, I found out that the principal shapori Shawarawë had died approximately three months before our visit in a sorcery attack from some Shamathari enemies. Early next morning, after spending the night in their spacious shapono, we began our long hike towards the Sheroana-theri shapono. Late afternoon, after about nine hours of walking, and having crossed many streams and swamp areas, we finally approached our destination. My heart accelerated when I heard their voices. We entered the shapono in the middle of a game of soccer. The players stopped their game immediately and everyone began shouting and gathering around me with welcoming smiles; they were in disbelief that it was really me. At that moment, I was also in disbelief that I was actually there. One Yanomami from our group commented that they had been eagerly expecting us, as they knew we were coming. Again and again, I was surprised how news spread so quickly even though to my knowledge nobody went ahead of our group that morning. I quickly spotted Ruweweriwë lying in his hammock. As I began walking towards him he quickly got up and we warmly embraced each other. He was very pleased to see me. I told him that he had not changed much in all those years. He smiled and replied: 'Awei pushika, wa pehetimou. Ya huya shoawe!' ('It is true my son, I am still an adolescent!'). I looked around, surprised by how much everything had changed; the shapono was still in the same place, albeit for me it was unrecognisable. What was once a traditional type of open communal house with a sloped circular roof had become a group of individual closed-type, rectangular houses with double-sloped roofs, unevenly scattered around the central area (Figure 9.1). The only familiar feature was Ruweweriwë's traditional house open towards the central area, the same as it was a decade ago. The hut to the left of his house was now a school where Platanal-trained teachers give classes to Sheroana-theri children.

Everyone now spoke Spanish and the majority of adolescents were wearing T-shirts, shorts and sport shoes. Soccer had become the main activity. Over the years, the Sheroana-theri population had doubled from twenty-nine inhabitants in 2000 to fifty-eight in 2012.

Ruweweriwë is still actively practising shaporimou and is now again the official headman of the community (in the year 2000, he had handed over his leadership to Maruwë). He spends lots of time in Toritha-theri where he has numerous relatives (Figure 9.2).

Arawë, whose initiation I described in Chapter Four, had lost interest in shaporimou and eventually stopped practising. Ruweweriwë had

Figure 9.1 Sheroana-theri, April 2012. *Back row, from left:* Ruweweriwë's son Mirko, the shapori Taramawë and Arawë. The author is in the middle. *Front row, from left:* Ruweweriwë's son-in-law Kiawë (now a shapori) and Maruwë an ex-headman.

Figure 9.2 The shapori Ruweweriwë and the author, Toritha-theri, April 2012.

subsequently initiated his son-in-law, Kiawë. Arawë's son Ronald, who was very young at the time of my fieldwork, was in 2012 attending school in Platanal. The Toritha-theri shapori Taramawë, who back in 2000 was assisting in Arawë's initiation, had settled permanently in Sheroana and had married. He is still an active shapori. The oldest Sheroana-theri woman, Mahekosi, was still alive when I visited, albeit in a very bad condition. She was lying in her hammock next to the fire, all alone in the corner of a house. As I approached her I called her by her name. She slowly lifted up her head and as I looked at her opaque eyes, I realised she was blind. At first she did not know who I was but then I said: 'Nape, kamiye këya! Misikiwë këya' ('Mother, it's me! I am Misikiwë') (the Yanomami name that was given to me)). 'Do you remember how we went together once to look for crabs and how I put my hand into the hole and instead of the crab took out wariomi [a type of tarantula]?' She wholeheartedly laughed and said: 'Awei pushika' ('Yes my son'). I was looking around for my dear friend whom I called Neboisa, who had claimed to be the only surviving Yanomami from the Wanapiwei-theri but could not see him. When I asked the Yanomami his whereabouts, they whispered that he had suddenly become very ill after visiting a distant community. Ruweweriwë said that õkã sorcerers had poisoned him and the situation had become critical. He was not able to help him so they took him to Platanal; the doctor was away so medical students had to take him to Mavaca where he died soon after, despite the doctor's attempts to save his life. Later on at SACAICET, I was told that he had died in 2009 and the doctor could not determine the cause of his death.

One day in Puerto Ayacucho, two months before visiting the Sheroana-theri, a Yanomami man across the street waved to me and called me to come. I waved back and approached him without really knowing who he was. He noticed that I was looking oddly at him and asked: 'Zeljko, do you know who I am?' 'I am Maruwë's son, Francisco, from Sheroana-theri'. It was Nano, who back in the year 2000 was approximately three years of age. He told me that he had been nominated by his community to be trained as a Yanomami Communal Primary Healthcare Worker (ACYAPS). The main idea behind the government's initiative to capacitate indigenous health workers had emerged as part of the strategy of the Yanomami Health Plan that was created in response to the 1993 Hashimú massacre. Due to the remoteness of the place where this tragic event had happened, the Venezuelan state was unable to provide effective medical and humanitarian aid to survivors. Three years after the massacre, the Yanomami came into focus again after a deadly epidemic of a viral haemorrhagic fever (Hantavirus) decimated the population of a remote village. In 1998, another lethal epidemic, this time of yellow fever, caused multiple deaths in many villages on both sides of the frontier (MSDS 2000: 7). The vulnerability of remote indigenous communities to deadly epidemics and the government's inability to provide adequate care led to a series of meetings between various health institutions. In 1999, the Venezuelan state, in front of the Inter-American Court of Human Rights, promised to create, finance and put into action through the Ministry of Health and Social Development a Programme of Comprehensive Health Care for the Yanomami people and allocate an annual budget managed by the Regional Health Council. In November that same year, a Colombian anthropologist, Martha Espinoza, backed by the OEPA, organised a workshop in Puerto Ayacucho called 'Health intervention strategies toward the Yanomami population, with emphasis on onchocerciasis' with major participation of various organisations involved in dealing with the Yanomami population. The main purpose of this event was to develop health intervention strategies for the Yanomami population, taking into account different degrees of cultural change among them. The workshop was followed by a series of consultations with indigenous representatives and non-indigenous organisations, which resulted in the creation of an initial document called: 'Strategic plan of integral health for the Yanomami people', which in 2001 became known as the Yanomami Health Plan (PSY). But it was not until 2005 that the PSY was put into action. To get the ball rolling, the Ministry of Health and Social Development organised a meeting where the creation of a programme for capacitating indigenous health workers was discussed, among other critical topics. In October that same year, Mark Wesley de Oliveira (former head of the Brazilian Yanomami Health District and coordinator of the Intercultural Education Programme CCPY), backed by the OEPA, collaborated with other institutions to devise a concrete plan of action. Two anthropologists, José Antonio Kelly, then coordinator of the PSY, and Javier Carrera Rubio, responsible for education, were contracted to carry out a specifically designed two-year long theoretical and practical course adapted to Yanomami socio-cultural and epidemiological reality. Altogether, thirty-three Yanomami adolescent male candidates were selected from various geographical areas and different socio-cultural contexts – that is, from communities with regular contact with national society and others with little or no contact. After completing the course they were to become reintegrated into their communities and incorporated within the Yanomami Sanitary District. This way, the regional health authorities sought to amplify the existing programmes of prevention and primary health care promotion and thus expand the overall health coverage. The course went ahead in July 2006 with twenty-four students (nine of them gave up for various reasons) and was taught mostly in the

Yanomami language; literacy was also taught in parallel with the health course to those who needed it. This course was not the first or the only attempt to capacitate Yanomami health promoters. Recall from Chapter One that in 1976 the first Yanomami were capacitated as Auxiliaries of Simplified Medicine[3] and there has been one at each health post working alongside doctors ever since. Later, in 1995, the first group of Yanomami from health posts in Ocamo, Mavaca, Platanal, Sierra Parima and Koyowë were trained as microscopists for malaria. However, the overall number of Yanomami working in the health sector was not enough for a population of nearly 15,000 (MSDS 2005). Subsequently, the idea of capacitating new Yanomami health workers (ACYAPS) from most parts of the territory emerged.

In the end, the first generation of nineteen out of twenty-four ACYAPS successfully completed the course and received their certificates on 15 August 2008 in a graduation ceremony held in La Esmeralda (the capital of the Upper Orinoco municipality). All important regional and national health authorities were present, including the Health Minister. A group of shapori from Mavaca were giving their recommendations to young graduates as to how to act responsibly in their new roles as health workers and how they should respect their elders along with traditional healing practices, which are complementary to medicine. Dr Carlos Botto, who was also present, told me about a rather touching moment at the end of the ceremony. The Health Minister was giving certificates to each of the 19 Yanomami when one of them requested the microphone; he thanked the minister and then approached him with a small gourd in his hand. Thinking it was a gift, the minister extended his hands to receive it, but to his surprise the young Yanomami dipped a piece of cloth inside the gourd, which contained red dye obtained from an annatto plant, and began decorating the minister's face with traditional designs. In continuation, other Yanomami approached the surprised Minister and put bracelets from the black curassow bird on his arms together with a monkey tail crown on his head (shaporis' garments). They also gave him a bow and arrows. It was possibly the minister's first direct contact with the Yanomami world and he appeared to be quite dazed. Subsequently, all these young men were reintegrated into their communities and have been putting their acquired knowledge into practice ever since. In addition to being a valuable aid to medical personnel in and around health posts, the ACYAPS also became an integral part of health teams visiting remote communities in three- to five-day operations carried out with the help of military helicopters. Part of my work for the OEPA was to accompany ACYAPS on those trips, assess their competence and observe the dynamics of their relationship with other health personnel in order to identify potential problems and difficulties. I conducted a series of interviews with ACYAPS, various doctors and medical students. OEPA was very interested in the whole project and provided support from the beginning, knowing that such health workers could greatly contribute to the distribution of Mectizan (among other things).

Their involvement and contribution as health assistants was deemed very positive, albeit with certain problems and difficulties. Communities with little outside contact are always a little fearful and mistrustful of outsiders, especially during the first visit. However, the fact that the ACYAPS are Yanomami greatly reduces initial tension and makes them an indispensable component of the health team. One of the main duties of the ACYAPS is to explain the main purpose of the visit and what tasks will be carried out. In addition, they assist doctors in many tasks, such as: vaccination, taking blood samples, setting up an IV drip, asking patients about their symptoms and translating thereof, distributing medicaments with simple instructions for their use in the Yanomami language, registering weight and helping with the population census. The vast majority of health staff reported that the ACYAPS are enthusiastic in their work and very keen to learn new things. While they were generally competent, one recurring problem for them was calculating the proper dose of medication per kilogram of body weight (or according to height in the case of Mectizan). Another problem for some ACYAPS was difficulty with the Spanish language. Additional issues included a fear of being poisoned through sorcery when visiting unknown communities; sometimes they would become paranoid and consequently stop collaborating.[4] While ACYAPS living near health posts have been able to interact with medical personnel, others from remote communities without any permanent medical presence, such as Haximú or Shitari in the Upper Ocamo, experienced difficulties due to a lack of supervision and a lack of radio communication with doctors or medical headquarters in La Esmeralda. In addition, logistical problems that the Health District was having in supplying medicine on a regular basis to those in faraway communities sometimes provoked a backlash from the community's inhabitants, which naturally placed the ACYAPS in a delicate situation. The initial course was only the beginning, and the original idea was to progressively continue capacitating new health assistants. In 2010, there was a two-week long reinforcement workshop held in Puerto Ayacucho for existing ACYAPS, who were already able to pass on their acquired knowledge and skills to new aspirants. After that, another short course was carried out in 2012, which Francisco from the Sheroana-theri had attended around the time I met him.

Another significant development in the Venezuelan Upper Orinoco region since my fieldwork has been the foundation of the 'Horonami'

Yanomami organisation in 2011. This was the first time that the Venezuelan Yanomami had created a legal body whose purpose was to protect their interests and voice their concerns. The establishment of the 'Hutukara' Yanomami Association in Boa Vista by Davi Kopenawa in 2004 was the main driving force behind the effort of the Venezuelan Yanomami to create a similar kind of organisation for themselves. In December 2007, Davi Kopenawa was invited by the NGO (non-governmental organisation) 'Wataniba'[5] to visit the Venezuelan Upper Orinoco region for the first time. I was then one of three anthropologists who had been contracted by this organisation to assess Yanomami needs, aspirations and rights regarding education and the demarcation of their territory. Davi and three of his close assistants spent ten days visiting various Yanomami communities (Koyowë, Ocamo, Mavaca and Platanal). In each community, they held public talks in front of large crowds of Yanomami about the importance of unity and the preservation of Yanomami culture. They also talked about the problems they faced in Brazil; about the Hutukara Association and the need to have a similar kind of Yanomami organisation in the Venezuelan Upper Orinoco. At the end, before he left, Davi invited some Yanomami leaders to visit his community of Watorikɨ, which they did the following year. By that time, the Venezuelan Yanomami were seriously considering the idea of having their own organisation because the existing SUYAO having been created and controlled by the missionaries had never truly been run by the Yanomami.

In November 2011, one of the emerging young Yanomami leaders Luis Shatiwë Ahiwei travelled to Boa Vista and participated in a meeting organised by Davi's Hutukara Yanomami Association in which they discussed the possibility of creating a similar organisation in Venezuela. One month later, the first general assembly was held in the community of Warapana near Mavaca with 2,585 Yanomami participants from 161 communities of the Upper Orinoco and Rio Negro municipalities. The main outcome of this historical meeting was the establishment of the Horonami Organisation Yanomami (HOY). After three days of discussions, Andrés Blanco from Sierra Parima was elected to be in charge of the organisation together with an executive board consisting of 22 general representatives (coordinators). Two months later, 'Horonami Organisation Yanomami' was officially registered in the State of Amazonas and has since been the unified voice of the Venezuelan Yanomami and the legal body representing their interests. It has become a fundamental instrument for defending the lives of new generations of the Yanomami people in their ancestral territory. Their main objective is to improve the quality of life and preserve their culture. As recognised in the Constitution of the Bolivarian Republic of Venezuela, the Yanomami are entitled to claim their rights as indigenous peoples, and intend to enforce them throughout their territory. Their main areas of focus are: education, the environment and territory, culture, sport and health. Horonami members are very proactive in promoting unity, solving problems and fighting for the rights of the Yanomami people. They also organise annual general assemblies (akin to their Hutukara Brazilian counterparts) to discuss any problems specific to illegal gold mining in their territory and to strategise health and education improvements. The presence of garimpeiros continues to pose a serious threat to the Yanomami population living in border areas with Brazil. In April 2010, some Yanomami leaders from Sierra Parima made a public announcement about reported deaths in the remote, previously unknown community of Momoi situated in the border area north of Sierra Parima. A few weeks later, multidisciplinary health teams and some government authorities were dispatched in military helicopters to the area, where they encountered a grave health situation in several communities. A recently abandoned mining camp was found nearby and all the equipment had been destroyed. More recently, in August 2012, the Horonami Organisation Yanomami announced the alleged massacre of Yanomami from the community of Irotha-theri, located near the headwaters of the River Ocamo, close to the border. A large-scale joint investigation led by Yanomami leaders and military personnel was carried out. Evidence of a massacre was never found, but the presence of various camps and environmental degradation was clearly evident. In October 2013, Hutukara and Horonami Yanomami Organisation representatives organised a joint forum in Puerto Ayacucho in commemoration of twenty years since the Hashimú massacre, where they discussed issues of health, indigenous rights and problems with gold mining. The main purpose of the meeting was to develop joint strategies to protect their people. They voiced their concern over the increased presence of garimpeiros continuing to generate violence as well as negatively impact the environment and cause unrest and epidemics. They asked their governments to help them protecting their lands, their health and their integrity essential for survival. Horonami representatives also called for the demarcation of the Yanomami territory in Venezuela. In Brazil, the Yanomami indigenous territory was officially demarcated in the 1990s.

Alongside the presence of garimpeiros, outbreaks of deadly epidemics of malaria and other introduced diseases continue to take their toll on the Upper Orinoco region. In April 2009, swine flu caused by the H1N1 influenza virus started in Mexico and triggered a global pandemic. In three months it had reached Brazil and Venezuela. Seven reported Yanomami deaths in the frontier region between the two countries were most probably caused by this virus. Around that time, there was an outbreak of severe respiratory infections in the Upper Orinoco region affecting more than 1,000 Yanomami. News of Yanomami deaths from suspected swine flu coincided with an epidemic and the regional office of the Ministry of Health together with SACAICET personnel sent an emergency team of epidemiologists to investigate suspicious cases reported in Mavaca and Platanal. Luckily, after examining the whole population, it was determined that the Yanomami were sick from standard flu. Epidemics of respiratory infections spread rapidly among the Yanomami, as we have seen in Chapter Seven, and they can often lead to potentially fatal secondary complications, such as pneumonia. New epidemics such as swine flu or any other new type of disease could have fatal consequences for the entire Yanomami population. Let us hope that such an occurrence never happens.

Notes

1. Onchocerciasis is an infectious disease caused by the parasite Onchocerca volvulus transmitted to humans through black fly bites. It is endemic in more than 160 Yanomami communities of the Upper Orinoco and Rio Negro municipalities and causes severe skin and eye lesions.
2. The name 'Batallon 51' (Brigade 51) was given to the first generation of fifty-one Venezuelan doctors who graduated from ELAM in 2005. Since 2005, many doctors arriving from other countries to work in Venezuela have been integrated into Batallon 51.
3. This role was created as part of the Programme of Simplified Medicine aimed at indigenous populations, which has been very successful since its establishment in 1962 (Sanchez-Salamé 2005). The manual of Auxiliaries of Simplified Medicine was used as the main point of reference in the ACYAPS course between 2006 and 2008.
4. During one of our visits to the remote community of Yaritha, belonging to the Hashimú sector near the Brazilian border, one of the ACYAPS suddenly became ill. He was shaking with fever all night while a shapori tried to heal him. The next morning, while he was asleep and evidently feeling better, the shapori came to us holding broken seeds in his hand, which he apparently took out of his body.
5. 'Wataniba' is the Organisation for the Multiethnic Human Development of the Amazon.

GLOSSARY OF YANOMAMI TERMS

A

ama ahi: type of tree (elizabetha princeps) used as an extra ingredient in the preparation of psychotropic snuff powder.

amahiri: underground ancestors; inhabitants of the subterranean cosmic stratum.

ãmo mɨsi: highest central point of a celestial cosmic stratum.

aroari këkɨ (mamocori): a poisonous plant (cyperus articulatis or corymbosus) used in *õkã* sorcery.

D

diosi (deosime): deriving from *Dios* (Spanish for 'God').

E

epena: general term for all types of conscious-altering snuff substances.

epenamou: group snuff-taking ritual.

H

hape: kinship term for father (haye: my father).

hariri: state of being ill.

haro këkɨ: a type of plant (cyperus distans (cyperaceae)) the root of which is used for treatment of diarrhoea and fever.

haya: deer; Hayariwë: Deer Ancestor.

haye hëri: sharp pain resulting from harmful magical actions.

heãhãtu: breeze; swirls of air; Heãhãturiwë: Breeze Hekura.

hehã: open central area of a shapono.

hei kë mɨsi: the actual (boa's) abdomen; terrestrial cosmic stratum.

hekɨ nini: a headache.

hekura: shaman; the shaman's helping spirits; original ancestors.

hekuramou: shamanistic practice; dealing with the hekura spirits.

hekurapraɨ: to transform into hekura; shamanistic initiation.

hërɨ: general term for a number of different magical substances and herbs.

hetu mɨsi: boa's abdomen (Yanomami macrocosm); celestial cosmic stratum (sky).

hetu mɨsi suwë pata: subterranean cosmic stratum ('the boa's abdomen of an old woman').

hetu mɨsi wakëmou: 'the sky has turned red' atmospheric phenomenon related to the sickness-bearing sky smoke.

hetu mɨsi wãro pata: old sky or current terrestrial stratum ('the boa's abdomen of an old man').

hetupera (hokoto): boa constrictor; Heturemariwë: Boa (Constrictor) Ancestor.

hikari thëka: open cultivated area; garden.

hisiõmɨ (yopo): a type of consciousness-altering snuff (anadanthera peregrina).

hoashi: white-faced capuchin monkey; Hoashiriwë: Ancestor of White-faced Capuchin monkey.

hoko: toucan spirit wings that enables the shaman to fly like a bird.

hõrãma: a small bush hen (crypturellus obsoletus).

hore mou: a lie.

horoi: white down from the curassow bird, used in shamanistic rituals.

horonami: Yanomami mythological ancestor and culture hero; Horonami Organisation Yanomami (HOY) in Venezuela.

hura: spleen; *(pei) hurapɨ (nini):* a local term for a painful spleen, associated with malaria.

hutukara: part of the sky from which the earth was born; Yanomami Association in Boa Vista (Brazil).

I

ihama: sloth (choloepus tridactilus); Ihamariwë: Sloth Ancestor.

ihirashi: cloud, morning mist.

ɨra (mashaema): jaguar; Ɨrariwë: Jaguar Ancestor.

iro sikɨ: T-shirt (skin of a red howler monkey).

iwa: caiman; Iwariwë: Caiman Ancestor.

K

kamakari: a general term for a deceased person; spirit being associated with death.

kõhõrõmɨ: earth worms used as fish bait; intestinal parasites or worms.

koro hamɨ: downriver; westwards; down (direction).

koro mɨsi: lower, western part of boa's abdomen (sky).

krii (shuu): diarrhoea.

kuramaɨ: shamanistic technique of inflicting illness on a victim through dreams while he or she is asleep at night.

kuratha: plantain, a member of the banana family and the Yanomami staple diet.

M

mahari: in dreams; dream content (see also *thapi*).

maharimou: to dream.

makɨ: mountain (rock face); *Pei Makɨ*: ceremonial mast; the shaman's corporeal mountain.

mamo wayu: eye infection.

mãrãshi: bush turkey (pipile pipile).

mashi: a group of interrelated kinsmen through the paternal side; patrilineage.

matohi: material goods of non-Yanomami origin (machetes, fabrics, saucepans).

matono: a voice box; a bottle.

mayepɨ: big-beaked toucan; *Mayepɨriwë*: Ancestor of Big-beaked Toucan.

mayo hëri: footprint sorcery; lethal sorcery technique involving manipulation of a person's footprint.

mɨ ãmo: central part, core; *pei mɨ ãmo*: constitutive bodily soul component, essence of a person and individual body parts and organs.

mɨshɨãkɨ (pei): breath.

mohomɨ: spotted eagle.

mõrã mahi: type of tree (burseraceae) from which a ceremonial mast is made during shamanistic initiation.

moshohara: a type of consciousness-altering snuff (justicia pectoralis).

mothoka: sun; *Mothokariwë*: Sun Ancestor.

motorema: whirlwind; *Motoremariwë*: Whirlwind Hekura.

motu: mythological reservoir of underground water.

N

naiki: meat hungry.

napë: non-Yanomami persons, including Westerners and members of other ethnic groups.

nape: kinship term for mother (naye: my mother).

Napërami: new type of hekura associated with white people.

nerõ: opossum; Nerõriwë: Opossum Ancestor.

nomai: 'to die' (biological or ritual death in shamanistic initiation); to enter trance.

no patapi: the ancients; original mythical humans; dead shamans.

no patapi tëhë: epoch of the ancestors; primordial time of creation.

no porepi: posthumous soul essences of the deceased.

noreshi: image, photo; *pei noreshi*: animal double, dualistic constitutive soul component. *Noreshi mou*: mimicry between an animal double and its human counterpart.

nosi: stale, weak (as in tobacco).

no uhutipi (pore): ghost of the dead.

no wãri: see *shawara*.

O

õi: black bee; Õiriwë: Black Bee Hekura.

õkã: harmful sorcery technique involving the use of poisonous *aroari* powder (see *aroari këki*).

oko shiki: (lit. crab intestines); a toxic plant that is pulverised, mixed with other ingredients then burned for the purpose of inflicting illness and death.

õmãyãri: spirit beings associated with rainbows, bitterness and bile; Õmãyãriwë: night hekura representative of these beings.

ora hami: upriver, eastwards; up (direction).

õrãmi nini: a sore throat.

ora misi: higher, eastern part of boa's abdomen (sky).

oshetiwë misi: young boa's abdomen (the topmost cosmic stratum).

P

pararo: Shamathari word for *hisiõmi* snuff; hekura custodian of this particular snuff.

pariki nini (pei): chest pain.

pãrimi: immortal, eternal.

paruri: nocturnal black curassow bird (crax alector).

pasho: spider monkey; Pashoriwë: Spider Monkey Ancestor.

paushi këkɨ: ear decoration.

pee nahe: tobacco.

pei ãmoku: liver; *pei ãmoku yori*: bile.

pei koko: comestible, sweet manioc; *pei koko wayu*: poisonous, bitter type of manioc.

pei yo: forest path; Hekura Path embodied during shamanistic initiation.

peripo: moon; Periporiwë: Moon Ancestor; *peripo hupëpi*: an old moon.

po: a flat rock used for grinding in the preparation of snuff powder.

pore hena: a plant 'ghost leaf' (crotalaria mucronata) from which *moshohara* snuff is made.

poshe: collared peccary (dicotyles tajacu); Posheriwë: Collared Peccary Ancestor.

prisɨprisɨmou: shivering from fever (as in a bout of malaria).

puhi: ethereal cosmic substance, mental capacity; *pei puhi*: constitutive bodily soul component of a person and his/her body parts and organs.

puriwa: a star; a dart; an adornment (earring).

R

rahara: a mythical giant snake who controls the waterways; Rahararithawë: original custodian of manioc and precursor of rahara.

rahara hena: 'leaf of a giant snake', a plant from which *moshohara* snuff is made.

rasha: peach palm (bactris gasipaes).

reahumou: funeral feast.

S

sayu kë kɨ: salt (from Sp. *sal*).

shamathari: collective name for a cluster of remote villages located in the proximity of the Siapa River.

shapono: Yanomami communal house.

shapori: shaman; the shaman's spirits assistants.

shaporimou: Yanomami shamanistic complex (see also *hekuramou*).

shawara: a generic term for epidemics of infecto-contagious diseases; inner fire associated with fever; *shawara wakeshi*: pathogenic shawara smoke; *shawarari*: malevolent beings associated with epidemics.

shereka: an arrow.

shiimi: stingy.

shitikari: stars, solar plexus.

shi wãri: feeling the effects of consciousness-altering epena snuff.

shopari wakë: eternal cosmic fire that devours souls of the dead who were stingy during their lifetime.

shori: a kinship term for brother-in-law but can also mean a friend.

siohamou: carrying out son-in-law duties and obligations.

si sãihõu: inner chill.

T

tapiri: a small provisional forest camp.

tararei: to encounter, to find.

temi: a state of being healthy.

tëpë: anteater (myrmecophaga tridactyla); Tëpëriwë: Anteater Ancestor.

thapi: dream content.

thapimou: to dream of distant places, spirits and people; shamanistic technique of dream recall.

theri: community; a member of a local community.

thõkõ thõkõ: cough.

thora: a tube used in snuff-taking.

titiri: Night Ancestor.

tutomou: the practice of a new shaman calling hekura spirits to come to him through chanting.

U

urihi: forest, territory.

urihiri: a dangerous forest spirit being.

W

wahari: cool wind.

wahati: feeling cold.

waika: relational term for upriver Yanomami; derogatory name for Yanomami who live far away with less contact with the outside world.

wãikõyã: anaconda (eunectes murinus); Wãikõyãriwë: Anaconda Ancestor.

waitheri: desirable personal attribute for men and women (brave, strong, fierce); aggressive and dangerous animal behaviour; strong quality (e.g., strong sun, strong tobacco).

wakeshi: smoke.

wakeshipɨ wayu: a gun ('lethal smoke that harms').

warapa koko: a tree sap obtained from the tree *warapa kohi* (crepidospermum rhoifolium (burseraceae)).

warë: white-lipped peccary (tayassu pecari); Warëriwë: White-lipped Peccary Ancestor.

wathapera: rainbow boa. Wathaperariwë: Rainbow Boa Ancestor.

watori: wind; Watoriwë: Wind Hekura.

watoshe: part of hekura attire: crown of light or halo.

watota peshiyë: hekura associated with clothing or textiles.

watupa: vulture; Watupariwë: Vulture Hekura.

wayu: harmful pathogenic substance; disease (*wayu wayu*) warring party (*wayumou*); strong quality of something (e.g., tobacco).

wayuhi: muscle cramps.

wãyumɨ: seasonal food-gathering expedition.

weyari: malevolent nocturnal spirit beings associated with Night Ancestor Titiri.

Y

yai thëpë: a class of invisible non-human beings causing illness and death.

yãkoana (ayukuma): a type of consciousness-altering snuff (virola elongata).

yãmirã: lightning.

yao: ocelot (leopardus pardalis); Yaoriwë: Ocelot Ancestor.

yaro: meat, game.

yãru: thunder.

yarushe: South American coati (nasua nasua solitaria); Yarusheriwë: Hekura Ancestor of the South American Coati.

yashokaɨ: shamanic rite of sickness expulsion and body purification of someone who has had bad dreams, using a tree branch.

yawari: subaquatic spirit beings.

yɨ kë kɨ: hammock.

yopo: an Arawakan word for psychotropic snuff– it is now widely used among the Yanomami alongside the local term *epena*.

yopri: fever.

BIBLIOGRAPHY

Albert B. 1985. 'Temps du Sang, Temps des Cendres: Représentation de la Maladie, Système Rituel et Espace Politique chez les Yanomami du Sud-est (Amazonie Brésilienne)', Ph.D. dissertation. Paris: Université de Paris.

———. 1988. 'La Fumée du Métal: Histoire et Représentations du Contact chez les Yanomami (Brésil)', *L'Homme* 28(2–3): 87–119.

Albert, B. and F.M. Le Tourneau. 2007. 'Ethnography and Resource Use among the Yanomami: Toward a Model of "Reticular Space"', *Current Anthropology* 48(4): 584–92.

Alès, C. and J. Chiappino. 1985. 'Medical Aid, Shamanism and Acculturation among the Yanomami of Venezuela', in M. Colchester (ed.), *The Health and Survival of the Venezuelan Yanoama* (IWGIA document 53). Copenhagen: ARC/IWGIA/SI, pp. 73–90.

Anderson, R. 1996. *Magic, Science, and Health: The Aims and Achievements of Medical Anthropology.* New York: Harcourt Brace.

Anduze, P.J. 1960. *Shailili-ko – Descubrimiento de las Fuentes del Orinoco – Relato de un Naturalista que También Llegó a las Fuentes del Río Orinoco.* Caracas: Ministerio de Justicia de Venezuela.

Anisimov, A.F. 1963. 'The Shaman's Tent of the Evenks and the Origin of the Shamanistic Rite', in H. N. Michael (ed.), *Studies in Siberian Shamanism.* Toronto: University of Toronto Press, pp. 84–123.

Aserinsky, E. and N. Kleitman. 1955. 'Two Types of Ocular Motility Occurring in Sleep', *Journal of Applied Physiology* (8): 1–10.

Ashburn, P.M. and F.D. Ashburn. 1980 [1947]. *The Ranks of Death: A Medical History of the Conquest of America.* Philadelphia: Porcupine Press.

Atkinson, J.M. 1992. 'Shamanisms Today', *Annual Review of Anthropology* 21: 307–30.

Baars, B.J., W.P. Banks and J.B. Newman (eds). 2003. *Essential Sources in the Scientific Study of Consciousness.* Cambridge, MA: MIT Press.

Barandiarán, D. 1965. 'Mundo Espiritual y Shamanismo Sanema', *Antropológica* 15: 1–28.

Barandiarán, D. and B. Brandli. 1983. *Los Hijos de la Luna.* Caracas: Arte Impresión.

Basilov, V.N. 1997. 'Chosen by the Spirits', in M. Mandelstram Balzer (ed.), *Shamanic Worlds: Rituals and Lore of Siberia and Central Asia.* New York: M.E. Sharpe, pp. 3–48.

Basso, E. 1987a. *In Favor of Deceit: A Study of Tricksters in an Amazonian Society.* Tucson: University of Arizona Press.

———. 1987b. 'The Implications of a Progressive Theory of Dreaming', in B. Tedlock (ed.), *Dreaming: Anthropological and Psychological Interpretations.* Cambridge: Cambridge University Press, pp. 86–104.

Berwick, D. 1992. *Savages: The Life and Killing of the Yanomami.* London: Hutchinson.

Biocca, E. 1971. *Yanoáma: The Narrative of a White Girl Kidnapped by Amazonian Indians.* New York: E.P. Dutton.

Bourget, S. 2005. 'Hot-Cold Medicine Revisited: Another Look at the Debate Over its Origin', honours thesis. Jupiter: Wilkes Honors College of Florida Atlantic University.

Buchillet, D. (ed.). 1991. *Medicinas Tradicionais e Medicina Occidental na Amazônia*. Belém: Edições CEJUP.

Bulkeley, K. 2008. *Dreaming in the World Religions: A Comparative History*. New York: New York University Press.

Burridge, K. 1969. *New Heaven New Earth: A Study of Millenarian Activities*. Oxford: Basil Blackwell.

Butcher, G. 1990. *Malaria: the Intelligent Guide*. Canberra: ANUTECH.

Butler, R. 2012. 'Fires in the Rainforest'. Retrieved 9 October 2013 from http://rainforests.mongabay.com/0809.htm

Butt Colson, A.B. 1976. 'Binary Oppositions and the Treatment of Sickness among the Akawaio', in J.B. Loudon (ed.), *Social Anthropology and Medicine* (A.S.A. Monograph 13). New York: Academic Press, pp. 422–99.

Butt Colson, A. and C. de Armellada. 1983. 'An Amerindian Derivation for Latin American Creole Illnesses and their Treatment', *Social Science and Medicine* 17: 1229–248.

———. 1985. 'El Origen de la Etiología de Enfermedades y su Tratamiento en la America Latina', *Revista Montalbán UCAB* 16: 5–45.

Caballero-Arias, H.R. 2003. 'Engaging in Politics: Yanomami Strategies in the Face of Venezuela's National Frontier Expansion', Ph.D. dissertation. Tuscon: The University of Arizona.

Cardozo, J.I. and H. Caballero. 1994. 'La Situación del Niño y la Mujer Yanomami', in *Diagnóstico del Niño Amazónico*. Caracas: UNICEF.

Carrier, A.H. 1989. 'The Place of Western Medicine in Ponam Theories of Health and Illness', in S. Frankel and G. Lewis (eds), *A Continuing Trial of Treatment: Medical Pluralism in Papua New Guinea*. Dordrecht: Kluwer, pp. 155–80.

Chagnon, N. 1968a. *Yanomamo: The Fierce People*. New York: Holt, Rinehart and Winston.

———. 1968b. 'Yanomamo Social Organization and Warfare', in M. Fried, M. Harris and R. Murphy (eds), *War: The Anthropology of Armed Conflict and Aggression*. New York: Natural History Press, pp. 109–59.

———. 1973. *Magical Death*. Documentary film (16mm, 29 minutes) distributed by Documentary Educational Resources. Pennsylvania State University.

———. 1974. *Studying the Yanomamo*. New York: Holt, Rinehart and Winston.

———. 1992. *Yanomamo: The Last Days of Eden*. New York: Harcourt Brace Jovanovich.

Chaumeil, J.P. 1992. 'Varieties of Amazonian Shamanism', *Diogenes* 158: 101–13.

Chernela, J.M. 1988. 'Righting History in the Northwest Amazon: Myth, Structure, and History in an Arapaço Narrative', in J.D. Hill (ed.), *Rethinking History and Myth: Indigenous South American Perspectives on the Past*. Chicago: University of Illinois Press, pp. 35–49.

Chiappino, J. 1995. 'El Coloso Yanomami Frente al "Nuevo" El Dorado. Representaciones de ser Humano y del Medio Ambiente: Un Envite de la Participación Comunitaria al Desarrollo Regional', in A. Carillo and M.A. Perera (eds), *Amazonas Modernidad en Tradición: Contribuciones al Desarrollo Sustentable en el Estado Amazonas, Venezuela*. Caracas: GTZ/CAIAH-SADA AMAZONAS, pp. 175–204.

———. 1997. 'Cosmos y Espíritus: Palabras de un Shamán Yanomami', in J. Chiappino and C. Alès (eds), *Del Microscopio a la Maraca*. Caracas: Ex Libris, pp. 29–31.

———. 2002. 'Participación Comunitaria al Control de la Salud: Experiencia de Producción de Documentos Didácticos en el Amazonas Venezolano', *Götenborg*

University, Faculty of Arts. Retrieved 11 November 2012 from http://hdl.handle. net/2077/3233

'Church World Service'. 1998. 'Brazil – Roraima Fires and Drought'. Retrieved 9 October 2013 from http://reliefweb.int/report/brazil/brazil-roraima-fires-and-drought

Classen, C. 1993. *Inca Cosmology and the Human Body*. Salt Lake City: University of Utah Press.

Cocco, L. 1972. *Iyëwei theri: Quince Años entre los Yanomamos*. Caracas: Edición Escuela Técnica Popular 'Don Bosco'.

Colchester, M. 1981. 'Myths and Legends of the Sanema', *Antropológica* 56: 25–126.

———. 1982. 'The Cosmovision of the Venezuelan Sanema', *Antropológica* 58: 97–174.

Colchester, M. (ed.). 1985. *The Health and Survival of the Venezuelan Yanoama* (IWGIA document 53). Copenhagen: ARC/IWGIA/SI.

Conklin, B.A. 2002. 'Shamans versus Pirates in the Amazonian Treasure Chest', *American Anthropologist* 104(4): 1050–61.

Cooper, J.C. 1992. *Symbolic and Mythological Animals*. London: Aquarian Press.

Crapanzano, V. 1977. 'Introduction', in V. Crapanzano and V. Garrison (eds), *Case Studies in Spirit Possession*. New York: John Wiley, pp. 1–40.

Crocker, J.C. 1985. *Vital Souls: Bororo Cosmology, Natural Symbolism, and Shamanism*. Tucson: University of Arizona Press.

Csordas, T. 1990. 'Embodiment as a Paradigm for Anthropology', *Ethos* 18(1): 5–47.

Cultural Survival. 1991. '"I Fight Because I Am Alive": An Interview with Davi Kopenawa Yanomami'. Retrieved 29 August 2013 from http://www.culturalsurvival.org/publications/ cultural-survival-quarterly/brazil/i-fight-because-i-am-alive-interview-davi-kopenawa-y

D'Andrade, R. 1961. 'Anthropological Studies of Dreams', in F.L.K. Hsu (ed.), *Psychological Anthropology: Approaches to Culture and Personality*. Homewood, IL: Dorsey, pp. 296–332.

Dardel, E. 1984. 'The Mythic', in A. Dundes (ed.), *Sacred Narrative: Readings in the Theory of Myth*. Berkeley: University of California Press, pp. 225–43.

Davies, J. and D. Spencer (eds). 2010. *Emotions in the Field: The Psychology and Anthropology of Fieldwork Experience*. Stanford, CA: Stanford University Press.

De Heusch, L. 2007 [1971]. 'Possession and Shamanism', in L. De Heusch *Why Marry Her? Society and Symbolic Structures*. Cambridge: Cambridge University Press, pp. 151–64.

Dement, W. and N. Kleitman. 1957. 'Cyclic Variations in the EEG during Sleep and their Relation to Eye Movements, Body Motility, and Dreaming', *EEG Clinical Neurophysiology* 9: 637–90.

De Pedro, M. 1980. *Iniciación de un Shamán*. Documentary film (70 minutes). Caracas: Cochano Films.

Dow, J. 1986. *The Shaman's Touch: Otomi Indian Symbolic Healing*. Salt Lake City: University of Utah Press.

DuBois, T. 2009. *An Introduction to Shamanism*. Cambridge: Cambridge University Press.

Dundes, A. 1988. 'The Flood as Male Myth of Creation', in A. Dundes (ed.), *The Flood Myth*. Berkeley: University of California Press, pp. 167–82.

Early, J.D. and J. Peters. 2000. *The Xilixana Yanomami of the Amazon: History, Social Structure and Population Dynamics*. Gainesville: University Press of Florida.

Eguíllor García, M.I. 1984. *Yopo, Shamanes y Hekura: Aspectos Fenomenológicos del Mundo Sagrado Yanomami*. Puerto Ayacucho: Vicariato Apostólico de Puerto Ayacucho.

Eliade, M. 1960. *Myths, Dreams and Mysteries*. London: Harvill Press.

———. 1965. *The Myth of the Eternal Return*. New York: Pantheon.

———. 1989 [1951]. *Shamanism: Archaic Techniques of Ecstasy*. London: Arcana.

Ferguson, B. 1992. 'A Savage Encounter: Western Contact and the Yanomami War Complex', in B. Ferguson and N. Whitehead (eds), *War in the Tribal Zone: Expanding States and Indigenous Warfare*. Santa Fe: School of American Research Press, pp. 199–227.

———. 1995. *Yanomami Warfare: A Political History*. Santa Fe: School of American Research Press.

Foster, G. 1987. 'On the Origin of Humoral Medicine in Latin America', *Medical Anthropology Quarterly* 1: 355–93.

———. 1994. *Hippocrates' Latin American Legacy: Humoral Medicine in the New World*. Amsterdam: Gordon and Breach.

Frazer, J. 1979 [1922]. 'Sympathetic Magic', in W. Lessa and E.Z. Vogt (eds), *Reader in Comparative Religion: An Anthropological Approach*, 4th ed. New York: Harper and Row, pp. 337–52.

Freire, G. (ed.). 2011. *Perspectivas en Salud Indígena: Cosmovisión, Enfermedad y Políticas Públicas*. Quito: Ediciones Abya-Yala.

Furst, P. 1987. 'South American Shamanism', in M. Eliade (ed.), *Encyclopedia of Religion (vol. 13)*. New York: Collier MacMillan, pp. 219–23.

———. 1994. 'Introduction: An Overview of Shamanism', in G. Seaman and J.S. Day (eds), *Shamanism in Central Asia and the Americas*. Colorado: University Press of Colorado and Denver, Museum of Natural History, pp. 1–28.

Gilberg, R. 1984. 'How to Recognize a Shaman among other Religious Specialists', in M. Hoppal (ed.), *Shamanism in Eurasia (part 1)*. Gottingen: Herodot, pp. 21–27.

Gillet, J.D. 1971. *Mosquitoes*. London: Weidenfeld & Nicolson.

Goulet, J.G. and B.G. Miller (eds). 2007. *Extraordinary Anthropology: Transformations in the Field*. Lincoln, NE and London: University of Nebraska Press.

Goulet, J.G. and D.E. Young. 1994. 'Theoretical and Methodological Issues', in D.E. Young and J.G. Goulet (eds), Being Changed by Cross-Cultural Encounters: The Anthropology of Extraordinary Experience. Peterborough, ON: Broadview, pp. 298–335.

Gow, P. 2001. *An Amazonian Myth and its History*. Oxford: Oxford University Press.

Green, E. 1999. *Indigenous Theories of Contagious Disease*. Walnut Creek: AltaMira Press, Division of Sage.

Grof, S. and J. Halifax. 1977. *Human Encounter with Death*. New York: Dutton.

Gurwitsch, A. 1974 [1967]. 'Husserl's Theory of Intentionality of Consciousness in Historical Perspective', in A. Gurwitsch (ed.), *Phenomenology and the Theory of Science*. Evanston: Northwestern University Press, pp. 210–40.

Halifax, J. 1979. *Shamanic Voices*. New York: Dutton.

Harner, M. 1972. *Jivaro: People of the Sacred Waterfalls*. New York: Anchor.

Heckenberger, M., et al. 2003. 'Amazonia 1492: Pristine Forest or Cultural Parkland?', *Science* 301(5640): 1710–714.

Heinen, D. 1991. 'Lathrap's Concept of "Interfluvial Zones" Applied to the Analysis of Indigenous Groups in the Venezuelan Amazon', *Antropológica* 75–76: 61–92.

Herzog-Schröder, G. 1999. 'Yanomami: Nacidos de la Pantorrilla', in *Orinoco-Parima – Comunidades Indígenas de Venezuela* La Colección Cisneros. Ostfildern-Ruit: Hatje Cantz Verlag, pp. 34–49.

Hobson, J.A. 2001. 'The New Neuropsychology of Sleep', in K. Bulkeley (ed.), *Dreams: A Reader on Religious, Cultural, and Psychological Dimensions of Dreaming*. New York: Palgrave, pp. 322–32.

Holy Bible. 1979. Authorised King James Version. Salt Lake City: Church of Jesus Christ of Latter-Day Saints.

Homan, J. 2011. 'Charlatans, Seekers, and Shamans: The Ayahuasca Boom in Western Peruvian Amazonia', MA thesis. Lawrence: University of Kansas.

Honko, L. 1984. 'The Problem of Defining Myth', in A. Dundes (ed.), *Sacred Narrative: Readings in the Theory of Myth*. Berkeley: University of California Press, pp. 41–52.

Hugh-Jones, S. 1988. 'The Gun and the Bow: Myths of White Men and Indians', *L'Homme* 28(2–3): 138–55.

Hultkrantz, A. 1973. 'A Definition of Shamanism', *Temenos* 9: 25–37.

Humphrey, C. and U. Onon (eds). 1996. *Shamans and Elders: Experience, Knowledge, and Power among the Daur Mongols*. Oxford: Clarendon Press.

Hunt, H. 1989. *The Multiplicity of Dreams: Memory, Imagination, and Consciousness*. New Haven and London: Yale University Press.

———. 1995. *On the Nature of Consciousness: Cognitive, Phenomenological and Transpersonal Perspectives*. New Haven: Yale University Press.

Husserl, E. 1960 [1906]. *Cartesian Meditations: An Introduction to Phenomenology*. Dordrecht: Martinus Nijhoff.

———. 1985. *The Paris Lectures*. Dordrecht: Kluwer Academic Publishers.

Jackson, M. 1989. *Paths toward a Clearing: Radical Empiricism and Ethnographic Enquiry*. Bloomington: Indiana University Press.

———. 1998. *Minima Ethnographica: Intersubjectivity and the Anthropological Project*. Chicago: University of Chicago Press.

Jauregui. I.P. 1993. 'Reflexiones Sobre la Muerte del Humanismo Entre Los "Napes"', unpublished report. Puerto Ayacucho: Memorias del CAICET III (1, 2), pp. 29–37.

Job, S. 2010. 'Without Ends Facing the End: Of Aztec Revivalists and Anthropologists'. (Panel 4) in S. Job and L. Connor (eds), *Online Proceedings of the Symposium Anthropology and the Ends of Worlds (Vol. 1)*. Sydney: Department of Anthropology, University of Sydney, pp. 85–95. Retrieved 15 December 2013 from http://anthroendsofworlds.files.wordpress.com/2013/11/sass-vol-1_job2.pdf

Jokic, Z. 2006. 'Cosmo-genesis or Transformation of the Human Body into a Cosmic Body in Yanomami Shamanistic Initiation', *Shaman: Journal of the International Society for Shamanistic Research* 14(1–2): 19–39.

———. 2008a. 'Yanomami Shamanistic Initiation: The Meaning of Death and Postmortem Consciousness in Transformation', *Anthropology of Consciousness* 19(1): 33–59.

———. 2008b. 'The Wrath of the Forgotten Ongons: Shamanic Sickness, Spirit Embodiment and Fragmentary Trancescape in Contemporary Buriat Shamanism', *Sibirica: Interdisciplinary Journal of Siberian Research* 7(1): 23–50.

———. 2014. 'Shamanic Battleground: Magic, Sorcery and Warrior Shamanism in Venezuela', *Social Analysis Special issue: War Magic and Warrior Religion: Sorcery, Cognition and Embodiment* 58(1): 107–26.

Kahan, T. 2001. 'Consciousness in Dreaming: A Metacognitive Approach', in K. Bulkeley (ed.), *Dreams: A Reader on Religious, Cultural, and Psychological Dimensions of Dreaming*. New York: Palgrave, pp. 333–60.

Kalweit, H. 2000. *Shamans, Healers, and Medicine Men*. Boston: Shambhala.

Kapferer, B. 1997. *The Feast of the Sorcerer: Practices of Consciousness and Power*. Chicago and London: University of Chicago Press.

———. 2002. 'Outside All Reason: Magic, Sorcery and Epistemology in Anthropology', in B. Kapferer (ed.), Beyond Rationalism: Rethinking Magic, Witchcraft and Sorcery. New York and Oxford: Berghahn Books, pp. 1–30.

Kelly, J.A. 2011. State Healthcare and Yanomami Transformations: A Symmetrical Ethnography. Tuscon: The University of Arizona Press.

Kilborne, B. 1987. 'On Classifying Dreams', in B. Tedlock (ed.), Dreaming: Anthropological and Psychological Interpretations. Cambridge: Cambridge University Press, pp. 171–93.

Kopenawa, D. and B. Albert. 2013. The Falling Sky: Words of a Yanomami Shaman. Cambridge, MA: Belknap Press of Harvard University Press.

Kracke, W. 1987. 'Myths in Dreams, Thought in Images: An Amazonian Contribution to the Psychoanalytic Theory of Primary Process', in B. Tedlock (ed.), Dreaming: Anthropological and Psychological Interpretations. Cambridge: Cambridge University Press, pp. 31–54.

La Berge, S. 1985. Lucid Dreaming. Los Angeles: Jeremy P. Tarcher.

Lacan, J. 1977. 'The Mirror Stage as Formative of the Function of the I as Revealed in Psychoanalytic Experience', Écrits: A Selection (trans. A. Sheridan). London: Tavistock, pp. 1–7.

Lathrap, D. 1970. The Upper Amazon. New York: Praeger.

Laughlin, C.D. 1994. 'Psychic Energy and Transpersonal Experience: A Biogenetic Structural Account of the Tibetan Dumo Yoga Practice', in D.E. Young and J.G. Goulet (eds), Being Changed by Cross-cultural Encounters: The Anthropology of Extraordinary Experience. Peterborough, ON: Broadview, pp. 99–134.

Laughlin, Jr., C.D., J. McManus and E.G. d'Aquili. 1992. Brain, Symbol and Experience: Towards a Neurophenomenology of Human Consciousness. New York: Columbia University Press.

Layrisse, M. and J. Wilbert. 1966. Indian Societies of Venezuela: Their Blood Types (Monograph 13). Caracas: Fundación La Salle de Ciencias Naturales.

Leach, E. 1969. Genesis as Myth and Other Essays. London: Jonathan Cape.

Levi-Strauss, C. 1963. 'The Effectiveness of Symbols', Structural Anthropology. New York: Penguin Books, pp. 186–205.

———. 1964. The Raw and the Cooked: Introduction to a Science of Mythology (Vol. 1). London: Jonathan Cape.

———. 1996. The Story of Lynx. Chicago: The University of Chicago Press.

Levy-Bruhl, L. 1965 [1928]. The 'Soul' of the Primitive. London: George Allen & Unwin.

Lewis, I.M. 1971. Ecstatic Religion: An Anthropological Study of Spirit Possession and Shamanism. Harmondsworth: Penguin Books.

———. 1984. 'What is a Shaman?', in M. Hoppal (ed.), Shamanism in Eurasia (part 1). Gottingen: Herodot, pp. 3–12.

———. 1988. 'Shamanism', in S. Sutherlandet al., The World's Religions. London: Routledge, pp. 825–35.

Lewis-Williams, D. 2002. The Mind in the Cave: Consciousness and the Origins of Art. London: Thames & Hudson.

Lizot, J. 1974. El Hombre de la Pantorrilla Preñada (Monografía no. 21). Caracas: Fundación La Salle de Ciencias Naturales.

———. 1975. Diccionario Yanomami-Español (trans. R. Lizarralde). Caracas: Universidad Central de Venezuela.

———. 1976a. Le Cercle des Feux. Paris: Editions du Seuil.

———. 1976b. The Yanomami in the Face of Ethnocide (IWGIA document 22). Copenhagen: ARC/IWGIA/SI.

————. 1984. 'Histoire, Organisation et Évolution du Peuplement Yanomami', L'Homme, 24(2): 5–40.

————. 1985. Tales of the Yanomami: Daily Life in the Venezuelan Forest. Cambridge: Cambridge University Press.

————. 1988. 'Los Yanomami', in J. Lizot (ed.), Los Aborígines de Venezuela (Vol. 3). Caracas: Fundación La Salle de Ciencias Naturales, pp. 479–583.

————. 1989. No Patapi Tëhë: En Tiempos de los Antepasados: Texto de Lectura – 2. Puerto Ayacucho: Vicariato Apostólico de Puerto Ayacucho.

————. 1994 'Words in the Night: The Ceremonial Dialogue – One Expression of Peaceful Relationships among the Yanomami', in L. Sponsel and T. Gregor (eds), The Anthropology of Peace and Nonviolence. London: Lynne Rienner, pp. 213–40.

————. 1996. Introducción a la Lengua Yanomami: Morfología. Caracas: Vicariato Apostólico de Puerto Ayacucho.

————. 1998. 'Situación cultural y acción sanitaria: el caso Yanomami', La Iglesia en Amazonas 19(81–82): 30–36.

————. 2004. Diccionario Enciclopédico de la Lengua Yãnomãmi. Puerto Ayacucho: Vicariato Apostólico de Puerto Ayacucho.

————. 2007. 'El Mundo Intelectual de los Yanomami: Cosmovisión, Enfermedad y Muerte con una Teoría sobre el Canibalismo', in G. Freire and A. Tillett (eds), Salud Indígena en Venezuela (Vol. 1). Caracas: DSI- MPPS, pp. 269–324.

Ludwig, A. 1966. 'Altered States of Consciousness', Archives of General Psychiatry 15: 225–34.

Luzar, B.J. and J.M.V. Fragoso. 2013. 'Shamanism, Christianity and Culture Change in Amazonia', Human Ecology 41(2): 299–311.

MacMillan, G. 1995. At the End of the Rainbow? Gold, People, and Land in the Brazilian Amazon. New York: Columbia University Press.

Madsen, W. 1955. 'Hot and Cold in the Universe of San Francisco Tecospa, Valley of Mexico', Journal of American Folklore 25: 89–138.

Magris, M. 2004. 'Malaria Control Trial using Lambdacyhalohrin-Treated Nets in Yanomami Communities in Amazonas State, Venezuela', Ph.D. dissertation. London: London School of Hygiene and Tropical Medicine.

Magris, M., et al. 2007. 'Community-Randomized Trial of Lambdacyhalohrin-Treated Hammock Nets for Malaria Control in Yanomami Communities in the Amazon Region of Venezuela', Tropical Medicine and International Health 12(3): 392–403.

Malinowski, B. 1954. Magic, Science and Religion: And Other Essays. New York: Doubleday Anchor.

Marcano, T.J., et al. 2004. 'Cross-sectional Study Defines Difference in Malaria Morbidity in Two Yanomami Communities on Amazonian Boundary between Brazil and Venezuela', Memorias do Instituto Oswaldo Cruz 99(4): 369–76. Retrieved 26 October 2012 from http://www.scielo.br/scielo.php?script=sci_arttext&pid=S0074-02762004000400005

Maury, A. 1848. 'Des hallucinations hypnagogiques, ou des erreurs des sens dans l'etat intermediaire entre la veille et le sommeil', Annales Medico-Psychologiques du système nerveux 11: 26–40.

Mavromatis, A. 1987. Hypnagogia: The Unique State of Consciousness between Wakefulness and Sleep. London: Routledge & Kegan Paul.

McEwan, C., C. Barreto and E. Neves (eds). 2001. Unknown Amazon. London: The British Museum.

McGovern, U. (ed.). 2007. Chambers Dictionary of the Unexplained. Edinburgh: Chambers Harrap.

McLean, A. and A. Leibing (eds). 2007. *The Shadow Side of Fieldwork: Exploring the Blurred Borders between Ethnography and Life*. Oxford: Blackwell.

Merleau-Ponty, M. 1962. *The Phenomenology of Perception*. London: Routledge & Kegan Paul.

Merleau-Ponty, M. 1964a. *Signs*. Evanston: Northwestern University Press.

———. 1964b. 'The Child's Relation with Others', in J.M. Edie (ed.), *Primacy of Perception and Other Essays on Phenomenological Psychology, the Philosophy of Art, History and Politics*. Evanston: Northwestern University Press, pp. 96–155.

———. 1973. 'Phenomenology and the Sciences of Man', in M. Natanson (ed.), *Phenomenology and the Social Sciences (Vol. 1)*. Evanston: Northwestern University Press, pp. 47–108.

Merrill, W. 1987. 'The Raramuri Stereotype of Dreams', in B. Tedlock (ed.), *Dreaming: Anthropological and Psychological Interpretations*. Cambridge: Cambridge University Press, pp. 194–219.

Messer, E. 1987. 'The Hot and Cold in Latin American Indigenous and Hispanicized Thought', *Social Science and Medicine* 25(4): 339–46. Chicago: University of Chicago Press.

Migliazza, E. 1972. 'Yanomama Grammar and Intelligibility', Ph.D. dissertation. Bloomington: Indiana University.

Mimica, J. 1988. *Intimations of Infinity: The Mythopoeia of the Iqwaye Counting System and Number*. Oxford: Berg.

Ministerio de Salud y Desarrollo Social (MSDS). 2000. 'Proyecto de Salud Pueblo Yanomami'. Puerto Ayacucho: Dirección Estadal de Salud y Desarrollo Social del Estado Amazonas.

———. 2005. 'Plan de Salud del Pueblo Yanomami'. Puerto Ayacucho: Dirección Estadal de Salud y Desarrollo Social del Estado Amazonas.

Murdock, G.P. 1980. *Theories of Illness*. Pittsburgh: University of Pittsburgh Press.

Myers, F.W.H. 1903. *Human Personality and its Survival of Bodily Death (Vol. 1)*. London: Longmans, Green. Retrieved 24 January 2014 from https://archive.org/details/humanpersonality01myeruoft

Narby, J. and F. Huxley (eds). 2001. *Shamans through Time: 500 Years on the Path to Knowledge*. London: Thames & Hudson.

Newson, L. 1993. 'The Demographic Collapse of Native Peoples of the Americas, 1492–1650', in W. Bray (ed.), *The Meeting of Two Worlds: Europe and the Americas 1492–1650*. Oxford: Oxford University Press, pp. 247–88.

———. 2001. 'Pathogens, Places and Peoples: Geographical Variations in the Impact of Disease in Early Spanish America and the Philippines', in G. Raudzens (ed.), *Technology, Disease and Colonial Conquests, Sixteenth to Eighteenth Centuries*. Leiden: Brill, pp. 167–210.

Ortiz de Montellano, B. 1975. 'Empirical Aztec Medicine', *Science* 188(4185): 215–20.

Osborne, H. 1968. *South American Mythology*. Feltham: Paul Hamlyn.

Peck, S. 1978. *The Road Less Travelled*. London: Rider.

Pedro, M. de 1980. *Iniciación de un Shamán*. Documentary film (70 minutes). Caracas: Cochano Films.

Perrera, M.A. and P. Rivas. 1997. 'Medicina Tradicional Indígena, Medicina Occidental. Compatibilidades y Oposiciones', in M. A. Perrera (ed.), *Salud y Ambiente. Contribuciones al Conocimiento de la Antropología Médica y Ecología Cultural en Venezuela*. Caracas: UCV – Facultad de Ciencias Económicas y Sociales, pp. 7–30.

Peters, J.F. 1973. 'The Effect of Western Material Goods upon the Social Structure of the Family among the Shirishana', Ph.D. dissertation. Kalamazoo: Western Michigan University.

Peters, L. 1979. 'Shamanism and Medicine in Developing Nepal', *Contributions to Nepalese Studies* 6(2): 27–43.

Peters, L. and D. Price-Williams. 1980. 'Towards an Experiential Analysis of Shamanism', *American Ethnologist* 7(3): 397–418.

Price-Williams, D. 1987. 'The Waking Dream in Ethnographic Perspective', in B. Tedlock (ed.), *Dreaming: Anthropological and Psychological Interpretations*. Cambridge: Cambridge University Press, pp. 246–61.

Rabben, L. 1998. *Unnatural Selection: The Yanomami, the Kayapo and the Onslaught of Civilization*. London: Pluto Press.

Radin, P. 1972 [1956]. *The Trickster: A Study in American Indian Mythology*. New York: Schocken Books.

Ramos, A. 1972. 'The Social System of the Sanuma of Northern Brazil', Ph.D. dissertation. Madison: University of Wisconsin.

———. 1995. *Sanuma Memories: Yanomami Ethnography in Times of Crisis*. Madison: University of Wisconsin Press.

Rasmussen, K. 1979. 'A Shaman's Journey to the Sea Spirit', in W. Lessa and E. Z. Vogt (eds), *Reader in Comparative Religion: An Anthropological Approach* 4th ed. New York: Harper and Row, pp. 388–92.

Reichel-Dolmatoff, G. 1975. *The Shaman and the Jaguar: A Study of Narcotic Drugs among the Indians of Colombia*. Philadelphia: Temple University Press.

Restrepo, A. 1993. 'La Mujer Yanomami', *Ethnia* (Medellín: Universidad Pontificia Bolivariana – Instituto Misionero de Antropología (IMA)) 72: 1–59.

Rhodes, L.A. 1996. 'Studying Biomedicine as a Cultural System', in C.F. Sargent and T.M. Johnson (eds), *Medical Anthropology: Contemporary Theory and Method*. London: Praeger, pp. 165–80.

Riboli, D. and D. Torri (eds). 2013. *Shamanism and Violence: Power, Repression and Suffering in Indigenous Religious Conflicts*. Farnham, Surrey: Ashgate.

Riches, D. 1994. 'Shamanism: The Key to Religion', *Man* 29(2): 381–405.

Roe, P. 1982. *The Cosmic Zygote: Cosmology in the Amazon Basin*. New Brunswick: Rutgers University Press.

Rouget, G. 1985. *Music and Trance*. Chicago: The University of Chicago Press.

Saffirio, G. 1985. 'Ideal and Actual Kinship Terminology among the Yanomama Indians of the Catrimani River Basin (Brazil)', Ph.D. dissertation. Pittsburgh: University of Pittsburgh.

Salamone, F. (ed.). 1997. *The Yanomami and their Interpreters: Fierce People or Fierce Interpreters?* Lanham: University Press of America.

Sanchez, C. 1999. 'Consideraciones sobre la Educación para la Salud en el Área Yanomami-Ye'kuana', unpublished paper. Puerto Ayacucho: SACAICET.

Sanchez-Salamé, G.L. 2005. 'Community Health Workers among Indigenous People in Amazonas, Venezuela: Their Role in a Shifting Context', Ph.D. dissertation. London: London School of Hygiene and Tropical Medicine.

Sansonese, J.N. 1994. *The Body of Myth: Mythology, Shamanic Trance, and the Sacred Geography of the Body*. Rochester, VT: Inner Traditions.

Schilder, P. 1956. *The Image and Appearance of the Human Body: Studies in the Constructive Energies of the Psyche*. New York: International Universities Press.

Schrempp, G. 1992. *Magical Arrows: The Maori, the Greeks, and the Folklore of the Universe*. Madison: The University of Wisconsin Press.

Schultes, R.E. 1976. *Hallucinogenic Plants*. New York: Golden Press.

Shafton, A. 1995. *Dream Reader: Contemporary Approaches to the Understanding of Dreams*. Albany: State University of New York Press.

Shanon, B. 2002. *The Antipodes of the Mind: Charting the Phenomenology of the Ayahuasca Experience*. Oxford: Oxford University Press.

Sherwood, J. 1965. *The Fourfold Vision: A Study of Consciousness, Sleep and Dreams*. London: Spearman.

Sherwood, C. 1975. 'New Evidence for the Late Introduction of Malaria into the New World', *Current Anthropology* 16(1): 93–104.

Shirokogoroff, S.M. 1935. *Psychomental Complex of the Tungus*. London: Kegan Paul, Trench, Trubner.

Shulman, D. and G. Stroumsa (eds). 1999. *Dream Cultures: Explorations in the Comparative History of Dreaming*. Oxford: Oxford University Press.

Sinka, M.E., et al. 2010. 'The Dominant Anopheles Vectors of Human Malaria in the Americas: Occurrence Data, Distribution Maps and Bionomic Précis', *Parasites and Vectors* 3: 72. Retrieved 22 January 2014 from http://www.parasitesandvectors.com/content/3/1/72

Smole, W. 1976. *The Yanoama Indians: A Cultural Geography*. Austin: University of Texas Press.

Spiegelberg, H. 1969. *The Phenomenological Movement: A Historical Introduction (Vol. 1)*. The Hague: Martinus Nijhoff.

Stang, C. 2010. '"Anthropokaluptein": The End as Anthropological Revelation'. (Panel 6) in S. Job and L. Connor (eds), *Online Proceedings of the Symposium Anthropology and the Ends of Worlds (Vol. 1)*. Sydney: Department of Anthropology, University of Sydney, pp. 124–31. Retrieved 15 December 2013 from http://anthroendsofworlds.files.wordpress.com/2013/11/sass-vol-1_job2.pdf

Steinbock, A. 1994. 'The New "Crisis" Contribution: A Supplementary Edition of "Crisis" Texts', *The Review of Metaphysics* 47(3): 557–75.

Steinvorth-Goetz, I. 1969. *Uriji jami! Life and Belief of the Forest Waika in the Upper Orinoco*. Caracas: Asociación Cultural Humboldt.

Sullivan, L. 1988. *Icanchu's Drum: An Orientation to Meaning in South American Religions*. New York: Macmillan.

———. 1994. 'The Attributes and Power of the Shaman: A General Description of the Ecstatic Care of the Soul', in G. Seaman and J.S. Day (eds), *Shamanism in Central Asia and the Americas*. Colorado: University Press of Colorado and Denver Museum of Natural History, pp. 29–45.

Sumabila-Tachon, A. 1999. 'Malaria among the Cuiva of the Venezuelan-Colombian Borderland: A Political Economy Perspective', Ph.D. dissertation. Sydney: Macquarie University.

Tart, C. (ed.). 1969. 'The "High" Dream: A New State of Consciousness', in C. Tart (ed.), *Altered States of Consciousness*. New York: John Wiley, pp. 169–74.

Taylor, K.I. 1976. 'Body and Spirit among the Sanuma (Yanoama) of Northern Brazil', in D.L. Browman and R.A. Schwartz (eds), *Spirits, Shamans and Stars: Perspectives from South America*. The Hague: Mouton, pp. 201–21.

Tedlock, B. 1987. 'Zuni and Quiche Dream Sharing and Interpreting', in B. Tedlock (ed.), *Dreaming: Anthropological and Psychological Interpretations*. Cambridge: Cambridge University Press, pp. 105–31.

Tedlock, D. 1999. 'Mythic Dreams and Double Voicing', in D. Shulman and G. Stroumsa (eds), *Dream Cultures: Explorations in the Comparative History of Dreaming*. Oxford: Oxford University Press, pp. 104–18.

Torres, J., et al. 1988. 'Hyperactive Malarial Splenomegaly in Venezuela', *American Journal of Tropical Medicine and Hygiene* 39(1): 11–14.

———. 1997. 'Aspectos Especiales de la Epidemiología y Patogenía de la Malaria en Poblaciones Yanomamis Aisladas de la Cuenca del Alto Orinoco', in M.A. Perrera (ed.), *Salud y Ambiente: Contribuciones al Conocimiento de la Antropología Médica y Ecología Cultural en Venezuela*. Caracas: Central University of Venezuela, Facultad de Ciencias Económicas y Sociales, pp. 217–28.

Valero, H. 1984. *Yo soy Napëyoma: Relato de una Mujer Raptada por los Indígenas Yanomami* (Monografía No. 35). Caracas: Fundación La Salle de Ciencias Naturales.

Van Eeden, F. 1969 [1913]. 'A Study of Dreams', in C. Tart (ed.), *Altered States of Consciousness*. New York: John Wiley, pp. 145–58.

Velásquez, R. 1987. *Chamanismo, Mito y Religión en Cuatro Naciones Étnicas de América Aborigen (Vol. 97)*. Caracas: Academia Nacional de la Historia.

Vidal Ontiveros, S. 1993. 'Reconstrucción de los Procesos de Entogenesis y de Reproducción Social entre los Baré de Rio Negro (siglos XVI–XVIII), Ph.D. dissertation. Caracas: Instituto Venezolano de Investigaciones Científicas.

Vitebsky, P. 2003. 'From Cosmology to Environmentalism: Shamanism as Local Knowledge in a Global Setting', in G. Harvey (ed.), *Shamanism: A Reader*. London: Routledge, pp. 276–99.

———. 2005. *Reindeer People: Living with Animals and Spirits in Siberia*. London: HarperCollins.

Viveiros de Castro, E. 1992. *From the Enemy's Point of View: Humanity and Divinity in an Amazonian Society*. Chicago: University of Chicago Press.

———. 1998. 'Cosmological Deixis and Amerindian Perspectivism', *Journal of the Royal Anthropological Institute* 4(3): 469–88.

———. 2004 [unpublished]. 'The Forest of Mirrors: A Few Notes on the Ontology of Amazonian Spirits'. Retrieved 12 December 2013 from http://amazone.wikia.com/wiki/The_Forest_of_Mirrors

———. 2012. 'Cosmological Perspectivism in Amazonia and Elsewhere' (Masterclass Series 1). HAU Network of Ethnographic Theory, pp. 45–168. Retrieved 23 January 2014 from http://www.haujournal.org/index.php/masterclass/article/viewFile/72/54

Vogel, G., D. Foulkes and H. Trosman. 1966. 'Ego Functions and Dreaming During Sleep Onset', *Archives of General Psychiatry* 14: 238–48.

Wagner, R. 1991. 'The Fractal Person', in M. Godelier and M. Strathern (eds), *Big Men and Great Men: Personification of Power in Melanesia*. Cambridge: Cambridge University Press, pp. 159–73.

Walde, C. 1999. 'Dream Interpretation in a Prosperous Age? Artemidorus, the Greek Interpreter of Dreams', in D. Schulman and G. Stroumsa (eds), *Dream Cultures: Explorations in the Comparative History of Dreaming*. Oxford: Oxford University Press, pp. 121–42.

Wallon, H. 1984. 'Kinesthesia and the Visual Body Image in the Child', in G. Voyat (ed.), *The World of Henri Wallon*. New York: Aronson, pp. 115–31.

Walsh, R. 1990. *The Spirit of Shamanism*. New York: Tarcher/Putnam.

———. 2007. *The World of Shamanism: New Views of an Ancient Tradition*. Woodbury, MN: Llewellyn.

Wautischer, H. (ed.). 2008. *Ontology of Consciousness: Percipient Action*. Cambridge, MA: MIT Press.

Whitehead, N.L. 2002. *Dark Shamans: Kanaima and the Poetics of Violent Death*. Durham, NC: Duke University Press.

Whitehead, N.L. and R. Wright (eds). 2004. *In Darkness and Secrecy: The Anthropology of Assault Sorcery and Witchcraft in Amazonia*. Durham: Duke University Press.

Whitley, D. 2009. *Cave Paintings and the Human Spirit: The Origin of Creativity and Belief*. Amherst: Prometheus Books.

Wilbert, J. 1963. *Indios de la Región Orinoco-Ventuari*. Caracas: Fundación La Salle de Ciencias Naturales.

———. 1972. 'Tobacco and Shamanistic Ecstasy among the Warao Indians of Venezuela', in P. Furst (ed.), *Flesh of the Gods: The Ritual Use of Hallucinogens*. New York: Praeger, pp. 58–83.

Wilbert, J. and K. Simoneau (eds). 1990. *Folk Literature of the Yanomami Indians* (UCLA Latin American Studies 73). Los Angeles: Latin American Centre Publications, University of California.

Wright, R. and J. Hill. 1986. 'History, Ritual, and Myth: Nineteenth Century Millenarian Movements in the Northwest Amazon', *Ethnohistory* 33(1): 31–54.

Young, D.E. and J.G. Goulet (eds). 1994. *Being Changed by Cross-Cultural Encounters: The Anthropology of Extraordinary Experience*. Peterborough, ON: Broadview.

Zerries, O. 1964. *Waika: Die Kulturgeschichtliche Stellung der Waika-Indianer des Oberen Orinoco im Rahmen der Volkerkunde Sudamericas*. Münich: Klaus Renner Verlag.

Zinberg, N.E. 1977. 'The Study of Conscious States: Problems and Progress', in N.E. Zinberg (ed.), *Alternate States of Consciousness*. New York: The Free Press, pp. 1–36.

INDEX